D0129522

VISUAL QUICKSTART GUIDE

PINNACLE
STUDIO 10

FOR WINDOWS

Jan Ozer

 Peachpit Press

Visual QuickStart Guide
Pinnacle Studio 10 for Windows
Jan Ozer

Peachpit Press

1249 Eighth Street
Berkeley, CA 94710
510/524-2178
800/283-9444
510/524-2221 (fax)
Find us on the Web at www.peachpit.com
To report errors, please send a note to errata@peachpit.com
Peachpit Press is a division of Pearson Education

Copyright © 2006 by Jan Ozer

Project Editor: Suzie Nasol
Editor: Stephen Nathans
Copy Editor: Liz Welch
Tech Editor: Stephen Nathans
Production Editor: Becky Winter
Composition: Kate Kaminski, Happenstance Type-O-Rama
Cover Production: Ellen Reilly
Indexer: Emily Glossbrenner, FireCrystal Communications

Notice of rights
All rights reserved. No part of this book may be reproduced or transmitted in any form by any means, electronic, mechanical, photocopying, recording, or otherwise, without the prior written permission of the publisher. For information on getting permission for reprints and excerpts, contact permissions@peachpit.com.

Notice of liability
The information in this book is distributed on an "As Is" basis, without warranty. While every precaution has been taken in the preparation of the book, neither the author nor Peachpit Press shall have any liability to any person or entity with respect to any loss or damage caused or alleged to be caused directly or indirectly by the instructions contained in this book or by the computer software and hardware products described in it.

Trademarks
Pinnacle Systems and the Pinnacle Systems logo are trademarks of Pinnacle Systems, Inc., registered in the U.S. and other countries.

Visual QuickStart Guide is a registered trademark of Peachpit Press, a division of Pearson Education. Many of the designations used by manufacturers and sellers to distinguish their products are claimed as trademarks. Where those designations appear in this book, and Peachpit Press was aware of a trademark claim, the designations appear as requested by the owner of the trademark. All other product names and services identified throughout this book are used in editorial fashion only and for the benefit of such companies with no intention of infringement of the trademark. No such use, or the use of any trade name, is intended to convey endorsement or other affiliation with this book.

ISBN 0-321-37459-2

9 8 7 6 5 4 3 2 1

Printed and bound in the United States of America

Dedication

For the three girlies in my life: Barb, Whatley, and Rose.

Acknowledgements

This book, pulled together during the hazy, lazy days of summer, 2005, owes a huge debt to those who gave up evenings at the pool and Major League Baseball (go Sox! Go Braves!) to get it done, including Stephen Nathans (editor), Suzie Nasol, the Beck, and whoever else deserves credit that I don't know about. Thank you all for your efforts.

Special thanks to the Pinnacle folks, particularly Mike Iampietro and Travis White, for answering my frantic inquiries during the final stages of product testing.

As always, thanks to Pat Tracy for technical and other assistance.

CONTENTS AT A GLANCE

TABLE OF CONTENTS

TABLE OF CONTENTS

INTRODUCTION

If you're a chef at a fine white linen restaurant, I'm sure that when you have friends over for dinner, burgers on the grill just won't do. You have to impress, amuse and delight.

Well, I can't cook worth a hoot, but as a writer and reviewer in the digital video space, I feel a similar pressure to perform when it comes to home movies. The video has too look great, the editing must be crisp, the titles and effects amusing and enhancing and the background music just like they have on *60 Minutes* or *The Fantastic Four*. I have to make my little girlies laugh, the grandparent smile, friends remain awake, and most of all, please my wife so she doesn't mind the football sized camera I drag around on vacation and other family events.

We're talking pressure.

And the reason I like Pinnacle Studio so much is that it helps me deliver. Over the last three revisions, the program has evolved from a reasonably well featured, easy to use editor to an effects powerhouse with outstanding DVD authoring capabilities.

continues on next page

When I say effects, I don't really mean *Star Wars*-like effects, I mean color correction that can fix mistakes like the improper white balancing when I videotaped the kids at the Atlanta Zoo back in '03. Or bad lighting at the high school reunion dinner in '04 (and I'm not telling which one). Or stabilizing the parade and concert videos shot in '05. We're talking a pre-eminent ability to clean up your videos so they look like you knew what you were doing when you shot it. Hey, even cooks make occasional mistakes.

Of course, Studio excels when you actually start to edit your video, with multiple trimming options, great precision, an excellent titling tool, an amusing set of thematic transitions and an expanding base of *Star Wars* like effects when I decide I want to use them. Plus the ability to automatically generate background music and mix the background music with other audio tracks quickly and easily. The new Overlay track added in Studio 9 Plus gives me chromakey and picture-in-picture capabilities while pan and zoom features let's me use the images shot with that lovely Canon Digital Rebel that showed up last holiday season.

When it's time to build my DVD, Studio offers the most flexible authoring tool this side of $300 standalone authoring programs, with completely customizable menus.

I personally adore Studio because it helps me produce home videos that meet the expectations of my wife and kids, other family, and most importantly, me. And I'm sure it will help you do so, as well.

What's New?

Not much; how 'bout with you?

Sorry, couldn't resist. Actually there's lots new with Studio 10. Here are some highlights.

Most significantly, Pinnacle merged Studio's polished interface with the editing and rendering engine from big sister product Pinnacle Liquid Edition. In addition to providing support for new formats like Microsoft Windows Media video and high definition video (HDV), this professional strength technology delivers additional speed and robustness to the Studio product line.

If you shoot with a DVD camcorder, you'll be happy to hear that Studio can now capture your video, while all producers will appreciate the ability to capture video from non-copy protected DVDs (see Chapter 6 for this last item). Pinnacle also threw in Pinnacle Instant DVD Recorder to help you quickly convert analog and digital tapes to DVD (See Chapter 16). Also new is the ability to preview video output on a second monitor or television set, as detailed in Chapter 2, which provides a more accurate preview and more efficient editing workspace.

On the editing front, Pinnacle added the ability to control audio and video effects with keyframes, providing near infinite customizability (Chapter 9). Pinnacle also added several new cleaning effects to improve video quality, and many other audio and video effects.

continues on next page

INTRODUCTION

Other noteworthy features include the ability to "scrub" audio on the Timeline, the ability to output progressive scan DVDs for your new DVD Player, additional SmartMovie styles, and more choices for producing high quality, slow motion effects. If you're producing longer movies, you'll adore the new ability to record to Dual Layer (DL) DVDs.

Overall, when you throw in the additional Overlay track and pan and zoom capabilities introduced in Studio 9 Plus, the jump from Version 9 to Version 10 is both significant and impressive. Most importantly, Pinnacle retained Studio's straightforward, easy to use interface. Much more powerful, but with the same basic interface we've all come to know and love.

Using This Book

If you bought Studio 10 through a retail channel, you already have a manual that explains how to use the various components of the Studio interface. This book complements the manual in two ways.

First, like all *Visual QuickStart Guides*, this one is task oriented, describing and showing you how to perform most common video production tasks. The descriptions are precise and exhaustive, identifying with screen shots and text the best ways to get the job done.

In addition, having worked with digital video for many years, I know that video editing can be an incredible time sink, probably the main reason most folks simply don't edit their camcorder tapes. Thus many sections and tips focus on how to avoid problems and work as efficiently as possible. Sidebars address technical topics to help you make decisions.

INTRODUCTION

Making Movies with Studio

Within its uniquely unified video-editing/DVD-authoring interface, Studio gives you an unparalleled range of production activities. Depending on your equipment, you can capture footage from a digital or analog camcorder, edit the footage, integrate video from other sources, and output the results for streaming on the Internet, playing back on your desktop, or delivering via DVD or CD.

However, all good movies, regardless how they are delivered, must start with an appreciation of how to create movies worth watching. Chapter 1 explores the notion of creating *watchable* video, a primer aimed at teaching you the proper settings for your video camera and sound shooting techniques. Chapter 2 introduces you to the Studio interface and gets your computer ready for video production.

Editing and production

After you've shot your source videos using the proper camera settings and solid shooting techniques, the process of editing and production begins. It involves the following four steps:

- **Gathering assets**. This is where you capture your video, import still images, or grab them from your camcorder or captured video, and import any background audio files. These activities are covered in Chapters 3, 4, and 5.

- **Trimming and organizing**. In most instances, you won't want to include every minute that you shot in the final production. Accordingly, you trim unwanted sections, then place your video clips and still images in the desired order. Chapter 7 describes how to get this done.

◆ **Garnishing**. Here's where the true editing comes in. During this stage, you add transitions between clips, title tracks, still image overlays, and any special effects. You can also input a narration track, add music ripped from a CD, or create your own custom background track using SmartSound (a utility included with Studio). Chapters 8 through 11 cover these activities.

◆ **Rendering**. This is where you produce your final output. Though "encoding into a streaming format" may sound complicated, Studio includes easy-to-follow templates that simplify the task, making this stage the most mechanical of all. Chapter 14 describes how to output your videos as digital files for posting to a Web site, sending via email, or copying to CD-ROM.

If you're outputting to DVD there's another stage, of course, typically called *authoring*. This is when you create your menus, link videos and still image assets, and preview to ensure that your project flows as desired. Then you burn your disc. DVD production is covered in Chapter 12.

You can also write your production back to your camcorder, where you can dub copies for VHS or other analog players. I describe how to do this in Chapter 13. Finally, Chapter 15 details how to convert tape based videos to DVD with Pinnacle's Instant DVD Recorder.

INTRODUCTION

System Requirements

Most products ship with two sets of requirements, minimum and recommended. Here are Studio 10's minimum and recommended requirements:

◆ Intel Pentium or AMD Athlon 1.4 MHz or higher (2.4 GHz or higher recommended).

◆ 512MB RAM (1 GB recommended. 1 GB required for HD).

◆ Windows XP.

◆ DirectX 9 or higher compatible graphics card with 32 MB (ATI Radeon or Nvidia Geforce 3 or higher with 128 MB recommended for SD. 128 MB required for 720p HD. 256 MB required for 1080i HD).

◆ DirectX 9 or higher compatible sound card (Creative Audigy or M-Audio recommended).

◆ 500 MB of disk space to install software + 3 GB to install bonus content.

◆ DVD-ROM drive for installation.

◆ CD-R(W) burner for creating Video CDs or Super Video CDs.

◆ DVD-/+R(W) burner drive for creating DVDs.

◆ Sound card with surround sound output required for preview of surround sound mixes.

◆ 16:9 compatible camcorder for capture of 16:9 video.

◆ 4.5 GB of hard disk space for every 20 minutes of video captured at best quality.

◆ Hard disk capable of sustained throughput of at least 4 MB per second. All SCSI and most ultra direct memory access (UDMA) drives are fast enough; dedicated hard drive recommended. (Studio will automatically test your hard drive for sufficient speed for real-time video capture when you first enter Capture mode.)

Note that if you're going to edit HDV with Studio, you'll need a bear of a system, including a mind boggling 256 MB of video memory in your graphics card.

Disk requirements

A faster processor and more RAM are certainly better when it comes to video production, but the most significant area of potential trouble relates to disk requirements. Here's a quick example that illustrates how to estimate how much disk space you'll need for your projects.

Assume that you've shot 60 minutes of video that you want to edit down to a 30-minute production. You plan on including both a narration and background audio track, and will burn the result to DVD.

Table i.1, which presents a worst-case estimate of required disk space, assumes that you'll be applying edits to every single frame in the production footage. If you edit more sparingly, you'll need less space.

In 1994, the required 22 GB would have cost close to $30,000, and your electrical bill would jump significantly. Today, you can buy an 80 GB drive for well under $100, a great investment if you plan on pursuing multiple editing projects.

Table i.1

Calculating Disk Requirements			
ITEM	DURATION	MB/MINUTE	TOTAL
Capture footage	60 minutes	216	12.96 GB
Production footage	30 minutes	216	6.48 GB
Narration track	30 minutes	10.5	315 MB
Background audio	30 minutes	10.5	315 MB
DVD files	30 minutes	60	1.8 GB
Total disk space required:			21.87 GB

Some Final Notes

All things in life involve some compromise; balanced against an exhaustive survey of new features like HDV and DVD camcorder compatibility was an onerous deadline and other things like two little girls who like seeing their Daddy every once in awhile. I think we hit the high points, but I wish we could have done more.

But I do have in my possession a brand new Sony HDR-FX1 camcorder, so HDV testing will come, and I plan to bum a DVD camcorder from Sony for the next round of *PC Magazine* and *EventDV* testing. Hey, I know there's a lot of you out there using these devices, and I want to be responsive.

So I plan to write a few how to's regarding new formats and some of the newer programs that will be showing up in the Studio family like Jasc Paint Shop Pro and Steinberg's WavLab audio editor. Please check www.doceo.com for these updates as time goes by in 2005 and beyond. Until then, thanks again for buying this book, and may all your movies have happy endings.

Part I:
Getting Started

CREATING WATCHABLE VIDEO

A video editor is like a hammer. Knowing how to hammer nails, straight and true, is a noble skill, but it doesn't guarantee you can build a sturdy house. Similarly, knowing how to capture your video and add transitions and titles and perhaps a special effect or two doesn't guarantee your video is *watchable*—that family and friends will be able to watch it for more than two or three minutes without squirming in their chairs.

My goal with this book is not only to show you the capabilities of Studio, our metaphorical hammer, but to help you create watchable videos. This involves a range of skills, such as using the proper camcorder settings; framing your shots correctly; shooting the right shots; and capturing, trimming, and weaving your scenes into a polished video production.

Don't fret. I'm not talking Hollywood movies, MTV videos, or 30-second commercials here. If you're like me, you probably shoot most, if not all, of your videos of friends and family for viewing by that same group and have minimal or no commercial aspirations.

So this chapter doesn't throw a lot of advanced theory your way—just a small set of fundamentals that will change the way you shoot and edit, and hopefully increase your enjoyment of the process. It should also greatly improve the perceived quality of your video.

What *Is* Watchable Video?

For better or for worse, what's on television today defines what's "watchable." Next time you're watching television, pay attention to the following elements.

First, in most shows, note the relative lack of camera motion. Specifically, while the show shifts from camera to camera, there is very little *panning* (moving the camera from side to side) or fast *zooming* (changing the zoom magnification either into or away from the subject). You'll almost never see the shaking typical of a handheld camerawork.

Second, note how transitions are used as the behind-the-scenes producer shifts from camera to camera. *Transitions* are visual effects that help smooth the change from shot to shot. Inside of a scene, or within a series of shots from a single location during a single time period, most directors simply *cut* between the various clips. One camera angle stops, and the other starts.

When television shows use a transition to alert the viewer that the time or location is about to change, it's almost always a simple *dissolve* (an effect that briefly merges the current clip with the next clip and then displays the second) or *fade to black*. On kids' shows and "zany" sitcoms, you may see more "artistic" transitions, but they're not random. Typically, the effect relates to the subject matter of the show—for instance, a crocodile dragging the second clip over the first in *Crocodile Hunter*.

Finally, note the pace of change. Few, if any, shows (or movies) display a static screen for longer than 10 or 15 seconds. News and sports shows use multiple text streams to keep viewers' eyes occupied, along with frequent background updates and cuts to reporters in the field, while sitcoms and other shows change cameras and camera angles frequently.

So here's the bar: videos worth watching use stable shots filmed from multiple angles and don't introduce random special effects, but they still manage to introduce some element of change every 5 to 15 seconds. If you want to produce watchable video, that's your target.

You really can't produce watchable video without shooting well and capturing well. For the most part, this chapter discusses how to shoot well, while the remainder of the book covers the capture and editing side.

Make a .com
name with us!®

SAVE
10%

on your order at
GoDaddy.com!*

Simply enter source code **AMAZON5**
in your shopping cart, or mention the code
when you call, to receive your discount.

Domain names from
JUST $1.99**

with each and every new,
on-domain product you buy!

GODADDY.COM

Daddy®.COM

...ake a .com
...ame with us!®

SAVE 10%

on your order at
GoDaddy.com!*

Simply enter source code
AMAZON5 in your shopping
cart, or mention the code when
you call, to receive your discount.

FREE EXTRAS
with every domain!

- Quick Blog
- Hosting with Web site builder
- Complete Email ($9.99 value)
- Getting Started Guide
- And Much More!

2 ways to order:

online:
www.GoDaddy.com

call toll-free:
1-866-GoDaddy
(1-866-463-2339)

* Not applicable to any product renewals, dom
transfers, reduced-price or bulk-priced dom

** Plus ICANN® fee of 25 cents per domain
year. Certain TLD's only.

Watchable Video Guidelines

The building blocks of TV-quality video are very accessible. You simply need to follow a few guidelines (see the sidebar on the left).

Shooting for success

A key point to keep in mind in creating watchable video is the goal of your production. Let's start with one assumption: that not all occasions demand the same level of attention in either shooting or editing. Sometimes you bring the camera just to capture the day or the event and really just want to have fun without the pressure of creating a masterpiece. Still, you want the video you shoot to look as good as possible, so you definitely want to use the proper camera settings and compose your shots carefully.

Other times, for weddings, significant birthdays and anniversaries, graduations, and other events, you want to weave in advanced shot combinations that captivate and impress your viewers. You may even want to develop a short list of shots so that your video can follow a definite storyline. This takes a bit more planning up front and more editing time at the back.

Even though you don't need to concern yourself with advanced shot composition each time you dust off your camera, you should gain a fundamental knowledge of the basics that will improve all of your videos. Then you should learn some more advanced techniques, for those special occasions when you want to spread your creative wings.

Let's start at the top of the guidelines and then work our way through the other elements.

Guidelines for Creating Watchable Video

- Use a feature-rich video editor.
- Develop strong nonlinear editing skills.
- Choose the right camera settings.
- Apply basic shot composition.
- Apply advanced shot composition.

WATCHABLE VIDEO GUIDELINES

Definitions 101

Here are some terms that are critical to video production. I'll try to stick with the following definitions in this chapter and throughout the book to ensure that we're speaking a common language.

Shot composition: Composition is the arrangement of the primary subjects on the screen. The goal is to present the most aesthetically pleasing image possible without exceeding the ambitions and time constraints of your project.

Shooting, taping, or videotaping: These terms all refer to the process of pointing your camera, pressing the red Record button, and recording on tape. I may slip up sometimes and use the term *filming*, a definite faux pas since we're using a DV or other tape-based camcorder that doesn't have film, but the process described is the same.

Scene (during shooting): During shooting, the scene is the key area where the action takes place. In a crime drama, the murder scene takes place in the bedroom or boardroom or library. In a football movie, you'll have locker room scenes (tasteful, of course), scenes on the field, and finally the tickertape parade scene, in the center of town.

Shot: A shot typically is described in terms of what you're doing with the camera when you're shooting a particular scene. So in a long shot, the camera is very far from the subject (unless you're at the race track), while in a close-up shot, the camera is close to the subject. An establishing or wide shot typically shows the entire scene so that the viewer understands the environment relevant to that footage. You'll learn more about the different types of shots later in this chapter.

Scene (during editing): During editing, a scene is a discrete chunk of video composed of one or more shots. Typically, during editing, you identify the scenes you want to use in the final project and then assemble them with your video editor.

Clip: A clip is a generic term for a chunk of audio or video that you're editing in Studio's Movie window. It is often used interchangeably with *scene*.

Sequence: A sequence is a group of scenes pieced together. In a wedding video, for instance, you might have a sequence for the rehearsal dinner, a sequence for the ceremony, and a sequence for the reception. You piece these sequences together into a finished movie.

Movie: A movie is the end product of your shooting and editing—what you end up with after you've pieced together the various scenes and added all the transitions, titles, and special effects; it's the creative fruit you serve up to your audience.

Video: Typically refers to what's transferred from your camcorder to your computer. Video is also used interchangeably with the term *movie*.

Using a Feature-Rich Video Editor

The video editor serves two primary functions in the creation of watchable video. First, it provides an accessible workspace for cutting up your raw footage into the most watchable segments and then piecing them together into a compelling movie. As you'll see in Chapter 7, Studio excels in this regard.

Second, the video editor provides a multitude of elements for introducing change into your videos to satisfy the MTV-nurtured attention spans of viewers. Studio excels here, too. For example, Studio's between-scenes transitions are the best in the industry, as are its background-music features, and its titling tool makes creating attractive, professional-looking titles easy. You can also animate still images using pan and zoom effects (see "Inserting Pan and Zoom Effects" in Chapter 5), or let Studio automatically create a music video for you (see "Creating Music Videos Automatically" in Chapter 9).

Developing Strong Nonlinear Editing Skills

A great tool, like our metaphorical hammer, does little good if you don't know how to use it. The rest of this book will give you the details. Even while you're shooting, however, you should understand Studio's most valuable capability so that you can make the best use of this tool.

Simply stated, Studio, like all computer-based video editors, is a nonlinear tool, which means that you can move video scenes around freely, like checkers on a checkerboard. Consider **Figure 1.1**. At the upper left is the Video Album, which contains the scenes in the order that I shot them and later captured

them on my hard disk. At the bottom is the Storyboard, where I can assemble all the scenes that I want in the final movie. (I'm jumping ahead a bit here on the interface side; if you want to bone up on Studio's interface elements, you can take a quick look at "Using Edit Mode" in Chapter 2.)

This is the beginning of a video I'm creating with footage shot at the Fiddler's Convention here in Galax, where I live. This is the opening sequence that introduces the viewer to the yearly, world-famous gathering. Later sequences will highlight individual bands and music and instrument types, like bluegrass and mandolins, and some of the country dancing I shot at the event.

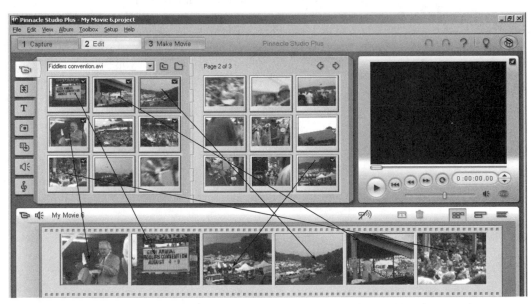

Figure 1.1 One of Studio's best features is that it's nonlinear, so you can cut and paste videos from anywhere to anywhere.

As you can see in the Studio Storyboard, Scene 1 shows an announcer introducing a band on stage. The next scene is the sign at the entrance to the Fiddler's Convention, which I shot first on the way in, so that the viewer instantly knows what the video is about.

Next, using the song from the background music in the first scene, I display several other scenes that visually illustrate the size of the festival: the hundreds of parked trailers and tents spread over about 20 acres, the thousands of people in the stands and milling about. (To make everything work together seamlessly, I use the Continuity system, described later in this chapter.).

Going to the Fiddler's Convention, I knew that I would need these shots to complete the video, but it wasn't convenient to shoot them all immediately when I arrived. Hey, I was being dragged around by two little girls who didn't give a hoot about continuity. No problem, though, because regardless of when I got the shots—later that night or even the next day—I could cut and paste them in Studio wherever and whenever I need them.

If you've never edited video before, you will find this is a huge paradigm shift that unleashes significant creative potential. As you'll discover throughout this chapter and later in the book, Studio's nonlinear nature is absolutely key to creating watchable videos.

That said, it all starts with the camera. So let's focus on that aspect of creating watchable video.

DEVELOPING NONLINEAR EDITING SKILLS

Choosing the Right Camera Settings

If you produced camcorders and sold them to untrained consumers, your primary goal (if you wanted to sell a lot of them) would probably be to allow your customers to produce the best possible videos right out of the box—no tweaking of controls required. Camcorder manufacturers are a bright group, and this is pretty much what they've attempted to do.

Still, in certain instances, you can improve the quality of your video if you tune the controls to match your surroundings and the goals of the shot. In addition, there are certain camera features you should always use, and some to avoid at all costs.

Finally, two realities of consumer camcorders—lighting and audio—have their own sets of challenges, which you should know about up front. This section briefly addresses these issues, and then we move on to shot composition.

It's all about exposure

No, this isn't a section about Janet Jackson and Justin Timberlake; it's about the exposure setting on your camera, which controls how much light gets to the charged coupled device (CCD) that captures the image. Virtually all consumer camcorders have automatic exposure settings that work well most of the time.

However, they also feature special *programmed auto-exposure (AE)* modes that can improve video quality in well-defined shooting conditions. For example, most Sony camcorders have the following programmed AE modes for specific shooting conditions:

- **Spotlight** prevents faces from being excessively white.

- **Portrait** sharpens close-up images and softens the background.

- **Sports** captures crisp images of fast-moving subjects.

- **Beach & Ski** prevents faces from appearing dark against the generally lighter background.

- **Sunset Moon** optimizes shooting controls for low-light conditions.

- **Landscape** focuses solely on faraway objects, softening any objects in the foreground.

Many DV cameras also have settings for backlit conditions, which, like the Beach and Ski mode, can prevent faces from appearing overly dark. In my experience, these modes work very well in their defined roles, improving image quality over fully automatic settings. For this reason, you should definitely identify the modes available on your camera and learn how to switch to them for the defined conditions.

The skinny on night-shot modes

Most DV cameras offer one or two low-light modes, which fall into two categories. The first is an infrared-assisted mode that creates a greenish "night-vision goggles" effect. This is very effective for capturing sleeping children or nocturnal animals, but you lose all the color in the shot—the image's colors consist of shades of green.

The other mode doesn't use infrared, but slows the shutter speed dramatically to ensure that sufficient light gets to the CCD. This preserves color, but even minimal motion produces extreme blurriness that usually makes the video unusable.

Depending on your goal, either or both modes work just fine. However, don't expect either to boost light under low-light conditions. That is, if you're shooting video at a quiet dinner party or dark restaurant, neither mode will improve your results. You need to either boost the ambient light in the room by turning on some lights or get a light for your video camera.

The white balance issue

White balance is kind of like bad cholesterol. It's not something you think about often, but whenever it comes up, it's generally bad news.

White balance is a problem because cameras perceive the color white differently based on the light source, whether fluorescent or incandescent light or sunlight. All cameras perform white balancing automatically, but under some circumstances, such as shooting in sunlight, under fluorescent lights, or under rapidly changing lighting conditions, the auto-sensing mechanisms may not be accurate, so you run a pretty significant risk that the colors will miss the mark.

For example, I once forgot to white balance my camera during a trip to Zoo Atlanta, and all of the video had a blue tone. Another time I switched from outdoor shooting to indoor shooting at a wedding without adjusting the white balance, and all whites appeared slightly pinkish, including the bride's wedding dress, which was a big hit, let me tell you.

Both problems could have been prevented with proper white balancing, and fortunately I was able to fix both problems using color correction, as discussed in "To Apply Automatic Color Correction" in Chapter 9. Still, it's always better to avoid these issues by white balancing before you start shooting.

The procedure is similar for most cameras: you zoom the camera into a white object like a wall, wedding dress, or piece of paper and press the white-balance button. Alternatively, many cameras have white-balance presets for indoor and outdoor shoots. Check your camera's documentation for details.

If this all sounds overly technical, you can also simply stay in automatic white-balance mode and point the camera at a white object for about 10 seconds or so whenever lighting conditions change, such as when you move into direct sunlight from the shade or move indoors from outside. This will give the automatic white-balance mechanism the best chance of operating correctly.

Automatic versus manual focus

Automatic focus is generally effective for keeping the video image sharp and in focus. Under certain conditions such as the following, however, manual focus produces superior results:

- Shooting a stationary subject from a tripod (where focus can inadvertently drift if the subject momentarily moves out of the picture).

- Shooting under low-light conditions (where the camera can lose focus and repeatedly adjust the focus back and forth to find it).

- Shooting through a window (where the camera may focus on the glass, rather than the objects behind the glass).

Check your camera's documentation to learn how to disable automatic focus and how to operate the manual focus controls.

When to use image stabilization

Image stabilization is a feature that minimizes minor hand shaking and other camera motion that might occur while walking or shooting from a moving car. While not always effective, image stabilization provides some benefit and should be used whenever you're not shooting from a tripod. When shooting from a tripod, however, most camera vendors recommend disabling this feature. Check your camera's documentation for recommendations regarding image stabilization and to learn how to enable and disable this mode.

CHOOSING THE RIGHT CAMERA SETTINGS

Other settings

Here are other controls to consider before shooting, along with some suggestions for using the best setting:

◆ **Date:** DV cameras imprint the date and time of each shot in the video, and Studio uses this information to detect scenes in the video. It's a great feature that makes setting the time and date on your camera a priority.

◆ **12-bit audio versus 16-bit audio:** Use 16-bit audio; 12-bit audio was created so that you could lay down two tracks of audio simultaneously while shooting, a capability that most cameras don't offer. The 16-bit audio setting creates larger files, so it requires more space on your hard disk. However, the additional audio data delivers better quality.

◆ **Digital zoom:** Unlike optical zoom, which uses the camera's lens to produce additional detail when zooming in, digital zoom simply zooms into the digital image, which creates obvious pixelation (jaggies) at extreme settings. Most pros disable digital zoom, and you should, too.

◆ **Standard play (SP) versus long play (LP):** With DV camcorders, you can record up to 90 minutes of video on a 60-minute tape using LP mode, which uses a slower tape recording speed (12.56 mm per second compared to 18.812 mm per second for standard play) to pack more video onto the same tape. The same video signal is stored in each mode; it's just that LP mode stores the same video on less tape, which is theoretically less safe. For example, if an inch of tape is damaged in LP mode, you'd lose 50 percent more video than you would in SP mode. Some pundits state that the slower tape speed actually decreases your chances for error, but also that LP modes are implemented slightly differently on different camcorders and shouldn't be used if the tape may later be played back on a different camera. For me, this was much more of an issue when DV tapes cost $25; now that they're under $4 in bulk, SP is probably a safer choice.

◆ **16:9 aspect ratio versus 4:3 aspect ratio:** Use 16:9 only if you have a widescreen television that can play it without distortion. Studio can edit video in both formats, but 16:9 video played on a normal TV will appear squashed.

◆ **Digital effects:** Many cameras offer digital effects such as sepia, mosaic, fade from black, and fade to black, plus primitive titling capabilities. You can produce these with much greater precision using Studio, so disable these effects on your camcorder.

The realities of shooting with consumer camcorders

There are two significant shortcomings of shooting with DV camcorders, particularly inexpensive consumer models. First, most camcorders produce suboptimal quality in anything other than extremely bright conditions. Second, it's very difficult to capture clear, crisp audio using solely the camcorder's microphone unless you're very close to the subject. Fortunately, you can minimize or resolve both problems with some advance planning and/or some inexpensive accessories.

Figure 1.2 Unless you're shooting participants in the witness protection program, poor lighting like this produces unacceptable images.

Let's look at the lighting problem first. This is a particular issue for me because my wife favors cozy, intimate family celebrations with minimal lighting, preferably candlelight. Unfortunately, under these conditions, it's impossible to shoot video that looks even remotely good. For example, **Figure 1.2** was taken at a wedding reception without ancillary lighting, and the subject's faces are very indistinct because of the low light.

Of course, under candlelight, the problem is obvious. The low-light issue is much more insidious under normal room lighting, which generally is still too dark for high-quality images. Here, however, the image on your LCD panel may look fine, and you won't discover that your images are too dark until you've captured your video to your computer's hard disk or viewed it on a television screen. Either way, it's too late to address the issue.

Figure 1.3 Lights like this one from Sony can go a long way toward reducing low-light quality issues.

Basically, there are two ways to solve the lighting problem. First, you can turn on every light in the room, sacrificing short-term intimacy for the long-term quality of your memories of the event. This generally works well in most homes, where lighting is plentiful, so long as you can get your spouse to agree.

In darker reception halls, restaurants, and similar venues, where you can't control the lighting, your best option is to purchase a video light like the Sony HVL-20DW2 shown in **Figure 1.3** (assuming your camcorder doesn't have a light, of course). This particular model attaches to the accessory shoe on top of the camera and draws power from the camcorder's battery. Alternatively, you can get a light that uses separate batteries.

Note that capturing good-quality video under low-light conditions is a serious, serious issue, probably mentioned more in most camcorder reviews than any other deficiency. Unfortunately, short of spending $3,000 for a camcorder that shoots great video in low light, there is no simple solution. Ignore it, and it will repeatedly degrade the quality of your indoor shots; take the steps discussed here, and you can minimize this problem.

Improving audio quality

As you would expect, the problem with camcorder-based audio starts with the microphone. First, since it's located on the camera body, it can easily pick up a host of operator noises such as the clicking of the zoom controls. More serious is the pickup pattern of the microphone, which defines the area from which the microphone gathers sound.

Typically, DV camcorders use microphones that prioritize all sounds in front of the camera equally. This pattern works well if you're shooting a group of people equidistant from the camera, but is useless if you're shooting a lecturer or speaker at the front of the room or anyone far away from the camera.

Here, you also have two options: either get closer to the speaker or purchase a separate microphone. For the latter, the options are almost limitless, but the easiest and cheapest alternatives are microphones that sit on the camera body itself, like the Sony ECM-MSD1 (**Figure 1.4**).

The MSD1 offers a narrower, front-focused pickup pattern that ignores ambient noise and captures audio primarily from the direction in which the camera is pointing. These types of microphones are also called shotgun or gun microphones.

Shotgun microphones probably won't help if you are shooting a lecturer from the back of the room. However, at a birthday party or wedding, you can shoot someone 10 to 15 feet away and clearly hear what the person is saying, which is almost impossible using solely the microphone on the camera body.

Figure 1.4 Microphones like this one from Sony help capture better audio when the audio source is distant from the camera.

CHOOSING THE RIGHT CAMERA SETTINGS

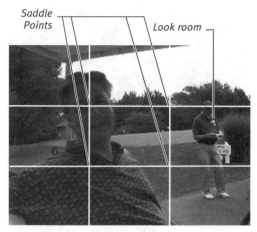

Figure 1.5 The rule of thirds. My golf buddy's head is located at the upper-left saddle point in the video frame, providing the necessary look room.

Figure 1.6 My other buddy is facing the opposite direction, so I placed him at the upper-right saddle point. Note how the eyes are above the top third of the frame.

Applying Basic Shot Composition

Once you get the camera settings down and deal with audio and lighting, it's time to start thinking about shot composition, which is the art of placing your subjects in the frame to create the most aesthetically pleasing image.

Here are four basic techniques to keep in mind while shooting. After you read this section, watch for them on TV and in the movies. Once you see how consistently the pros use these techniques, you'll be surprised that you never noticed them before.

The rule of thirds

According to the rule of thirds, you should divide each image into a tic-tac-toe grid, like that shown in **Figure 1.5**, and place the primary subject of the frame at one of the four saddle points, or intersections of the four lines. This rule has its roots in Greek architecture and Renaissance art and is based on the belief that certain shapes and proportions are more pleasing to the eye than others.

When you are shooting a subject that isn't moving, the image looks best when the open space is located in front of where the subject is facing, as shown in Figure 1.5 and **Figure 1.6**. This is called providing look room, or nose room.

When your primary subject is moving, place your subject in the back third of the frame, leaving lead room in the front. In **Figure 1.7**, my daughter is skating from left to right, so the lead room is on the viewer's right. Similarly, in **Figure 1.8**, my other daughter is moving from right to left, so the lead room is on the viewer's left.

A corollary to the rule of thirds is that the eyes should always be at or above the top third of the video. This holds true regardless whether the shot is taken from close up and includes the face only, or from farther back, as in Figures 1.5 to 1.8.

Like all aesthetic guidelines, the rule of thirds isn't fixed in stone; sometimes you simply have to shoot what looks appropriate at the time. For example, if the background is direction-neutral, I find it hard to apply the rule of thirds when shooting a subject looking straight at me, as in **Figure 1.9**.

That said, it's clear that the "center the image in the camera" instruction we learned when we got our first Instamatic is not universally applicable. Though it's impossible to apply the rule of thirds to every frame in your video, especially with moving subjects, use it as a guide, and you'll find your videos more aesthetically pleasing.

Motion techniques

One of the most striking differences between professional and amateur video is the amount and quality of the motion in the video. When you watch most television shows or movies, you'll notice two facts related to motion. First, most shots are either totally stable or have only slight, virtually unnoticeable motion. Second, if there is significant motion, it's very smooth.

Lead room

Figure 1.7 Whatley is skating from left to right, so I try to keep her in the back left of the frame, to provide lead room.

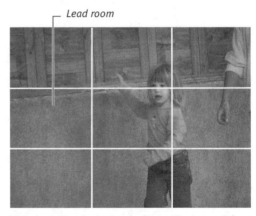

Lead room

Figure 1.8 Rose is skating (well, shuffling, actually) from right to left, so the lead room is on the other side.

APPLYING BASIC SHOT COMPOSITION

Figure 1.9 I find it hard to apply the rule of thirds on a subject facing directly at me, unless there's another object in the background that dictates it. Here the background is neutral, so this buddy is framed in the middle.

In contrast, most amateur videos are shot from unstable platforms that shake continuously, with fast zooms (using the camera's zoom controls to zoom into or out of the image), pans (moving the camera from side to side), and tilts (moving the camera up and down).

Obviously, the pros have multiple cameras and better equipment, making their jobs much easier. Still, if you follow these five rules, you can produce very similar results.

◆ Shoot from a stable platform. I'm not going to tell you to shoot with a tripod because I know it's impractical most of the time. However, you can buy an inexpensive monopod (a one-legged tripod) at a discount store for under $20 that will hold your camera at a steady height, making it much simpler to reduce the shake in the video. Folded up, it's only slightly longer than an umbrella, so it's easy to carry around. Even with a monopod, you should lean against something solid, like a wall, tree, or fence, whenever possible.

If you're shooting without a tripod or monopod, find the most comfortable sustainable position for the camera; usually this is about chest high, holding the camera with both hands and sighting with the viewfinder. If your camera has a shoulder strap, see if you can use this strap to support the weight of the camcorder when you're shooting. One of the best approaches is to lay the camera on a fixed object, like a desk, table, or shelf.

continues on next page

APPLYING BASIC SHOT COMPOSITION

- Zoom, pan, or tilt only to follow the action, not for dramatic effect. Don't try to zoom slowly into your spouse's face as he or she watches your daughter's gymnastics meet; frame the close-up shot and then start shooting. Don't pan from skyscraper to skyscraper in downtown Manhattan; shoot one building, stop, reframe the next building, and start shooting again (or cut the panning sequences between buildings during editing).

- Whenever possible, rehearse the necessary camera motion beforehand. This approach works exceptionally well at sporting events like baseball games or gymnastics meets, where the athlete has to follow a designated path, whether to first base or to the vault spring. While you're waiting for your child's turn, practice with other children. Not only does this improve the smoothness of your camera motion, but it also helps ensure that obstacles don't obscure your line of sight during that critical moment.

- For all shots that have motion, start at a stable position for a few seconds whenever possible, and hold the final shot for a few seconds to ensure that you have sufficient footage for editing.

- Use your waist for panning and tilting shots, not your hands or your feet. That is, to pan across a scene, hold the camera steady and swivel at the waist across the scene. To tilt up and down, hold the camera steady and bend forward and backward at the waist.

The Continuity system

Briefly, the Continuity system is a style of editing whose goal is to present a scene so that the cuts from scene to scene are unnoticeable to the viewer—that is, the progression of shots within the scene is logical, without any discontinuities that jar the viewer. It's a pretty complex system with lots of rules, so for our purposes here we'll focus on its absolutely critical points.

Most importantly, you need to start each sequence with an establishing shot that presents the watcher with a complete view of the setting. Then you can move into medium shots and close-ups, with periodic reestablishing shots to keep the viewer grounded. (See the sidebar "Taxonomy of Shots" later in this chapter for definitions of these types of shots.)

This sequence of shots is shown in **Figure 1.10**, taken from a television interview I participated in several years ago at a trade show. This was a two-camera shoot, so it's unlike what most of us do day to day, but the technique is instructive.

The first shot is the establishing shot: two guys talking, with the stage and people walking around behind us clear to the viewer. This gives the viewer a feel for the environment. This is Camera 1. Next is a medium shot of me with a title on Camera 2. Then Camera 1 tightens the framing to a medium two-shot of the friendly interviewer and me (note the adherence to the rule of thirds in the medium shot of me, but not in either the wide shot or the medium two-shot).

What's particularly instructive is the difference between the establishing shot and the medium two-shot. They look very similar, but in the establishing shot, you can clearly tell what's going on in the background—folks walking around with bags; must be a trade show. In the medium two-shot, you see only body parts walking around, and the environment is much less comprehensible to the viewer. That's okay, since the establishing shot has already clued the viewer into what's going on. In addition, the camera person periodically shifted back to a wider shot with this camera so that viewers entering in midstream would understand the context.

The clear lesson is this: Start every sequence with an establishing shot, or series of shots, that presents the environment to the viewer. Then shoot progressively closer so that you get scenes that present the detail you want without confusing the viewer. Next time you watch ESPN *SportsCenter* or the evening news, notice how the video follows this progression.

continues on next page

Establishing shot   Medium shot   Medium two-shot

Figure 1.10 The Continuity system in action. The first shot is an establishing shot that clearly shows we're at a trade show. The next is a cut to a medium shot and then to a medium two-shot.

APPLYING BASIC SHOT COMPOSITION

Let's apply this theory to our typical one-camera shoot, using the Fiddler's Convention video mentioned earlier. As shown in **Figure 1.11**, I start with a medium shot of the announcer, breaking the rules, but only for a second. Call this my nod to the *Tom Jones Show*, which always started with Tom's hand on the microphone before he broke into "It's Not Unusual." I always liked that dramatic effect.

The first shot is on the screen for only a moment or two, primarily to introduce the audio background track of the announcer and the band playing on the stage. Then I cut to the Fiddler's Convention sign, so the viewer immediately knows what's going on; then several wide shots showing the stage from the background, the acres of trailers and tents, and the thousands of folks in the stands; and then the stage.

After this, I can start adding medium shots and close-ups of the band members and interesting attendees because I've set the stage with the wide shot. Let's apply this approach to some common situations:

- **Birthday party:** Start with exterior shots of the house and interior shots of the party room showing all participants and decorations. Then move to medium shots of guests and the birthday celebrant.

- **Soccer game:** Set the stage with wide shots of the field, showing both goals, the location of both teams, and the grandstands. Then start working in views of your star forward, the team, the coach, and other participants.

- **Dance recital or play:** Use exterior shots of the gymnasium or theater to set the stage; then shoot the entire gym or stage to show the complete environment. Then add medium shots of the participants and, later, close-ups.

Figure 1.11 In my first video of the Fiddler's Convention, I used a series of wide shots to introduce the spectacle to the viewer before transitioning to medium shots of the band.

Remember to shoot an establishing shot each time you change the physical location of the scene. For example, if you're shooting a family wedding, you shouldn't shift from a scene in the chapel to a scene in the reception hall without an establishing shot of the reception hall. It also helps to shoot closing wide shots that you can fade to black during editing so that the viewer understands one sequence is ending and another is starting.

Once again, the lovely aspect of digital video is the nonlinear nature of the editing process. You don't have to shoot the establishing shots first; you can shoot them later and cut and paste them in at the proper location.

The Continuity system for audio

The Continuity rule for audio is a bit cerebral, but it's exceptionally important so bear with me for a moment. I'll use an example to illustrate the point.

Assume that you're at a wedding reception. You want to show people dancing and having a good time, so you shoot a bunch of shots of everyone dancing—say 10 minutes' worth taken over a 30-minute period.

You start editing and quickly realize that no one will watch 10 minutes of dancing, so you start trimming away footage to get down to a more palatable 4 minutes. Here's the problem: Since the band or DJ didn't play the same song all night, most shots of the revelers have different songs playing in the background. Though your viewers can accept visual cuts from person to person without a sense of discontinuity, audio cuts are a different matter—that is, cutting from 5 seconds of one song to 5 seconds of another song is a big red flag that signals a discontinuity.

To avoid this, when shooting, make sure that you capture at least one complete song that you can use as background for the entire finished dance sequence. Then, as described in "The Insert Edit" in Chapter 7, you can use that song as the background for the entire 4 minutes and cut and paste bits of other shots to complete the sequence.

In essence, you're fooling the audience into thinking that you took all of the shots during one song, simulating a multiple-camera shoot with one camera, which is incredibly effective. Sure, problems can arise—for example, if you choose a disco song and have footage of people slow dancing—but overall, this is a very powerful technique, with broad application.

For example, in the Fiddler's Convention video, I used the audio from the first scene as the background for the entire first sequence. In addition to the wide shots, I came back to medium and close-up shots of the band and pasted in other bits of people listening, dancing, and generally having a good time. These are all the shots I would use to convey the atmosphere of the event, and provide the visual context for later sequences. But because I captured one entire song on tape and used it to create essentially a music video, the presentation is much more polished than if I had pasted the same scenes together with disparate audio tracks, revealing to my viewers that the scenes aren't really continuous.

At a recent wedding, I kept the camera running during both the entry and exit processionals, which took about 10 minutes each. Then, using one song from each processional as the background, I condensed each sequence to about 2 minutes, which was much more palatable to viewers.

Applying Advanced Shot Composition

Advanced shot compositions typically involve different types of shots and shot combinations. You've seen them hundreds of times on TV; they're easy to implement and look very polished. Here's how to use some in your own movies.

Medium shot, point-of-view shot, reaction shot

Figure 11.12 starts with a medium shot of my wife and daughter, obviously staring at something. What is it? you find yourself asking. Then I cut to a point-of-view shot, which shows the action in the eyes of my daughter: her point of view. Then, as the horse draws nearer to her, she smiles in delight; that's the reaction shot.

As with all of the shots we're discussing, it's important to recognize that these shots were filmed out of order. I shot about 2 minutes of video before a horse carriage ride and pieced together these 15 or 20 seconds before we got on the carriage to show how Whatley was enjoying the day.

I used the background audio from the first and third shots for the entire sequence to preserve audio continuity. Then I pasted a shot of the horse, taken later, into the middle to show Whatley's point of view. It looks like I have two cameras to most untrained eyes, which was the effect I was seeking, but I had only my trusty Sony DCR-PC1.

Think, for a moment, about the unlimited potential for these types of shots. You're at a softball game and your daughter gets a hit. You catch the line drive on video and then want to switch to the crowd cheering and your spouse smiling like a fool.

But you can't physically move the camera fast enough to catch all this action. Thinking in advance, while other kids were at bat, you took several shots of the crowd cheering and your spouse smiling. You also took several shots of your spouse pensively watching the action, just to use when piecing together this video.

During editing, you start with the pensive shots of the spouse, then the line drive, and then the crowd and proud spouse shots. If you use the audio from the actual line drive for the whole sequence, it will look like you had multiple cameras working the entire game. It's not hard, it's not time consuming; you just need to plan ahead.

Medium shot   Point-of-view shot   Reaction shot

Figure 1.12 What's Whatley staring at? A horse? How delightful.

Over-the-shoulder shot, point-of-view shot

An over-the-shoulder shot is what you see on the left in **Figure 1.13**, a shot that includes the back of one of the subjects and the focus of the subject's attention. It's also an establishing shot, because it shows the elephant's environment at Zoo Atlanta.

Then you switch to a point-of-view shot that shows in detail what your subject is looking at. This is a great combination for involving your primary subject in your sequence while following the rules of continuity discussed earlier.

Over-the-shoulder shot   Point-of-view shot

Figure 1.13 Using the over-the-shoulder shot as an establishing shot; then cutting to a point-of-view shot of the elephant.

APPLYING ADVANCED SHOT COMPOSITION

Cutaways

A cutaway is a shot that relates to the primary subject of the video, but isn't the primary subject. For example, when ESPN interviews the winning coach after a football game, the coach might attribute the win to a goal-line stand late in the fourth quarter. During the interview, while the coach is still talking, ESPN switches to a view of the play and then cuts back to the coach once the play is done.

Or maybe it's the weatherperson describing the wonderful spring-like weather that just descended in mid-December. The shot starts with the weatherperson, and then cutaways show joggers running in shorts, couples sunning on the grass, and babies crawling on blankets. Then back to the weatherperson for tomorrow's forecast.

Here's what I like about cutaways. Number one, they allow you to show the flavor of the entire event. Rather than simply keeping the camera on little Sally during the softball game, you shoot the coaches cajoling, the parents praising, the shortstop shuffling, an uproar from the umpire—all the shots that make softball such a compelling game.

Second, cutaways can serve as patches for badly shot video that you can't cut from your sequence, as may occur when you're capturing an entire song, speech, or sermon to use as the background track for your audio as described earlier.

For example, **Figure 1.14** shows six images of a shot from the Fiddler's Convention. Much of the fun action occurs away from the stage, and this dynamic duo had generated an amazing amount of dancing, shuffling, and stomping. The main subjects of the video sequence were the two performers; all other shots not directly of them were cutaways.

Figure 1.14 Using cutaways. The primary subject here is the two-person band; the cutaways are the folks dancing.

Following the audio continuity system described previously, I filmed one entire song, moving from one side of the scene to the other while recording, and catching some of the dancing action as I went. Then I hung around for two other songs, shooting different, additional dance sequences.

Because I was moving around while filming the one background song, there was an awful lot of unusable footage, violent camera motion, and bad framing. Wherever necessary, however, I just pasted in a dance sequence to hide the bad footage, allowing me to produce one fairly cohesive 4-minute song.

Similarly, for a wedding video, you might want pictures of the proud parents watching the ceremonial first dance. So you shoot the entire ceremonial dance and later shoot the proud parents beaming at something else; you can then use these shots of the parents as cutaways to patch into the dance sequence.

My rule for cutaways is that you can never get enough of them. If your goal is advanced shot composition, spend a lot of time shooting subjects other than your primary ones.

APPLYING ADVANCED SHOT COMPOSITION

Taxonomy of Shots

Here's a list of shots and some suggestions for when to use them.

- **Establishing shot:** Any shot that provides the viewer with a visual overview of the environment of the shot.

- **Long shot:** Any shot that doesn't cut out any body part of the primary subject. For example, **Figure 1.15** is a long shot that shows a lovely straight left arm but a disturbing hint of a reverse pivot. This is about the shortest long shot you'll see; shots from farther away are also called medium or extreme long shots. Long shots are good for showing action and as establishing shots and are also called wide shots.

Figure 1.15 Here's a long shot that adheres to the rule of thirds. For those who care about such things, I parred this short par-three hole (that's my story and I'm sticking to it).

- **Medium shot:** Any shot that cuts away a portion of the primary subject, up to a close-up, which shows only the upper shoulders and face. These shots are also called mid-shots. Medium shots are good for introducing the viewer to the character and should be used before a close-up.

- **Close-up shot:** Any shot that shows only the shoulders and head, or closer in. These shots are good primarily for reaction shots. Use close-ups sparingly, for effect only; during most shoots, a medium shot is a much better choice to show people talking.

- **Over-the-shoulder shot:** Shows the upper shoulder of a subject and the primary subject of the video.

- **Point-of-view shot:** Shows the point of view of the immediately preceding subject on the screen.

- **Reaction shot:** Shows a subject's reaction to the immediately preceding shot.

APPLYING ADVANCED SHOT COMPOSITION

INTRODUCTION TO STUDIO 10

Though generally straightforward, Pinnacle Systems' Studio 10 has a few nooks and crannies that aren't obvious at first glance. Fortunately, Studio includes a comprehensive guided tour to get you familiar with the landscape fast. This chapter starts by showing you how to take the tour and then quickly introduces you to Studio's primary modes: Capture, Edit, and Make Movie. It also shows you how to undo or redo your work, use online help, and name and save your project files.

Studio 10 is a very accessible program, so it's tempting just to just in and get started. Still, for each project, a few options should be set beforehand. For example, you should choose the location for your captured video and auxiliary files, and you should perform a disk performance test to see if your system is up to the rigors of video editing. Most of these options are "set 'em and forget 'em": Studio will maintain them from project to project until you manually change them.

Note that Studio displays housekeeping options, such as file location settings, in the same dialog boxes that display configuration options such as capturing and transition rendering. This chapter focuses mainly on the housekeeping options; other options that you don't see in this chapter are covered later in this book.

Studio Overview

After you install Studio, you'll see the Studio launcher icon on your desktop (**Figure 2.1**). Double-click the icon and you'll see the Studio Launcher (**Figure 2.2**), which contains icons for launching the Studio editing application, which I'll cover in chapters 1–14, and the Pinnacle Instant DVD Recorder, which I'll cover in Chapter 15.

If you have the Pinnacle Media Manager loaded on your system, the Launcher will also contain an icon to run that program. You can also run the Studio Tutorial from the Launcher, which is a great way to get a quick fly-by of the program.

✔ Tip

■ In addition, many of the configuration screens you'll see in this chapter will be labeled Studio "Plus" configuration screens because I'm using the Plus version. If you have the standard version and notice differences in the screens, they probably relate to differences between the programs.

Figure 2.1 Here's the icon to launch Studio Launcher, which is one way to run Studio 10.

Run Studio   Run Instant   Run Tutorial
             DVD Recorder

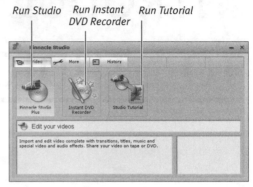

Figure 2.2 The new Studio Launcher, which you can use to run other Studio-related programs and view Studio's helpful tutorial.

Figure 2.3 Here's the second page of the Launcher for accessing Pinnacle support and home pages, as well as the Settings dialog.

Figure 2.4 If you use the Launcher, click this option to close the Launcher once you choose a program or task.

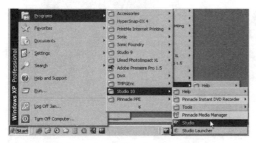

Figure 2.5 You can access Studio 10 and the Pinnacle Media Manager directly from the Start menu. Note the Studio 10 icon on my Quick Launch taskbar.

Click the More button in the Launcher to see the dialog box shown in **Figure 2.3**, which provides links to Pinnacle's Technical support and home page. Click Settings to access the Launcher Settings dialog (**Figure 2.4**), which lets you opt to close the Launcher after selecting a task (which I recommend enabling).

Since I use Studio primarily, and not the other functions available on the Launcher bar, I prefer to skip the Launcher and run Studio directly. Pinnacle makes this simple by including an icon for Studio in the Program group accessible from the Windows Start menu (**Figure 2.5**). Since I use Studio a lot, I created an icon for the program in the Quick Launch area of my Windows XP taskbar by dragging the icon from the Start menu to the taskbar.

Now let's jump directly into the Studio editing program.

Using Edit Mode

When you first enter Studio, you're in Edit mode (**Figure 2.6**), where you'll spend the bulk of your time. Capture mode and Make Movie mode, accessible via tabs at the upper left of the screen, enable their namesake activities.

The Edit mode interface is composed of three windows: the Album, the Player, and the Movie window. While in Edit mode, you have access to Undo, Redo, and Help buttons at the upper right of the screen.

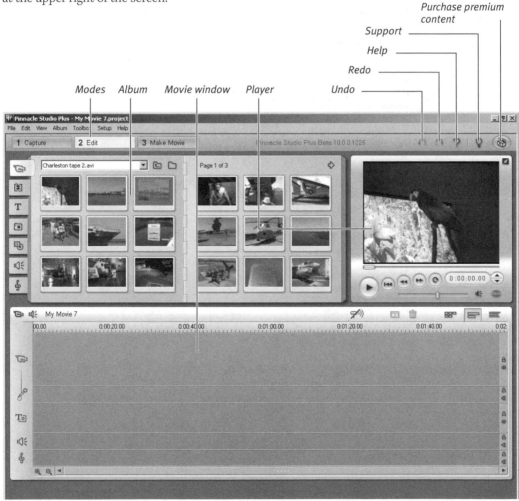

Figure 2.6 When you first run Studio, you're in Edit mode, where you'll spend most of your time.

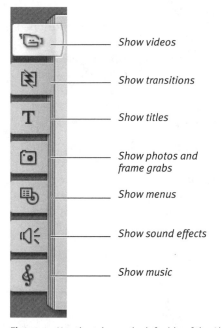

Show videos

Show transitions

Show titles

Show photos and frame grabs

Show menus

Show sound effects

Show music

Figure 2.7 Use the tabs on the left side of the Album to navigate among the various content types.

The Album

The Album consists of seven windows, which you can select using the icons on the left panel (**Figure 2.7**). Three of these windows are for collecting video, audio, and still image files so that you can include them in a project (for details on how to do this, see Chapter 6).

The other four windows contain libraries of effects supplied by Pinnacle, offering transitions, titles, sound effects, and disc menus. For information on how to apply and customize these, see Chapters 8, 10, 11, and 12, respectively.

The Player

The Player is where you preview content and effects contained in the various albums, as well as your editing progress in the Movie window (**Figure 2.8**). Click the DVD icon at the lower right, and you convert the Player into a DVD playback remote control for previewing your DVD titles. Note that this icon doesn't become active until you've added a DVD menu to your project (more on DVD authoring in Chapter 12).

In Studio, you can toggle to full-screen preview by clicking the arrow key at the upper-right corner of the Player, returning to the main screen by pressing Esc on your keyboard. As we'll see in "Setting Up a Dual-Monitor Display," later in this chapter, the arrow key also toggles between preview in the Player and preview in a second monitor.

Note that you can't detach or enlarge the Player, because like all interface components, it's fixed, for simplicity. Since the Player is integral to virtually all editing operations, its use is discussed in most of the chapters in this book.

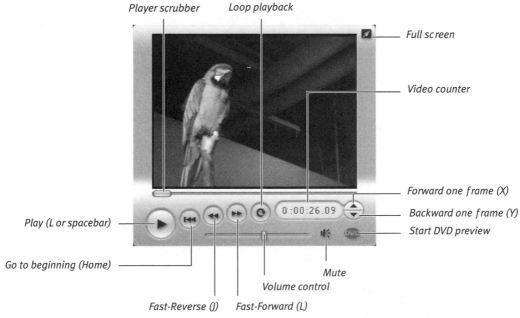

Figure 2.8 Polly want a cracker? The Player has the usual VCR-like playback controls, plus a scrubber that lets you manually move through the video files. The DVD button transforms the Player into a DVD remote control (see Chapter 12).

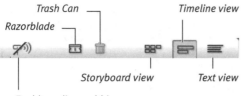

Trash Can

Razorblade

Timeline view

Storyboard view

Text view

Enable audio scrubbing

Figure 2.9 You can easily switch among the Timeline, Storyboard, and Text views of the Movie window. Note the omnipresent Razorblade, for splitting your videos, and the Trash Can, for deleting them.

The Movie window

The Movie window has three views—Timeline (shown in Figure 2.6), Storyboard, and Text (called Edit List view in the Studio menu)—that you toggle using controls in the upper-right corner of the Movie window (see **Figure 2.9**). See Chapter 7 to learn how and when to use these modes. Three icons, the Enable Audio Scrubbing (to hear audio as you drag your cursor through the clip), the Razorblade (for splitting clips), and the Trash Can (for deleting clips), are available in all three modes.

continues on next page

Using Edit Mode

Video toolbox. In the upper-left corner of the Movie window is a Camcorder icon (**Figure 2.10**), which you click to open the Video toolbox (**Figure 2.11**), revealing seven editing functions.

The Video toolbox offers the following functions:

◆ *Clip Properties.* Use this tool to trim video and still image content to the desired length (Chapter 7).

◆ *Create or Edit a Title.* Use this tool to design and edit titles (see Chapter 10).

◆ *Create or Edit a Disc Menu.* Use this tool to link menus to content and customize DVD menus (see Chapter 12).

◆ *Frame Grab tool.* Use this tool to grab still-frame images from your camcorder or disk-based video files (see Chapter 5).

◆ *Create a Music Video Automatically.* Use this tool to convert your footage to a music video automatically (see Chapter 9).

◆ *Edit Video Overlay.* Use this tool to create and edit Picture-in-Picture and Chroma Key effects (see Chapter 9).

◆ *Add an Effect to a Video Clip.* Use this tool to access Studio's color correction facilities and other special effects (see Chapter 9).

You can click through the various options at will; click the Camcorder icon or the X in the upper right of all tools to close the Video toolbox. When I first started using Studio, the controls located in this tab were the ones I "lost" most often. You might click this window open and shut a few times to burn the location of these critical controls into your mind.

Figure 2.10 The Camcorder icon opens and closes the Video toolbox.

Clip Properties

Create or Edit a Title

Create or Edit a Disc Menu

Frame Grab tool

Create a Music Video Automatically

Edit Video Overlay

Add an Effect to a Video Clip

Figure 2.11 The editing tools in the Video toolbox.

Using Edit Mode

Figure 2.12 The Speaker icon opens and closes the Audio toolbox.

Audio Clip Properties

Change the Volume of the Audio Tracks

Record a Voice Over Narration

Add Background Music from an Audio CD

Create Background Music Automatically

Add an Effect to an Audio Clip

Figure 2.13 The editing tools in the Audio toolbox.

Audio toolbox. If you hover the cursor over the right side of the toolbox, Studio reveals a Speaker icon in the upper-left corner of the Movie window (**Figure 2.12**). You can click this icon to open the Audio toolbox, which contains its own set of unique tools (**Figure 2.13**).

The Audio toolbox provides the following functions (see Chapter 11 for more information):

◆ *Audio Clip Properties.* Use this tool, which is selected in Figure 2.13, to trim audio files to the desired length.

◆ *Change the Volume of the Audio Tracks.* Use this tool to adjust the volumes of the audio tracks.

◆ *Record a Voice Over Narration.* Use this tool to record your narration.

◆ *Add Background Music from an Audio CD.* Use this tool to rip CD-Audio tracks to include in your projects.

◆ *Create Background Music Automatically.* Use this tool to create custom background music of any length.

◆ *Add an Effect to an Audio Clip.* Studio 10 includes a range of audio effects, which you can add to your project using this tool (see "Using Studio's Audio Effects" in Chapter 11).

✔ Tip

■ Double-clicking any icon in the Video or Audio toolbox returns you to the main Movie window.

USING EDIT MODE

Using Capture Mode

You enter Capture mode by selecting the Capture tab at the upper left of the Studio interface (Figure 2.6). Here you transfer video from a camcorder or other source to your computer. Studio has two interfaces for capturing: one for digital devices and one for analog camcorders and decks.

Studio includes a Frame Grab feature for capturing still images from your camcorder or captured video (see Figure 2.7). This feature is covered in more detail in "Capturing Still Images" in Chapter 5.

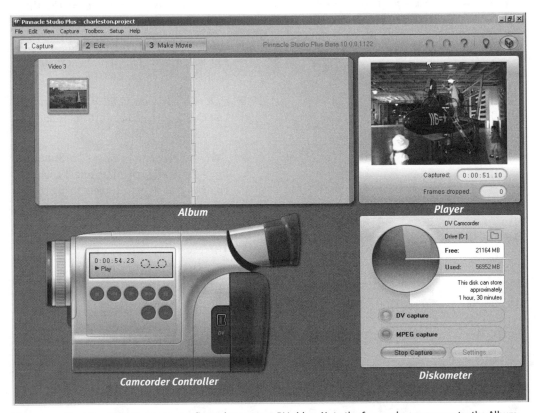

Figure 2.14 Meet the Capture screen, configured to capture DV video. Note the four major components: the Album, the Player, the Camcorder Controller, and the Diskometer.

Capturing from DV source devices

Figure 2.14 shows the four basic windows in Capture mode: the Album, the Player, the Camcorder Controller, and the Diskometer.

The **Album** holds the captured video files, which are added dynamically during capture when Studio detects additional scenes in your source video. After capture, you can change the comments associated with each scene (see Chapters 3 and 4) and thus search for scenes while in Edit mode. However, you can't play back your videos in Capture mode; you must switch to Edit mode.

The **Player** previews the captured video, providing information on capture duration and the number of frames dropped during capture, if any. As you can see, there are no playback controls, so you have to switch to Edit mode to play your captured video.

The **Camcorder Controller** lets you control your digital camcorder. One of the key advantages of these digital formats is the ability to control your camcorder over the same FireWire connection that transfers video from the camcorder to the computer (see the sidebar "FireWire to the Rescue" in Chapter 3). This ability makes capture from these sources much easier than when you use analog capture.

The **Diskometer** contains the controls for starting and stopping capture. It also provides features to let you select your capture drive and see how much disk space remains on your capture drive (in megabytes) and the amount of time remaining for the selected capture format. You can select several capture options on the face of the Diskometer; to choose all other relevant options, you click the Settings button.

USING CAPTURE MODE

Capturing from analog sources

Figure 2.15 shows Studio's interface for capturing analog video. As you can see, the Album and Player remain unchanged from DV capture, but two additional panels appear to the left and right of the Diskometer for adjusting the brightness and color of the captured video and for adjusting the incoming audio volume. These are unnecessary with digital source video, as you're simply transferring the digital video file from camera to computer.

Capturing from an analog source, however, usually involves some fine-tuning, especially for audio, and Studio provides a strong tool set for doing so. Also, when capturing analog video, you have to select the format for storing your video and, often, the quality options associated with that format—hence, the additional controls adjacent to the Diskometer.

If all this capturing business sounds scary, don't sweat. Capturing analog video is more meticulous than mysterious, and the process is spelled out in Chapter 4.

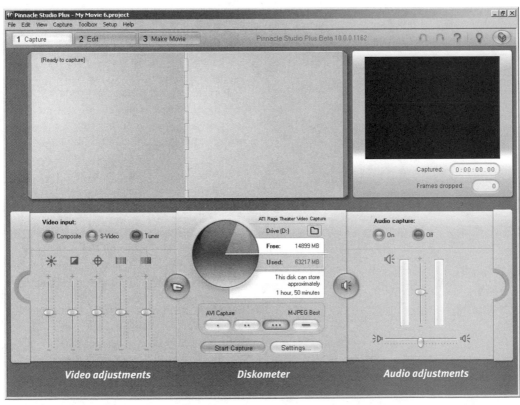

Figure 2.15 Here's the Capture screen, analog style. The controls let you adjust the incoming audio and video.

Using Make Movie Mode

You enter Make Movie mode (**Figure 2.16**) by selecting the Make Movie tab at the upper left of the Studio interface (see Figure 2.6). This takes you to the controls for outputting your work.

Note that Studio customizes the Make Movie interface based on output type. In Figure 2.16, I'm about to produce a DVD of a recent trip to Charleston. As you can see, Studio shows a Diskometer-like view of the amount of space available on the DVD, and clicking the Settings button launches a dialog box with options specific to the selected output medium (**Figure 2.17**).

As indicated on the vertical panel on the left of the Make Movie tab (see Figure 2.16), you can also output to tape (see Chapter 13) and produce digital files, including AVI, MPEG, and streaming media formats (see Chapter 14).

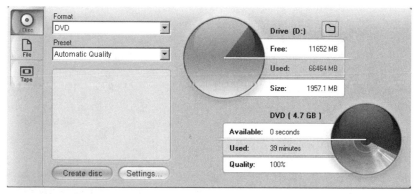

Figure 2.16 The Make Movie dialog box is your last stop in the production process. Note the tabs at the upper left that let you select the output type.

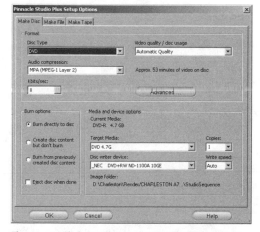

Figure 2.17 Click Settings to see the detailed encoding options for the selected output medium (here we see the settings for DVD output).

Using Undo and Redo

Experimentation is a major part of the video creation process, which means trying and discarding lots of options. Studio makes this process painless with an exhaustive Undo/Redo feature that saves up to 64 edit decisions made since the project was loaded for the current editing session. You can even save your project file and then undo previous edit decisions (a rare option in my experience) and, of course, redo them all if you change your mind again. Note that the redo and undo functions don't work on a movie once you've rendered it and output it to AVI, MPEG, or some other digital video format.

Figure 2.18 Video requires lots of experimentation, so Studio gives you several options if you change your mind, such as an Undo icon.

To undo an edit:

◆ To undo the immediately preceding edit that you've made, do *one of the following*:

  ▲ Click the Undo icon in the upper-right corner of the Studio interface (**Figure 2.18**).

  ▲ Select Edit > Undo.

  ▲ Press Ctrl+Z on your keyboard to activate the Undo keyboard shortcut.

  Studio will undo the last edit—in this case, an inserted clip.

  Note that Studio stores edits sequentially, so if you want to undo the third previous edit, you must first undo the two most recent edits.

Figure 2.19 Changed your mind again? Simply click the Redo icon.

To redo an edit:

◆ To redo an edit, do *one of the following*:

▲ Click the Redo icon in the upper-right corner of the Studio interface (**Figure 2.19**).

▲ Select Edit > Redo.

▲ Press Ctrl+Y on your keyboard to activate the Redo keyboard shortcut.

Studio will redo the last edit—in this case, a trim end.

As with edits, Studio stores Undo commands sequentially, so you must apply Redo commands sequentially if you want to reverse previously applied Undo commands.

USING UNDO AND REDO

Using Online Help

Studio includes extensive online help—
essentially a digital version of the product
manual. Studio also provides Tool Tips, those
little flags that explain an icon's function
when you hover over the icon with your cursor for a moment or two. If you find these
irritating, Studio lets you disable them.

In addition, Studio provides keyboard shortcuts for many common activities. Studio
offers an online list of shortcuts, which you
can access as described in the following
tasks.

To open Studio's Help screen:

◆ Do *one of the following:*

▲ Press the F1 key.

▲ Click the Question Mark icon in the
upper-right corner of the screen (see
Figure 2.14).

▲ Choose Help > Help Topics
(**Figure 2.20**).

Studio's Help screen appears (**Figure 2.21**).

Figure 2.20 Here's how you open Studio's online Help
screen.

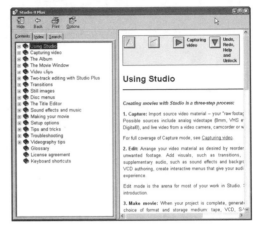

Figure 2.21 What you get is essentially an online
version of the manual.

Figure 2.22 If you find Tool Tips irritating, you can disable them.

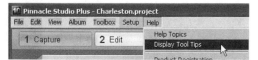

Figure 2.23 Tool Tips are disabled when the check mark is gone from the side of the menu item.

Figure 2.24 If you're a fan of keyboard shortcuts, Pinnacle makes them easy to learn by posting them in the Help file.

To disable Studio's Tool Tips:

◆ Choose Help > Display Tool Tips (**Figure 2.22**).

When you select Display Tool Tips, the check mark beside the Display Tool Tips menu item is removed (**Figure 2.23**). You can reenable Tool Tips by selecting Display Tool Tips in the Help menu again.

To view Studio's keyboard shortcuts:

◆ With Studio Help Topics open, select Keyboard Shortcuts at the bottom of the Contents menu.

A list of keyboard shortcuts appears in the display window (**Figure 2.24**).

Now let's take a look at the steps you should take before starting your initial project.

USING ONLINE HELP

Selecting Your Capture Drive

Most video old-timers use systems with two or more hard disk drives: one for the operating system and applications and one for captured video and project files. This model arose in the days of underpowered computers and cranky, low-capacity disk drives that were barely up to the task of capturing video.

Things have changed since then. Most computers purchased since 2000 are more than capable of video capture and editing as is. Still, with 300-gigabyte (GB) drives costing under $300, most video producers should consider purchasing a separate drive, especially for long projects or DVD production.

To select your capture drive:

1. From the Studio menu, choose Setup > Capture Source (**Figure 2.25**).

   The Pinnacle Studio Setup Options dialog box appears, set to the Capture Source tab.

2. In the Data Rate box (at the lower right of the Pinnacle Studio Setup Options dialog box), click the yellow Folder icon (**Figure 2.26**).

   The Select Folder and Default Name for Captured Video dialog box appears.

3. To change drives and select a destination folder on your preferred capture drive, click the Save In list box at the top of the screen (**Figure 2.27**).

   The list of available drives drops down.

4. Click to select the target drive and folder (**Figure 2.28**).

Figure 2.25 Choose Setup > Capture Source to access disk selection and test settings.

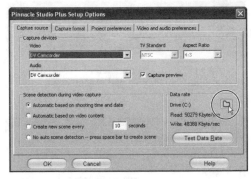

Figure 2.26 Click the yellow Folder icon to select your capture drive and folder.

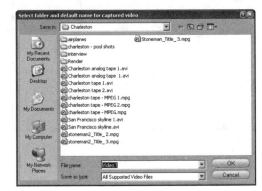

Figure 2.27 Click the Save In list box to change capture drives.

✔ Tips

■ Even if you're running a fast network at home, don't select a network drive as your capture disk. Performance is best with a local drive.

■ If you have multiple drives, sometimes it's helpful to label your capture drive "Video Disk."

SELECTING YOUR CAPTURE DRIVE

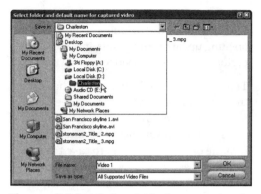

Figure 2.28 Select the target drive for your captured video.

Figure 2.29 Click the Create New Folder icon to create a new folder.

Figure 2.30 Give your folders descriptive names so that you can remember what's in them.

To create a new folder and name your clips:

1. At the top of the Select Folder and Default Name for Captured Video dialog box, click the yellow Folder icon to the right of the selected disk drive.

   When you hover the mouse over the icon, the Create New Folder Tool Tip appears (**Figure 2.29**).

2. Studio creates a new folder, which you can name at will (**Figure 2.30**).

3. If desired, type the name of the captured file in the File Name box.

   If you capture sequential files, Studio simply updates the file from Video 1 to Video 2, and so on.

✔ Tips

- Don't stress about what to name your files at this point, as you'll revisit this topic during the capture process.

- Try to make your folder names descriptive; otherwise, six months from now you'll have trouble figuring out what's in them.

SELECTING YOUR CAPTURE DRIVE

Defragmenting Your Capture Drive

Although most current computers (that is, those manufactured from 2000 onward) have enough power to handle digital video capture and editing, Studio includes a performance test so that you can be sure your computer has what it takes. Run this test as soon as you install Studio to identify any problems that may prevent smooth operation.

If you're using a disk that contains lots of data for your capture and edit drive, you should defragment the drive before performing this test. During normal disk operation, Windows copies and deletes files all over the drive, sometimes splitting up longer files when writing them to disk. *Defragmenting* the

drive reunites all file components and packs the files efficiently together on the drive, opening up large contiguous spaces for the performance test and video editing projects.

The Windows Disk Defragmenter has a tool that lets you analyze the drive to see if it needs defragmenting. We'll skip that test and defragment anyway, just to be sure your disk is in the optimal condition to take the performance test—even if you're not in dire need of defragmenting, it can only help.

To defragment your capture drive:

1. From the Windows desktop, choose Start > Accessories > System Tools > Disk Defragmenter (**Figure 2.31**).

   The Disk Defragmenter application window appears.

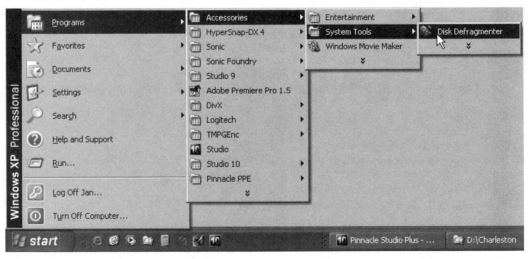

Figure 2.31 The long and winding road to the Disk Defragmenter utility, a hard drive's best friend.

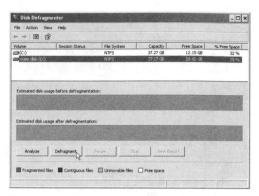

Figure 2.32 Select your target drive and click the Defragment button to get started.

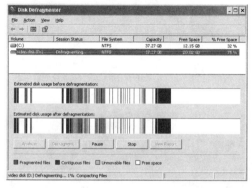

Figure 2.33 The Disk Defragmenter first analyzes your file and then starts to consolidate files, compacting them to the inner tracks of the drive.

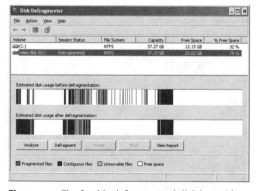

Figure 2.34 The freshly defragmented disk has wide open spaces, perfect for efficient video capture.

2. Choose the video capture disk by selecting it in the application window; then click the Defragment button (**Figure 2.32**).

While you're waiting, go get a cup of coffee. You're pretty much done, but if you care to watch, here's what you should be seeing:

The program analyzes disk usage before defragmenting. Although you can't see it in the black-and-white screen shots, most of the small lines surrounded by white spaces are fragmented files that will be consolidated during the defragmentation process (**Figure 2.33**).

In the defragmented disk, which is ready for testing, all files are consolidated and efficiently packed, leaving plenty of contiguous disk space (**Figure 2.34**).

✔ Tips

- Depending on the size of the drive and how much data is on the disk, defragmenting can take anywhere from 30 seconds to several hours, during which time you shouldn't use your computer. Keep this in mind before starting this operation.

- Turn off all background programs and don't use the computer when you're defragmenting the drive. If any program writes data to disk while the system is defragmenting, the Disk Defragmenter may stop and then restart, extending the completion time significantly.

- Large files slow the disk defragmentation process. If you have large video files or other files on the capture drive that you don't need, delete them and any other extraneous files before defragmenting.

DEFRAGMENTING YOUR CAPTURE DRIVE

Testing Your Capture Drive

Now that your drive is freshly defragmented, let's see how it performs in the Studio drive test.

For perspective, keep in mind that DV streams from a camera at about 3.6 megabytes (MB) of video data per second. To capture DV successfully, a disk must be able to write, or store, at least 3.6 MB of data per second. To transfer DV back to the camera, the disk must be able to read at least 3.6 MB of data per second.

As you'll see, the video disk on my HP xw4100 workstation can far exceed these requirements. In all likelihood, your computer will also pass this test with flying colors, but it's better to test early to identify any problems than to experience balky operation during capture and editing.

To test your capture drive:

1. From the Studio menu, choose Setup > Capture Source (**Figure 2.35**).

    The Pinnacle Studio Setup Options dialog box appears, set to the Capture Source tab.

2. Click the Test Data Rate button in the lower-right corner of the Capture Source tab (**Figure 2.36**).

    Studio starts the test, and the Data Rate Test dialog box appears (**Figure 2.37**). The test should take no longer than about 10 seconds, and then a Data Rate Test results dialog box appears (**Figure 2.38**). I passed!

Figure 2.35 Choose Setup > Capture Source to access Studio's disk test utility.

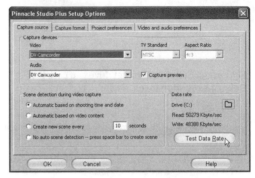

Figure 2.36 Click the Test Data Rate button in the lower-right corner to check disk performance.

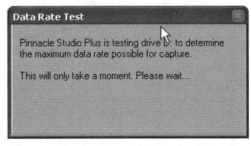

Figure 2.37 You should see this dialog box for 10 to 15 seconds.

Figure 2.38 Voilà! I passed the test and am almost ready to get started.

Figure 2.39 Studio notes the results in the Capture Source tab's Data Rate section.

Studio lists these results on the Capture Source tab (**Figure 2.39**). You can retest at any time. For example, if you start experiencing dropped frames during capture or you can't write video back to the camera, retest and make sure that performance is up to par.

✔ Tip

■ I've noticed big ranges in test rates when I test several times in sequence. So don't sweat it—expect some variance, and recognize that any score over 10,000 kilobytes per second (Kbyte/sec) should be fine.

Optimizing System Disk Performance

Is your computer's performance not up to snuff? The most frequent cause of poor disk performance is too many programs loaded into background memory. You'll know this is the culprit if the Windows taskbar on the bottom right of your screen has more icons than a NASCAR racer. You can attack this problem in two ways. First, click each icon, thus loading each corresponding program. In the properties or similar window, you should find a control for disabling the background process. For example, to disable QuickTime, choose Edit > Preferences and make sure that QuickTime System Tray Icon is not selected. While you wouldn't want to disable your virus checker, you probably don't need RealPlayer, QuickTime Player, the Microsoft Office taskbar, and other items running all the time.

If this doesn't solve the problem, check my Web site at www.doceo.com/stable_editing_workstation.html, where I detail a number of measures that can help you get rid of programs running in the background.

TESTING YOUR CAPTURE DRIVE

Setting Project Preferences

Studio 10 offers several sophisticated preferences that require consideration before you begin editing. These range from how your projects are saved, to using Studio's new dual-monitor capabilities to electing whether to use background rendering and choosing a format. I know this stuff is boring, and you're itching to get started with your first video project, but bear with me on this; I think you'll find it worthwhile.

We'll start with your project preferences.

To open the project preferences dialog box:

◆ From the Studio menu, choose Setup > Project Preferences (**Figure 2.40**).

The Pinnacle Studio Setup Options dialog box appears, open to the Project Preferences tab (**Figure 2.41**).

Figure 2.40 Choose Setup > Project Preferences to access basic editing default settings.

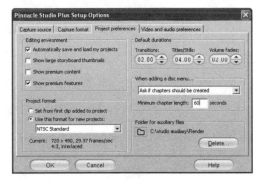

Figure 2.41 Here are your project preferences. We'll start by discussing the top preference in the editing environment category, which relates to how you save your files.

Saving Your Projects

The first preference, Automatically Save and Load My Projects, relates to a new feature that requires some explanation. As mentioned in the Introduction, the most significant under-the-hood change in Studio 10 is that it now uses components of sibling prosumer editor Pinnacle Liquid Edition. One of Edition's best features is that it continually saves all edit decisions as you make them, with undo capabilities, of course. That way, if the program or your computer crashes, you should be totally covered–no lost work.

Studio now has that same capability, which is a great thing, and you can use it in one of two ways. That is, when the Automatically Save and Load My Projects checkbox is disabled, which is the default condition that exists when you first load the program, Studio will act pretty much like previous versions of Studio, except that all edits will be stored in real time. If you check the checkbox, Studio will act more like Edition.

continues on next page

With Automatically Save and Load Disabled

Specifically, when this option is disabled, Studio performs as follows:

◆ Each time you run Studio, the program starts a new project with an automatically assigned name that you can change when you first save the project.

◆ When you start a new project, Studio immediately creates and names a new project file, which you can change when you first save the project.

◆ If you attempt to close Studio or start another project, Studio will prompt you to save your project (even though all edits are already saved).

Talking to the product management folks at Pinnacle, I learned that they made this the default option because it would be most familiar to Studio users, who may feel uncomfortable leaving the program without "saving" their work (even if in reality, their work was already saved).

With Automatically Save and Load Enabled

When you enable the Automatically Save and Load feature, Studio works as follows:

◆ When you first run the program, Studio loads the project you were last working on—a nice convenience.

◆ When you start a new project, Studio prompts you for a name to assign to the new project.

◆ When you exit the program, Studio won't prompt you to save your work, because it's already saved. You might find this disconcerting at first.

I like the second approach (Automatically Save and Load enabled) because I like naming projects at the start, and because 99 percent of the time I run Studio, I'll be editing the last project that I worked on anyway. Note that even if you started a project with Automatically Save and Load disabled, you can switch over at any time, just by clicking the checkbox.

Either way, it's great to know that your edits are being saved in real time, and that random crashes won't cost you your work. If you do crash, when you rerun Studio, you'll see the error message shown in **Figure 2.42**; simply click Continue, and you'll be back where you were before the crash.

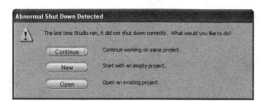

Figure 2.42 If Studio crashes, you'll see this dialog box the next time you run the program. Click Continue and you should pick up where you left off.

There is one caveat, however. I've worked with Liquid Edition, and like the automatic save feature, but there's one scenario where it's kind of a pain. Specifically, with Studio 9, you could save your project and then try something totally wacky like applying six different filters to a clip to produce a bizarre effect. At the end, if you decided that you didn't like the effect, you could simply exit the project and elect not to save your changes.

With Liquid Edition, and Studio with this feature enabled, you can't simply exit and not save the project, since all your work is already saved. Instead, you have to undo each and every edit, which can get cumbersome after you've made 50 or 60 adjustments. Still, it's a pretty small price to pay for the security this feature provides.

Once again, if you opted to have Studio automatically save and load your projects, you'll save your file when you first select a new project, and never again. If you elected to save and load manually, you'll need to get familiar with most of the following procedures.

To enable automatic save and load:

1. From the Studio menu, choose Setup > Project Preferences (Figure 2.40).

    The Pinnacle Studio Setup Options dialog box appears, open to the Project Preferences tab (Figure 2.41).

2. Click the Automatically Save and Load My Projects checkbox.

To save a project for the first time:

1. Do *one of the following*:

   ▲ Choose File > Save Project.

   ▲ Choose File > Save Project As.

   ▲ Press Ctrl+S.

   The Save As dialog box opens (**Figure 2.43**).

2. Find the folder where you'd like to store your project, and assign your project a file name; then click Save.

   Studio saves the project as an STX file, which is the file type used for all Studio 10 project files.

Figure 2.43 You know this drill; name the file and click Save. Note the nifty new .stx extension.

✔ Tip

■ Studio 10 can load projects from Studio 9, but once saved into Studio 10's STX project format, Studio 9 can no longer open them.

To save a project after naming it:

◆ Choose File > Save Project, or press Ctrl+S.

To save a project to a new name or location:

1. Choose File > Save Project As.

   The Save As dialog box opens.

2. Select a folder, type the desired file name, and click Save.

   Studio saves the project file.

✔ Tip

■ Note that when you use the Save Project As command, you are creating a totally separate project, and Studio duplicates all auxiliary files. If you just want to change the name, use the File > Rename Project command, shown in the next task.

SAVING YOUR PROJECTS

Figure 2.44 Here's where you start to rename your project.

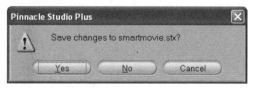

Figure 2.45 Type the new name, click OK, and you're done.

Figure 2.46 You'll only see this if you elect not to have Studio automatically save and load your projects (though Studio will save them automatically even if you don't).

To rename a project:

1. Choose File > Rename Project (**Figure 2.44**).

   The Rename Project dialog box opens (**Figure 2.45**).

2. Type the desired New Project Name.

3. Click OK to close the dialog box.

   Studio renames the project, storing all auxiliary files under the new name (and not duplicating them as with the Save Project As command).

To respond to Studio's automatic save functions:

1. Attempt to exit Studio by doing *one of the following*:

   ▲ Choose File > Exit.

   ▲ Click the X icon in the upper-right corner of the screen.

   The dialog box shown in **Figure 2.46** appears.

2. Do *one of the following*:

   ▲ Click No.

   Studio exits.

   ▲ Click Cancel.

   You return to Studio.

   ▲ Click Yes.

   The Save As dialog box opens.

3. Select a folder and type the desired file name.

4. Click Save.

   Studio saves the project file.

SAVING YOUR PROJECTS

Deleting Projects

Also new in Studio 10 is a project delete function, which is a fast way to delete the STX file associated with your project and all auxiliary files. This function does not delete the source files that you've incorporated into your project, however.

Note that you can't delete the project that you're currently editing, so the first step in this process is to exit the project you want to delete and either start a new project or open an existing project.

To delete a project:

1. Choose File > Delete Projects (**Figure 2.47**). Studio opens the Delete Projects dialog box (**Figure 2.48**).

2. Select the project you want to delete.

3. Click Delete.

    Studio deletes the project file and all auxiliary files.

4. Do *one of the following*:

    ▲ Repeat steps 2 and 3 to delete another project or projects.

    ▲ Click Close to close the dialog box.

Figure 2.47 Step one toward deleting your projects.

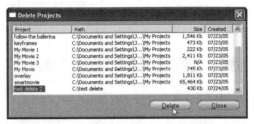

Figure 2.48 The Delete Projects window. Just select the project you no longer want and click Delete.

✔ Tips

■ My tests revealed that the size provided in the Delete Projects window is not accurate, at least in the version of software I was using. Specifically, the project "test delete 2" selected in Step 2 actually had about 95 MB of auxiliary files that were deleted in the process, which is much more than the 430 KB shown in Figure 2.48.

■ Studio also allows you to delete project auxiliary files; see "Working With Auxiliary Files," later in this chapter.

■ Once again, this function does not delete the source files you've included in your project. To better manage these files, I typically capture or copy all files I use in a project into one folder that I can delete easily after project completion.

Hiding Premium Content and Features

Pinnacle sells multiple versions of its software, each with different feature sets, and also sells additional effects and transitions. In previous Studio versions, the program displayed these extra features and effects, and let you know that you could upgrade or buy the additional components at Pinnacle's Web site.

In Studio 10, Pinnacle allows you to hide features and effects you can't use by deselecting the Show Premium Content and Show Premium Features checkboxes in the Setup Options dialog box (**Figure 2.49**).

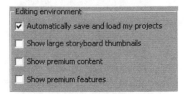

Figure 2.49 If you don't want to see premium features you can't use, deselect the bottom two preferences in the Editing Environment section of the Setup Options dialog box.

Figure 2.50 To change a default duration, you can click and enter the desired duration.

Figure 2.51 Or use the arrows to increase or decrease the duration.

Setting Default Durations

When you insert transitions, titles, still images, and audio fades into your video projects, Studio assigns default durations to these assets. You can modify these defaults for each asset or effect during editing, but here's how you set the default values.

To set default durations:

1. From the Studio menu, choose Setup > Project Preferences (Figure 2.40).

    The Pinnacle Studio Setup Options dialog box appears (Figure 2.41).

2. To change the default duration for transitions, titles, still images, or volume fades, do *one of the following*:

    ▲ Click the number you want to change and enter a new number (**Figure 2.50**).

    ▲ Use the arrow controls beside each duration to adjust the numbers manually (**Figure 2.51**).

✔ Tip

■ Note that these durations are in seconds and frames, not seconds and milliseconds. Since video displays at 30 frames per second, to produce a 2.5-second transition, select 2.15, not 2.5, which Studio wouldn't let you enter anyway (since there are only 30 frames a second). If you click through the durations using the number control, you'll find that after 29 frames, Studio adds a second in duration, and zeros out the frames.

Setting the Project Format

Studio can produce projects in a variety of formats, most notably standard (4:3 aspect ratio) and widescreen (16:9 aspect ratio). Studio can now also mix video files for both formats in the same project, though when rendering, the program must output one format or the other.

Once a project is started, you can't change the format. What you can do, however, is control the format for new projects via the controls shown in **Figure 2.52**. As shown in the figure, you can let the first clip added to the project set the format, or choose the new format from the drop-down list.

If you're only working in one format, like most producers, you should choose the second option using your usual format. If you're mixing formats, like 16:9 and 4:3 video, you should also choose the second option, selecting your target output format as the designated format.

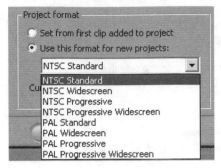

Figure 2.52 You can't change the format of your current project, but you can specify the format for new projects.

About 16:9 Mode

The designation 16:9 is what's called an *aspect ratio*, which defines the relationship between horizontal and vertical display units in a display technology such as a television set. For example, all camcorders sold in the United States shoot in an aspect ratio of 4:3, because that's the aspect ratio most domestic television sets use to display video.

In addition to supporting 4:3, most new DV camcorders also support the 16:9 aspect ratio. The 16:9 mode captures video in a widescreen format like that used in Hollywood movies, making it ideal if you have a widescreen television or high-definition television (HDTV) that supports widescreen footage. Check the documentation that came with your camcorder to learn how to enable and disable this shooting mode.

When's the Right Time for 16:9?

Before shooting in 16:9 format, consider where you and others will view your project. This format works best with older widescreen televisions and newer HDTVs. In addition, most software DVD players like Sonic Solutions' CinePlayer and InterVideo's WinDVD can play both 16:9 and 4:3 video.

However, some standard TV sets (neither widescreen nor HDTV) will stretch the video vertically to full screen, distorting its appearance. You'll likely get similar results if you output your video to analog tape such as VHS. So while 16:9 may look great in your own living room, it might not look so great on grandma's older TV set, a definite factor to consider when choosing your shooting format. If you're unsure of the capabilities of the television or other device that will play your upcoming project, the best course is to test before shooting a major production. Shoot some video in 16:9 format and then capture and render to DVD, to tape, or to whatever format you intend to distribute. Make sure that the video is displayed correctly on your target device. Otherwise, you may be in for a nasty surprise when you show your video masterpiece.

SETTING THE PROJECT FORMAT

Working with Auxiliary Files

Auxiliary files are the files Studio creates when producing your project. These can include background audio files, narration tracks, DVD image files, and the other file detritus associated with project development.

A few points about auxiliary files. First, they can be quite large in size, easily 20–30 GB for a one-hour DVD project. For this reason, you probably want them on your largest drive, and not on your system (C:\) drive if at all possible. You probably also want them where you can find them, so you can delete them manually if necessary.

Second, you don't want to change the location of your auxiliary files from project to project, especially if you've got multiple projects under way. Though this option is presented as a "project" preset, it doesn't attach to a particular project.

So if Project A has 10 GB of auxiliary files (like the DVD files you've been planning to use to burn additional discs), and you change the auxiliary file location while working on Project B, Studio deletes all of the auxiliary files for Project A (and the auxiliary files for all other projects at that location, for that matter). While you can still run Project A, you've lost all the fruits of your previous rendering, which could add hours to your project rendering time.

Accordingly, my strategy for auxiliary files is this: I choose a folder on the root directory of my largest disk and store all auxiliary files in that location. I don't change this from project to project.

In the past, since Studio didn't have a command for deleting auxiliary files, I deleted them manually. This will probably change now that Studio has an auxiliary file delete function, described in this section.

Figure 2.53 Here's where you set the location of your auxiliary files.

Figure 2.54 I always try to name this folder something creative, like the Studio Auxiliary folder.

To set the auxiliary file location:

1. From the Studio menu, choose Setup > Project Preferences (see Figure 2.40).

   The Pinnacle Studio Setup Options dialog box appears (**Figure 2.53**).

   The Folder for Auxiliary Files section of the dialog box at the lower right contains a yellow Folder icon.

2. Click the yellow folder to open the Browse for Folder dialog box (**Figure 2.54**).

3. Click the desired drive and folder for your auxiliary files.

4. Click OK to close the Browse for Folder window and return to the Setup Options dialog.

✔ Tip

■ Note that Studio's Browse for Folder function can't create a new folder, so do that first in Windows Explorer if you need to create a new folder for the auxiliary files.

To delete auxiliary files:

1. From the Studio menu, choose Setup > Project Preferences (see Figure 2.40).

   The Pinnacle Studio Setup Options dialog box appears (Figure 2.41).

2. In the bottom right of the dialog, in the Folder for Auxiliary section, click Delete.

   The Delete Auxiliary Files dialog box appears (**Figure 2.55**).

3. Do *one of the following*:

   ▲ Click Delete Auxiliary Files for Current Project.

   ▲ Click Delete Auxiliary Files for All Other Projects.

   ▲ Click Delete Auxiliary Files for All Projects.

4. Click OK to close the dialog box.

✔ Tip

■ The delete function only relates to files stored at the current selected location for auxiliary files. If you change locations for these files, the delete function won't go back and delete files at the old location, another reason to choose a single location and stay there.

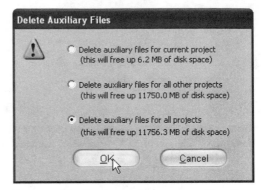

Figure 2.55 Studio can now delete your auxiliary files for you with this dialog box.

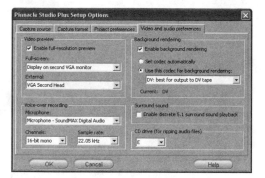

Figure 2.56 We're on the home stretch, on our final window of preferences.

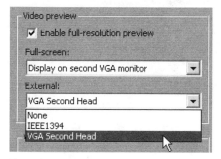

Figure 2.57 Your options for external full-screen preview.

Setting Up a Dual-Monitor Display

Most of the options in the Video and Audio Preferences tab of the Setup Options dialog box (**Figure 2.56**), are addressed later in the book. Most notably, I discuss background rendering in "Working With Background Rendering," in Chapter 8, and I discuss voice-over recording discussed in "Recording Narrations," in Chapter 11. Here, we'll discuss a new feature of Studio 10: the ability to display the video window in a second monitor.

There are three possible configurations for achieving this dual-monitor display, which I'll address in turn (**Figure 2.57**).

◆ First, you can display the video preview out the IEEE1394 (or FireWire) port of your computer, which normally connects to a DV camcorder with a television attached. This provides preview on a TV, which is great when you're producing for DVD, since TVs and computer monitors differ slightly in color and detail. On the other hand, using this approach, your effects must render in the background before you can preview them, which promotes accuracy but can slow you down.

continues on next page

◆ Second, you can display the output on a second computer monitor. This doesn't require background rendering, so it's quicker than the first alternative, but you don't get to see how your video looks on a television set, a negative if you're producing for DVD.

◆ Third, if you have a television tuner card like ATI Technologies' All-in-Wonder, you can treat the television output as the second monitor, and send it directly to a television set. This offers the best of both worlds, because you can preview on a TV without waiting for the video to render.

Whatever approach you select, there are two challenges to setting up the dual-monitor display. First, your Windows desktop must configured for dual-monitor display, in a mode where the second monitor extends the desktop, rather than duplicates the first (which is called clone mode). Techniques for setting this up will vary by graphics card; check your product documentation for guidance. **Figure 2.58** shows the proper mode with the ATI All-in-Wonder.

Once in the proper dual-screen display mode, you must use Studio controls to send the video preview to the second monitor. Here's how you do it.

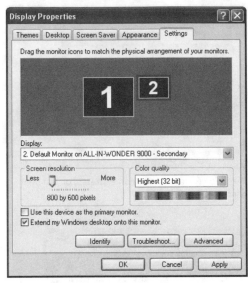

Figure 2.58 Windows has to have dual monitors enabled with the desktop spread over both monitors (not clone mode).

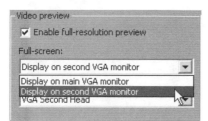

Figure 2.59 To display video on the second monitor, choose this option.

Toggle video display to second monitor

Figure 2.60 Once you've got the preferences set, use the arrow to toggle between modes.

Figure 2.61 This icon means video should be displaying in your second display device.

To configure the second monitor:

1. From the Studio menu, choose Setup > Video and Audio Preferences.

   The Pinnacle Studio Setup Options dialog box appears open to the Video and Audio Preferences tab (Figure 2.56).

2. Click the Full-screen drop-down list, and select Display on Second VGA Monitor (**Figure 2.59**).

3. Click the External drop-down list, and choose the appropriate device (Figure 2.57).

4. Click OK to close the dialog box.

✔ Tip

- If video playback isn't fast enough, uncheck the Enable Full-Resolution Preview option in the Video and Audio Preferences tab (Figure 2.56).

To toggle video on the second monitor on and off:

1. In the upper-right corner of the Player, click the arrow icon (**Figure 2.60**).

   Studio displays video on the second monitor and displays the Pinnacle logo on the Player (**Figure 2.61**).

2. To return the video back to the Player, do *one of the following:*

   ▲ Press the Esc key on your keyboard.

   ▲ In the upper-right corner of the Player, click the arrow icon.

SETTING UP A DUAL-MONITOR DISPLAY

Part II: Gathering Your Assets

CAPTURING DV

DV offers better video quality than most analog camcorders, and since DV camcorders record the time and date of each shot, Studio 10 can divide captured DV footage into scenes, making it easier to find the clips you want.

Since DV is a digital format, *capturing* from a DV camcorder is more like a file transfer; some even refer to the process as a file import. Call it what you will, getting DV video from your camcorder to your computer is a snap. No video resolution to set or audio volume to adjust—just press Start and Stop.

The same cable that carries the DV video to your computer lets you control the camera, so you can start, stop, rewind, and fast-forward your DV camera within Studio—a useful capability unavailable with most analog camcorders. All of these factors make DV capture quick, painless, and highly functional.

Note that capture operation is identical whether you shot your footage in 16:9 or 4:3 mode. However, the first video you insert into the project determines the aspect ratio that Studio uses for that project. In addition, Studio won't let you capture 16:9 and 4:3 footage from the same tape into the same project. Studio's Capture Album does have the ability to display 16:9 and 4:3 footage at the proper aspect ratios, an option we'll explore in this chapter.

The DV Capture Interface

Let's have a quick look at the tools you'll use to control and monitor DV capture. Note that the interface is different when you're capturing from a DV camcorder than it is when you're capturing from an analog camcorder. (See Chapter 4 for the scoop on analog capture.)

You access the main capture window by clicking the Capture tab at the upper left of the Studio interface (**Figure 3.1**). In Capture mode, Studio has four main components: the Album, where Studio displays the captured clips; the Player, which displays video during capture; the Camcorder Controller; and the Diskometer.

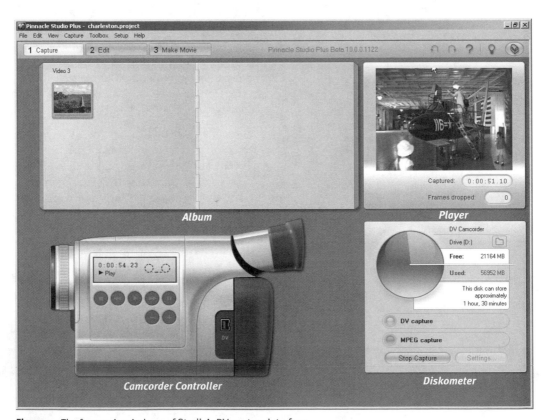

Figure 3.1 The four main windows of Studio's DV capture interface.

Stop

Rewind/Review

Play

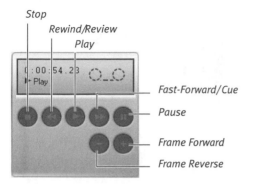

Fast-Forward/Cue

Pause

Frame Forward

Frame Reverse

Figure 3.2 The Camcorder Controller lets you control the playback of your DV camcorder.

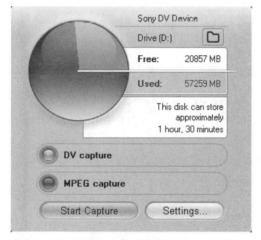

Figure 3.3 The Diskometer tells you how much video you can store on your capture drive, lets you choose among the three capture options, and contains the Start Capture button.

The Album. The Album contains your captured clips, though you can't play them back while in Capture mode. If you enable scene detection (see the sidebar "Making the Scene with Scene Detection," later in this chapter), each scene from that file appears in the Album, thus accounting for the multiple scenes in the Album in Figure 3.1. Had you captured more scenes than could fit on the two pages in the Album, you would see a little white arrow at the upper right of the second page of the Album, indicating that more scenes are stored on subsequent pages.

Studio stores captured files either during capture or, in the case of MPEG files, immediately after capture. Either way, no user intervention is needed to store the files. Once you start to capture another file, your previously captured files disappear from the Album—but don't worry; they are safely stored and accessible in Edit mode.

The Player. Note the lack of playback controls in the Player window. The Player's role during capture is to let you preview the incoming video and give you information about dropped frames. To play the captured files, you have to switch to Edit mode.

The Camcorder Controller. The controls in the Camcorder Controller mimic those on your camcorder (**Figure 3.2**). Use these to navigate through the tape to find the scenes you want to include in your project.

The Diskometer. The Diskometer serves multiple purposes. First, the wheel and associated text describe how much additional video you can store on the capture drive at the selected format and capture quality. For example, **Figure 3.3** shows about 21 GB of space left on the capture drive, which means the drive has enough available space to hold 1.5 hours (at 13 GB per hour) of video recorded in DV format.

continues on next page

THE DV CAPTURE INTERFACE

In the middle of the Diskometer are controls for toggling between DV and MPEG capture—options discussed later in this chapter (see the section "Choosing Your Capture Format"). You also control capture from the Diskometer, clicking Start Capture to start. After you start the capture, this button changes to Stop Capture, which you click to stop the capture (**Figure 3.4**).

Click the Settings button in the lower-right corner to open the Pinnacle Studio Setup Options dialog box. The Capture Format tab is where you choose your capture parameters if you capture in a format other than DV (**Figure 3.5**).

The Capture Source tab is where you select your capture device and scene-detection options (**Figure 3.6**). This is also where you choose and test the capture drive (see "Testing Your Capture Drive" in Chapter 2).

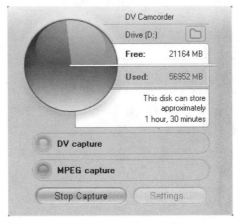

Figure 3.4 The Start Capture button changes to Stop Capture during capture. You can also press the Esc key on your keyboard to end capture.

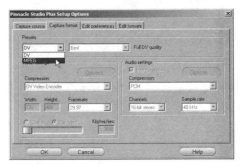

Figure 3.5 The Capture Format tab. Since DV is a standard format, there are no options, but you'll have to select options here when capturing in MPEG or preview format.

Figure 3.6 Here's the Capture Source tab again. Chapter 2 explained how to select and test the capture drive from this screen; this chapter explores the scene-detection options and how to choose among various capture devices.

THE DV CAPTURE INTERFACE

Making the Scene with Scene Detection

Sifting through your scenes and finding the ones to include in your final project can be extraordinarily time consuming. Fortunately, Studio automates much of the process with its comprehensive scene-detection feature.

Studio offers four scene-detection modes (Figure 3.6), accessed via the Capture Source tab in the Pinnacle Studio Setup Options dialog box (click Settings on the Diskometer or choose Setup > Capture Source). The mode I've found most useful is Automatic Based on Shooting Time and Date, an option that analyzes time codes embedded on the DV tape to identify new scenes.

Here's how it works: I chronicle family events with my DV camcorder continuously, usually taking two or three months to complete a 60-minute tape of holidays, school events, and other camera-worthy moments. When it's time to produce a video, I have Studio use the Automatic Based on Shooting Time and Date scene-detection mode to scan the tape, examine the time codes, and break the captured video into multiple scenes that appear in the Album. Without scene detection, I'd have to view the video and perform that work manually, which is time consuming and tedious. Although the scenes are all part of a single video file, during editing they look and act like discrete files, so I can easily pull one or more scenes into the Timeline for editing. For many productions, the amount of time saved is enormous.

The Automatic Based on Video Content option analyzes the video frame by frame, identifying a scene change when the amount of interframe change is significant. This mode is useful for DV cameras when the source video contains one long scene with no breaks—for instance, when you're dubbing a tape from analog to DV or using a single camera to film one long event.

You can also have Studio break a scene into regular intervals of 1 second or more, by choosing the Create New Scene Every *x* Seconds option, or you can eschew automated scene detection and manually create scenes by choosing No Auto Scene Detection and pressing the spacebar to create scenes as you watch the video play.

THE DV CAPTURE INTERFACE

Connecting for DV Capture

Before setting up for DV capture, quickly review the sections "Selecting Your Capture Drive," "Defragmenting Your Capture Drive," and "Testing Your Capture Drive" in Chapter 2.

I'm assuming that you have a FireWire connector or card installed in your computer. If you don't, start there, and make sure it's up and running. Don't spend too much on the connector; for your purposes, virtually all cards will serve equally well, from the $19 variety on up, and they all plug into an available PCI card slot inside your PC. Choosing one with at least two ports will allow you to connect both your camcorder and a FireWire hard drive, as needed, for additional storage space for your captured video.

Note that if you have an HDV camcorder, it should perform identically to a DV camcorder during capture. Specifically, you connect it the same way, and control the camera the same way as shown on these pages.

FireWire to the Rescue

FireWire technology was invented by Apple Computer and then standardized by the Institute of Electrical and Electronic Engineers as IEEE 1394. Sony's name for FireWire is i.Link, and companies refer to the connectors as FireWire, DV, or IEEE 1394. Whatever the name, they should all work together seamlessly.

Some newer DV cameras, like the Canon GL2, have Universal Serial Bus (USB) ports to transfer still images from camera to computer, but that doesn't work for DV video. To capture DV, ignore this connector (and the traditional analog connectors) and find the FireWire plug.

While most computers use a six-pin port, some computers (like my Dell Latitude D800 laptop) use a four-pin connector identical to that in most cameras. Identify which connector you have before buying a cable; cables come in three varieties: four-pin to six-pin, four-pin to four-pin, and six-pin to six-pin.

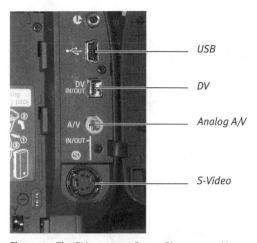

USB

DV

Analog A/V

S-Video

Figure 3.7 The DV port on a Canon GL2 camera. Note the single analog A/V connector for composite video and both audio channels.

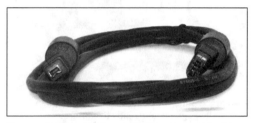

Figure 3.8 A four-pin (on the left) to six-pin DV cable. DV cables also come with dual four-pin and dual six-pin connectors.

FireWire connectors

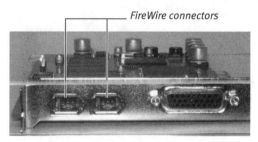

Figure 3.9 The typical six-pin DV connectors (on the left) are found on most—but not all—computers.

To connect your camera and computer for DV capture:

1. Plug in your DV camcorder to AC power. Battery power should work, but it doesn't work with all cameras.

2. Make sure that the camcorder is in VCR, VTR, or Play mode.

3. Connect your FireWire cable to the camera's DV connector (**Figure 3.7**).

   Virtually all cameras use a tiny four-pin connector like that on the left side of the cable in **Figure 3.8**.

4. Connect the FireWire cable to your computer using one of the two slots shown on the left in **Figure 3.9** and the larger six-pin connector shown on the right in Figure 3.8. Some computers—laptops especially—come with a four-pin FireWire port installed. For these, you'll need a FireWire cable with four-pin connectors on each end.

   You're now ready to run Studio and enter Capture mode.

✔ Tip

■ Speaking of buying a cable, basic FireWire cables are priced between $12 and $50, depending on brand and store. If you're buying, check out www.cables.com, which offers a complete line of FireWire cables (including those with four-pin connectors at each end) at very reasonable prices.

CONNECTING FOR DV CAPTURE

Entering DV Capture Mode

As the name suggests, Capture mode is where Studio manages all video capture activities. Entering Capture mode isn't as simple as it sounds.

As soon as you click the Capture tab, Studio checks to ensure that your DV capture device is running properly and your camera is connected, turned on, and in the proper mode.

If everything is configured and connected properly, the process will be invisible to you—you'll simply be ready to capture. If there are problems, however, this section can help you tackle them.

To enter DV Capture mode:

1. Run Studio, and at the upper left, click the Capture tab (Figure 3.1).

   You are in Capture mode. If this is the first time you've entered Capture mode, Studio runs a quick diagnostic test on your system disk to determine if it's fast enough to capture video (**Figure 3.10**).

   If Studio reports that your drive is too slow to capture video, defragment your drive as detailed in "Defragmenting Your Capture Drive" in Chapter 2, and test again. If the drive can't meet these minimum requirements, you need to diagnose and fix the problem, or get a new computer or drive. After successfully completing the check, Studio attempts to load the DV capture driver and find the DV camera.

   If Studio finds the driver and the camera, the LCD panel in the Camcorder Controller will show the time code position of the tape in the DV (**Figure 3.11**). You are clean, green, and ready for takeoff. Proceed to Step 2.

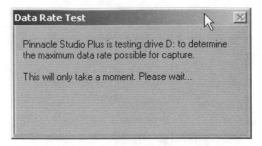

Figure 3.10 Studio runs a quick test on your system disk the first time you enter Capture mode. To read about selecting and testing your capture disk, see "Testing Your Capture Drive" in Chapter 2.

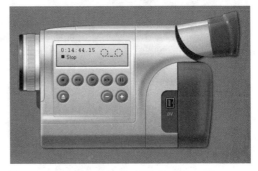

Figure 3.11 Time code in the DV camcorder means you're clean, green, and ready to capture.

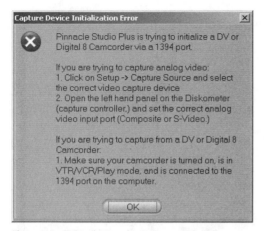

Figure 3.12 Ruh-roh, Scooby-Doo, rumpring's rong... This is what you see when Studio can't find the driver or camera.

Figure 3.13 The blank camera LCD means you're in Capture mode, but Studio can't "see" your DV camcorder.

Figure 3.14 When you see video in the Player, your setup is working and you're ready to capture.

If Studio doesn't find either the driver or the camera, an error message appears (**Figure 3.12**). If you click OK, you enter Capture mode, but the camera LCD is completely blank and you can't capture (**Figure 3.13**). Take the steps recommended in the error message:

▲ Turn the DV camera off and on.

▲ Disconnect and reconnect the FireWire cable.

▲ Restart Windows and try again.

After each step, see if you can enter Capture mode without error. If so, proceed to Step 2; if not, check Studio's Help files for troubleshooting information.

2. Click the Play control button, the middle button on the top row (Figure 3.11).

   Video should appear in the Player window, signifying that you're ready to capture (**Figure 3.14**). Pause the video and turn to the next section for instructions on capturing.

   If you can't see video in the Player window, check Studio's Help files for troubleshooting information.

✔ Tip

■ Studio doesn't pass audio through the system during DV capture, so don't sweat it if you don't hear audio during capture. Besides, unlike when you capture from an analog device, it's virtually impossible to transfer the DV video without the audio: it's stored in the same file in the camera.

Time Code: What You Need to Know

As you shoot, your DV camcorder stamps each frame with a sequential that looks like this:

`01:02:03.04`

Here's what it stands for:

`Hours:minutes:seconds.frames`

Time code gives your DV camcorder and programs like Studio the ability to locate and access any particular frame on the DV tape.

Note that DV tapes don't come with time code embedded; these codes are stored on the tape by the camera as you shoot. Ideally, time code is consecutive from start to finish, so each frame is unique. If there is a break in time code, the camera starts counting again at 00:00:00:01, which means duplicate time codes and potential confusion.

Duplications can occur, for example, when you watch video that you've recorded on your camcorder and play past the end point of the recorded video. If you start recording anew from that subsequent point, the camera restarts the time code from the beginning.

Studio handles time code breaks fairly well, but other programs don't—especially higher-end programs that use continuous time code for features like batch capture. For this reason, it's good practice to maintain a continuous time code on each recorded tape. You can accomplish this in two ways:

◆ Put each tape in your DV camcorder with the lens cap on and record from start to finish. Then rewind and start your normal shooting, which will overwrite the previously recorded frames but maintain the time code structure.

◆ Whenever you shoot with your DV camcorder, be sure you don't start beyond the last previously written time code segment. You've gone beyond the time if you see nothing but lines in the time code field.

Don't confuse time code with the time and date stamp the DV format uses to produce scene changes, which are stored on a different part of the tape. On many camcorders, including most Sony DV camcorders, you can see time and date stamps by pressing the data code control.

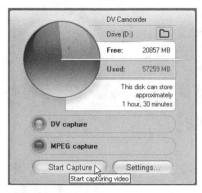

Figure 3.15 Click the Start Capture button on the Diskometer.

Figure 3.16 You can name your file before capture and elect to capture for a specified interval. This is useful, for example, when you want to capture a 60-minute tape while you're away from the computer.

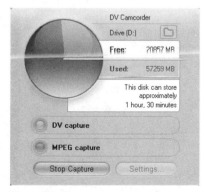

Figure 3.17 To stop capture, click Stop Capture on the Diskometer or press the Esc key on your keyboard.

Capturing DV Video

There are several capture options and other settings that you could mess with, but let's capture some video using Studio's default settings and return to the key capture options later in the chapter.

Begin by working your way through the steps in the last two tasks. Once you enter Capture mode, the Camcorder Controller should appear, with live time code information. If it doesn't, run through the steps in the previous two tasks again.

Note that it doesn't matter whether you're capturing 16:9 or 4:3 video; Studio will automatically adjust accordingly. You don't need to set any switches or controls to make this happen.

To capture DV video:

1. Click the Capture tab to enter Capture mode.

2. Use the Camcorder Controller to move the DV tape in the camera to the desired starting point.

3. Click the Start Capture button on the Diskometer (**Figure 3.15**).

   The Capture Video dialog box opens (**Figure 3.16**), and the Start Capture button changes to Stop Capture (**Figure 3.17**).

4. For this test, enter a duration of 1 minute and 00 seconds in the Capture Video dialog box, as shown in Figure 3.16.

   When the Capture Video dialog box first appears, it displays the maximum duration of video your disk can store, which is limited by the available space on your hard disk, the file system used in your capture drive, or the version of Windows you're running. (For more information, see the sidebar "Windows File Size Limitations," later in this chapter.)

continues on next page

If the maximum duration shown in your program is less than one minute, either your capture disk is almost full or you're pointing toward the wrong disk. See "Selecting Your Capture Drive" in Chapter 2.

5. If desired, click the Create "SmartMovie" Automatically After Capture checkbox shown in Figure 3.16.

   For more information on SmartMovies, see "Creating Music Videos Automatically," in Chapter 9.

6. Click Start Capture in the Capture Video dialog box to start capturing.

7. If an error message appears (**Figure 3.18**), you've already captured some video using the same file name. Do *one of the following:*

   ▲ Click Yes to overwrite the file and start the capture.

   ▲ Click No to return to the Capture Video dialog box and rename the file. Then click Start Capture to start capturing.

   ▲ Your DV camera starts playing, and capture begins.

8. Studio should capture one minute of video. To stop capture before then, do *one of the following:*

   ▲ Click Stop Capture on the Diskometer.

   ▲ Press the Esc key on your keyboard.

   ▲ After the capture stops, a file labeled Tape 1 (or whatever name you may have chosen) appears in the Album (**Figure 3.19**). You'll see multiple files if any scene changes occurred in the source video during the one-minute capture. (See the sidebar "Making the Scene with Scene Detection," earlier in this chapter, for scene-detection options.)

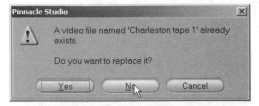

Figure 3.18 Studio won't automatically overwrite previously captured files—a nice feature.

Figure 3.19 Your captured file appears in the Album, with a separate icon for each scene identified by Studio during capture.

CAPTURING DV VIDEO

Figure 3.20 Studio won't capture 4:3 and 16:9 footage from the same tape during the same capture session.

Windows File Size Limitations

A consistent thorn in the side of video developers has been file size limitations inherent to Windows. Depending on a bunch of arcane rules, such as which version of Windows you're running and how you formatted your drives, the maximum file size your system can store may be 2 GB (about 9 minutes of video) or 4 GB (about 19 minutes of video). In these instances, you'll have to divide your capture into 2-GB or 4-GB chunks to capture an entire 60-minute DV tape.

Fortunately, Windows XP and Windows 2000 have no file size limitations as long as you format your drives using the Windows NT file system. That's why most video developers have moved to these versions. When it comes time to format a hard disk, you'll usually see two options for file system: FAT 32 and NTFS. Choose NTFS.

If you're running Windows 98 or Me, however, you're probably using a fairly old computer with lots of out-of-date drivers and other code bits and fragments. Upgrading to Windows XP and reformatting your capture drive will allow you to capture files of any size and will provide a cleaner starting point for your programs.

Whichever version of Windows you're running, Studio should automatically list the maximum duration you can capture in the Capture Video dialog box (Figure 3.16).

✔ Tips

- If you attempt to capture 4:3 and 16:9 footage from the same tape during the same capture session, you'll see the error message displayed in **Figure 3.20**.

- You can't view your captured video in Capture mode. To play back your captured file, see the section "Viewing Your Captured Video," later in this chapter.

- Note the Frames Dropped counter at the bottom of the Player in Figure 3.14. Dropped frames are frames that the computer couldn't capture, usually because the disk wasn't fast enough to keep up with the incoming video. This counter updates in real time during capture. If you drop more than one or two frames, stop capturing and attempt to resolve the problem. Often, running other applications while capturing will cause Studio to drop frames, which should be reason enough not to do so.

- The first several hundred times I used Studio, I would start the video rolling, click the Start Capture button, and get frustrated when Studio asked me for a file name before starting capture, since the video I wanted to capture would be speeding by while I named the file. Then the nickel dropped in my brain, and I realized that I should simply move the video to the desired spot and let Studio do the rest by following the procedures in the preceding task.

- When you capture DV video, Studio's default scene-detection mode automatically detects scenes based on time code. If you desire, change this option on the Capture Source tab, accessible from the Studio menu by choosing Setup > Capture Source.

Choosing Your Capture Format

The previous exercise explained how to capture in DV format, which is appropriate for the vast majority of users and projects. However, when you are capturing DV video from a DV camcorder, Studio gives you one additional option: MPEG full-quality capture.

MPEG Full-Quality Capture. Capturing using the MPEG option saves file space and production time if you're producing a DVD, VideoCD (VCD), or Super VideoCD (SVCD) project with MPEG video.

However, the algorithm that Studio uses to encode MPEG during capture is optimized for speed, not quality, so that Studio can store the video to disk in as near to real time as possible. In contrast, when Studio outputs to MPEG format during final project rendering, say for DVD production, the algorithm is optimized for quality, not speed.

Note also that when you insert effects such as transitions, titles, or color correction into captured MPEG video, Studio implements the effects and then re-encodes the affected portions of the video into MPEG format. So if your edits affect substantial portions of the video, your production-time savings will be minimal. In addition, the edited sections are encoded in MPEG format twice—once during capture and once during rendering—which is the digital equivalent of photocopying a photocopy. Also, if you choose a capture bitrate (or quality setting) that ends up being too high to fit all the video you produce for DVD on your disc, Studio will also have to re-encode your video at the lower rate, again negating your time savings.

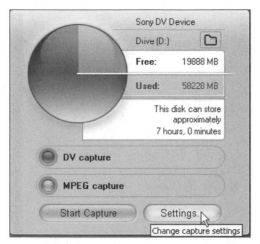

Figure 3.21 Click the Settings button to access your MPEG configuration options.

So unless you're extremely short on hard disk space or expect your edits to be minimal—and production time is absolutely critical—you should capture in DV format and then render in MPEG format after editing. This approach will maximize production quality, even as it may extend production time.

This leaves DV video as the best capture format for virtually all projects.

To choose your capture format:

◆ On the Diskometer, click the button for the desired capture format (**Figure 3.21**).

▲ The light to the left of the button lights up.

▲ If you choose DV Full-Quality Capture, you're all set; there are no other options to select.

▲ If you choose MPEG Full-Quality Capture, you need to set several options before capture. (See the following section for more information.)

Capturing DV Video to MPEG Format

The most obvious time to capture directly into MPEG format is when you're creating projects using MPEG-formatted video, such as in DVDs, VCDs, and SVCDs. Studio simplifies these captures with presets that deliver the properly formatted video for each project.

However, remember that during MPEG capture, Studio defaults to an encoding algorithm optimized for encoding speed rather than quality, so quality will be optimized if you capture with DV and encode in MPEG format during final rendering.

In addition, remember that if your edits affect significant portions of the video in the project, you will have to re-render these anyway before producing your disc. If this is the case, capturing in DV format will produce better overall quality with minimal increase in production time.

Knowing all of these caveats, if you still want to capture in MPEG format, here's how.

To capture DV video in MPEG format:

1. Open the Pinnacle Studio Setup Options dialog box to the Capture Format tab by doing *one of the following*:

   ▲ From the Studio menu, choose Setup > Capture Format (Figure 3.21).

   ▲ In Capture mode, click the Settings button on the Diskometer.

2. Click the text in the first list box in the Presets section and confirm that MPEG is the chosen option (**Figure 3.22**).

3. In the second list box in the Presets section, choose *one of the following options:*

   ▲ If encoding for a DVD project, choose High Quality (DVD).

   ▲ If encoding for an SVCD project, choose Medium Quality (SVCD).

   ▲ If encoding for a VCD project, choose Low Quality (VideoCD).

   ▲ If you want to customize your encoding settings, choose Custom (but be sure to read the following tips first).

4. Click OK to close the Pinnacle Studio Setup Options dialog box.

5. If you're not in Capture mode, click the Capture tab.

continues on next page

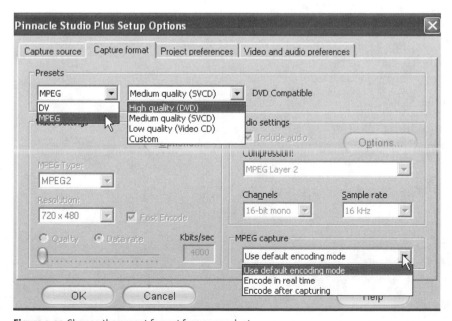

Figure 3.22 Choose the preset format for your project.

CAPTURING DV VIDEO TO MPEG FORMAT

6. Use the Camcorder Controller to move the DV tape in the camera to the desired starting point.

7. Click the Start Capture button on the Diskometer.

The Capture Video dialog box opens, and the Start Capture button changes to Stop Capture.

8. If you desire, change the duration of the video capture and/or change the name of the captured file.

9. Click the Start Capture button in the Capture Video dialog box to start capturing.

10. If the error message appears (refer to Figure 3.18), do *one of the following:*

▲ Click Yes to overwrite the file and start the capture.

▲ Click No to return to the Capture Video dialog box and rename the file. Then click Start Capture.

Your DV camera starts playing, and capture begins.

11. Allow capture to proceed through the specified duration or, to stop capture before then, do *one of the following:*

▲ Click Stop Capture on the Diskometer.

▲ Press the Esc key on your keyboard.

Unless you have a fast computer, it may take Studio a while to compress the DV footage into MPEG format, and you'll see a message like the one shown in **Figure 3.23**.

After encoding stops, a file labeled Video 1 (or whatever name you may have chosen) appears in the Album. You'll see multiple files if any scene changes occurred in the source video during the capture.

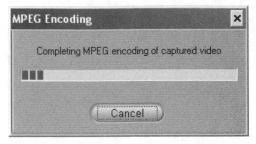

Figure 3.23 On all but the fastest computers, Studio requires a few moments to finish encoding after you stop the tape.

✔ Tips

■ Don't modify the MPEG capture parameters at the lower right of the Capture format screen (Figure 3.22), since this could lead to dropped frames. In default mode (Use Default Encoding Mode), Studio chooses the optimal mode (either Encode in Real Time, or Encode After Capturing), based upon your computer's CPU and the data transfer rate of your hard disk.

■ The Custom option mentioned in Step 3 should be used only by advanced users, since it presents additional encoding controls unfamiliar to most users.

■ If you're capturing video to include on DVD, VCD, or SVCD, stick to the presets and avoid the custom settings. These optical formats define video parameters very tightly, and custom settings could render your video files unusable in these projects.

■ If you're using the same captured video in different types of projects—for instance, to create both a DVD and VCD—use the lowest-common-denominator format. For instance, DVDs can incorporate video encoded for VCD and SVCD, but VCDs can't integrate video encoded for SVCD or DVD.

■ If you're capturing video in MPEG format simply to distribute it on CD-ROM or via the Internet, note that virtually every computer on the planet can now play back MPEG-1 files, since MPEG-1 decoders have been standard on Windows and Macintosh computers for years. However, MPEG-2 decoder capabilities are much less prevalent and generally not available for free. Thus, MPEG-1 is a much better format for general sharing.

Supported Capture Formats

In Studio 10, Pinnacle added support for HDV camcorders, a nice addition, as well as the ability to retrieve video from DVDs, a capability documented in "Importing Content from DVDs," in Chapter 6.

Pinnacle dropped support for the MMV format, which was used solely by Sony's small line of MicroMV camcorders. If you have one these camcorders, your options are to capture digitally using a different program or to capture using your camera's analog outputs.

Customizing Album Views

While your time spent using the Capture Album is usually brief, Studio helps you get as comfortable as possible by providing options for customizing the view.

I've captured some 16:9 footage to illustrate 16:9 views in the Album. **Figure 3.24** shows the Album post-capture in the default mode, which is Scene View with 4:3 images. I'll show you how to switch to 16:9 view in a moment.

To switch between Scene and Comment views:

◆ Right-click anywhere in the Album and choose Comment View (**Figure 3.25**).

The Album switches to Comment view. See the next section, "Adding Scene Comments," to learn how to add comments to your scenes.

Note that if you touch the Album in a gray area, and not on a picture, you get only the options shown in Figure 3.25. To get the complete list of options shown in **Figure 3.26**, you must right-click a picture.

To switch back to Scene view, right-click and choose Scene View.

To switch between 4:3 and 16:9 views:

◆ Right-click a picture in the Album and choose Aspect Ratio 16x9 (Figure 3.26).

The Album switches to 16:9 view. To switch back, right-click and choose Aspect Ratio 4x3.

✔ Tip

■ Note that changing views does absolutely nothing to the captured file; it just changes the way that Studio displays it. It does not convert the file from 4:3 to 16:9, or vice versa.

Figure 3.24 The default Album view: Scene view in 4:3 mode.

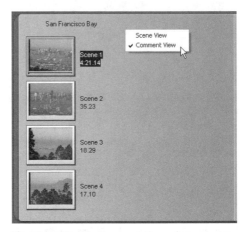

Figure 3.25 Now in Comment view, where you can annotate your scenes.

Figure 3.26 Now in 16:9 mode, converting your project to the 16:9 aspect ratio.

Figure 3.27 To add or change scene comments, slowly double-click the text to make it editable.

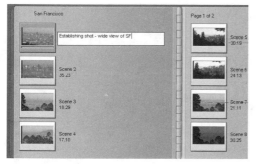

Figure 3.28 Then type your description.

Adding Scene Comments

Immediately after capture, you can annotate your captured scenes in the Album while in Capture mode. This is useful for flagging a specific scene that you want to recall later when you're actually editing.

If you intend to add comments to your scenes, note that Studio updates the Album each time you capture, so if you start another capture before changing the scene comments, Studio stores the captured file and associated comments and clears the Capture Album to make room for the next capture. Don't worry; you can easily find your captured files and comments in the Album in Edit mode and edit your comments there (see "Working with Scene Comments" in Chapter 6).

To add scene comments to your captured video:

1. In the Album, slowly click twice the text immediately to the right of the Video icon to make it editable (**Figure 3.27**).

2. Type the desired comment (**Figure 3.28**).

3. Save your comment by doing *one of the following:*

   ▲ Press Enter.

   ▲ Click anywhere outside the comment box on the Studio interface to set the comments.

✔ Tips

■ You're not actually changing the file name; you're merely editing text that can be seen only inside Studio.

■ If you plan to combine your scenes on the Edit tab of the Album, note that Studio blows away all screen comments when you combine scenes. You might want to look at "Combining Scenes" in Chapter 6 before you invest much time in naming your captured scenes.

ADDING SCENE COMMENTS

Viewing Your Captured Video

If you're like me, the first thing you want to do after capture is watch the video. To do this, switch to Edit mode and use the Player there.

To view your captured video:

1. Select the Edit tab at the upper left of the Studio interface.

   Studio enters Edit mode.

2. In the Album, double-click the video you want to play (**Figure 3.29**).

   The video starts playing in the Player.

3. Use the controls beneath the Player to stop, rewind, fast-forward, go to the beginning of the video, and move through your video frame by frame.

✔ Tip

■ If you captured using scene detection and the Album contains multiple scenes, the Player automatically plays from one scene to the next without breaks.

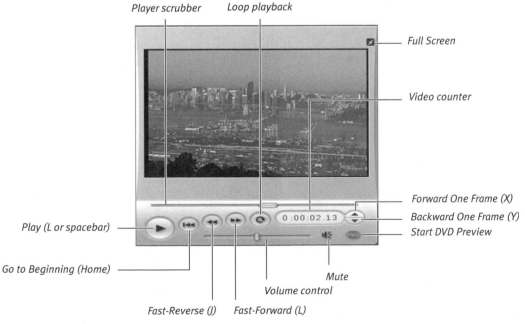

Player scrubber   Loop playback

Full Screen

Video counter

Forward One Frame (X)
Backward One Frame (Y)
Start DVD Preview

Play (L or spacebar)

Go to Beginning (Home)

Mute
Volume control

Fast-Reverse (J)   Fast-Forward (L)

Figure 3.29 You have to jump to Edit mode to play your captured videos.

CAPTURING ANALOG VIDEO

4

While DV capture is a simple file transfer with few settings to worry about, analog capture involves a plethora of controls, including resolution, quality, brightness, volume, and much, much more. To paraphrase Zorba the Greek, the sheer number of options can easily turn analog capture into "the whole catastrophe."

Fortunately, Studio simplifies the process with some well-designed presets and an excellent interface for making all the choices and adjustments necessary to capture analog video at top quality. With some care and frequent checking of your captured files, you should be in great shape.

Note that while DV capture interfaces are relatively standard among different cameras and FireWire devices, analog capture devices and their software interfaces can be as different as snowflakes. Although Pinnacle attempts to present a standard approach for analog capture in Studio, differences among the various devices abound. The best approach is to use this chapter as a guide and then consult the manual or Help files that came with your analog capture card for fine-tuning.

Because 16:9 is primarily a DV-enabled format, you most likely won't want to capture 16:9 video in analog mode. But if you do, Studio can definitely handle it, as you'll discover near the end of this chapter.

The Analog Capture Interface

As you would expect, Studio's analog capture interface (**Figure 4.1**) contains various controls for adjusting your analog capture. Its three main components perform the following roles:

The Album. Your captured clips go directly into the Album, though you can't play them back while in Capture mode. Only one captured file appears in the Album at a time. If you enable scene detection, however (see the sidebar "Scene Detection with Analog Video" later in this chapter), each scene from that file appears in the Album, thus accounting for the multiple scenes (**Figure 4.2**). Had you captured more scenes than could fit on the two pages in the Album, you would see a

little white arrow on the upper-right corner of the Album, which lets you know more scenes are stored on subsequent pages.

Studio may store captured files during capture, or it may store them immediately after capture, as in the case of MPEG files, which must be converted before storage. Either way, no user intervention is needed to store the files. Once you start to capture another file, your previously captured files disappear from the Album—but don't worry; they are safely stored and accessible in Edit mode.

The Player. Note the lack of playback controls in the Player window. The Player's sole role during capture is to preview the incoming video and provide information about dropped frames; you have to switch to Edit mode to actually play the captured files.

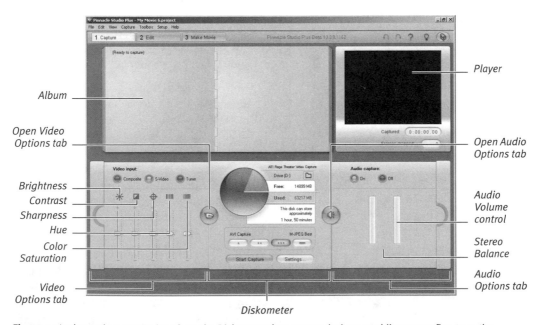

Figure 4.1 In the analog capture interface, the Diskometer has sprouted wings, enabling you to fine-tune the incoming video and control audio volume.

Figure 4.2 The Album, with scene detection enabled.

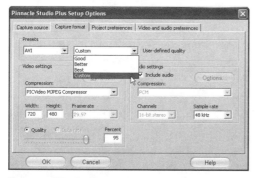

Figure 4.3 Here's where you set your analog capture options.

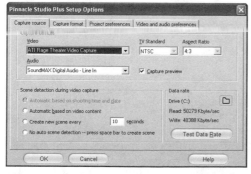

Figure 4.4 Here's where you select your analog video and audio capture devices, as well as scene-detection options.

The Diskometer. If you study the analog capture interface in Figure 4.1, you'll see that the Camcorder Controller, present in the DV interface, is missing in action. That's because the lack of a FireWire or similar connection for analog capture prevents Studio from controlling the camcorder.

The Diskometer for analog capture looks vaguely similar to the DV-capture version, at least on top, where it displays the space remaining on the capture drive. However, the DV, MPEG, and preview capture options are replaced with Good, Better, Best, and Custom quality settings.

In addition, the Diskometer has sprouted wings, with controls for selecting and customizing analog video source and input on the left, and controls for enabling audio capture and setting volume on the right. You open and close these wings by clicking the TV and Speaker icons on the sides of the Diskometer (video on the left and audio on the right). You'll learn how to operate these controls later in this chapter.

Click the Settings button at the lower right of the screen to open the Setup Options dialog box. It will open to the default Capture Format tab (**Figure 4.3**), where you select your analog capture parameters. The tab to the left is the Capture Source tab (**Figure 4.4**), where you choose your capture device and scene-detection options.

Scene Detection with Analog Video

With analog footage, sifting through and finding the scenes to include in your project can be extraordinarily time consuming. When you're using DV footage, on the other hand, you can set Studio to analyze the time and date codes on the tape and identify scene changes by noting when you stop and start the camera. This makes choosing the scenes to include in your final project a lot easier.

Because analog consumer camcorders don't store time code, you don't have this option (that's why the option Automatic Based on Shooting Time and Date is dimmed in Figure 4.4). Fortunately, Studio provides three analog options that can help you find the scenes you want:

◆ If you choose the first available option, Automatic Based on Video Content, Studio identifies scene changes based on significant changes between frames. For example, if one second you're filming the birthday cake and the next your child's delighted face, Studio breaks the two Kodak moments into separate scenes.

◆ If you choose the next option, Create New Scene Every x Seconds, you can break the scene into regular intervals of one second or more.

◆ Finally, when all else fails, you can watch the video and manually create scenes by pressing the spacebar at the appropriate moments during capture. (Choose the option No Auto Scene Detection.) Though this is obviously the most time-consuming method, you get reacquainted with all the best moments of your video—helpful when you're editing several months (or years) after filming.

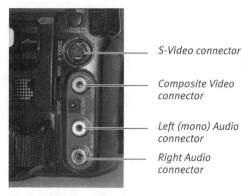

S-Video connector

Composite Video
connector

Left (mono) Audio
connector

Right Audio
connector

Figure 4.5 The business end of my venerable Sony Hi-8 camcorder has separate outputs for S-Video and composite analog video as well as stereo audio.

Figure 4.6 An S-Video cable. Use S-Video whenever it's available, because you'll definitely get higher quality than with composite video.

Connecting for Analog Capture

Although not quite as simple as setting up for DV capture, connecting for analog capture is pretty easy if you can follow color codes and fit square pegs into square holes (metaphorically speaking).

Before taking the steps that follow, make sure that your analog capture card is installed and running. In addition, quickly review the sections "Selecting Your Capture Drive," "Defragmenting Your Capture Drive," and "Testing Your Capture Drive" in Chapter 2.

To connect the camera and computer for analog capture:

1. Plug in your analog camcorder to AC power.

   Battery power should work, but it doesn't always with some cameras.

2. Make sure that the camcorder is in VCR, VTR, or Play mode.

3. Connect your video cables to the camera (**Figure 4.5**) by doing *one of the following:*

   ▲ If both your camera and analog capture device have S-Video connectors and you have the necessary cable (**Figure 4.6**), use the S-Video connector.

continues on next page

▲ If S-Video is not available and your analog camera or deck has a separate composite video port (Figure 4.5), use the composite video connectors with a cable like the one shown in **Figure 4.7**. In most instances, composite video connectors are yellow, and most three-headed cables are coded yellow (composite video), red (right audio), and white (left audio and mono audio). Follow the color coding at both ends and you'll speed your installation.

▲ If S-Video is not available and your camera has a specialty A/V port, use the composite video connectors with a specialty cable. You should have received a specialty cable that looks like that shown in **Figure 4.8**. Plug the single end into your camera.

4. Connect your audio cables to the camera by doing *one of the following:*

▲ If your camera has separate audio connectors (Figure 4.5), connect a cable like that shown in Figure 4.7, being careful to match the colors of the connectors and output ports when applicable.

▲ If your camera has a specialty A/V port, you should have a specialty cable that looks like the one in Figure 4.8. Plug the single end into your camera.

Figure 4.7 The typical three-headed analog cable with separate RCA connectors, for composite video and left and right audio. Fortunately, most cables are color-coded to help you make the right connections.

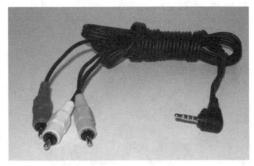

Figure 4.8 If your camcorder has a specialty A/V plug, you'll need a specialty cable. Note the three rings on the single connector: one for each of the three outputs.

5. Connect your video cable to the capture card in your computer.

Most capture cards have input ports and output ports. For example, the ATI All-in-Wonder 9000 PRO card installed in my HP Workstation xw4100 uses a separate breakout box for analog input, with ports for S-Video and composite video and right and left audio (**Figure 4.9**), but a different port and cable for outputting productions back to analog tape. If you see two sets of analog connectors, either in a break-out box like the All-in-Wonder or on the bracket of the internal card itself, check the product's documentation to determine which connector is input and which is output.

6. Connect your audio cables to the computer by doing *one of the following:*

▲ If your analog capture card has separate audio inputs, use the audio input on your capture card.

▲ If your analog capture card doesn't have separate audio inputs, use your sound card's Line In connector (**Figure 4.10**).

Most computers have single-pin stereo audio inputs (Figure 4.10) rather than separate RCA connectors (Figures 4.7 and 4.8). To convert RCA inputs into stereo audio inputs, you'll need a Y-connector like the one shown in **Figure 4.11**, or a similar adapter. You can find these at Radio Shack or on the Web at www.cables.com.

You're now ready to run Studio, set the appropriate software options, and start capturing.

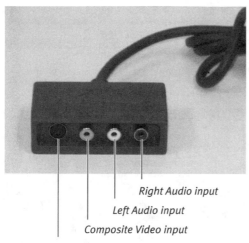

Right Audio input

Left Audio input

Composite Video input

S-Video input

Figure 4.9 The breakout box for ATI's All-in-Wonder graphics card. This box accepts analog inputs.

Figure 4.10 A representation of the bracket on my sound card. Use the Line in connector, not the Mic in (microphone), for your analog audio input.

Figure 4.11 Use a Y-connector to convert the two RCA-type analog connectors to one stereo connector compatible with your sound card.

CONNECTING FOR ANALOG CAPTURE

Choosing Your Analog Capture Parameters

Now that the hardware side is squared away, it's time to start working on the software side by first selecting your capture source and then setting and adjusting your capture parameters.

To select your capture source:

1. Run Studio and enter Capture mode by selecting the Capture tab at the upper left of the screen (Figure 4.1).

2. From the menu bar, choose Setup > Capture Source (**Figure 4.12**).

   The Pinnacle Studio Setup Options dialog box appears.

3. In the Video Capture Devices drop-down menu, select your analog video capture device (**Figure 4.13**).

4. In the Audio Capture Devices drop-down menu, select your analog audio capture device (**Figure 4.14**).

5. Select the desired scene-detection option.

   Remember that the option Automatic Based on Shooting Time and Date is unavailable because analog tapes don't store this information.

6. Click OK to return to Capture mode.

   If your analog capture card has audio input, it should be one of the listed options. Since in this example the system's sound card is used, Line In is selected on the SoundMax sound card.

   At this point, you should be in analog Capture mode, and your screen should look identical to Figure 4.1.

Figure 4.12 Getting to the Capture Source screen.

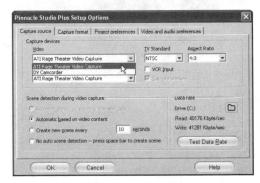

Figure 4.13 Choosing your analog video capture device.

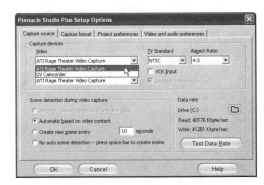

Figure 4.14 Selecting your analog audio capture device. Remember to use Line In!

Figure 4.15 Getting to the Capture Format screen via the Setup pull-down (or you can just click the Capture Format tab in the Setup Options screen).

Figure 4.16 For more information on these settings, read the sidebar "Navigating Your Analog Capture Format Options."

✔ Tips

■ If the video and audio capture controls are not open, open them by clicking the icons on the sides of the Diskometer (Figure 4.1).

■ If you see the Camcorder Controller, you're in DV Capture mode. Go back and reselect your capture source (Step 3 in the preceding task).

■ If your analog capture source appears in the drop-down menu, it's properly loaded and running under Windows. If it's not listed, it's not properly installed, and you have some work to do before you can start capturing. Go back to "Connecting for Analog Capture" earlier in this chapter and try again.

To configure your capture parameters:

1. Open the Studio Setup Options dialog box set to the Capture Format tab by doing *one of the following:*

   ▲ Click the Settings button on the Diskometer.

   ▲ From the Studio menu, choose Setup > Capture Format (**Figure 4.15**).

   The Capture Format tab appears (**Figure 4.16**).

2. Choose the appropriate preset—Good, Better, or Best—for your project.

   Studio also offers a Custom option that lets you customize capture options at will. See the sidebar "Navigating Your Analog Capture Format Options" for assistance with selecting the best preset or customized parameters.

3. Click OK to return to the capture interface.

Navigating Your Analog Capture Format Options

The most critical options to consider during analog capture are the video resolution, or the width and height of the captured video in pixels, and the frame rate, or number of frames per second (fps) captured. For example, when you capture at a resolution of 320 x 240 pixels, you produce a captured file that's 320 pixels wide and 240 pixels high. Similarly, when producing an MPEG-1 file that requires 29.97 fps, you must capture at this frame rate.

When determining the best resolution to use during capture, the most important factor is your intended output resolution. For example, suppose you intend to create a DVD using MPEG-2. This high-quality format generally outputs at a resolution of 720 x 480. In contrast, MPEG-1 files, typically used for posting to the Web or sharing on CD-ROM, generally have a resolution of 320 x 240. If you're creating a RealVideo file to post for streaming at modem speeds, the resolution may be as low as 176 x 120.

The general rule for selecting capture resolution is always to capture at the exact output resolution whenever possible. If not, capture at the next available *higher* resolution. Similarly, for frame rate, the general rule is to capture at the exact output frame rate.

Although all capture devices use different Good, Better, and Best presets (and sometimes name them slightly differently), those in ATI's All-in-Wonder capture card provide an example.

◆ Good: 176 x 120 at just under 14.985 fps. Use this preset for all streaming output when your target audience is primarily on dialup modems.

◆ Better: 352 x 240 at 14.985 fps. This preset has little use, primarily because it captures at 14.985 fps, which is insufficient for the 30 fps used by MPEG-1. To capture for AVI video or for MPEG-1 video displayed on a computer (as opposed to a television set via Video CD), I would customize the capture parameters to 320 x 240 at 30 fps. To produce VideoCD discs for display on TV sets, I would use 354 x 240.

◆ Best: 720 x 480 at 29.997. Use this for MPEG-2 and DVD projects.

Adjustments Defined

Here are definitions for the analog capture adjustments that Studio provides. Precise controls vary by capture device.

◆ **Hue:** This is the visual property that allows you to distinguish colors. The slider biases all the colors in a clip toward red (left) or green (right). This can be especially useful for correcting flesh tones.

◆ **Saturation:** This is the quantity of pure color, ranging from zero (no color at all, or grayscale) to fully saturated (the maximum color intensity your output system can deliver). Move the slider to the left for a tonally reduced, washed-out look, or to the right for extra vibrancy.

◆ **Brightness:** This is the relative intensity of light, without regard to color. Try adjusting both brightness and contrast to correct video that is underexposed or overexposed.

◆ **Contrast:** This is the range of light and dark values in a picture or the ratio between the maximum and minimum brightness values. Moving the slider to the left lowers contrast, forcing all areas of the image toward medium brightness values. Moving the slider to the right increases contrast, making dark areas darker and bright areas brighter.

◆ **Sharpness:** Increases the contrast of edges in the image, making them appear sharper.

To capture audio and configure video input:

1. At the top of the Video Options tab (Figure 4.1), select the icon that corresponds to your physical cable connection (in this case, S-Video).

2. At the top of the Audio Options tab, choose the On button to enable audio capture, to make sure that the audio is up and running.

   Once you know it's working, you can disable it if you want by choosing the Off button.

3. The moment of truth has arrived. Press Play on your camcorder.

   You should see video in the Player and hear audio over your speakers. If you do, you've jumped a significant hurdle. Now you're ready for analog capture.

   If you don't get video and audio right away, take heart. I've installed hundreds of capture cards and rarely gotten it right the first time. Run through the steps in this and the previous task one more time. If you still have no signal, check your capture card installation.

CHOOSING YOUR ANALOG CAPTURE PARAMETERS

Tuning the Incoming Video Signal

Because DV video is digitized by the camera, digital video capture is a simple file transfer from camera to computer. In contrast, analog capture involves an analog-to-digital conversion, which is something like a negotiation between two parties speaking a common language with slightly different accents.

This is how it works: The analog camera outputs an analog signal that it perceives as representing reality, adjusting the brightness, color, and contrast accordingly. Then, using factory-preset values, the analog capture card looks for and captures a signal that it perceives as representing reality. Seldom do the two realities match.

This is a long way of saying that if you're going to capture analog video, most of the time you will have to mess with the analog input controls to get the video looking right. Compare the image in **Figure 4.17**, which used the default settings, with the image in **Figure 4.18**, which used optimized settings. As you can see, the differences can be dramatic.

As Figure 4.1 shows, Studio provides the adjustments for brightness, contrast, sharpness, hue, and color saturation, but these technical terms don't tell the story (see the sidebar "Adjustments Defined"). The only way to become skilled at capturing analog video that looks as it should is to play with the controls during each capture and fine-tune as you go along.

Figure 4.17 With brightness and contrast at their default settings, here I am speaking at a trade show. Pretty dark, eh?

Figure 4.18 Here's the new me, with enhanced brightness and contrast. These controls make a huge difference in the ultimate quality of your video projects.

To adjust incoming video:

1. On your camcorder, press Play to start the video playing. Try to find frames that contain objects with known color and brightness values, such as faces or clothing.

2. Using the Video Options tab, adjust the various sliders up and down until the picture quality is where you want it (Figure 4.1).

3. Note the adjusted values used during capture so that you can re-create your results if necessary.

   These adjustments would be easier if Studio offered numerical presets, but it doesn't. Instead, you need to note the relationship of the slider to the midline. For example, the adjustments in Figure 4.18 would have a brightness value of approximately +14 and a contrast value of +5.

✔ Tips

■ Studio lets you modify these same video options settings during editing. However, adjusting color and brightness during editing can degrade quality and takes time, so it's better done while tweaking parameters before capturing your video files.

■ If your tape contains radically different scenes, you should adjust the video options for each scene.

■ Encoding often darkens video slightly. To make sure that your video is bright enough after encoding, encode a short segment in the final format as early as possible. If you'll be viewing the video on a range of output devices, such as laptops or projectors, you might test playback on these as well.

Adjusting the Incoming Audio Volume

Pop quiz: You've just captured some analog video and you play it back to check the volume. Unfortunately, it's way too low. But why? Some of the possibilities follow:

a) Your speaker system is too low.

b) Your Windows volume control is too low.

c) You didn't boost audio volume sufficiently during capture.

d) All of the above.

Hmmm. Tough one. The answer is, unless you checked your speakers and playback volume before capture, you don't really know. So don't roll your eyes and skip through the following steps; it's all about the process.

To adjust incoming audio volume:

1. Make sure that your system sound speakers are set at an appropriate playback volume. Disable any treble, bass, or similar boosts, since your ultimate viewer may not have the same tools.

2. Open your computer's volume control by doing *one of the following:*

▲ Click the Speaker icon in the Windows taskbar (**Figure 4.19**).

▲ From the Windows Start menu, choose Programs > Accessories > Entertainment > Volume Control (**Figure 4.20**).

The Volume Control dialog box opens (**Figure 4.21**).

3. Make sure that the Volume Control slider, at the far left of the screen, is not muted and is set somewhere near mid-volume.

Figure 4.19 Click the Speaker icon to open the Volume Control dialog box.

Figure 4.20 Or take the long route to the Volume Control.

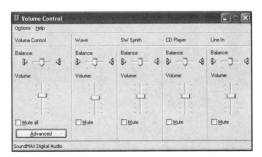

Figure 4.21 Whichever way you get here, make sure that the Volume Control slider at the far left of the Volume Control dialog box is set at approximately mid-level during capture.

4. Make sure the slider that controls your capture source (typically, Line In) is not muted. Studio will adjust the Line In volume as described in Step 8 of this exercise, but you may not hear (or capture) any audio if the control is muted here.

5. Make sure that the Wave slider is not muted and is set somewhere near mid-volume.

   This is the slider that controls the playback volume of the Wave audio captured with the video file.

   Settings for all other sliders are irrelevant. I typically don't mute them because when I later try to play a CD or MIDI music, I forget I turned them off and spend 20 minutes trying to figure out why there's no sound.

6. Close the Volume Control dialog box and return to Studio.

7. Press Play on your camcorder.

8. Use the Audio Volume control (on the Audio Options tab; see Figure 4.1) to adjust the volume during capture so that the lights occasionally reach into the yellow bar but never into the red (**Figure 4.22**). Be sure to test both high- and low-volume regions of the clip.

9. After capture, periodically play back your captured files to check the audio volume level.

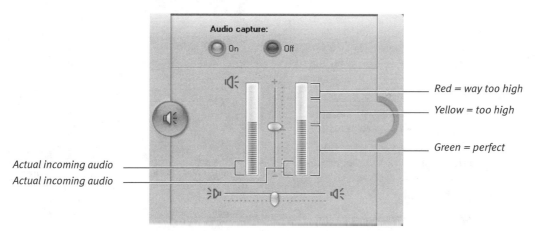

Figure 4.22 Adjust incoming audio volume until it's in the middle-to-upper regions of the green zone.

Capturing Analog Video

The big moment is finally here. It's time to capture some analog video.

To capture analog video:

1. Using your camcorder controls, position your tape about 30 seconds before the initial frame you want to capture.

2. Click the Start Capture button on the Diskometer (**Figure 4.23**).

   The Capture Video dialog box opens (**Figure 4.24**), and the Start Capture button changes to Stop Capture (**Figure 4.25**).

3. For this test, enter a duration of 1 minute and 00 seconds in the Capture Video dialog box, as shown in Figure 4.24.

   When the Capture Video dialog box first appears, it displays the maximum duration of video your hard disk can store, which is limited by either the file size or the version of Windows you're running or the file system your hard disk is using (for more information, see the "Windows File Size Limitations" sidebar in Chapter 3).

   If the duration shown in your program is less than 1 minute, either your capture disk is almost full or you're pointing toward the wrong disk. (See "Selecting Your Capture Drive" in Chapter 2 for more information.)

4. Press Play on your camcorder to start the video rolling.

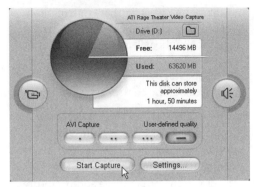

Figure 4.23 Click the Start Capture button on the Diskometer to start capture.

Figure 4.24 You can name your file before capture and elect to capture for a specified interval. Capturing for a particular interval is useful, for example, when you want to capture a 60-minute tape while you're away from the computer.

Figure 4.25 Click the Stop Capture button on the Diskometer to stop capture, or press the Esc key on your keyboard.

Figure 4.26 After analog capture, Studio takes a moment to detect scenes in the content.

5. Watch the video in the Player and click Start approximately 10 to 15 seconds before you actually want capture to begin.

Some capture devices take a few seconds to start capturing; starting early ensures that you capture the desired frames and provides additional frames for fade-in and fade-out or for inter-scene transitions during editing. You can always trim out any unwanted footage later on.

6. Studio will capture one minute of video. To stop capture before then, do *one of the following:*

▲ Click the Stop Capture button on the Diskometer.

▲ Press the Esc key on your keyboard.

Assuming that you enabled scene detection by video content, Studio takes a moment after capture stops to rescan the file for scene changes (**Figure 4.26**). Then your captured scenes appear in the Album (**Figure 4.27**).

Note that this footage was shot in 16:9 mode. However, it appears in Figure 4.27 in 4:3 mode because the default view in the Album is Scene view in 4:3 mode. To ensure that Studio recognizes that this footage is actually 16:9 video, we'll change to 16:9 view in the next section.

continues on next page

Figure 4.27 Then your scenes appear in the Album in all their glory. Note that the scenes are in default Scene view in 4:3 mode.

CAPTURING ANALOG VIDEO

111

✔ Tips

■ You may not always hear audio during capture (I didn't using All-in-Wonder). Even if you do, there's no guarantee that the audio was properly captured in the file. For this reason, check the presence, quality, and volume of audio frequently during the capture process.

■ If you attempt to capture 4:3 and 16:9 footage from the same tape during the same capture session, you'll see the error message displayed in **Figure 4.28**.

■ Note the Frames Dropped counter under the Player in Figure 4.27. Dropped frames are frames that the computer couldn't capture, usually because the hard disk wasn't fast enough to keep up with the incoming video. This counter updates in real time during capture; if you drop more than one or two frames during capture, stop capturing and consult the Studio Help files to diagnose and fix your problem.

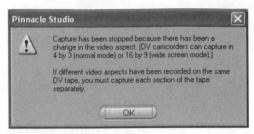

Figure 4.28 Studio won't capture 4:3 and 16:9 footage from the same tape during the same capture session.

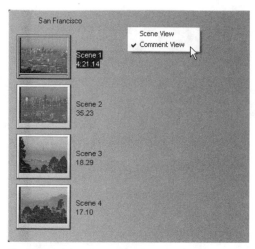

Figure 4.29 Comment view, where you can annotate your scenes.

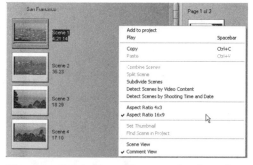

Figure 4.30 Now in 16:9 mode, converting the project to the 16:9 aspect ratio.

Customizing Album Views

While time spent using the Capture Album is usually brief, Studio helps you get as comfortable as possible by providing options for customizing the view.

I've captured some 16:9 footage to illustrate 16:9 views in the Album. Figure 4.27 shows the Album post-capture in the default mode, which is Scene view with 4:3 images.

To switch between Scene and Comment views:

◆ Right-click anywhere in the Album and choose Comment View (**Figure 4.29**).

The Album switches to Comment view. See the following section, "Adding Scene Comments," to learn how to add comments to your scenes.

Note that if you click the Album in a gray area rather than on a picture, you get only the options shown in Figure 4.29. To get the complete list of options shown in **Figure 4.30**, you must click a thumbnail.

To switch back to Scene view, right-click and choose Scene View.

To switch between 4:3 and 16:9 views:

◆ Right-click a picture in the Album and choose Aspect Ratio 16 x 9 (Figure 4.30).

The Album switches to 16:9 view. To switch back, right-click and choose Aspect Ratio 4 x 3.

✔ Tip

■ Changing views does absolutely nothing to the captured file; it just changes the way that Studio displays it. It does not convert the file from 4:3 to 16:9, or vice versa.

CUSTOMIZING ALBUM VIEWS

Adding Scene Comments

If you want to rename or annotate your captured scenes to make them easier to find and use in your final production, go to the Album in Capture mode.

If you intend to add comments to your scenes, note that Studio updates the Album each time you capture, so if you start another capture before changing the scene comments, Studio stores the captured file and associated comments and clears the Capture Album to make room for the next capture. Don't worry; you can easily find your captured files and comments in the Album in Edit mode and edit your scene comments there (see "Working with Scene Comments" in Chapter 6).

To add scene comments to your captured video:

1. In the Album, slowly double-click the text immediately to the right of the Video icon to make it editable (**Figure 4.31**).

2. Type the desired comment.

3. Save your comment by doing *one of the following* (**Figure 4.32**):

   ▲ Press the Enter key on your keyboard.

   ▲ Click anywhere outside the comment box on the Studio interface to set the comments.

✔ Tips

■ You're not actually changing the file name; you're editing text that can be seen only inside Studio.

■ If you plan to combine your scenes on the Edit tab of the Album, note that Studio blows away all screen comments when you combine scenes. You might want to look at "Combining Scenes" in Chapter 6 before you invest much time in naming your captured scenes.

Figure 4.31 To add or change scene comments, click the text twice slowly.

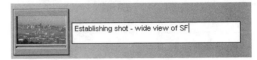

Figure 4.32 Then type in your description.

Viewing Your Captured Video

If you're like me, the first thing you want to do after capture is watch the video. To do this, switch to Edit mode and use the Player.

To view your captured video:

1. Select the Edit tab at the upper left of the Studio interface (Figure 4.1).

    Studio enters Edit mode.

2. In the Album, double-click the video you want to play (**Figure 4.33**).

    The video starts playing in the Player.

3. Controls beneath the Player let you stop, rewind, fast-forward, go to the beginning of the video, and move through each frame of your video.

✔ Tip

■   If you capture using scene detection and the Album contains multiple scenes, the Player automatically plays from one scene to the next without breaks.

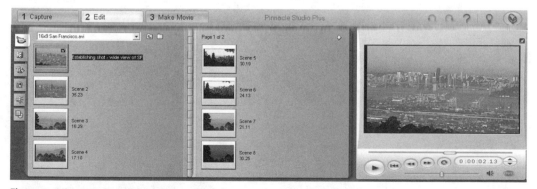

Figure 4.33 Once you're in Edit mode, you can play your captured videos by clicking the icons in the Album.

WORKING WITH STILL IMAGES

I absolutely adore capturing still images from my digital videotapes, especially when shooting videos of the young 'uns. Why? Because although my Kodak DC4800 takes much higher-quality, 3.2-megapixel images, it can shoot only about once every six seconds. When you've got DV tape rolling, this gives you about 180 chances to get the shot you really want, compared to one shot with the Kodak.

On the other hand, some days I just don't want to mess with my camcorder, and I grab the Kodak instead. With my 1-GB flash memory card, I can take pictures all day long and usually find many nuggets worth keeping. Of course, these are huge images that often need to be cropped, cut, or reduced in resolution to work optimally in Studio.

This chapter covers three topics: grabbing images from your camcorder or movie files, prepping images for use in a video production, and adding motion to your still images. These motion-related features are typically called pan-and-zoom effects, or Ken Burns effects, after the director who popularized their use in documentaries like *The Civil War* and *Baseball*.

Ultimately, you'll build your slideshow on the Timeline, as described in Working with Still Images, in Chapter 7. This chapter will provide the building blocks so you can hit the ground running when you're ready to work in the Timeline.

Capturing Still Images

To capture images from your camcorder, you need to have everything connected, tested, and turned on (see Chapters 3 and 4). Operation is similar for digital video (DV) and analog camcorders, so this section covers both. Studio can also grab still images from movie files on disk, whether previously captured within Studio or sourced from another location.

When it comes to capturing still images, DV cameras have one killer feature: the ability to pause on a single frame for multiple seconds without distortion. This makes frame capture from your DV camera frame-accurate. In contrast, most analog camcorders can't pause for more than a moment or two without some image distortion, making it difficult to capture the precise frame you're seeking. For this reason, when you have images you'd like to grab on DV tape, go ahead and grab them from the camera.

On the other hand, if you have images on analog tape that you'd like to capture, the easier, faster, and more accurate approach is to capture the video to disk first and then grab the frame from the captured file.

To capture still images from your camcorder:

1. Click the Edit tab at the upper left of the Studio interface.

   Studio switches to Edit mode.

2. At the top left of the Movie window, click the Camcorder icon to open the Video toolbox (**Figure 5.1**).

   The Video toolbox opens.

Figure 5.1 Click the Camcorder icon to open the Video toolbox.

CAPTURING STILL IMAGES

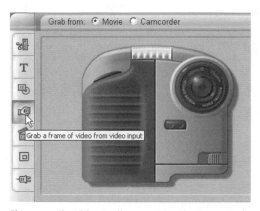

Figure 5.2 The Video toolbox contains the Frame Grab tool. Note that when you're using an analog camcorder, there are no camcorder controls.

3. Click the Frame Grab icon to open the Frame Grab tool (**Figure 5.2**).

4. Click the Video Input radio button, located at the top of the window, to capture from your camcorder.

5. Use the Camcorder Controller controls to start your DV camcorder, or press Play on your analog camcorder to start the video rolling. Watch the video in the Player window; then do *one of the following*:

▲ If you have a DV camcorder, you can pause (not stop) at the exact frame you want to capture (**Figure 5.3**).

▲ If you have an analog camcorder, try pausing at the desired capture frame using camcorder controls. If the frame is clear and undistorted, you can move to Step 6. However, many analog devices can't pause on a frame without distortion, so you'll have to capture by playing the video in real time, and then pressing the Grab button as the desired frame passes by, which is obviously less accurate.

continues on next page

Figure 5.3 When you're using a DV camcorder, Studio provides software controls for getting to the desired frame. Let's get this one of Whatley at the Charleston Aquarium petting zoo.

CAPTURING STILL IMAGES

6. Click the Grab button to capture the frame visible in the Player.

The frame appears in the Frame Grab window (**Figure 5.4**).

7. Do *one or both of the following*:

▲ Click the Add to Movie button to add the frame to a movie.

Studio adds the movie to the Video track at the first blank location (**Figure 5.5**).

▲ Click the Save to Disk button to save the still image.

Studio opens the standard Save As dialog box, which is configured to store the frames on your default capture drive (**Figure 5.6**).

8. In the Save as Type drop-down box, choose Bitmap Files. (For more information on choosing formats, see the tips that follow.)

9. In the Save Grabbed Frame in This Size drop-down box, choose Original Size. (See the tips that follow for more information about choosing resolutions.)

10. Name the file and click Save (or press Alt+S).

11. At the top left of the Movie window, click the Camcorder icon to close the Video toolbox (Figure 5.1).

Figure 5.4 Click the Grab button, and Studio grabs the image.

Figure 5.5 Click the Add to Movie button, and Studio places it in the Video track.

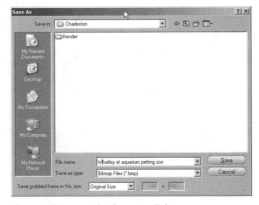

Figure 5.6 Or save the frame to disk.

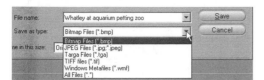

Figure 5.7 Among Studio's many format choices, your best bet usually is Bitmap Files (*.bmp); choose this option unless you have a strong need to use another.

Figure 5.8 You can scale your image up or down at will, but Studio scales it anyway, if necessary, once the image is loaded on the Timeline. To avoid potential distortion, save your image in its original size.

✔ Tips

- If you're capturing still images from an analog camcorder and the camera won't pause without distorting the image, you're better off capturing the video to disk and then grabbing your still image from the captured file, as detailed in the next task.

- Most camcorders don't include frame-advance controls on the camcorder body, but do on the camcorder remote, usually with other nice controls such as slow motion.

- Studio lets you save a still image in a number of formats (**Figure 5.7**). Generally, if you plan on using the image in your video production, choose bitmap (BMP), Targa, TIFF, or Windows Metafile format, which are all uncompressed. I like BMP because it's the format most widely recognized by other programs, giving me more flexibility if I decide to use the image again. If you're capturing an image to send via email, you might want to go with JPEG, since it produces a smaller, compressed file (though Studio doesn't have the optimization tools offered by most still-image editors).

- Studio also lets you save your still images at a number of different resolutions (**Figure 5.8**). Generally, if you plan on using the image in your video production, your best choice is Original Size, which stores the image at its actual capture resolution.

To capture still images from a file on disk:

1. Click the Edit tab at the upper left of the Studio interface.

   Studio switches to Edit mode.

2. Drag the video containing the target frames from the Album to the Movie window (**Figure 5.9**).

   If you're in the Timeline view, drag the video to the Video track. In the other two views, it doesn't matter where you drag the file, so long as it's in the Movie window.

3. At the top left of the Movie window, click the Camcorder icon to open the Video toolbox.

   The Video toolbox opens, most likely to the Clip Properties tool.

CAPTURING STILL IMAGES

Figure 5.9 To capture a frame from a video on disk, load the video into the Movie window. Here's the U.S.S. Clamagore, a WW II submarine serving as a Museum Ship at Patriots Point in Charleston Harbor.

Figure 5.10 Select the Movie button to capture frames from the selected movie.

4. Click the Frame Grab icon at the left to open the Frame Grab tool.

5. Select the Movie radio button at the top of the screen to grab frames from the Movie window (**Figure 5.10**).

6. Use the Player controls or the Timeline scrubber (**Figure 5.11**) to move to the target frame.

   You can use the Jog controls to the right of the Player counter (up and down arrows) to move one frame at a time. If the Player controls aren't active, you didn't select the Movie radio button in Step 5.

continues on next page

Timeline scrubber   *Player controls*

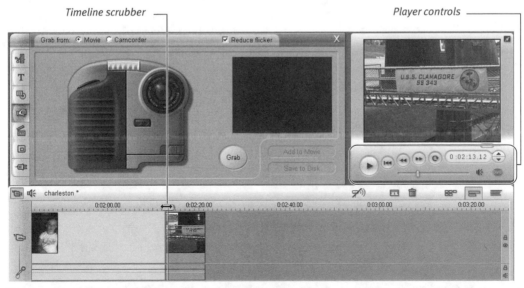

Figure 5.11 Use the Timeline scrubber or the Player controls to move to the desired frame, or the Jog controls to move one frame at a time.

CAPTURING STILL IMAGES

7. Click the Grab button to capture the frame visible in the Player.

The frame appears in the Frame Grab window (**Figure 5.12**).

8. Do *one or both of the following*:

▲ Click the Add to Movie button to add the frame to the movie.

▲ Studio adds the movie to the Video track at the first blank location.

▲ Click the Save to Disk button to save the still image.

Studio opens the standard Save As dialog box, which is set to store the frames on your default capture drive.

9. In the Save as Type drop-down box, choose Bitmap Files (Figure 5.6). For more information on choosing formats, see the tips from the previous task.

10. In the Save Grabbed Frame in This Size" drop-down box, choose Original Size. (See the tips from the previous task for more information on choosing resolutions.)

11. Name the file and click Save (or press Alt+S).

12. At the top left of the Movie window, click the Camcorder icon to close the Video toolbox.

✔ Tips

■ Still-image capture in 16:9 mode works just fine for disk-based files and when grabbing the frames from your DV camcorder via DV or analog connectors, with 16:9 images stored at 853 x 480 resolution.

■ Note the flicker reduction option on the right of Figure 5.8. I tested this feature with multiple frame grabs, storing the files at number of different resolutions and formats. I found that flicker reduction helped slightly when capturing from a DV camcorder or a DV file, but hurt image quality significantly when capturing via an analog connection. However, this testing falls far short of a scientific study, and your results may vary. When you're grabbing still frames for your productions, try toggling the Reduce Flicker button on and off, and use whichever setting produces the best possible quality.

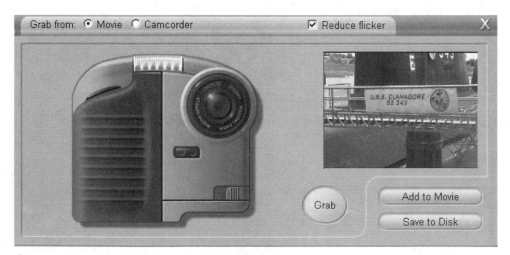

Figure 5.12 Once again, click Grab, and you've got your frame.

Rosie 1   Rosie 2   Rosie 3

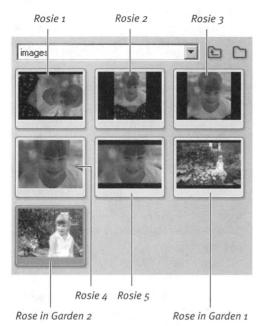

Rosie 4   Rosie 5

Rose in Garden 2   Rose in Garden 1

Figure 5.13 The black bars beside Rosie 2 and Rosie 3 are Studio's way of telling you that the image resolution isn't optimal.

0:00:00.00

Figure 5.14 Here's the big view of Rosie 2. let's get a bit closer.

Editing Still Images

Okay, the question on the table is this: Your digital camera takes shots at a princely resolution of, say, 2160 x 1440 pixels. The maximum DVD video resolution is 720 x 480. How do you resolve the difference?

To answer this question, let's first get a bird's-eye view of how Studio works with still images and then explore the different ways you can crop your images so that you can present them most effectively in Studio.

How Studio works with images

Studio takes an admirably laissez-faire approach to images, basically displaying them as you place them in the movie. It doesn't try to fill the screen with your image, stretching it horizontally or vertically, or trim your image to fit; it simply makes your image larger or smaller to fit the screen without changing the aspect ratio. If this means that your image doesn't completely fill the 720 x 480–pixel DVD frame, so be it. At least there's no distortion.

Studio also provides excellent visual cues about what your image will look like when it's finally produced. Let's take a look at **Figure 5.13** to get a sense of how this works.

Rosie 1 is the original 2160 x 1440–pixel image, shot by turning the camera to the side to capture Rosie's glam pose Rosie 2 is the same image rotated 90 degrees to the left.

If you click Rosie 2 to preview her in the Player, you see large areas of black to her left and right, which is precisely the way the image would appear in the final DVD or video (**Figure 5.14**). This is Studio's way of telling you that the image doesn't match the final resolution of your project, and Studio is not going to squish or otherwise distort the video to make it appear full screen. Note that these same black areas show up on the Still Images tab of the Album, providing the same message.

Optimizing Rosie

The Rosie picture presents two opportunities. To go with the original impulse of the photographer, you can crop away the bottom of the image to get a bit closer while retaining the vertical, portrait look, as shown in Rosie 3 (**Figure 5.15**). She's a bit more prominent in the screen, but you still have those black areas on the sides. The other alternative is the full-screen, fetching face shot. Here the image has been cropped so that Rosie fills the entire screen, making all involved thankful that she takes after her mother, not her father (**Figure 5.16**).

The obvious question is, what image resolution must you use to totally fill the Player window and eliminate those black bars? Since picture resolutions vary immensely among different cameras, the answer isn't a particular resolution, but a specific aspect ratio, which must be 4:3.

Figure 5.15 Rosie 3. I've cropped most of the bottom, making Rosie slightly bigger.

Figure 5.16 Rosie 4. Full-screen Rosie, providing a much closer look and filling the screen.

Figure 5.17 The secret's in the tool: Ulead's PhotoImpact lets you constrain an image to a 4:3 aspect ratio, so that you can easily grab the best image.

Figure 5.18 Your brain says 720 x 480 resolution, but those black bars above and below the image say no, no, no.

What this means is that for every 4 horizontal pixels, you must grab 3 vertical pixels. To grab the image of Rosie, the capture resolution was 1120 pixels across and 840 pixels high. If you divide 1120 by 4, you get 280. Multiply 280 by 3 and you get 840.

It's a pain, but keep a calculator open on your desktop when you're grabbing still images. Once you find the optimal horizontal resolution for your images, divide by 4, multiply by 3, and you've calculated the ideal height. Or find an image editor like Ulead Systems' excellent PhotoImpact XL, which does the math for you (**Figure 5.17**). The little Lock icon in the top tool panel constrains the crop tool to the selected shape, Digital Camera (4:3).

The other obvious question is, why can't you capture at an aspect ratio of 4:2.66, which is the aspect ratio for 720 x 480 pixels—the ultimate resolution at which you'll be displaying the video? The complete answer is long, confusing, and involves arcane differences between how computers and televisions display video data.

The quick, empirical answer is this: If you capture at the 4:2.66 aspect ratio and enter the result, Studio tells you via black bars at the top and bottom of the screen that you're not totally filling the screen (**Figure 5.18**). These bars aren't present when the 4:3 aspect ratio is used, so 4:3 must be the optimal setting (Figure 5.16).

✔ Tip

■ Note that Studio's relatively new (since Studio 9 Plus) pan and zoom features allow you to zoom into the image and eliminate the black edges, so you don't have to perform this work in your image editor. See Inserting Pan and Zoom Effects later in the chapter.

Finding the Rose in the Garden

Now it should be easy to tackle the problem in the second example: a picture of Rose in her mother's garden. It's a wonderful shot of the garden, but this slide show is actually about Rose, not her mother's green thumb. (**Figure 5.19**).

To zoom in on Rose, I cropped the image using the fixed aspect ratio of 4:3, while following the rule of thirds to place her in the back right of the image with look room on the left. This dramatically increases the size, making Rose much more prominent. (**Figure 5.20**).

✔ Tip

- When fine-tuning your images, always crop to a resolution that matches the desired aspect ratio. Never change the aspect ratio of an image or resize an image to make it fit a specific area.

Figure 5.19 Here's Momma's garden, but where is the Rose?

Figure 5.20 The benefit of working with megapixel images is that I can zoom in without distortion. Once again the screen is filled by cropping the photo to create an aspect ratio of 4:3.

Quick Image Fixes in Studio

Image editors like PhotoImpact and Photoshop Elements provide the perfect environment for perfecting your images, but sometimes it's faster to perform quick fixes in Studio. Here are the two corrections you can make quickly and easily within Studio.

To rotate your image:

1. Start with the Movie window in Timeline view and the Album window open to the Still Images tab.

2. Drag the image into the Timeline (**Figure 5.21**).

continues on next page

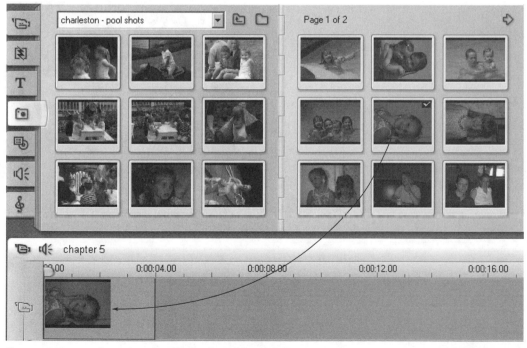

Figure 5.21 To get an image into the Timeline, just click and drag.

3. Double-click the image.

Studio opens the Clip Properties tool (**Figure 5.22**). Here's Whatley looking natural for the camera.

4. Click the Rotate icons as required to rotate the photo into the desired position (**Figure 5.23**).

Studio rotates the image to the desired position (**Figure 5.24**).

✔ Tips

- To understand why there are black bars around the image in Figure 5.24, see "How Studio works with images," earlier in this chapter.

- To remove the black bars, zoom into the image until they disappear, as described in "To insert a pan and zoom effect," later in this chapter.

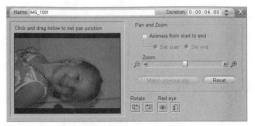

Figure 5.22 This image needs to be rotated to the left.

Figure 5.23 Rotate the image by clicking these controls.

Figure 5.24 The corrected image.

QUICK IMAGE FIXES IN STUDIO

To remove red eye in an image:

1. Start with the Movie window in Timeline view and the Album window open to the Still Images tab.

2. Drag the image into the Timeline.

3. Double-click the image.
   Studio opens the Clip Properties tool (Figure 5.22).

4. Do *one* or *both of the following* to zoom into the region of the image containing the red eye:

   ▲ Use the zoom slider to zoom into the image (**Figure 5.25**).

   ▲ Click and drag the image to the desired position.

continues on next page

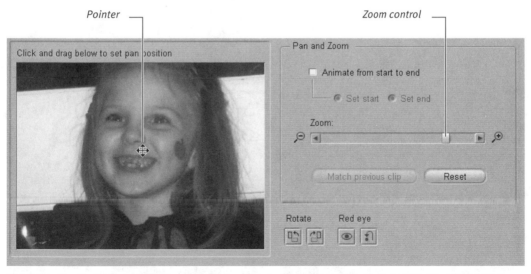

Pointer

Zoom control

Click and drag below to set pan position

Pan and Zoom

☐ Animate from start to end

◉ Set start   ◉ Set end

Zoom:

Match previous clip   Reset

Rotate   Red eye

Figure 5.25 Use the Zoom slider to zoom into the image and grab the image directly to move it around the frame.

QUICK IMAGE FIXES IN STUDIO

5. Click the Red Eye icon (**Figure 5.26**).

6. Click and drag a rectangle around the eye or eyes containing the red eye (**Figure 5.27**).

Studio removes the red eye (**Figure 5.28**).

✔ Tips

■ Studio worked best for me when I eliminated the red eye from both eyes at once.

■ If two or more subjects in the picture have red eye, fix them sequentially, using the pan cursor to move around the image as necessary.

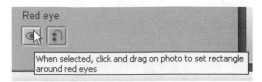

Figure 5.26 Click here to remove red eye.

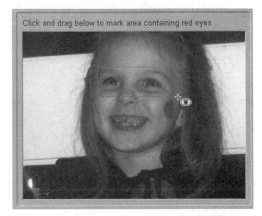

Figure 5.27 Then drag the rectangle around both eyes.

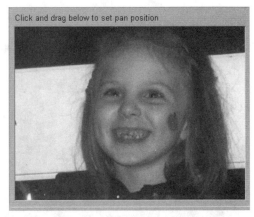

Figure 5.28 Works like Visine (though it's not apparent here in the grayscale image).

Inserting Pan and Zoom Effects

At a high level, Studio's workflow for panning and zooming within an image has two simple steps. First you pick a starting position for the pan and zoom effect, then you choose the end position. When rendering the effect, Studio builds a movie from the starting point of the image to the ending point.

This start-to-finish approach works well with some pictures, but sometimes you'll want to make more complicated passes through an image. For example, in the image shown in **Figure 5.29**, shot outside of historic Dollywood, I want to move to three different locations within the image, from daughter to mother to daughter.

To facilitate this, Pinnacle added a button called Match Previous Clip to Studio to simplify multi-point panning within an image. This section demonstrates both single-point and multiple-point pan and zoom effects.

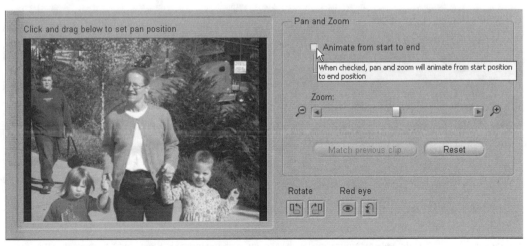

Figure 5.29 Now let's pan and zoom around this image; daughter to mother to daughter.

INSERTING PAN AND ZOOM EFFECTS

To insert a pan and zoom effect:

1. Start with the Movie window in Timeline view and the Album window open to the Still Images tab.

2. Drag the image into the Timeline.

3. Double-click the image.

   Studio opens the Clip Properties tool (Figure 5.29).

4. Click the Animate from Start to End checkbox.

   The Set Start button is automatically selected.

5. Do *one* or *both of the following* to set the start position:

   ▲ Use the Zoom slider to zoom into or away from the image.

   ▲ Click and drag the image to the desired position (**Figure 5.30**).

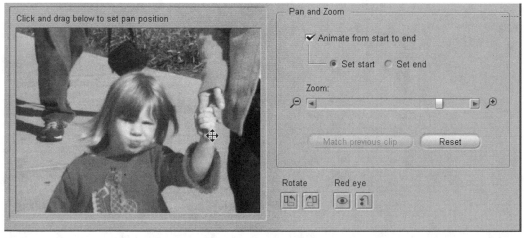

Figure 5.30 The zoom slider sets magnification levels, and you grab the image in the window to move it to the desired position.

INSERTING PAN AND ZOOM EFFECTS

6. Click the Set End checkbox (**Figure 5.31**). Studio resets the image to its original position.

7. Do *one* or *both of the following* to set the end position:

▲ Use the Zoom slider to zoom into or away from the image.

▲ Click and drag the image to the desired position.

✔ Tip

■ At this point, if you exit the Clip Properties window by clicking X in the upper-right corner or closing the Video Toolbox, the pan and zoom effect is set. But I've only zoomed into two of the three faces in the picture. To zoom seamlessly into a third image, see below.

Set end radio button

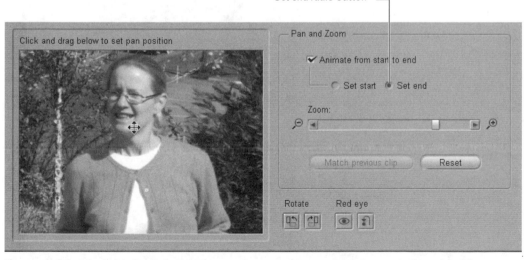

Figure 5.31 Select the Set end radio button, then use the pan and zoom controls to move to the end position.

To insert multi-point pan and zoom effects:

1. After inserting the first point of the multi-point pan and zoom effect, click the Open/Close Video Toolbox icon (Figure 5.4) to close the Video Toolbox.

   Studio returns to the Album window open to the Still Images tab.

2. Drag the same image to the Timeline (**Figure 5.32**).

3. Double-click the image.

   Studio opens the Clip Properties tool (**Figure 5.33**).

4. Click the Animate from Start to End checkbox.

   The Set Start button is automatically selected.

5. Click the Match Previous Clip button.

   Studio matches the Set Start pan and zoom location to the end point of the previous image.

6. Click the Set End checkbox.

7. Do *one* or *both of the following* to set the end position:

   ▲ Use the Zoom slider to zoom into or away from the image.

   ▲ Click and drag the image to the desired position (**Figure 5.34**).

✔ Tip

■ At this point, if you exit the Clip Properties window by clicking X in the upper right corner or closing the Video Toolbox, the pan and zoom effect is set.

Figure 5.32 To get to the second daughter, you have to drag the same video to the Timeline.

Figure 5.33 Click the Match Previous Clip button and Studio aligns the starting point of the second clip to the ending point of the first clip.

Figure 5.34 Then pan and zoom over to the second daughter.

COLLECTING ASSETS IN THE ALBUM

The Album is an integral component of Studio's interface: a place for loading video, still images, and audio files—the basic assets that comprise your project—into separate, tab-selected folders before integrating them into your projects. The Album also contains transitions, titles, and menus—effects discussed in subsequent chapters.

The Album isn't a true bin or library, like those found in many programs, that stores the imported assets in a project file. Rather, the Album simply displays the files in the currently selected directory.

One Album feature is critical to users working with 16:9 video. Although Studio should detect 16:9 video during capture, it may not if you load 16:9 video from another source, such as a previously captured file. In such instances, you can now switch the Album to 16:9 viewing mode, directing Studio to process the video in 16:9 mode.

Otherwise, the Album's features—compared with the flexible Storyboard, bountiful transitions, and other rich features that lie beyond—are not Studio's most impressive. However, the Album is unquestionably one of Studio's most valuable tools. You could easily spend the bulk of your time just finding the assets to put into your project; working efficiently in the Album reduces this time considerably.

Opening the Album to Video Scenes

Few things in life are easier than getting to the Video Scenes component of the Album. So let's get right to it ourselves.

To open the Album to Video Scenes:

◆ Do *one of the following*:

▲ If you're not running Studio, load the program. Once Studio loads, you're in Edit mode, and the Album opens to the Video Scenes tab. Click a scene to select it (**Figure 6.1**).

▲ If you're running Studio and you're in Capture or Make Movie mode, select the Edit tab in the three-tab menu at the top of the Album. Once you're in Edit mode, the Album opens to the video scenes you've accessed or captured most recently.

▲ If you're in Edit mode and working on any Album tab other than Video Scenes, click the Camcorder icon at the top of the column of icons along the left side of the Album window (**Figure 6.2**). The Album switches to Video Scenes.

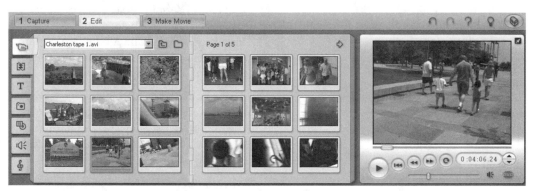

Figure 6.1 Here's Studio in Edit mode, with the Album containing footage from my Charleston trip.

Figure 6.2 If you're on any other Album tab in Edit mode, click the Camcorder icon to get to the Video Scenes tab.

Figure 6.3 Click here to move up one level, and see other video files in this folder.

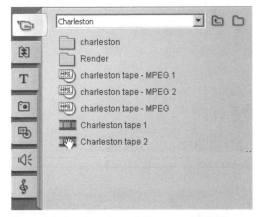

Figure 6.4 The Album lists all files stored in the selected folder, making it easy to switch among captured files. Double-click the video that you want displayed.

Loading Video Files

Before you can split, combine, or annotate your video files, you have to load them into the Album. Here's how.

To load captured files into the Album:

◆ If you just finished capturing video files, select the Edit tab to enter Edit mode.

  The most recently captured video file appears in the Album.

To display other captured files in the Album:

1. Click the Move Up One Level folder icon (**Figure 6.3**).

  Studio displays a list of other files captured in that folder.

2. Double-click the file you want to display (**Figure 6.4**).

  The selected file appears on the Video Scenes tab (**Figure 6.5**). Note that if it hasn't already done so, Studio performs scene detection on the new clip using whatever option is currently selected on the Capture Source tab (see Figure 3.6 in Chapter 3).

Figure 6.5 Presto—there's the video I want, covering our visit to Patriots Point in Charleston Harbor.

To display other videos in the Album:

1. Click the Directory icon to the right of the Album list box (**Figure 6.6**).

   A standard Open dialog box appears (**Figure 6.7**).

2. Navigate to the folder that contains the target file (**Figure 6.8**).

3. Do *one of the following*:

   ▲ Double-click the target file.

   ▲ Select the target file with the pointer and click Open (**Figure 6.9**).

   If it hasn't already done so, Studio performs scene detection on the selected clip using whatever option is currently chosen on the Capture Source tab.

   If Studio can't display all of the scenes from that video on one page, it creates multiple pages. Move through the pages by clicking the arrows at the upper right and upper left of the Album pages.

✔ Tips

- Studio imports only AVI, MPEG-1, and MPEG-2 video files. Studio cannot import RealVideo, Windows Media, or QuickTime files or files saved in animated formats such as Autodesk's FLC format.

- The Album can display only one video at a time. Although the Album can display multiple scenes from one video, you cannot import, combine, or otherwise display scenes in the Album from more than one video at a time.

- You can't delete scenes or change their order in the Album. However, Studio provides a great tool for choosing and rearranging the order of your videos: the Storyboard view in the Movie window, which is discussed in Chapter 7.

Figure 6.6 To select files in other folders, click the Directory icon to the right of the drop-down box.

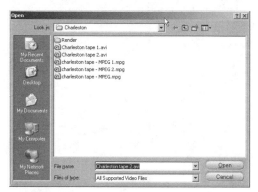

Figure 6.7 A standard Open dialog box appears.

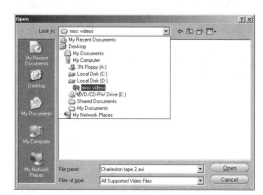

Figure 6.8 Navigate to the folder that contains the new files.

Figure 6.9 Select the target file and click Open.

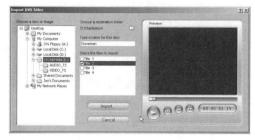

Figure 6.10 To import a DVD title, select Import DVD Titles from the File menu.

Figure 6.11 The Import DVD Titles window opens.

Importing Content from DVDs

One essential feature that appeared in Studio 9.4 and continues in version 10 is the ability to import video from DVD-Video discs. This can be a quick and easy way to reclaim short bits of footage from previous productions where you no longer have the source assets on your hard disk. In theory, you do lose a bit of quality when working from video retrieved from DVDs, since it's already been encoded once, but it's usually difficult to tell.

You can't import video from DVDs with the kind of specificity or sequential access you get when you capture from your camcorder. Video is stored on DVDs in groups of clips called Titles, and that's exactly how it appears to Studio as it retrieves content from a DVD. When you instruct Studio to import video from a DVD, you have to select it by title, because Studio can't drill into the title and find the specific five-minute scene you want. Once you've imported the content as a video file, however, you'll be able to move through and edit it just like any other video file you work with in Studio.

Note that Studio can't retrieve video from copy-protected DVDs like those distributed by Hollywood studios, so if you're looking to spice up your videos with the deli scene from *When Harry Met Sally* ("I'll have what she's having"), or some other favorite scene ("Rosebud..."), you're out of luck.

To import DVD titles:

1. Choose File > Import DVD Titles (**Figure 6.10**).

   The Import DVD Titles window opens (**Figure 6.11**).

   continues on next page

2. In the Choose a Disc or Image window, click the DVD drive containing the DVD-Video to import (or the directory containing the disc image).

3. In the top center of the Import DVD Titles dialog box, click the folder to choose a destination folder for the imported content.

Studio opens a Browse for Folder window (**Figure 6.12**).

4. Select the destination folder and then click OK.

5. Type a name for the disc in the designated line.

Studio stores the imported content as an MPEG file using the following convention: name_title_title number.mpg. For example, Studio assigned the following name to the file imported from the settings shown in Figure 6.11: "Stoneman_Title_2.mpg."

6. Check the title or titles to import.

If you click and highlight a title, you can play the content from that title in the Preview window to confirm that it contains the target video.

7. After choosing the titles, click Import.

Studio displays an Importing DVD Titles dialog box (**Figure 6.13**) and imports the content. Once complete, Studio closes the Import DVD Titles dialog box.

After Studio imports and stores the file, you can load the video file into the program as described in the previous section, "Loading Video Files."

✔ Tip

■ Studio worked very quickly during our tests, importing 51 minutes of video in under 10 minutes on a dual-processor computer. Quality was excellent since Studio merely imports the video, and doesn't convert it in any way.

Figure 6.12 Select the target folder for your imported DVD title.

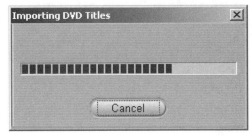

Figure 6.13 Studio imports the DVD title.

Playing Videos

It's tough to select the right scenes for your project without playing the video. For this reason, the Album works closely with the Player to let you view and move through your video scenes.

To play your videos:

1. Do *one of the following:*

   ▲ Double-click the scene you want to play.

   ▲ The video immediately starts to play in the Player.

   ▲ Click the scene you want to play.

   The border around the video turns from white to blue. If you're in Comment View mode (see "Working with the Album's Views and Tools," later in this chapter), the scene comments immediately to the right of the video are also highlighted. In addition, the initial frame of the scene appears in the Player (**Figure 6.14**).

   continues on next page

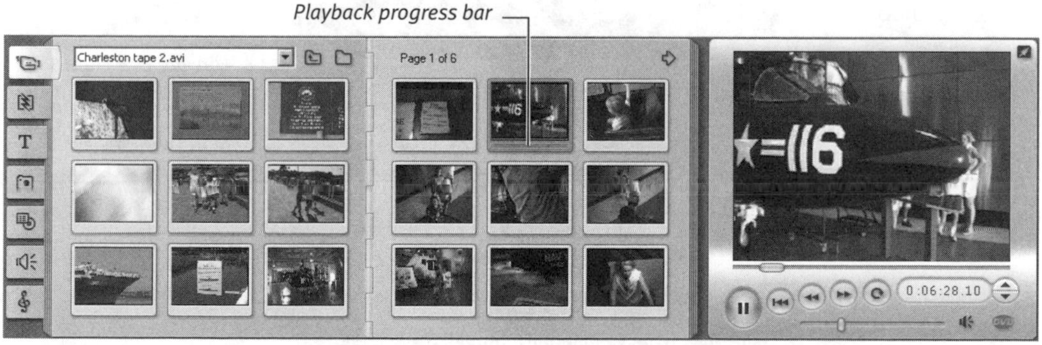

Playback progress bar

Figure 6.14 To play any video file in the Album, double-click it, or click it once and click Play in the Player.

2. Under the Player, click Play to start video playback and use the other controls to navigate through the video (**Figure 6.15**). Playback shifts automatically from scene to scene when multiple scenes are present.

The progress bar, a white line underneath the thumbnail in each scene in the Album that fills as the Player progresses through the scene, represents the position of playback within each scene. The Player scrubber represents the position of playback within the entire video.

✔ Tip

■ Keyboard shortcuts are really helpful for playing back video in the Player from both the Album and the Movie window. Here are the relevant commands:

▲ *Spacebar* Play and stop

▲ *J* Fast-reverse (press multiple times for faster speed)

▲ *K* Stop

▲ *L* Play

▲ *L* Fast-forward (press multiple times for faster speed)

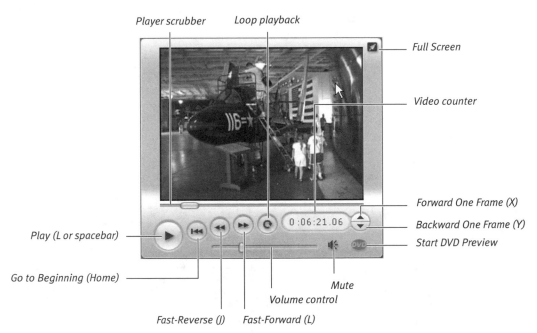

Figure 6.15 To move manually through the scenes, use the familiar VCR playback controls or the Player scrubber.

PLAYING VIDEOS

Combining Scenes

Scene detection is a great feature, but often you'll want to combine multiple scenes before moving the composite clip to the Timeline, or perhaps you'll want to consolidate scenes to reduce clutter in the Album. After all, it's always easier to keep track of one asset than five.

Studio's Combine Scenes feature has one significant limitation: you can combine only contiguous scenes captured from a single video, preventing serious rearranging. But the good news is that Studio has a great Storyboard feature that's perfect for extensive reorganizing.

To combine scenes:

1. Select the scenes to combine by doing *one of the following:*

   ▲ While holding down the Shift key, use the pointer to select the desired contiguous scenes.

   ▲ Drag to select all scenes under the marquee, starting with the pointer over a gray area (not a scene).

   ▲ While holding down the Shift key, click a scene with the pointer and then press the arrow keys to select the desired scenes.

   ▲ Choose Ctrl+A to select all scenes on all pages of the Album.

   ▲ Choose Edit > Select All to select all scenes on all pages of the Album.

2. Once the scenes are selected, do *one of the following:*

   ▲ From the Studio menu, choose Album > Combine Scenes.

   ▲ Place the pointer over one of the scenes you want to combine; then right-click and choose Combine Scenes (**Figure 6.16**).

continues on next page

Figure 6.16 To combine multiple scenes into one, you can hold down the Shift key while clicking the desired contiguous scenes. In this example, I'm combining three scenes of helicopters on the deck of the aircraft carrier Yorktown into a single scene.

COMBINING SCENES

Studio combines all selected scenes (**Figure 6.17**). Had you selected any non-contiguous scenes, Studio would have ignored those selections and combined only the contiguous scenes.

In addition, had you left any contiguous scenes unselected, Studio would have combined all selected contiguous scenes on either side of the unselected scenes into separate groups, excluding the unselected scene.

✔ Tips

■ If you customize scene comments for a scene (see "Working with Scene Comments," later in this chapter) and later combine the scene with another scene, Studio deletes the customized comments and reverts to the default naming convention: scene number, date and time of shooting, and duration. Similarly, though you can later subdivide clips and reestablish the original scenes, Studio won't recall your custom comments. If you plan on customizing scene comments, do so after combining or splitting your clips (see the next section, "Splitting Scenes").

■ After combining scenes, Studio automatically renumbers all scenes that follow the combined scenes. For example, if you combine Scenes 1 through 5, the consolidated scene becomes Scene 1, and the old Scene 6 becomes Scene 2. Keep this in mind if you've been cataloging your scenes based on automatic names.

■ No matter what method you use to select scenes, Studio ignores the order of selection, combining only the selected contiguous scenes in their original order.

■ Don't group scenes if you plan to trim frames from scenes (see Chapter 7) or add transitions between them (see Chapter 8), as Studio will simply make you re-split them to access the individual scenes.

Figure 6.17 Now we have one scene we'll later call "Helicopters."

COMBINING SCENES

Splitting Scenes

In addition to a feature for combining your scenes, Studio gives you three options for dividing up scenes in the Album: splitting, subdividing, and scene detection. Splitting is the manual process of dividing one scene into two or multiple scenes, convenient when automatic scene detection doesn't yield useful results. Subdividing involves cutting your clips into regular intervals, useful when working with long continuous videos with no natural breaks. Finally, automatic scene detection breaks the video into intervals based on scene changes in the content or discontinuities in the shooting time and date of the video.

These three options are available during capture and can be accessed in the Album for scenes captured with scene detection disabled, captured clips with scenes that were manually combined, or videos that were imported. Note that making scene changes based on discontinuities in the shooting date and time requires DV source video, since MPEG and non-DV source AVI files don't contain the necessary time code.

To split scenes manually:

1. Select the video to split.

2. Use the Player controls to move to the desired initial frame of the second scene (**Figure 6.18**).

continues on next page

Scene to be split

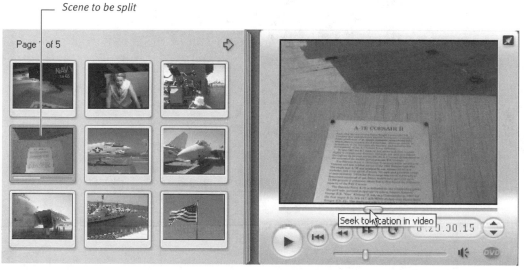

Figure 6.18 Here I shot the nameplate and walk-bys of two jets in one scene. To separate the footage into multiple scenes, I move the Player controls to the desired initial frame of the second scene.

SPLITTING SCENES

3. Do *one of the following:*

▲ From the Studio menu, choose Album > Split Scene.

▲ Place the pointer over the video you want to adjust; then right-click and choose Split Scene (**Figure 6.19**).

Studio splits the scene into two scenes, with the selected frame as the initial frame of the second scene (**Figure 6.20**).

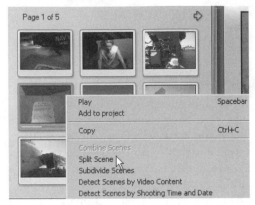

Figure 6.19 Then right-click and select Split Scene.

Figure 6.20 Now we have separate scenes for the A7E Corsair (on the left) and F8K Crusader, two key jets in the post WWII era.

SPLITTING SCENES

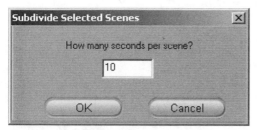

Figure 6.21 Select the desired interval (the minimum is 1 second, default is 5) and click OK.

Figure 6.22 When the progress bar appears, Studio is analyzing the clip using the selected scene-detection method.

To subdivide scenes into intervals:

1. Select the video to subdivide.

2. Do *one of the following:*

   ▲ From the Studio menu, choose Album > Subdivide Scenes.

   ▲ Right-click and choose Subdivide Scenes.

   The Subdivide Selected Scenes dialog box appears.

3. Type the desired interval in the dialog box, with the minimum interval being 1 second (**Figure 6.21**).

4. Click OK.

   Studio splits the video into scenes of the specified interval, with any remaining time placed in a separate scene. The new scenes are added to the Album.

To detect scenes in your clips:

1. Select the video to be adjusted.

2. Do *one of the following:*

   ▲ In the Studio menu, choose Album > Detect Scenes by Video Content *or* Detect Scenes by Shooting Time and Date.

   ▲ Right-click and choose Detect Scenes by Video Content or Detect Scenes by Shooting Time and Date.

   Studio implements the selected scene-detection option. First you see a dialog box with a bar tracking Studio's progress (**Figure 6.22**); then the new scenes appear in the Album.

continues on next page

SPLITTING SCENES

✔ Tips

- Studio has much more precise tools for trimming, or the process of cutting unwanted frames from the beginning and end of each video clip. Accordingly, use splitting for rough cuts and for making the scenes in the Album easier to manage, and use the tools in the Movie window for fine-tuning.

- If you customize comments for a scene and later split, subdivide, or use scene detection for that scene, Studio deletes the customized scene comments and uses the default naming convention. If you plan on customizing scene comments, do this after splitting or combining your scenes.

- Splitting also updates the order of all Album scenes, so if you split Scene 1 into two scenes, the former Scene 2 becomes Scene 3. Keep this in mind if you've been cataloging your scenes-based upon automatic names.

Working with the Album's Views and Tools

The first time you load Studio, the Album opens in Scene view, where each scene is represented by an icon: essentially a thumbnail of the initial frame in the scene. However, Studio lets you customize this view to make your videos more accessible. Here's how.

To change from Scene view to Comment view:

◆ Do *one of the following*:

▲ Hold the pointer over any gray area in the Album; then right-click and choose Comment view (**Figure 6.23**).

▲ Hold the pointer over any thumbnail in the Album; then right-click and choose Comment view.

▲ From the Studio menu, choose Album > Comment view.

The Album switches to Comment view (**Figure 6.24**).

The scene comments to the right of each video list the scene number, duration, and date and time the scene was shot. As you'll see in the next section, you can customize these comments so that you can more easily find relevant scenes during production.

(Note that while working with the beta program, we noticed the scene information seemed to change randomly. So if you see different information from what is shown in Figure 6.24, don't be surprised.)

Figure 6.23 To switch to Comment view, hold the pointer over any gray area in the Album, right-click, and choose Comment view.

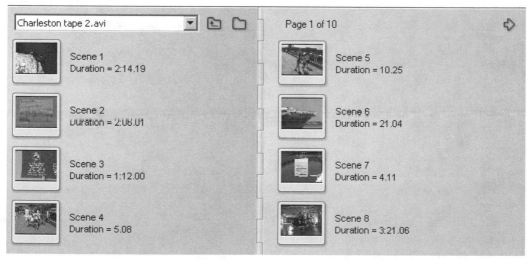

Figure 6.24 The Album switches to Comment view.

WORKING WITH THE ALBUM'S VIEWS AND TOOLS

To switch between 4:3 and 16:9 views:

◆ Right-click on a picture in the Album and choose Aspect Ratio 16:9 (**Figure 6.25**). The Album and Player switch to 16:9 view (**Figure 6.26**). To switch back to 4:3, right-click and choose Aspect Ratio 4:3 view.

✔ Tip

■ Note that changing views does nothing to the captured file; it just changes how Studio displays the file.

WORKING WITH THE ALBUM'S VIEWS AND TOOLS

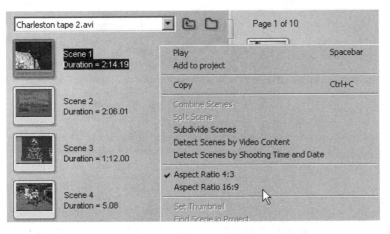

Figure 6.25
Here's how you switch back and forth between 16:9 and 4:3 modes.

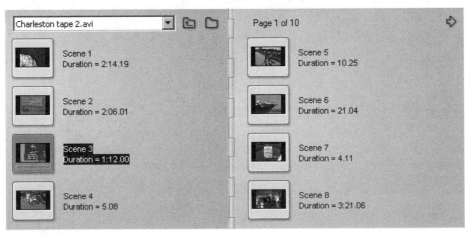

Figure 6.26 Here's the Album in 16:9 mode.

To change the video thumbnail:

1. Click the target video.

   Studio highlights the scene in the Album and displays the initial frame in the Player (**Figure 6.27**).

2. Use the Player controls to move to the frame you want to use as the new thumbnail image (**Figure 6.28**).

3. Do *one of the following:*

   ▲ From the Studio menu, choose Album > Set Thumbnail (Figure 6.28).

   ▲ Place the pointer over the video you want to adjust; then right-click and choose Set Thumbnail.

   Studio changes the thumbnail image to the new frame (**Figure 6.29**).

Figure 6.27 Here's the original thumbnail of this scene, which is not descriptive enough.

Figure 6.28 Looks equally nondescript, but now we see the coil that holds the wire that catches the plane when it lands on the deck of the aircraft carrier. Miss this one (the third of three) and you're in trouble.

Figure 6.29 It's much easier to tell what this is when I'm scanning for thumbnails in Scene view.

To locate a clip from the Album in a production:

1. Click any scene with a green check mark in the upper-right corner (**Figure 6.30**). The check mark identifies scenes that are included in the production.

2. Do *one of the following*:

   ▲ From the Studio menu, choose Album > Find Scene in Project (Figure 6.30).

   ▲ Place the pointer over the scene you want to find; then right-click and choose Find Scene in Project.

   Studio highlights the selected scene in the Movie window (**Figure 6.31**).

✔ Tip

■ If you hold the pointer over any scene for a moment, Studio displays the start time and duration of the scene (**Figure 6.32**). Keep in mind that this and other helpful information found by hovering over a scene or other icon works only with the Tool Tips feature enabled—be sure the Display Tool Tips option is checked in the Help pull-down menu.

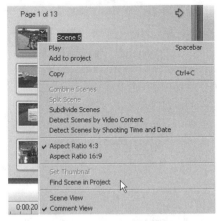

Figure 6.30 The green check mark tells you that you've used the scene somewhere in the production. To find it, select the scene, right-click, and choose Find Scene in Project.

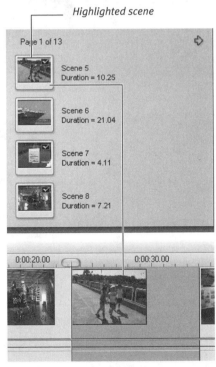

Figure 6.31 Studio shifts the Timeline to make the scene visible in the Movie window (if necessary) and highlights the scene.

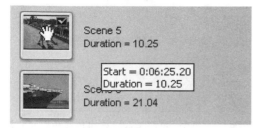

Figure 6.32 The pop-up box that appears when you hold the pointer over a scene's thumbnail identifies the scene's starting time and duration in the captured video.

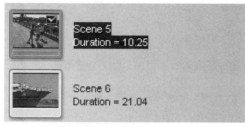

Figure 6.33 Changing scene comments helps you find videos fast. Start by clicking the scene.

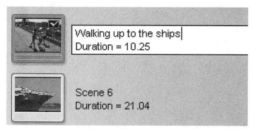

Figure 6.34 Then type the desired text.

Working with Scene Comments

In smaller productions, it's easy to keep track of videos and scenes, but when you're tracking multiple videos over many months, finding the scenes you want can be harder. This is where the ability to add descriptive comments to scenes and later search for these scenes can be immensely helpful.

To change scene comments:

1. In Comment View mode, click the target video and click again on the comments box.

   The outline around the video turns blue, and the scene comments are highlighted (**Figure 6.33**).

2. Click the comments box again.

   It turns white, signifying that it's ready for editing.

3. Type the desired scene comments (**Figure 6.34**).

4. To save the scene comments, press Enter or click anywhere in the Studio interface outside the comments box.

   Studio saves the scene comments.

✔ Tips

- With a long video like this shoot from the trip to Charleston, I take the time to label every clip so that I know both what the content is and how I might use the shot. This way, relevant scenes will be easy to search for, as you'll see in the next section.

- I typically leave the duration information in the description, since this is useful to know when assembling videos.

To select scenes based on keywords:

1. From the Studio menu, choose Album > Select Scenes by Name.

   The Select Scenes by Name dialog box appears (**Figure 6.35**).

2. Enter the keywords you want to search for.

3. Do *one of the following:*

   ▲ Select And to find all scenes containing all of the words typed in the Keywords box.

   ▲ Select Or to find all scenes containing any of the words typed in the Keywords box.

   ▲ Select Not and And to find any scenes that don't contain all of the words typed in the Keywords box.

   ▲ Select Not and Or to find any scenes that don't contain any of the words typed in the Keywords box.

   The Album highlights the scenes that meet the specified criteria (**Figure 6.36**). You'll have to page through the Album to locate the highlighted clips; Studio doesn't move them to a new location.

✔ Tips

■ Studio's search function searches only scenes in the video currently loaded in the Album, not other videos saved to disk. This somewhat limits its functionality except with extremely large capture files.

■ Unlike Windows Explorer, the Album doesn't prevent you from using duplicate names. Your files won't self-destruct; you'll just end up with different scenes with identical names.

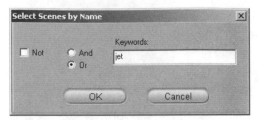

Figure 6.35 Type the words you want to search for and specify the conditions.

Figure 6.36 Studio highlights the conforming clips.

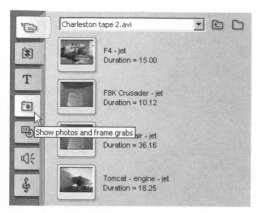

Figure 6.37 Let's click the Camera icon and throw in some still shots from the pool.

Working with the Still Images Tab

The Still Images tab is where you load still images from all sources for deployment in your projects. The Album's functions in this area are extremely limited; you can't combine, arrange, or annotate the images in the Album. Don't worry; there's plenty of functionality for that in the Movie window.

To open the Album to the Still Images tab:

1. Open Studio in Edit mode.

    When you first open Studio, Edit mode is the default.

    If you're running Studio and are in Capture or Make Movie mode, select the Edit tab.

2. Click the Camera icon, the fourth icon from the top along the left side of the Album window (**Figure 6.37**).

    The Album switches to the Still Images tab and displays any images in the currently selected folder (**Figure 6.38**). Click any image, and Studio will display it in the Player.

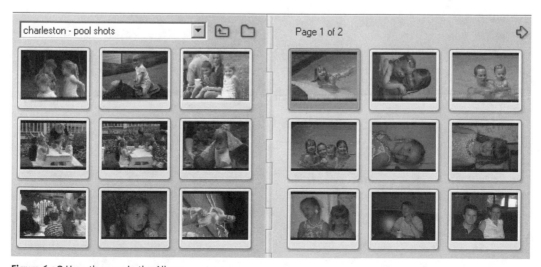

Figure 6.38 Here they are in the Album.

To display file names:

◆ Hover the pointer over any image.

The pointer immediately changes to a hand and then (with Tool Tips on) displays the image's file name (**Figure 6.39**).

To load files from a different location:

1. Click the Directory icon to the right of the Album's list box (**Figure 6.40**).

   A standard Open dialog box appears (**Figure 6.41**).

2. Navigate to the folder that contains the files to be imported and select any file in the folder; then click the Open button (**Figure 6.42**).

   Studio loads all files in the folder (**Figure 6.43**).

Figure 6.39 Hover the pointer over an image, and Studio tells you its name.

Figure 6.40 To load files from a different directory, click the Folder icon.

Figure 6.41 Once the Open dialog box appears, navigate to the desired location.

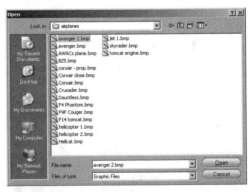

Figure 6.42 Select any file and click Open.

WORKING WITH THE STILL IMAGES TAB

✔ Tips

- If you select a subdirectory with many high-resolution images, it may take several minutes for Studio to create the thumbnails to display in the Album, during which time your hard drive will be chugging like crazy, and your computer will feel extremely sluggish. If your still image folders contain lots of images, consider moving the images you want to incorporate into your production to a separate folder for input into Studio.

- Studio can import files in the following formats: bitmap (BMP), JPEG (JPG, JPEG), Targa (TGA), TIFF (TIF), Windows Metafiles (WMF), and files created by Title Deko, Studio's titling utility. This pretty much covers the majors, but if you want to use a GIF image or Photoshop document (PSD), you have to convert to one of the supported formats in another program first.

Figure 6.43 Studio loads all of the directory's images into the Album. Here are some of the aircraft I saw on the U.S.S. Yorktown.

Working with the Sound Effects Tab

The Sound Effects tab is where you load audio files for deployment in your projects. As with the Still Images tab, the Album's functions in this area are extremely limited; you can't combine, arrange, or annotate the audio files in the Album, nor can you adjust volume. All this and more are possible in the Movie window; the Album is here simply to help you collect and deploy.

To open the Album to the Sound Effects tab:

1. Open Studio in Edit mode.

   When you first open Studio, Edit mode is the default.

   If you're running Studio and are in Capture or Make Movie mode, select the Edit tab.

2. Click the Speaker icon, the fifth icon from the top on the left side of the Album window (**Figure 6.44**).

   The Album switches to the Sound Effects tab and displays all supported files in the current folder (**Figure 6.45**).

To display file duration:

◆ Hover the pointer over any audio file.

   The pointer immediately changes to a hand and then, in a moment, displays the file duration (**Figure 6.46**).

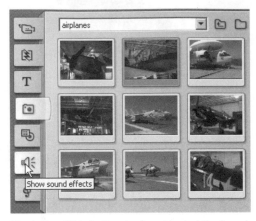

Figure 6.44 Click the Speaker icon to select the Sound Effects tab, where you load audio files into the project.

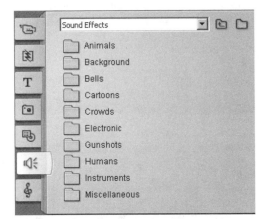

Figure 6.45 The Album defaults to folders containing sound effects that Pinnacle includes with Studio 10.

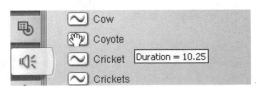

Figure 6.46 As with still images, the Album features for audio files are light, but (with Tool Tips on) you can ascertain file duration by hovering the pointer over the icon.

Figure 6.47 You know the drill by now. To open new audio files, click the Folder icon.

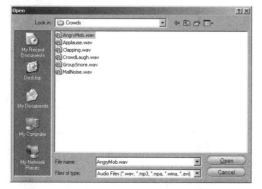

Figure 6.48 Choose any file and click Open.

Figure 6.49 Studio displays all compatible audio files in the Album.

To play any audio file:

◆ Click any file on the Sound Effects tab. The file immediately plays through to the end. Use the controls in the Player to replay, rewind, or move through the scene.

To load files from a different location:

1. Click the Directory icon to the right of the Album list box (**Figure 6.47**).
   A standard Open dialog box appears.

2. Navigate to the folder containing the files to be imported, select any file in the folder, and click Open (**Figure 6.48**).
   Studio loads all compatible files in the folder into the Album (**Figure 6.49**).

✔ Tip

■ Studio can import WAV files, MP3 files, and audio from AVI files. Notable missing formats include QuickTime, RealAudio, and Windows Media files. The lack of the latter two is a pain given that many folks who collect digital audio files use these formats extensively for their collections.

WORKING WITH THE SOUND EFFECTS TAB

Part III: Editing

PRODUCING VIDEOS IN THE MOVIE WINDOW

7

Once you've captured your video, still image, and audio assets, you will have created a huge collection of files—usually far more than you'll want to include in your final production. The next steps are to cut out the fat and assemble the basic pieces of your project, all of which you do in Studio's Movie window.

The Movie window showcases the most flexible part of Studio's interface, providing three views of your assembled assets: Storyboard, Timeline, and Text view (called Edit List view on the Studio menu). This chapter discusses the strengths of each view and then teaches you how to customize and work efficiently within the Storyboard and Timeline views. Considering how much time you'll be spending in the Movie window—particularly the Timeline—learning the basics now will save you hours of work later.

Looking at Movie Window Views

The Movie window offers three views: Storyboard (**Figure 7.1**), Timeline (**Figure 7.2**), and Text (**Figure 7.3**).

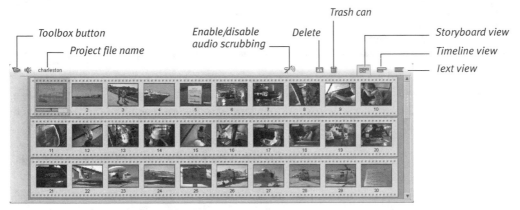

Trash can

Toolbox button *Enable/disable audio scrubbing* *Delete* *Storyboard view*

Project file name *Timeline view*

Text view

Figure 7.1 The Storyboard view, the best view for initially loading and sequencing your assets.

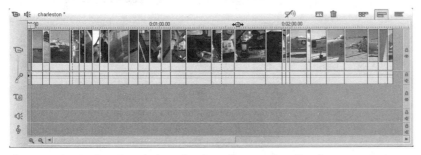

Figure 7.2 The Timeline view, the best view for pulling together all project components.

	Name	Trimmed start	Movie duration	Movie start
1	Video clip: 'Signage	3:03:02.11	0:00:01.23	0:00:00.00
	Audio clip: 'Signage	3:03:02.11	0:00:01.23	0:00:00.00
2	Video clip: 'Establishing shots - carrier	3:02:54.01	0:00:04.27	0:00:01.23
	Audio clip: 'Establishing shots - carrier	3:02:54.01	0:00:04.27	0:00:01.23
3	Video clip: 'Walking up to the ships	3:06:26.29	0:00:03.06	0:00:06.20
	Audio clip: 'Walking up to the ships	3:06:26.29	0:00:03.06	0:00:06.20
4	Video clip: 'Closer establishing shot - Yorktown	3:06:36.15	0:00:09.11	0:00:09.26
	Audio clip: 'Closer establishing shot - Yorktown	3:06:36.15	0:00:09.11	0:00:09.26
5	Video clip: 'Signage - Yorktown	3:07:00.21	0:00:01.09	0:00:19.07
	Audio clip: 'Signage - Yorktown	3:07:00.21	0:00:01.09	0:00:19.07
6	Video clip: 'Jet - F9F Couger - walk inside	3:07:02.00	0:00:02.29	0:00:20.16
	Audio clip: 'Jet - F9F Couger - walk inside	3:07:02.00	0:00:02.29	0:00:20.16
7	Video clip: 'Jet - F9F Couger - walk inside	3:07:13.12	0:00:02.12	0:00:23.15
	Audio clip: 'Jet - F9F Couger - walk inside	3:07:13.12	0:00:02.12	0:00:23.15
8	Video clip: 'Jet - F9F Couger - walk inside	3:07:23.06	0:00:03.18	0:00:25.27

Figure 7.3 The Text view (also called Edit List), for those who prefer working in text rather than using visual tools.

Figure 7.4 Switch among views using the Studio menu or the icons at the top of the Movie window.

Briefly, the Storyboard view uses a thumbnail image to represent each asset in a project. This is a great view for sequencing your assets and inserting transitions between them, but little else, since you can't access tracks for titles, narration, or background music.

The Timeline view is a graphical representation of an entire project, with the length of each clip on the Timeline representing the duration of that clip. Although Timeline view lets you recognize bits and pieces of clips, you won't be able to recognize most of the smaller clips, especially if you've zoomed out to get a bird's-eye view. So it's best to sequence your videos in Storyboard view and then switch to Timeline view for serious editing such as adding titles, background music, and other elements.

The Text view is appropriate for those who enjoy working with text descriptors rather than visual assets. I don't work that way and have seldom found uses for this view, so I won't elaborate on it.

To switch among Movie window views:

◆ Do *one of the following*:

   ▲ At the upper right of the Movie window, click the appropriate button for the desired view (Figure 7.1).

   ▲ In the Studio menu, choose View and the desired view (**Figure 7.4**).

Working on the Storyboard

In traditional video productions, a storyboard is a large chart or series of charts with images representing the various scenes of a project. It's a great tool for conceptualizing the content and flow of your movie, and it's even better in digital form, since it makes rearranging your assets easy.

If you're at all unsure of the order of your scenes, Studio's Storyboard is a very convenient place for shuffling them around until you've decided. You can even add transitions and preview your project on the fly to view the rough cut. However, when it's time to trim your videos and perform other more sophisticated editing, you'll need to use the superior tools available only in Timeline view.

Note that by default, Studio maintains audio and video synchronization in all Movie window views by automatically tying the Audio track to the Video track through all edits. Accordingly, if you move, delete, split, or combine scenes in the Video track, the audio automatically follows. (Later in this chapter, you'll learn how to adjust this default, so that you can delete the Audio track or perform advanced editing operations that let you edit the Audio and Video tracks separately.)

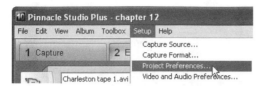

Figure 7.5 Getting to the Pinnacle Studio Setup Options screen.

Figure 7.6 With the Project Preferences tab selected, check Show large storyboard thumbnails.

To customize the Storyboard view:

1. From the Studio menu, choose Setup > Project Preferences (**Figure 7.5**).

   The Pinnacle Studio Setup Options screen appears, open to the Edit tab (**Figure 7.6**).

2. In the Storyboard Thumbnails section, select the Large radio button to increase the size of the images on the Storyboard.

   Studio increases the size of the individual images and decreases the number of images shown from 27 to 12 (**Figure 7.7**). Use the scroll bar on the right to scroll down to see the additional thumbnails, or use the Page Up and Page Down keys to move through the pages of the Storyboard.

Figure 7.7 Select Large Storyboard Thumbnails to see more detail in your thumbnails. Note the scroll bar on the right, which you'll use to access the rest of your assets.

To drag video clips to the Storyboard:

1. On the Video Scenes tab, hold down the mouse button and select one or more contiguous or noncontiguous scenes.

   The borders turn from white to blue, and a small hand appears over the scenes (**Figure 7.8**).

2. Drag the scenes toward the empty frame at the upper left of the Storyboard.

   A green box appears around the empty frame, and a small plus sign and box appears below the pointer (**Figure 7.9**). (You won't be able to see the green frame in Figure 7.9, but you will when you try this in Studio.)

3. Release the mouse button.

   Studio inserts the scenes in the high-lighted Storyboard frame (**Figure 7.10**).

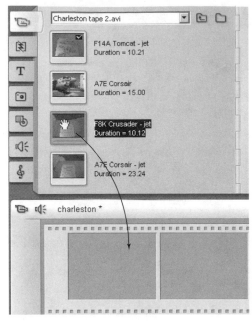

Figure 7.8 Getting videos into the Movie window is as simple as selecting and dragging.

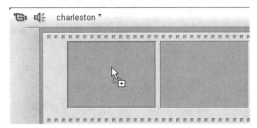

Figure 7.9 The green border and plus sign are your clues that it's safe to drop the asset in the selected frame.

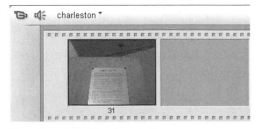

Figure 7.10 Voilà. There's your clip.

Figure 7.11 Other placement cues include the universal "prohibited" sign, indicating that you can't arrange your clips on the Video Scenes tab.

✔ Tips

- Studio provides visual cues regarding where you can drop all assets. As shown in **Figure 7.11**, if you attempt to drop a scene in a prohibited zone, such as another location on the Video Scenes tab, Studio displays the universal "prohibited" sign.

- Studio drops video and still image assets in the first available space at the beginning of a project. Although you can reorder at will once the assets are on the Storyboard, Studio doesn't let you create gaps in your projects in any Movie window view.

- To create a black scene at the start of your video, create a full-screen blank title and drag it to the Video track (see "To create a single-color background" in Chapter 10).

- You can also use the Cut and Paste commands to move videos and still images to and around the Movie window, but dragging and dropping is much more intuitive.

To insert a video clip between two scenes in the Storyboard:

1. On the Video Scenes tab, hold down the mouse button and select one or more scenes.

   The borders turn from white to blue, and a small hand appears over the scene.

2. Drag the scenes to the desired location.

   A green line appears between the video scenes, and a small plus sign appears below the pointer (**Figure 7.12**).

3. Release the mouse button.

✔ Tip

■ Studio inserts the scene between the existing scenes (**Figure 7.13**), pushing back all clips after the newly inserted clips. No clips are deleted or otherwise truncated.

Figure 7.12 The green line and a small plus sign tell you that you can drop the assets in that location.

Figure 7.13 The assets, successfully inserted and shifted.

Selected clip

Figure 7.14 Here I want to drag the scene containing the F-4 Phantom plaque in front of both video clips, rather than between them. To start, I click the clip.

Figure 7.15 When you see that green line and the small box under the arrow, you can drag the clip to the desired location and drop it.

Figure 7.16 Done. This ease of sequencing is why the Storyboard view is great for arranging your assets.

Figure 7.17 Since the Storyboard view doesn't visually convey duration-related information, Studio provides it when you hover your mouse over the asset. Top duration is the total for the scene; bottom is the duration of video actually included in the project.

To arrange assets in Storyboard view:

1. On the Storyboard, hold down the mouse button and select one or more scenes.

   Studio highlights the clip in blue, and a small hand appears over the scene (**Figure 7.14**).

2. Drag the scenes to the desired location.

   A green line appears each time you cross an available space to drop the new scenes, and a small box appears below the pointer (**Figure 7.15**).

3. Release the mouse button at the desired location.

   Studio inserts the scene in the specified location (**Figure 7.16**).

To see clip-related information on the Storyboard:

◆ On the Storyboard, hover the pointer over a clip for a moment.

   The scene name and duration appear in a yellow box beneath the scene (**Figure 7.17**). The top duration is the total duration of the clip. The bottom one is the duration of the clip remaining in the sequence after trimming. (For more information, see "Trimming with the Clip Properties Tool," later in this chapter.)

WORKING ON THE STORYBOARD

To preview your video clip on the Storyboard:

1. Select the scene you want to play back. Studio highlights the clip in blue.

2. Start playback by doing *one of the following:*

   ▲ In the Player, click Play (**Figure 7.18**). The Play key switches to Pause mode, which you can click to stop playback.

   ▲ Press the spacebar to start playback. Press the spacebar again to stop playback.

   ▲ Press the L key to start playback. Press K to stop playback.

Playback shifts automatically from scene to scene when multiple assets are present. During playback, Studio displays a progress bar beneath the scene.

The progress bar represents the position of playback within each scene; the Player scrubber represents the position of playback within the entire video.

✔ Tips

■ Here are some keyboard shortcuts:
   Press L for fast-forward (press L multiple times to accelerate the effect).
   Press J for fast-reverse (press J multiple times to accelerate the effect).

■ You can always use the Player scrubber to move around in the video file.

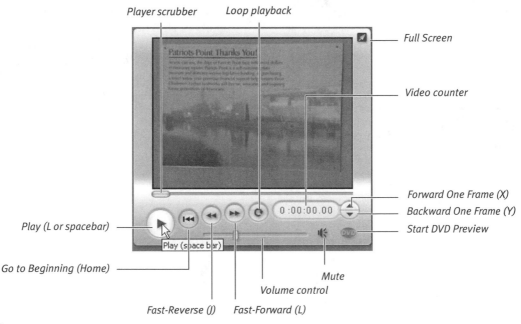

Figure 7.18 The Player is your preview window.

Getting Video Clips to the Timeline

Timeline view is where you'll spend the bulk of your editing time. Although it's not quite as straightforward as Storyboard view, its operational advantages quickly become apparent.

This section identifies the various Timeline tracks and explains how to get video scenes to the Timeline. If your Timeline starts getting cramped or otherwise out of control, skip ahead one section to learn how to customize your Timeline view.

As mentioned earlier, in default mode Studio automatically inserts the audio that was originally captured with the video file on the appropriate track when you transfer the video, so you don't have to worry about manually moving the audio track yourself.

The components of the Timeline and other components of the Studio interface that are important in using the Timeline effectively are summarized here (**Figure 7.19**):

◆ **Timescale:** Shows the absolute time of the assets displayed in Timeline view. You can modify the Timescale to show more or less detail (see "Customizing Your Timeline View," later in this chapter).

continues on next page

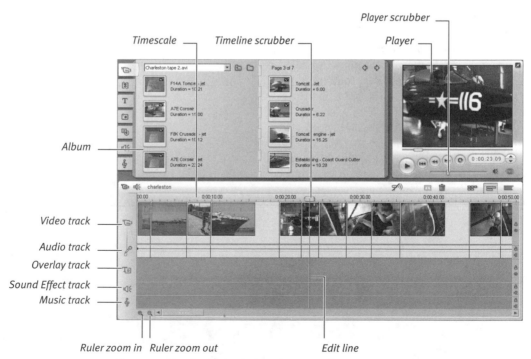

Figure 7.19 The Timeline and other relevant Studio components. Take a good look around; you'll be spending lots of time here.

- **Menu track:** Appears only after you add a DVD menu to the Timeline. (For details on DVD authoring, see Chapter 12.)

- **Video track:** The only track that can display video; it can also display still images.

- **Audio track:** Contains only the audio that was captured with the video clip. Note that Studio 8 referred to the Audio track as the Original Audio track, and still does in the Help files. However, Tool Tips refer to it as the Audio track. For the purposes of this book I also refer to it as the Audio track, though I may slip and mention Original Audio track occasionally.

- **Overlay track:** Contains titles and Studio 10 still image and video overlays. (For more information on creating titles, see Chapter 10. For more information on video overlays, see "Studio's Overlay Effects" in Chapter 9.)

- **Sound Effect track:** Studio places all voice-over recordings on this track, or you can insert audio from any source. For example, to insert only the audio from a captured video file into the production, simply drag it to this track. Note that the Studio 10 Help files may refer to this as the Sound Effect and Voice Over track, but I'm sticking with what the Tool Tips call it. If I happen to refer to it in the same way the Help files do, you'll know I'm talking about the Sound Effect track.

- **Music track:** Studio places background music produced by the SmartSound utility or from any source on this track. To learn how to set audio levels for the three Audio tracks, see "Using the Volume Tool" in Chapter 11.

- **Edit line:** The current editing position on the Timeline and the frame currently visible in the Player.

- **Timeline scrubber:** A tool used to drag the edit line to different positions on the Timeline.

- **Player scrubber:** A tool used to move the edit line through the project.

- **Timeline slider:** A tool used to drag the visible area on the Timeline forward and backward through the project.

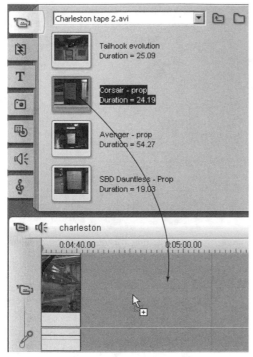

Figure 7.20 More placement cues. A green box defines the duration of the video clip on the Timeline, and the plus sign says it's okay to drop the file here.

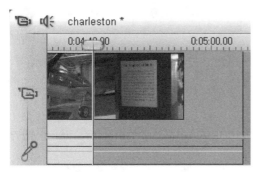

Figure 7.21 There's your scene, ready to go.

To drag video clips to the Timeline:

1. On the Video Scenes tab, hold down the mouse button, and select one or more contiguous or noncontiguous scenes.

   The borders turn from white to blue, and a small hand appears over the scenes.

2. Do *one of the following:*

   ▲ Drag the scenes to the Video track.

   ▲ Drag the scenes to the Sound Effect track.

   ▲ Drag the scenes to the Music track.

   A green rectangle representing the duration of the clip appears in the first open space on the Timeline, and a small plus sign appears below the pointer (**Figure 7.20**).

3. Release the mouse button.

   Studio inserts the scenes on the selected track (**Figure 7.21**).

continues on next page

GETTING VIDEO CLIPS TO THE TIMELINE

✔ Tips

- As shown in **Figure 7.22**, when you drag a video into the Overlay track, Studio adds new Video and Audio tracks, and opens a new Title track that can contain titles and still images (but no additional video files).

- If you drop a video on the Video track, Studio always inserts the associated audio on the Audio track. To delete the Audio track, lock the Video track and delete the associated Audio track. See "Advanced Timeline Editing" later in this chapter for details on locking tracks.

- If you drop a video file on either the Sound Effect track or the Music track, only the audio, not the video, is inserted on the track.

- Studio provides the same visual cues on the Timeline to show where you can drop all assets as it does on the Storyboard. If you attempt to drop scenes on prohibited tracks, such as the Title track, you'll see red lines instead of green, a "prohibited" sign, and the error message "Only titles, photos and transitions on title track" above the Timescale (Figure 7.22).

- As with the Storyboard, Studio always drops video and still image assets in the first available space at the beginning of a project. Although you can reorder assets at will once they're on the Storyboard, you can't create gaps in your projects in any of the Movie window views.

Figure 7.22 Here's the fully tricked-out Studio timeline with separate Overlay and Title tracks. The error message notes that you can insert titles, photos, and transitions into the Title track, but not videos.

To insert video clips between two clips on the Timeline:

1. On the Video Scenes tab, hold down the mouse button and select one or more scenes.

   The borders turn from white to blue, and a small hand appears over the scenes.

2. Drag the scenes to the desired location.

   Two vertical green lines appear between the two selected video clips, and a small plus sign appears below the pointer (**Figure 7.23**).

3. Release the mouse button.

   Studio inserts the scene between the existing scenes (**Figure 7.24**).

✔ Tips

■ Note that Studio inserts the new clip between the selected clips, pushing back all clips after the newly inserted clips (potentially out of your current view of the project). No clips are deleted or otherwise truncated.

■ You can normally insert a clip only at the beginning or end of another clip, not in the middle of a clip. Both of the "To perform an insert edit" tasks later in this chapter show you how to insert a clip in the middle of a different clip, a process called insert editing.

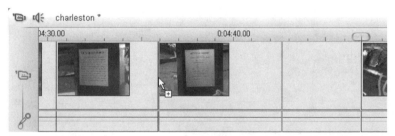

Figure 7.23 Studio won't let you drop a clip in the middle of another one. Move the pointer until you see the green lines and plus sign.

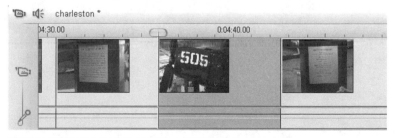

Figure 7.24 Release the mouse button, and there you go.

To arrange video clips on the Timeline:

1. On the Video track, hold down the mouse button and select one or more scenes.

    Studio highlights the clip in blue, and a small hand appears over the scene (**Figure 7.25**).

2. Drag the clip to the desired location.

    Studio displays green lines at the beginning and end of the clip that you're arranging, and a small box appears below the pointer (**Figure 7.26**).

3. Release the mouse button.

    Studio inserts the scene in the specified location (**Figure 7.27**).

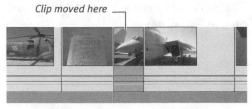

Clip moved here

Figure 7.25 You move clips on the Timeline the same way you do on the Storyboard, with slightly different cues. Here I'll move the front shot of the F-14 Tomcat in front of the zoom into the engine air intake. I'll start by selecting the clip.

Figure 7.26 Move the clip to the desired space, watching for the green lines and plus sign, and then release the mouse button.

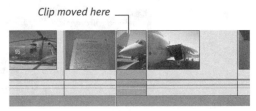

Clip moved here

Figure 7.27 Studio inserts the clip and pushes all clips behind it to the back of the line.

Timeline scrubber

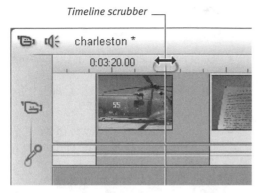

Figure 7.28 Get familiar with the Timeline scrubber, which shifts the edit line and controls the frames viewed in the Player.

To preview your video clip on the Timeline:

1. Do *one of the following*:

    ▲ Select the scene you want to play back.

      Studio highlights the clip in blue and positions the Timeline scrubber at the start of the scene.

    ▲ Drag the Timeline scrubber to the desired start location (**Figure 7.28**).

2. Start playback by doing *one of the following*:

    ▲ In the Player, click Play.

      The Play key switches to Pause mode, which you can click to stop playback.

    ▲ Press the spacebar to start playback. Press the spacebar again to stop playback.

    ▲ Press the L key to start playback (ignore the Tool Tip). Press K to stop playback.

    Playback shifts automatically from scene to scene when multiple assets are present.

    During playback, the Timeline and Player scrubbers advance with the video.

✔ Tips

■ Here are some relevant keyboard shortcuts:

    ▲ Press L for fast-forward (press L multiple times to accelerate the effect).

    ▲ Press J for fast-reverse (press J multiple times to accelerate the effect).

    ▲ Press K to stop playback.

■ You can always use the Player scrubber to position video playback.

■ If your mouse has a wheel, you can use it to scroll through the video. Note that if you press and hold down the Ctrl key as you're doing it, you'll move through the video frame by frame.

Customizing Your Timeline View

As you've probably already noticed, as you place additional videos on the Timeline, it gets increasingly difficult to see the big picture. Fortunately, Studio supplies several tools that help you control your Timeline environment.

First, a slider bar at the bottom of the Timeline makes it easy to move through your production. In addition, Studio can stretch the Timeline so that it represents a longer period (and thus shows more video clips, or longer stretches of a single video clip) to provide a high-level view. Or you can shrink down the Timeline to a frame-by-frame view, which is helpful when synchronizing production elements such as audio and the main video.

To move around on the Timeline:

◆ Do *one of the following*:

  ▲ Drag the Timeline slider at the bottom of the Timeline to the right to reveal the video clip inserted after the last visible track (**Figure 7.29**).

  ▲ Press the Page Down key to move from the beginning to the end of the Timeline, or the Page Up key to move from the end to the beginning.

  ▲ Press the right arrow key to move forward to the next scene on the Timeline, and the left arrow key to move backward from scene to scene.

✔ Tips

■ The Timeline slider is not movable until the project assets exceed the space then visible on the Timeline.

■ The Timeline slider will shrink as the project gets longer, essentially representing the size of the video visible at that time on the Timeline relative to the entire project.

Ruler zoom in

Ruler zoom out

Timeline slider

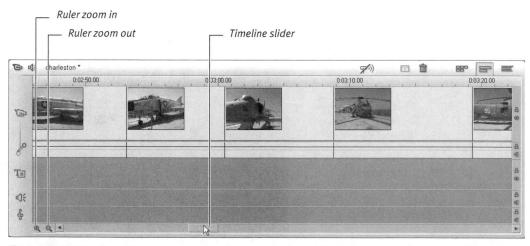

Figure 7.29 The Timeline slider moves you around your production, while the two ruler tools zoom you into and out of your project.

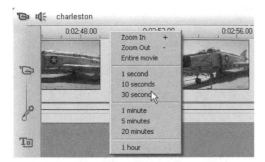

Figure 7.30 Here's another way to adjust the Timescale, giving you control over the duration of the video in the project you can see on the Timeline at one time.

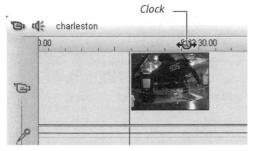

Figure 7.31 Here's another. Just click the yellow Timescale anywhere but on the Timeline scrubber, and the clock appears.

To adjust the Timescale of the Timeline:

◆ Do *one of the following:*

▲ On the bottom left of the Timeline, click the Ruler zoom in and Ruler zoom out icons (Figure 7.29).

▲ Place your pointer over the yellow Timescale on the Timeline and right-click. Studio opens a menu that lets you select the desired duration visible on the Timeline (**Figure 7.30**).

▲ Press the plus (+) or minus (–) key to make the Timescale larger or smaller.

▲ On the yellow Timescale bar, place the pointer anywhere except directly over the edit line until a small clock with arrows appears (**Figure 7.31**). Drag the clock left to expand the Timescale and show more video clips or right to compress the Timescale and see more detail.

✔ Tips

■ If you choose Entire Movie (Figure 7.30), Studio places the entire movie in the visible area of the Timeline. This is the best way to see your whole production fast.

■ When you set the Timescale at the highest magnification, each tick mark on the Timescale represents an individual video frame (although Studio shows only the initial frame on the Timeline). When performing precision trims on the Timeline, this level of detail can be extremely useful, though you'll have to view the frames in the Player, not on the Timeline.

CUSTOMIZING YOUR TIMELINE VIEW

Common Tasks

As you'd expect, Studio has common commands for many housekeeping tasks you perform in the Storyboard and Timeline views. Here are the major ones, shown in the Timeline view for simplicity.

In terms of workflow, I like to drag videos quickly to the Timeline to get a "rough draft" of the movie, then start removing what I absolutely don't need and fine-tuning the rest. This means deleting and splitting clips, covered here, and trimming, covered in the next three major sections.

With most home videos, I find that less is more, and I'm sure you'll agree. This makes these sections among the most important in the book.

Figure 7.32 When deleting clips from the main Video and Audio tracks, click Delete to ripple edit and Delete (Leave Gap) to leave a gap.

Figure 7.33 On other tracks, it's the reverse. Click Delete to leave a gap, and Delete (Close Gap) to ripple edit.

Studio's Delete-ist Behaviors

Before you start deleting clips, you should first understand Studio's behavior regarding subsequent clips on that track. On the main Video and Audio tracks, Studio's tendency is to avoid gaps when deleting clips. Accordingly, if you delete a clip on either of these tracks, Studio will automatically perform a "ripple" edit, closing the gap by moving all subsequent Audio and Video clips to the left. On all other tracks, even the Overlay track, Studio doesn't worry about gaps; it simply deletes the clip, and doesn't ripple the remaining content to the left.

New in Studio 10 is the ability to reverse these tendencies. For example, in **Figure 7.32**, when you select a clip on the main Video track, you'll see the Delete (Leave Gap) option in addition to the normal Delete command. This option lets you leave a gap open in the Video track, perhaps to fill in with other content, or to delete normally and ripple all subsequent contents to close the gap.

In **Figure 7.33**, I've selected a title on the Overlay track. Here, the default behavior accomplished via the Delete command is to delete the title without rippling subsequent titles over to close the gap. Sometimes, however, you'll want subsequent titles to ripple back. For example, suppose you created a slide show with a title for each slide. If you delete one slide from the project, you'd probably want all subsequent slides to ripple over to close the gap. If so, you'd also want the associated titles to ripple to the left, in which case you'd choose Delete (Close Gap).

COMMON TASKS

To delete assets on the main Video and Audio tracks:

1. Select the asset you want to delete. Studio highlights the clip in blue.

2. To delete the assets and close the gap (ripple edit), do *one of the following:*

   ▲ Press the Delete key.

   ▲ From the Studio menu, choose Edit > Delete.

   ▲ Right-click, and choose Edit > Delete (Figure 7.32).

   ▲ On the top right of the Timeline, click the Delete icon (Figure 7.1).

3. To delete the assets and leave a gap (no ripple edit), do *one of the following:*

   ▲ Press the Ctrl and Delete keys.

   ▲ From the Studio menu, choose Edit > Delete (Leave Gap).

   ▲ Right-click, and choose Edit > Delete (Leave Gap) (Figure 7.32). Studio deletes the clip from the Timeline, but not from the Album or your hard disk.

To delete assets on all other tracks:

1. Select the asset you want to delete. Studio highlights the clip in blue.

2. To delete the assets and leave a gap (no ripple edit), do *one of the following:*

   ▲ Press the Delete key.

   ▲ From the Studio menu, choose Edit > Delete.

   ▲ Right-click, and choose Edit > Delete (Figure 7.33).

   ▲ On the top right of the Timeline, click the Delete icon (Figure 7.1).

3. To delete the assets and close the gap (ripple edit), do *one of the following:*

   ▲ Press the Ctrl and Delete keys.

   ▲ From the Studio menu, choose Edit > Delete (Close Gap).

   ▲ Right-click, and choose Edit > Delete (Close Gap) (Figure 7.33).

   Studio deletes the clip from the Timeline, but not from the Album or your hard disk.

✔ Tip

■ In addition to the options on the Edit and right-click menus, you can use keyboard commands to cut (Ctrl+X), copy (Ctrl+C), and paste (Ctrl+V) files.

To split clips:

1. Use Player controls or the Timeline scrubber to move the edit line to the initial frame of the desired second clip (**Figure 7.34**).

2. Split the clip by doing *one of the following*:

   ▲ Click the Razorblade icon at the top the Movie window.

   ▲ Right-click the selected clip and choose Split Clip (**Figure 7.35**).

   ▲ Press the Insert key.

   Studio splits the clips at the edit line (**Figure 7.36**).

Razorblade icon

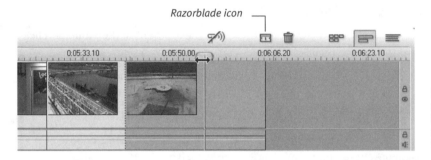

Figure 7.34 To split a clip, move the edit line to the desired location and click the Razorblade icon.

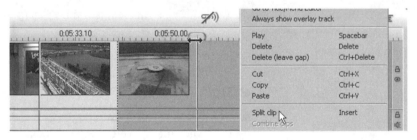

Figure 7.35 Or, for you right-click fans, choose Split Clip.

Figure 7.36 Either way, you now have two clips where formerly there were none.

To combine scenes:

1. Select the scenes to combine by doing *one of the following:*

   ▲ Hold down the Shift or Ctrl key and select two or more scenes (**Figure 7.37**).

   ▲ Starting with the pointer over a gray area (and not a scene) on the Storyboard or Timeline, drag to select all scenes within the marquee (**Figure 7.38**).

▲ From the Studio menu, choose Edit > Select All to select all scenes on the Storyboard or Timeline.

▲ Press Ctrl+A to select all scenes on all pages of the Album.

2. Position the pointer over one of the selected scenes; then right-click and choose Combine Clips (**Figure 7.39**). Studio combines all selected scenes (**Figure 7.40**).

continues on next page

Selected clips

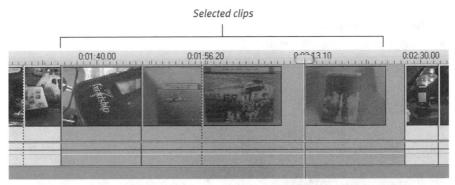

Figure 7.37 To combine scenes, hold down the Shift key while clicking two (or more) clips.

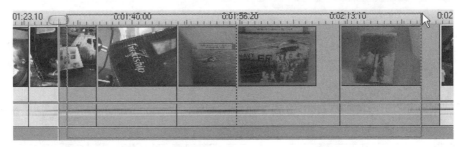

Figure 7.38 You can also drag on the Timeline to include the desired clips.

COMMON TASKS

✔ Tips

■ If you select noncontiguous scenes from the same or different capture file, Studio ignores these selections and combines only the contiguous scenes. To help you in this process, Studio identifies contiguous scenes with a dotted vertical line between them on the Timeline (Figure 7.38).

■ You can't combine two scenes if transitions have been inserted between them, even if they are contiguous. To combine them, delete the transition.

■ You can't combine scenes if you've trimmed any frames from the beginning or end of either scene. To combine, restore each scene to its original length.

■ If you trim a scene that has many clips after it on the Timeline, Studio has to shift all subsequent clips to the left to eliminate any gaps on the Timeline (unless you're in Leave Gap mode—see the earlier sidebar, "Studio's Delete-ist Behaviors"). Depending on the project length, this process can cause perceptible delays. To avoid this, trim soon after you place individual clips on the Timeline rather than waiting until all clips are in place.

■ The Clip Properties tool edits the original audio along with the video.

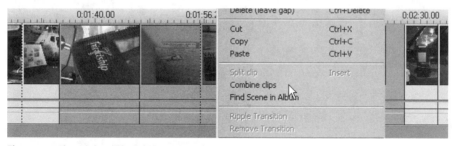

Figure 7.39 Then right-click and choose Combine Clips.

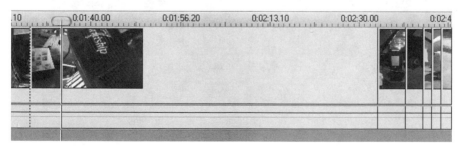

Figure 7.40 Studio combines the clips.

COMMON TASKS

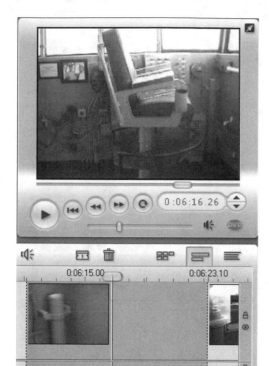

Figure 7.41 A thumbnail should tell you what's in a scene at a glance. Here the thumbnail shows a pole, while the shot is of the captain's chair. I'll find a more descriptive image by clicking the clip and moving the Timeline or Player scrubber to a better frame.

To change the thumbnail image:

1. Use Player controls or the Timeline scrubber to move the edit line to the image you want to use as the thumbnail (**Figure 7.41**).

continues on next page

2. Right-click the selected clip and choose Set Thumbnail (**Figure 7.42**).

Studio sets the new thumbnail image (**Figure 7.43**).

✔ Tips

■ Setting a new thumbnail in the Movie window doesn't reset the thumbnail in the Album. It also doesn't set it as the thumbnail for use when making your DVD.

■ To reset the thumbnail to the original location, Undo doesn't work, even though it appears as an option in the usual spot, under Edit. You'll need to move the scrubber to the original location and repeat Step 2.

Figure 7.42 Then right-click the clip and choose Set Thumbnail.

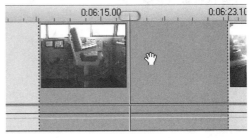

Figure 7.43 The new thumbnail. No problem telling what's in this video now.

Figure 7.44 If you ever need to find the clip you're editing back in the Album, right-click the clip and choose Find Scene in Album.

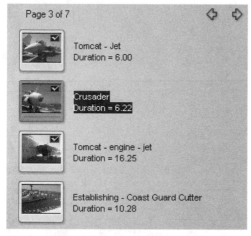

Figure 7.45 Studio locates the scene, even if it's in a different video clip.

To find a scene in the Album while in the Movie window:

1. Select the scene you want to locate.

2. Right-click and choose Find Scene in Album (**Figure 7.44**).

   Studio opens the Album to the page containing the scene and highlights the scene and scene comments (**Figure 7.45**). If another video file is loaded, Studio loads the necessary video clip to locate the scene.

Trimming with the Clip Properties Tool

Trimming video is the process of removing unwanted frames from the beginning and end of your captured scenes, often referred to as the *heads* and *tails*. Since this is probably the most common editing activity, Studio's Clip Properties tool (**Figure 7.46**), a mechanism for trimming your clips, is accessible in all three Movie window views. See **Table 7.1** for a list of the controls that the Clip Properties tool provides.

You can also trim your videos directly on the Timeline (see "Trimming a Clip on the Timeline," later in this chapter), although generally you have greater precision with the Clip Properties tool.

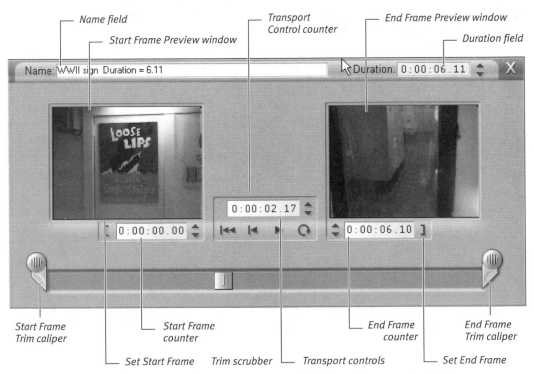

Name field — Transport Control counter — End Frame Preview window

Start Frame Preview window — Duration field

Start Frame Trim caliper — Start Frame counter — End Frame counter — End Frame Trim caliper

Set Start Frame — Trim scrubber — Transport controls — Set End Frame

Figure 7.46 The Clip Properties tool is great for precision trimming of video, still image, and audio files.

Table 7.1

Controls in the Clip Properties Tool	
CLIP PROPERTIES	TOOL CONTROLS
Name field	Contains the scene name specified in the Album.
Duration field	Displays the video duration with new start and end frames.
Start Frame Preview window	Displays the currently selected start frame.
End Frame Preview window	Displays the currently selected end frame.
Transport controls	Like the Trim scrubber, can be used to move loaded video to any desired frame, or can play back the trimmed clip.
Transport Control counter	Displays the current edit point in the video.
Set Start Frame	Sets the start frame to the current edit point.
Start Frame counter	Displays the current start frame location in standard hours:minutes:seconds.frame format. You can select the desired start frame by entering the time code directly or by adjusting the start frame position using the jog controls at the right.
Set End Frame	Sets the end frame to the current edit point.
End Frame counter	Displays the current end frame location in standard hours:minutes:seconds.frame format. You can select the desired end frame by entering the time code directly or by adjusting the end frame position using the jog controls at the right.
Start Frame Trim caliper	Shows the location of the currently selected start frame; can be dragged to the desired location.
Trim scrubber	Reflects the edit point of the currently loaded video. You can use the scrubber to drag video to any desired frame to set the frame as the start or end frame using the appropriate icon or keyboard command. As you scrub through the video, frames appear in the Player window to the right of the Clip Properties tool, not in the Start or End Frame Preview window. These displays change only as you move the Start and End Frame Trim calipers or the clocks beneath them.
End Frame Trim caliper	Shows the location of the currently selected end frame; can be dragged to the desired location.

Planning Your Trimming Activities

Before trimming your clips, consider whether you intend to fade into the first scene, fade out of the final scene, and/or use transitions between the scenes. If you use any of these effects, you need to account for them in your trimming.

Briefly, transitions are animated effects inserted between video scenes either to smooth or emphasize the passage from one clip to the next (for details, see Chapter 8). The most commonly used transition is a cut, which is actually the absence of a transition: the video simply jumps from the last frame of the first clip to the first frame of the second clip. Other frequently used transitions are dissolves, wipes, and fades, which you implement using frames that overlap between two clips.

If you were trimming two clips to be joined by a cut, the end frame for your first video clip would be the last frame you want to appear in the production. Similarly, the start frame for the second video clip would be the initial frame you want visible.

continues on next page

TRIMMING WITH THE CLIP PROPERTIES TOOL

Planning Your Trimming Activities *(continued)*

For example, one fun scene for me that I shot during the Fiddler's Convention here in Galax shows my daughters looking at some dodo-bird puppets (**Figure 7.47**). The visual is key because of the comment my eldest daughter made at the time: "Daddy, can we take these due-due birds home?" This brought a lot of chuckles from those around us.

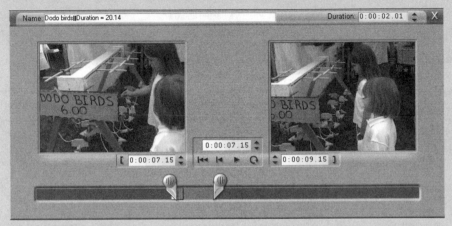

Figure 7.47 Two seconds can make a huge difference. If I cut into this clip at 7 seconds, 15 frames in, viewers see DODO BIRDS and get the joke. If I transition in using a 2-second transition, the first complete frame viewers see is O BIRDS, and the context of the joke is lost.

Anyway, if I cut from the previous scene into this scene, the frame shown on the left of Figure 7.47, which is located at 7 seconds and 15 frames into the scene, will be the first one shown, so the viewer will understand the visual context of the remark. In contrast, if I transition from the previous scene using Studio's default 2-second transition, the first completely visible frame will be 2 seconds later, shown on the right of Figure 7.47, located at 9 seconds, 15 frames into the clip. As you can see, "DODO BIRDS" is no longer visible (extinct, so to speak), and though the audio is still there, the visual context is lost.

What this boils down to is that you need to leave sufficient frames at the front of the scene so that the target frame becomes the first visible frame after the transition. If you're using 2-second transitions or fades, this means 2 seconds before the target start frame.

Of course, the same approach applies at the end of the scene if you plan to fade out or transition into another scene. Specifically, if you're using a 2-second transition or fade, leave 2 seconds of video after the last frame to be completely visible before the transition or fade.

A similar approach is a good rule to use when shooting and capturing your video in general. Always start shooting 5 to 10 seconds before you think you actually want to start and let the camera roll for a similar duration after the end of the shot. When capturing, always start the capture a few seconds before the target first frame and continue a few seconds after the target last frame to provide the extra footage needed during editing.

TRIMMING WITH THE CLIP PROPERTIES TOOL

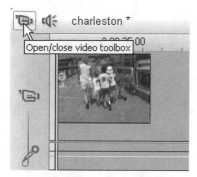

Figure 7.48 Click the Camcorder icon to open the Clip Properties tool for video or still images.

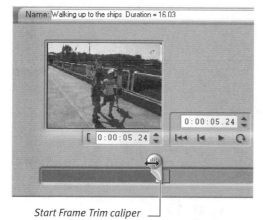

Start Frame Trim caliper

Figure 7.49 The fastest way to set the start frame is with the Start Frame Trim caliper.

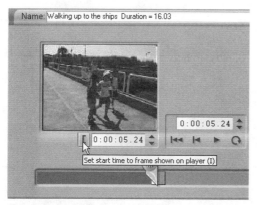

Figure 7.50 Or you can use the Transport controls to find the perfect frame and click the Set Start Frame icon.

To open the Clip Properties tool:

◆ Do *one of the following*:

   ▲ Double-click the video you want to trim.

   ▲ Select a clip and click the Camcorder icon at the top left of the Movie window (**Figure 7.48**).

Studio opens the Video toolbox, which contains the Clip Properties tool. If the toolbox doesn't open to the Clip Properties tool, click the Scissors icon at the upper left of the screen to open it.

If you haven't yet trimmed the clips, the tool opens with the start frame time set to 0:00:00.00 and the end frame time set to the final frame of the clip. If you have trimmed the clip, the values will be those set in the previous session.

To set a new start frame:

◆ Do *one of the following*:

   ▲ Click the Start Frame Trim caliper and drag it to the desired start frame (**Figure 7.49**) or enter the desired start frame in the Start Frame counter either manually or via the jog controls.

   ▲ Studio immediately sets the new start frame, shifting to the left all videos placed after the edited clip to close any gaps on the Timeline.

   ▲ Move the Trim scrubber to the desired start frame by manually dragging the Trim scrubber to the desired start frame or by using the transport controls located in the center of the Clip Properties tool to play or advance the video until it reaches the frame you want. Then set the new start frame by clicking the Set Start Frame icon to the left of the Start Frame counter (**Figure 7.50**) or pressing the I (for in) key.

To set a new end frame:

◆ Do *one of the following*:

▲ Drag the End Frame Trim caliper to the desired end frame (**Figure 7.51**), enter the desired end frame in the End Frame counter either manually or via the jog controls, or enter a new duration in the duration field either manually or by using the jog controls.

▲ Studio sets the new end frame, shifting to the left all videos placed after the edited clip to close any gaps on the Timeline.

▲ Move the Trim scrubber to the desired end frame by dragging it or using the Transport controls located in the center of the Clip Properties tool. Then set the new end frame time by clicking the Set End Frame icon to the right of the End Frame counter or pressing the O (for out) key.

✔ Tips

■ Trimming doesn't affect the actual captured video file in any way. You're not really deleting any frames; you're just telling Studio to use a different start frame and end frame when incorporating the scene into your production. For this reason, you can easily reverse your trims by clicking the Undo icon or using the steps in the preceding tasks to locate new start and end frames.

■ Once you're in the Clip Properties tool, you can select additional clips to trim by clicking them or moving the Timeline scrubber to another clip.

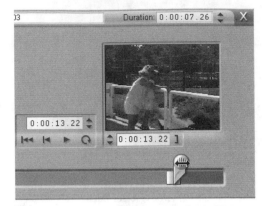

Figure 7.51 To set the end frame, drag the End Frame Trim caliper to the desired shot.

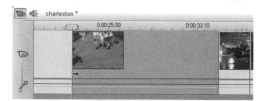

Figure 7.52 Trimming on the Timeline is much faster than trimming using the Clip Properties tool, but it is a touch more difficult to precisely select the desired start and end frames.

Figure 7.53 The arrow becomes bidirectional when you can edit in both directions.

Trimming a Clip on the Timeline

The Clip Properties tool lets you make trims with great precision. However, trimming on the Timeline is generally much quicker and provides much more interactivity with other project elements (audio, video, and so on). Most producers use both tools extensively when crafting their videos.

Trimming on the Timeline is generally easier when you're zoomed into the project and the Timescale covers a relatively short duration, since grabbing and moving the edge shifts only a few frames at a time. When long stretches of video are showing on the Timeline, grabbing and moving the edge may shift a few seconds at a time, making precise adjustments much more difficult to make. If you're going to trim on the Timeline, be sure to adjust the Timescale to a comfortable view (see "Customizing Your Timeline View," earlier in this chapter).

To trim a single video on the Timeline:

1. Select the clip you want to trim by placing the pointer on the right edge of the clip.

   The pointer becomes an arrow pointing right (**Figure 7.52**), or a bidirectional arrow if you previously trimmed the clip (**Figure 7.53**).

2. While holding down the mouse button and watching the video frames displayed in the Player, drag the arrow to the desired end frame.

3. Release the mouse button to set the trim.

   Studio sets the end frame to the new location.

   As soon as you shift a single frame to the left, the single arrow becomes bidirectional, signifying that you can now drag the edge both ways.

Trimming Multiple Clips on the Timeline

Studio offers two approaches to trimming when two scenes are adjacent on the Timeline: the ripple edit and the rolling edit.

Performing a ripple edit is very much like trimming a single clip on the Timeline—only that clip's duration is changed. However, the effect of the trimming *ripples* through the remainder of the project to compensate for the change in the trimmed clip. For example, if you trim 2 seconds from a clip, you shorten the entire project by 2 seconds.

In contrast, in a rolling edit you trim two contiguous scenes simultaneously. As a result, the duration changes to both clips off-set each other, so the overall project duration doesn't change.

Studio handles ripple editing—the program's default mode—very well, rippling not only the Video track but all other associated tracks. This ensures that titles, overlays, and sound effects remain synchronized with the underlying video.

Sometimes, however, you don't want the project duration to change each time you trim a video. For example, if you create a narration or Music track closely synchronized to a video, a series of ripple edits would likely destroy synchronization. Or if you committed to delivering exactly 2 minutes of video, ripple edits would make this difficult. For this reason, Studio supports both ripple and rolling edits. The following tasks show you how to perform each type.

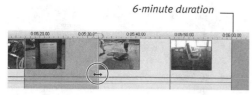

6-minute duration

Figure 7.54 You can also trim clips within the production by dragging the edge of the clip. Note the 6-minute duration.

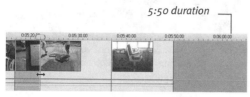

5:50 duration

Figure 7.55 The ripple trim affects all clips behind it on the Timeline, reducing duration from 6 minutes to 5:50.

To perform a ripple edit on the Timeline:

1. Select the clip you want to trim and place the pointer over the right edge of the clip.

   The pointer becomes an arrow pointing left or, in this case, a bidirectional arrow because the clip was previously trimmed (**Figure 7.54**). The project duration is approximately 32 minutes.

2. Holding down the mouse button and watching the video frames displayed in the Player, drag the arrow to the left to shorten the clip (**Figure 7.55**) or to the right to lengthen the clip.

3. Release the mouse button.

   Studio shortens the clip. The project duration is now approximately 31 minutes, as Studio shifted all clips to the left.

TRIMMING MULTIPLE CLIPS ON THE TIMELINE

To perform a rolling edit on the Timeline:

1. Pressing either the Ctrl or Shift key, select two contiguous clips.

2. Position the pointer over the connection point between the two clips.

   The pointer becomes a bidirectional arrow with a vertical line in the middle (**Figure 7.56**).

3. Drag the pointer to the desired location.

4. Release the mouse button.

   Studio shortens the first clip and extends the second clip backward to fill the gap. The overall project duration remains at approximately 6 minutes.

✔ Tips

■ Rolling edits are limited to the start and end of the original scene. When Studio reaches this limit, it displays a unidirectional arrow (**Figure 7.57**).

■ When performing a rolling edit, Studio displays the start frame of the second video in the Player. Ideally, you would also see the final frame of the first video, but there's no way to display both simultaneously.

■ Studio can't perform a rolling edit when there's a transition between the two target clips. To perform a rolling edit, delete the transition, perform the edit, and then reinsert the transition.

Figure 7.56 Avoid messing up synchronization by using the rolling edit tool, which trims without affecting the overall video duration.

Figure 7.57 As with all video trims, your edit can't go beyond the starting or ending point of the original video.

TRIMMING MULTIPLE CLIPS ON THE TIMELINE

Advanced Timeline Editing

Okay, you've worked through Timeline 101; now it's time for the advanced course. As previously mentioned, in its default state, Studio maintains synchronization of the video file and the original audio file captured with the video, and as a default, uses global ripple edits to maintain the relative position of assets on the main Video and Audio tracks on the Timeline. This setup works well in most common editing situations, but there are times when you will want to undo both defaults. Fortunately, through the use of *locked tracks,* Studio allows just that.

When a track is locked, all assets on the track are locked, and edits that would normally affect these assets have no effect on them. Lock the Video track, for example, and you can delete the Audio track and keep the Video track. Similarly, if you lock the Title track, you can add, trim, or delete video clips, and the titles will stay in place.

Locked tracks enable some interesting edits that can add a professional touch to any production. Let's take a brief look at one of these, the insert edit, before moving on to the nuts and bolts of locking tracks and performing advanced edits.

The insert edit

An insert edit is a technique that lets you insert just the video portion of one clip into another larger clip, while using the background audio from the larger clip. It's a useful technique in a variety of circumstances. You might shoot an entire song, for instance, so that you can create a music video composed of the original video shot with the song, plus video scenes pasted in from earlier or later shots.

A good example of such a project is a music video I pieced together from footage from the aforementioned Fiddler's Convention, which I touched on in "Applying Basic Shot Composition" in Chapter 1. In this sequence, I introduce viewers to the entire spectacle of the event—from the acres of trailers and tents to the capacious grandstands with thousands of attendees watching, listening, and dancing—using the complete audio from one of the first songs I shot as the background music and video bits I shot later cut and pasted into the composite clip.

Another useful application of the insert edit is to seamlessly shorten the duration of some aspect of an event, such as the opening and closing processionals at a wedding, graduation, or other ceremony. If you use the audio you captured at a wedding ceremony during the closing processional, for example, and then trim out segments when not much is going on or when no one is on camera, you can shorten the sequence dramatically, yet still retain the highlights. And because the audio plays continuously, no one will even notice.

Figure 7.58 Here's the clip containing the Music track I'm going to use for this music video. We'll be cutting out segments of video and replacing them with other scenes shot after this video.

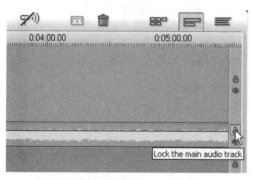

Figure 7.59 Click here to lock the Audio track.

To lock the Audio track:

1. Drag the clip containing the background audio onto the Timeline (**Figure 7.58**).

2. At the far right of the Timeline, click the Lock the Main Audio Track button (**Figure 7.59**).

   Studio turns the lock red and dims the Audio track (**Figure 7.60**). If you attempt to select this audio track thereafter, Studio posts the error message: "Can not select clip when track is locked" (Figure 7.60).

   At this point, you can freely cut the video above the locked Audio track, and Studio won't snap the remaining video together to fill the gaps. You can paste in other video scenes, and Studio will ignore the audio associated with the pasted clip.

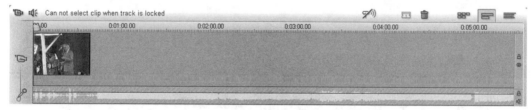

Figure 7.60 The locked Audio track is gray, and the lock at the far right shines a bit red.

THE INSERT EDIT

203

To insert video scenes into original video and audio:

1. Move the edit line to the target insertion point for the second video clip and split the clip by doing *one of the following:*

   ▲ Click the Razorblade icon at the top of the Movie window (Figure 7.34).

   ▲ Right-click the selected clip and choose Split Clip (Figure 7.35).

   ▲ Press the Insert key.

   Studio splits the clip into two parts (**Figure 7.61**).

2. Move the edit line to the approximate point at which the inserted clip should end and then create another split (**Figure 7.62**).

3. Hover the pointer over the segment to be replaced and delete it by doing *one of the following:*

   ▲ Press the Delete key.

   ▲ From the Studio menu, choose Edit > Delete.

   ▲ Right-click and choose Delete.

   Studio deletes the segment (**Figure 7.63**).

First split

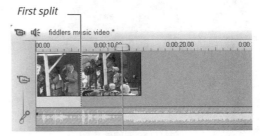

Figure 7.61 Split the clip at the first frame where you want to paste in another video scene.

Figure 7.62 Next, move the edit line to the desired end point, and split the clip again to create a section you can delete.

Gap

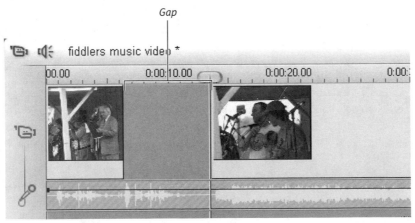

Figure 7.63 Hover the pointer over the unwanted segment and delete it. You should see a gap like the one shown here.

THE INSERT EDIT

4. Drag the segment to be inserted from the Album into the gap created by the deleted segment.

Studio inserts the segment (**Figure 7.64**).

If the new segment is too large for the slot you created, Studio fits it into the slot. You can then use the trimming tools discussed earlier to resize all elements of the composite clip.

If the new segment is too small for the slot you created, manually close the gap by dragging the original clip segments to the edge of the inserted scene.

5. Repeat Steps 1 through 5 until you've inserted all the clips you want in your video. When you've finished, your Timeline will look like **Figure 7.65**.

continues on next page

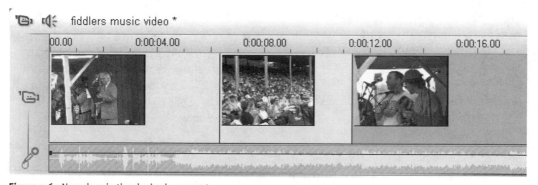

Figure 7.64 Now drag in the desired segment.

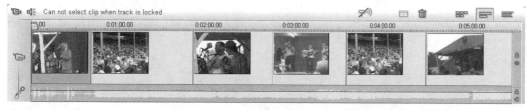

Figure 7.65 Here's the first minute of my music video, containing 11 different scenes. This amounts to a scene change about every 5 seconds, which definitely helps keep the viewer's interest.

THE INSERT EDIT

✔ Tips

- I use this insert technique to hide bad camera moments, such as when I'm moving the camera from subject to subject, or zooming in and out to frame a shot. It's generally easiest for me to go through the clip, excise all the bad camera spots, and then fill these gaps with other video scenes.

- If you plan on doing this type of cutting and pasting, it really pays to annotate your clips when you bring them into the Edit window (see "Working with Scene Comments" in Chapter 6). Annotating allows you to work much more efficiently by allowing you to quickly identify the scenes you want to insert.

- To make your music video look good, all the parts of the original video clip you retain must remain synchronized with the background audio. This isn't really relevant with the dancing and clapping scenes you insert, since there's almost no way to tell if they're synchronized or not, at least with foot-stomping country music or most other fast dancing. However, if the singer's lips are moving and you can't hear any singing, you've got a problem.

- Note that once you lock the Audio track, Studio will let you move the Video track above it, and if you do, you may lose synchronization. So be mindful of this when you're cutting, pasting, and trimming, and remember never to move the original video.

- To insert audio in the Audio track, you follow the same procedure, except that you need to lock the Video track first and then cut the Audio track. Of course, you can also drag the intended audio insertion to either of the other tracks and then mute the Audio track (see "Using the Volume Tool" in Chapter 11).

- You can easily insert a still image into a video clip: just drag the image to the Title track and resize it (see "To change the duration of a still image on the Timeline," later in this chapter).

- You can lock any track or combination of tracks except the Menu track, which appears when you're creating DVD menus.

- Get in the habit of unlocking tracks immediately after performing any edits that require locked tracks. Otherwise, when you try to select a clip track later, nothing will happen, and you'll see the error message shown in Figure 7.60.

To shorten a wedding processional:

1. Load the video clip that contains the processional.

2. Lock the Audio track (see "To lock the Audio track" earlier in this section).

   The clip should appear as in **Figure 7.66**.

3. Move the edit line to the end of the first sequence and split the clip by doing *one of the following*:

   ▲ Click the Razorblade icon at the top of the Movie window (Figure 7.34).

   ▲ Right-click the selected clip and choose Split Clip (Figure 7.35).

   ▲ Press the Insert key.

   Studio splits the clip into two parts (**Figure 7.67**). As you can see in the Player at the upper right, the bride and groom have walked past the camera. Now it's time to find a starting point for the next group to walk back up the aisle.

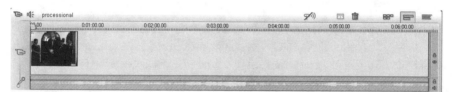

Figure 7.66 Here's the scene containing the entire processional I want to transparently condense. I've already locked the Audio track.

Figure 7.67 The first usher has already walked by me, so most likely it's time to delete some video. Start by splitting the clip just after the usher leaves the camera view.

4. Drag the starting point of the second clip to the first frame of the next group to come down the aisle (**Figure 7.68**).

5. Drag the entire second clip to the left until it abuts the initial clip (**Figure 7.69**).

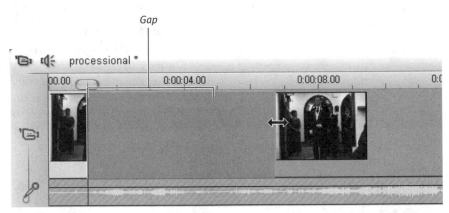

Figure 7.68 No use watching the ushers just standing there waiting. Delete this footage by clicking the second clip and dragging the clip to the start of the next usher to walk back up the aisle. This creates a gap in the video that you'll fill in a moment.

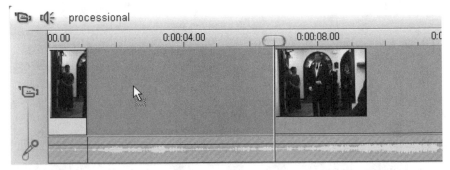

Figure 7.69 Here I'm dragging the second clip to abut against the first. This shaves only about 6 seconds, but multiply that times the number of bridesmaids, ushers, and family members—plus time spent waiting for the blushing bride—and it can add up to significant time savings.

6. Repeat Steps 3, 4, and 5 for each group in the processional. At the end of the exercise, your Timeline should look like **Figure 7.70**.

This example shaved almost a minute off the sequence, and the trick is totally transparent to the viewer.

7. Unlock the Audio clip.

8. Move the edit line to the end of the video and split the audio clip using one of the techniques discussed in Step 3.

Studio splits the audio clip (**Figure 7.71**).

9. Select and delete the second (unneeded) audio clip.

For details, see the "To delete assets" tasks earlier in this chapter.

✔ Tips

■ When performing these types of edits, consider inserting a short (like 0.5 seconds) dissolve transition between the clips to smooth the visual flow. See "Using Transitions" in Chapter 8 for more details.

■ With most processional videos, you'll probably have to drag the audio backward or forward so that "Here Comes the Bride" sounds as she starts walking down the aisle.

Figure 7.70 Repeat as necessary. Here I shaved two minutes off the processional time and no one in the audience will notice a thing because the audio is continuous.

Split audio clip here

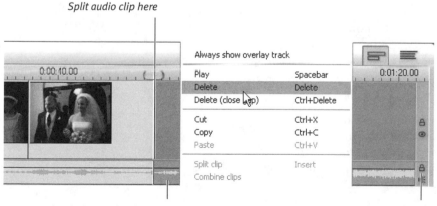

Delete balance of audio track   *Unlock track here*

Figure 7.71 Now unlock the audio clip, split it at the end of the processional, and delete the excess.

THE INSERT EDIT

Producing split edits

Split edits are transitions between two clips in which the audio and video start playing at different times. There are two basic types of split edits: L-cuts and J-cuts.

In an *L-cut*, the audio from the first video continues while the second video starts playing. One very common use is in interviews. Imagine Larry King asking O.J., "Did you do it?" Clearly, at that point, you want to see the reaction on O.J.'s face, not Larry King's. I've used an L-cut in an interview with Dr. Don T. Sumie. As you'll see, while I'm asking Dr. Sumie a question, the video will cut to a shot of Dr. Sumie's face.

In a *J-cut*, the audio from the second video precedes the appearance of the actual frames. In the J-cut task that follows, I've maintained the camera on Dr. Sumie while switching the audio to that from the next clip, the sounds of him examining a patient. This inserts an audio transition to the next event, presaging the action to come. Though all this may sound complicated, Studio makes short work of both kinds of edits.

To create an L-cut:

1. Load two clips onto the Timeline and select the first clip.

2. Hover the pointer over the connection point between the two clips.

   The pointer becomes an arrow pointing left, or a bidirectional arrow if you previously trimmed the clip.

3. Holding down the mouse button and watching the video frames displayed in the Player, drag the arrow to the left until you reach the last frame to be displayed (**Figure 7.72**).

Figure 7.72 To create an L-cut, trim the first video back to the last video frame that you want to appear.

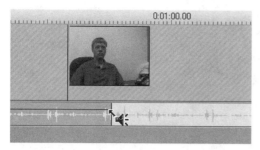

Figure 7.73 When dragging the audio track, select anywhere but the middle line, which is the Volume control that produces a Speaker icon.

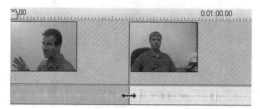

Figure 7.74 To drag the audio to the right, select the audio at the connection line, converting the pointer to a bidirectional arrow.

The L

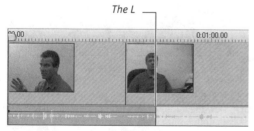

Figure 7.75 Then just drag the audio to the right, creating the L pattern.

4. Hover the pointer over the Camcorder icon on the Video track and then click the Camcorder button to lock the Video track.

5. Use the pointer to select the Audio track from the first clip.

6. Hover the pointer over the connection line between the two clips, being careful to avoid the blue horizontal line (which is the Volume control) in the middle of the audio clips.

Hovering the pointer over the line converts the pointer to a Speaker icon, which will change the volume—something you don't want to do here (**Figure 7.73**).

The pointer becomes a bidirectional arrow (**Figure 7.74**).

7. Drag the audio file to the right, to the desired starting point from the second clip.

Studio extends the audio from the first clip under the video to the second clip, forming the namesake *L* appearance (**Figure 7.75**).

✔ Tips

- If, during Step 6, you accidentally click the blue horizontal Volume control, you may inadvertently adjust the track volume. If so, you'll see a small blue dot in the middle of the line. You can undo this volume change by choosing Undo from the Edit menu, by clicking the Undo button at the upper right, or by pressing Ctrl+Z.

- If you've already performed some additional edits that you don't want to undo, you can click the blue dot (the pointer becomes a Speaker icon when placed over the Audio track) and drag it straight down, thus deleting the dot.

To create a J-cut:

1. Load two clips on the Timeline.

2. Click the second scene. While watching the Player window, drag the second clip to the first target frame to be displayed after the cut (**Figure 7.76**).

   In Figure 7.76, the first target frame to be displayed in the second clip is the shot where Dr. Sumie is listening to my daughter's heartbeat. Once the tracks are locked, I'll drag the audio I just trimmed under the first clip, a process similar to the one described in Steps 6 and 7 of the previous task.

3. Click the lock at the far right of the Video track to lock the track (**Figure 7.77**).

4. Hover the pointer over the connection line between the two clips.

   The pointer becomes a bidirectional arrow.

5. Drag the audio file to the left, to the desired starting point within the first clip.

   Studio extends the audio from the second clip to the desired position under the video track of the first clip, forming the namesake *J* appearance (**Figure 7.78**).

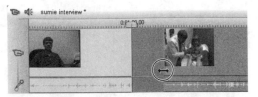

Figure 7.76 Drag the second clip to the first frame to be displayed after the video cut.

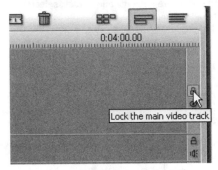

Figure 7.77 Lock the main Video track.

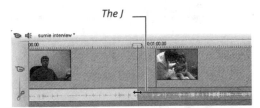

Figure 7.78 Drag the audio from the second clip to the first. Now the audience will hear the sounds of the examination before it appears on screen.

Working with Still Images

Studio handles still images in two completely different ways, depending on where you drop the file. Drop an image in the Title track, and it can serve as the background for a DVD menu or contain a logo or watermark to blend into the Video track. Drop an image into the Video track, and it can serve as the foreground video, usually in the form of a slide show. We deal with the latter scenario in this section.

When you drop images into the Video track, Studio treats the image files almost the same way as it treats video files, except that there are no duration limits or associated audio files. Accordingly, all the techniques described in the previous sections for getting videos into the Movie window, moving them around, trimming them on the Timeline, and splitting and deleting them apply equally to still images. There are just a couple of differences to note.

First, you set the default duration for all images inserted into your projects in the Pinnacle Studio Setup Options box, using a process described in "Setting Default Durations," in Chapter 2. This section also explains two ways to modify the default duration and how to create a slide show.

Studio 10 also has two mechanisms for adding motion to still images in what's generally referred to as the Ken Burns effect (a term that surfaced after filmmaker Ken Burns created his *The Civil War* and *Baseball* documentaries entirely out of still images). This effect is detailed in "Inserting Pan and Zoom Effects," in Chapter 5.

To change the duration of a still image on the Timeline:

1. Do *one of the following:*

   ▲ Trim the still image on the Timeline using the same techniques as for trimming video files, described in "Trimming a Clip on the Timeline," earlier in this chapter.

   ▲ Launch the Clip Properties tool by selecting the still image with the pointer and clicking the Camcorder icon at the top left of the Movie window (Figure 7.48).

   Studio opens the Video toolbox.

   If you don't see the Clip Properties tool, click the Scissors icon at the upper left of the screen to open it.

2. At the upper right of the tool, adjust the duration by typing a new value in the Duration field or by using the jog controls at the right (**Figure 7.79**).

Duration field

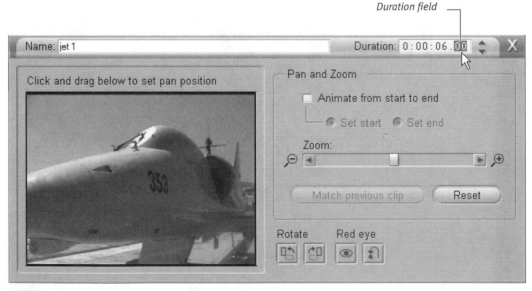

Figure 7.79 You can change the duration of a still-image file. For more detail on Pan and Zoom controls see "Inserting Pan and Zoom Effects," in Chapter 5.

To create a slide show:

1. Start with the Movie window in Storyboard view and the Album window open to the Still Images tab.

2. Do *one of the following*:

   ▲ Drag images one by one onto the Storyboard.

   ▲ To select all images on the Still Images tab and drag them to the Storyboard, choose Edit > Select All from the Studio menu or press Ctrl+A.

   ▲ To select multiple sequential images, click the first image, hold down the Shift key, and click the final image.

   ▲ To load multiple nonsequential images, click the first image, hold down the Ctrl key, and click additional target images (**Figure 7.80**).

   ▲ To select groups of images, click any gray area in the Album and drag over the target images.

Once your images are on the Storyboard, add, delete, and arrange them as desired via drag and drop (see "To arrange assets in Storyboard view," earlier in this chapter).

✔ Tip

■ For the ultimate in professional-looking slide shows, learn how to add motion to your images in "Inserting Pan and Zoom to Images" in Chapter 5 and how to insert a ripple transition between images in "Ripple Transitions for Slide Shows" in Chapter 8.

Figure 7.80 Hold down the Ctrl key to select still images that are out of order. Here I'm selecting all the jets on the first page of the still image album.

Working with Audio Files

Studio includes many different methods to capture and integrate audio into your production. Whether you're ripping music from a CD, adding a narration track, or creating background music from SmartSound, Studio places the results directly on the Timeline for you—no muss, no fuss. (These activities are covered in Chapter 11.) On the other hand, if you're using audio files you previously produced, you'll have to import them into the Album (see "Working with the Sound Effects Tab" in Chapter 6) and then get them to the Timeline.

Studio treats audio files almost identically to video files and still images, with exceptions noted in the sidebar, "Tracking the Audio Tracks," later in this chapter. Otherwise, all of the techniques described earlier for getting videos into the Movie window, moving them around, trimming them on the Timeline, and splitting and deleting them apply to audio files.

This section takes a quick look at the Audio Clip Properties tool, demonstrates how to load only the Audio track from a captured video file into a project, and describes where to drag your audio files (see the sidebar "Tracking the Audio Tracks," later in this chapter).

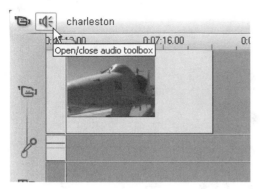

Open/close audio toolbox

Figure 7.81 Click here to open the Audio Clip Properties tool.

To change the duration of an audio file on the Timeline:

1. Do *one of the following:*

   ▲ Trim the audio file on the Timeline using the same techniques as for trimming video files, described in "Trimming a Clip on the Timeline," earlier in this chapter.

   ▲ Launch the Clip Properties tool by selecting the audio file and clicking the Speaker icon at the top left of the Movie window (**Figure 7.81**), or by double-clicking the audio clip.

   Studio opens the Audio toolbox.

   If you don't see the Audio Clip Properties tool, click the Scissors icon at the upper left of the screen to open it.

2. To adjust the start and end points of the audio file, use the controls described in "Trimming with the Clip Properties Tool," earlier in this chapter (Figure 7.46).

   Note in particular that most CDs have several seconds of silence at the end of each track. To avoid this gap in your production, trim this space as shown in **Figure 7.82**.

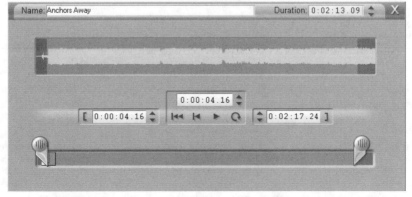

Figure 7.82 How does "Anchors Away" sound as background music for a slide show on carrier-based airplanes?

To add only the audio from a video file:

◆ From the Video Scenes tab in the Album window, drag a video file to either the Sound Effect track or the Music track.

Studio inserts only the audio from the video file. See Chapter 11 for more on audio.

✔ Tip

■ Studio lets you drag an audio file into a clip in the Storyboard and Text views. However, since there is no indicator of duration, results are unpredictable, so you should work with audio in Timeline view.

Tracking the Audio Tracks

Here are some rules of the road for Studio's audio tracks. (See Chapter 11 for much more on audio.)

◆ To add an audio file to your production, drag it to either the Sound Effect track or the Music track.

◆ Be careful, however, if you intend to use Studio's narration recording, CD-ripping, or SmartSound Music track features, because they require that a specific track be open for the files they produce. For narration recording, the Sound Effect track must be open; for CD-ripping and SmartSound, the Music track must be open. So if you drag an audio file onto the Sound Effect track, for example, you won't be able to record a narration track for that segment.

◆ To add the audio track from a captured video file to your production—without the video—drag it to either the Sound Effect track or the Music track.

◆ Studio prevents you from adding an audio file to either Audio track if the audio is present. However, if you delete the audio clip by locking the Video track and deleting the audio, Studio lets you add audio to either Audio track as well.

◆ Studio lets you place audio files anywhere in a production, even if it creates a gap in the playback audio. Be careful to avoid these unintended gaps when you place audio files.

◆ If you drag one audio file into another, Studio always trims the clip you're dragging. This makes it easy to accidentally truncate a clip by dragging it into another clip. (With video files, dragging doesn't trim a clip at all; you have to activate the trim handles.)

8

USING TRANSITIONS

Transitions are effects placed between video clips to help smooth the movement from one scene to another. We've all seen transitions, even if we don't recognize them by that name. In movies, for example, when the screen fades to black at the end of a dramatic scene and then fades back in from black to the next scene, the filmmaker is using a *fade* transition. When two scenes blend together for a moment before the second scene appears clearly, the filmmaker is using a *dissolve* transition.

On *Monday Night Football,* when the half-time stats swing back, down, and under, revealing Al and John, that's a transition, too. However, in most film and television productions, the most frequent transition is a *cut,* which is actually the absence of a transition, or the instantaneous jump from the last frame of the first clip to the first frame of the second clip.

Studio 10 provides three transition collections: Standard Transitions, Alpha Magic, and Hollywood FX for Studio. This chapter describes each group, discusses when to use them, and then explains how to apply and customize them.

Looking in the Box

You access the three transition groups from the Transitions tab of the Album, opened by clicking the Lightning Bolt icon on the left panel of the Album (**Figure 8.1**). In defining how these transitions work, I'll call the first video Video A, and the second Video B.

Standard Transitions: As you would expect, the Standard Transitions group includes the common transitions used in most video editing. In addition to the dissolves and fades already mentioned, the Standard group includes the following types of transitions:

◆ *Wipes:* Both Videos A and B remain fixed while an effect hides Video A and reveals Video B. Imagine you're pulling down a shade between two videos. With a wipe, both videos would remain static, and the shade simply hides Video A and reveals Video B. On Studio's Transitions tab, any transition with an arrow that appears to be pulling Video B over Video A, with the arrow visible in both videos, is a wipe.

◆ *Slides:* Video B slides in over Video A. With the shade example, Video B would be playing on the shade and slowly appear, bottom first, as you pulled the shade down. As with a wipe, Video A remains static and is simply covered up by Video B. On Studio's Transitions tab, any transition with an arrow that appears to be pushing Video B over Video A, with the arrow contained completely in Video A, is a slide.

◆ *Pushes:* Video B pushes Video A off the screen. If you were pulling down a shade between two videos, Video B would push Video A down, very much like a slide, except that Video A doesn't get covered up; it gets pushed off the screen. On Studio's Transitions tab, any transition with two arrows moving in the same direction is a push.

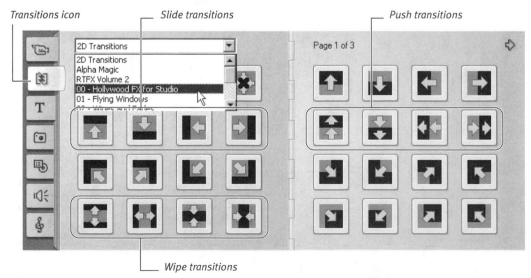

Figure 8.1 You access the Transitions tab by clicking the Lightning Bolt icon. Note how Studio differentiates Push, Slide, and Wipe transitions in the Standard Transitions group.

Figure 8.2 The word PRO is a watermark and will show up in your transition unless you upgrade to Hollywood FX Pro.

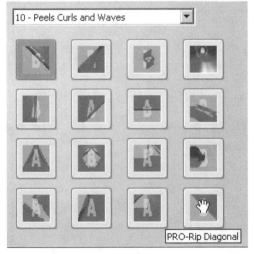

Figure 8.3 Hover your mouse over the Hollywood FX transitions and you can see which version of Hollywood FX you need to use the transition sans watermark. You'd need the Pro version for this transition.

The Standard Transitions collection includes many other transitions not characterized in these three major groups, so you should definitely explore what else is there. Just click the white arrows at the top of each page to navigate to the next page.

Alpha Magic: Technically, Alpha Magic transitions are wipes that use organic forms as masks to create the effect. In plain English, they're generally more artistic than the standard transitions and often more whimsical.

Hollywood FX: All transitions in the Hollywood FX for Studio collection are yours to use as you wish. However, most transitions in the Hollywood FX collections below this are watermarked, so you can use them, but the annoying watermark will appear in your video unless you purchase upgrades to either Hollywood FX Plus or Pro at www.pinnaclesys.com. For example, the PRO shown in **Figure 8.2** is a watermark.

Pinnacle includes the required version of Hollywood FX in the name, so if you hover your mouse over a transition, you can see if it's a BAS transition (included with Studio), a PLS transition (in the FX Plus collection), or a Pro transition (in the FX PRO collection; **Figure 8.3**).

✔ Tip

■ To see how a transition looks, click it and it will play in the Player window.

Understanding Transitions

As you'll see, using and customizing transitions is easy. Using them effectively is also easy, if you keep three simple concepts in mind.

A little goes a long way

Recognize that you don't have to insert a transition between every two scenes on the timeline. Rather, use a transition only when it highlights a change in place or time that you want the viewer to perceive.

For example, if you're shooting your child's birthday party, you may have a bunch of shots in the dining room: kids eating, shouting, and blowing their horns; parents watching and smiling; and Uncle Ernie discreetly grabbing his third piece of chocolate cake. When you edit these clips, you should simply cut from clip to clip—sans transitions— because they all occur at the same place in time. However, the next major scene is opening presents in the living room. When you move from the dining room to the living room, there is a change in place and time, so a transition is appropriate.

Like meets like

All your transitions should match the extent of change in place and time. For example, when you move from the dining room to the living room, the change is pretty minor. Here you might use a dissolve, or a simple motivated transition, discussed later in this chapter. But you shouldn't fade to black and then fade back in to the dining room scene because a fade to black suggests a very significant change in place and time. However, if the entire birthday party sequence, from start to finish, was part of a longer video, you might fade to black at the end of the party and then fade in from black at the next major scene: Thanksgiving or that trip to Disneyland.

Keep it simple or motivate

Transitions should either be motivated or kept very simple. When I say motivated, I mean a transition that relates to the content of the video or one that moves the viewer from one scene to the next with particular aplomb. This final concept is probably the most difficult to accept, especially if you've been eagerly eyeing Studio's capacious quantity of transitions.

Motivated transitions go a long way toward engaging the audience, and they add a lovely professional touch. For example, in past productions, I've used a snowflake transition between songs at a holiday concert, a golf-tee transition between holes at a golf outing, and a bottle-of-bubbly transition between the wedding ceremony and wedding reception.

Had I not had these motivated Hollywood FX transitions, I would have used a simple fade or dissolve instead. That's because random, complicated transitions that don't relate to the content of the videos confuse and possibly irritate the viewer.

This is the primary reason that I'm such a fan of Hollywood FX: because it allows me to add a fun and professional touch to my videos. Pinnacle offers some alluring transitions in the Basic pack, which is freely accessible to Studio 10 users, and in the free Extra pack you get for registering your copy of Studio with Pinnacle. However, as you'd expect, Pinnacle saves the best Hollywood FX transitions for the optional Plus and PRO upgrades. In addition to the extra transitions, the Plus upgrade offers extensive customization options, and the PRO upgrade lets you customize transitions and even build your transitions from scratch.

If you find yourself using lots of transitions, explore the Hollywood FX samples and consider upgrading to either the Plus or Pro versions.

KEEP IT SIMPLE OR MOTIVATE

Using Transitions

The next few pages cover the basics of transitions. Once you've mastered these, you'll be ready to move on to the subsequent sections that illuminate advanced topics: customizing transitions, working with Hollywood FX transitions, and using ripple transitions for slide shows.

To set the default transition duration:

1. Choose Setup > Project Preferences to open the Studio Setup Options screen to the Project Preferences tab (**Figure 8.4**).

2. Change the Transitions default duration value to the desired setting by doing *one of the following*:

   ▲ Use the jog controls (up and down triangles) to the right of the duration.

   ▲ Click the duration to make it editable and directly enter the desired setting.

3. Click OK to close the dialog box.

To identify and preview a transition effect in the Album:

1. If you're at a different panel, click the Lightning Bolt icon in Edit mode to open the Transitions tab in the Album (Figure 8.1).

2. Hover the pointer over the transition to preview it.

   Studio displays the transition name in a Tool Tip (**Figure 8.5**).

3. Click the transition to preview it in the Player.

   In the preview, A represents the first clip, and B represents the second clip. In Figure 8.5 you can see the heart-shaped transition, with Video B opening up into Video A. Use only for weddings and on Valentine's Day, please.

Figure 8.4 Here's where you change the default transition duration in the Project Preferences window.

Figure 8.5 Hover your mouse over a transition, and Studio tells you its name; click it, and Studio plays it in the Player. Note the Video A/Video B nomenclature in the Player.

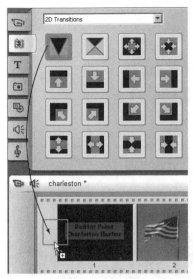

Figure 8.6 To use a transition in a production, just drag it and drop it at the desired spot, aided by Studio's visual cues.

Figure 8.7 There you go, fading into a clip.

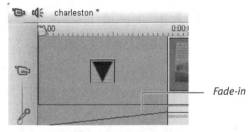

Figure 8.8 Here's the same transition in Timeline view. Note that Studio fades in the audio, too, saving you some work.

To fade into or out of a clip:

1. With at least one clip in the Movie window, drag a fade transition into the Timeline or Storyboard in front of the first clip (to fade in) or behind the last clip (to fade out).

   Studio displays a green box on the Storyboard (**Figure 8.6**) or two vertical green lines on the Timeline whenever you roll over a location where you can apply the effect. You'll also see a small transparent box and plus sign under the pointer.

2. Release the mouse button.

   Studio inserts the fade effect (**Figure 8.7**).

✔ Tips

- You can apply transitions in any Movie window, though the Storyboard and Timeline views are probably most appropriate. **Figure 8.8** shows the fade transition shown in Figure 8.7 in the Timeline view.

- Studio also fades in the audio component when it applies a fade effect. This can be a great convenience, but if you want to do something different with your audio, you can find more detailed information in Chapter 11.

USING TRANSITIONS

To insert a transition between two clips:

1. With at least two clips in the Movie window, drag any transition between any two clips.

   Studio displays a green box on the Storyboard or two vertical green lines on the Timeline whenever you roll over a location where you can apply the effect. Studio also adds a small transparent box and plus sign to the pointer (**Figure 8.9**).

2. Release the mouse button.

   Studio inserts the transition (**Figure 8.10**).

✔ Tips

- Whenever Studio inserts a transition between two clips, it also inserts a cross-fade between the two audio clips, simultaneously reducing the volume on the first clip from 100 percent to 0 percent and boosting the volume on the second clip from 0 percent to 100 percent. These changes are reflected on the Audio track (**Figure 8.11**). This behavior is appropriate, since most transitions help you move smoothly from one scene to another, and the audio treatment should follow that of the video. However, if you want to reverse this effect and customize your audio treatment, see Chapter 11 for instructions.

- The only exception to Studio's audio cross-fade approach occurs during the fade transition, where Studio fades the scene completely to black (or white) before starting to show the second scene. Here, Studio also fades out the old audio completely to zero before boosting audio on the second track (see Figure 8.20). This behavior is appropriate given that fades are generally used to emphasize the ending of one scene and the beginning of another.

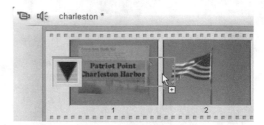

Figure 8.9 When you drag a transition between two clips, a box and a plus sign let you know where you can safely drop the transition.

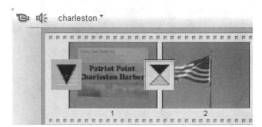

Figure 8.10 The completed dissolve transition.

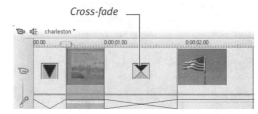

Figure 8.11 The same transition in Timeline view. Note the automatic audio cross-fade.

USING TRANSITIONS

Transition

Figure 8.12 To preview the transition, select it on the Timeline and click Play. Here the helicopter is pushing the jet plane off the screen.

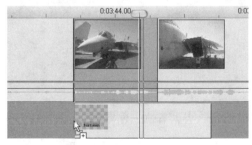

Figure 8.13 Inserting a fade into a title uses the same basic technique as for video clips: drag the transition, drop it, move on to the next edit.

To preview a Standard or Alpha Magic transition:

1. Click the transition to make it active (**Figure 8.12**).

2. To start the preview, click the Play button in the Player (or press the spacebar or L).

✔ Tip

■ Virtually all Standard and Alpha Magic transitions preview in real time, playing both audio and video, so you can immediately determine whether you like the effect. The Hollywood FX transitions are more complicated; many require rendering (see "Working with Background Rendering" later in this chapter).

To fade into or out of a title or other element on the Title track:

1. With at least one title or other element on the Title track, drag a fade transition in front of the target (to fade in) or behind the target (to fade out).

   Studio displays a green box on the Storyboard or two vertical green lines on the Timeline whenever you roll over a location where you can apply the effect. Studio also adds a small transparent box and a plus sign to the pointer (**Figure 8.13**).

2. Release the mouse button.

   Studio inserts the fade effect (**Figure 8.14**).

continues on next page

USING TRANSITIONS

✔ Tips

- You preview a fade-in on the Title track in the same way you preview effects dragged to the Video track.

- You can also apply a transition between titles or other elements on the Title track, as shown in **Figure 8.15**. The process is identical to that for inserting a transition between two clips on the Video track.

To change transitions on the Video or Title track:

1. Drag another transition on top of the existing transition.

   Studio shows the same green box or lines and the cursor with the box and plus sign (**Figure 8.16**).

2. Release the mouse button.

   Studio replaces the previous effect, and you're ready to preview (**Figure 8.17**).

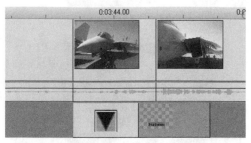

Figure 8.14 The completed fade transition into the title.

Figure 8.15 You can also insert transitions between titles and other images on the Overlay track by following the same basic instructions as for video clips.

Figure 8.16 To use a different transition, simply drag it and drop it over the old transition.

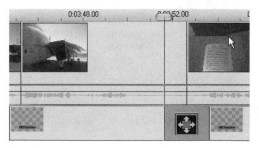

Figure 8.17 The new transition.

USING TRANSITIONS

Transition Timing

Quick question: If you set your default transition time to 2 seconds, how many seconds of video does your transition take? Well, if you guessed 2 or 4, you're right (I'm trying to make this book a positive experience)—but only part of the time (sorry).

The obvious answer is 2, since the transition should take 2 linear, real-time seconds to play. That's true for every transition except fade transitions, where Studio fades out for 2 seconds and then in for 2 seconds. In that case, the total transition time is 4 seconds.

For example, **Figure 8.18** shows two clips, each 6 seconds long, totaling 12 seconds. Then a 2-second dissolve is added between the two clips (**Figure 8.19**). However, if a fade is added, the entire transition takes 4 seconds: 2 seconds to fade out, and 2 to fade in (**Figure 8.20**).

What's also intriguing about Figure 8.19 is that the transition starts at the 4-second point in the first clip, and also that somehow the overall clip is shortened from 12 to 10 seconds (this didn't occur with the fade transition).

continues on next page

Figure 8.18 Two clips, 6 seconds each, 12 seconds total.

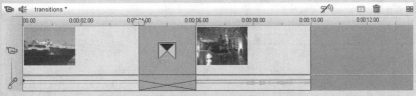

Figure 8.19 Insert a 2-second dissolve, and we're down to 10 seconds. Hey, what happened? See Figure 8.21.

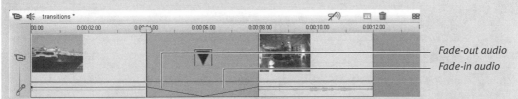

Fade-out audio
Fade-in audio

Figure 8.20 Insert the cross-fade, and the transition takes 4 seconds, though the default duration is 2. Hey, at least the movie is still 12 seconds. Note the complete audio fade-out before the audio fades back in.

Transition Timing *(continued)*

What happened? To show you, I loaded the same clips into an older version of Adobe Premiere, which offers what's called an A/B editing view that shows both the clips on the Timeline and the transition (**Figure 8.21**). (This transition works the same in Premiere as in Studio; it's just presented differently in the Timeline.)

This screen shot reveals that during the 2-second dissolve transition, Studio uses the last 2 seconds of the first clip and the first 2 seconds of the second clip. Since segments from both clips are being used simultaneously, this shortens the video from 12 to 10 seconds.

In contrast, the fade transition—since it doesn't use simultaneous portions of the two clips—allows the clip to stay at 12 seconds (**Figure 8.22**). Obviously, if you used a cut, or no transition between the clips, there would be no overlap at all, and the video would still be 12 seconds long.

Beyond the riddles, what are some practical ways to apply this information?

First, if you plan on using transitions other than cuts, be sure to trim your clips accordingly, leaving the planned durations of your transitions and fades at the beginning and end of each affected clip.

Second, if you're planning on a tight narration or Music track, remember that two 6-second clips don't add up to 12 seconds of video if you have a 2-second dissolve between them. Though it's possible to do the math and compute the duration and precise starting points of each clip, it's generally easier to get the video lined up exactly the way you want it and then produce your audio.

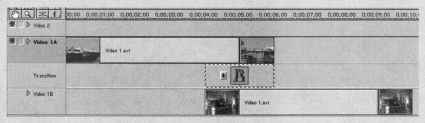

Figure 8.21 A screen shot from Adobe Premiere tells the story. The 2-second dissolve transition overlaps 2 seconds in each video, which is why the video is shorter overall.

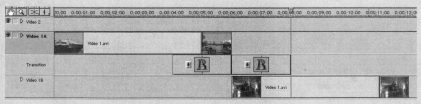

Figure 8.22 The clip isn't shortened with the fade-out and then fade-in, since there is no overlap.

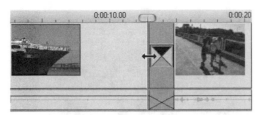

Figure 8.23 The easiest and most visual way to modify transition duration is to use the Timeline, where you can see the key frames in the two affected videos.

Customizing Transitions

Unless you upgrade to Hollywood FX Plus or Pro, Studio allows you to customize only two aspects of a transition: duration and direction.

This section explains how you can change the duration of a transition by dragging the transition to the desired length on the Timeline or by using the Clip Properties tool. It also explains how to reverse the direction of the effect, which can only be done using the Clip Properties tool.

To edit transition duration on the Timeline:

1. Select the target transition and place the pointer over either edge.

   The pointer becomes a bidirectional arrow (**Figure 8.23**).

2. Holding down the mouse button and watching the video frames displayed in the Player, drag the transition to the desired duration.

3. Release the mouse button to set the new duration.

✔ Tip

- If you drag the transition to the right, the Player shows the first frame of the second clip that will appear after the transition finishes. If you drag it to the left, the Player shows the last frame in the first clip that will appear before the transition starts. This is a great way to fine-tune the starting and ending points of your transition.

To edit transition duration in the Clip Properties tool:

1. Open the Transitions Clip Properties tool by doing *one of the following*:

   ▲ Double-click the target transition (or right-click it and select Clip Properties from the menu that appears).

   ▲ Select the target transition and then click the Video Toolbox icon at the top left of the Movie window (**Figure 8.24**).

   The Video toolbox opens to the Clip Properties tool for transitions (**Figure 8.25**).

Figure 8.24 You can also open the Video toolbox and use the Clip Properties tool to modify duration.

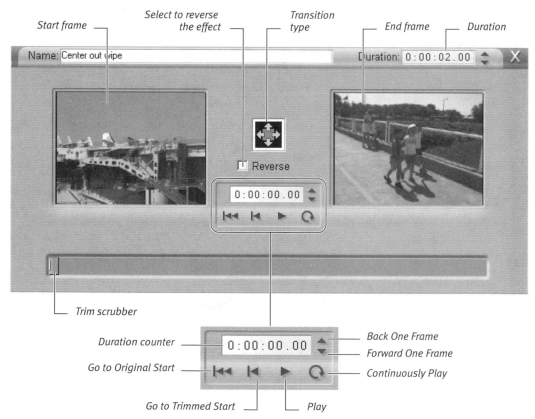

Figure 8.25 Set duration at the upper right, by using the jog controls or by clicking the duration number and typing a new one.

Figure 8.26
Checking the Reverse box reverses the effect you applied. In this case, Studio converts the selected effect, the center-out wipe, to an outside-to-center wipe.

2. At the upper right, change the duration value to the desired setting by doing *one of the following:*

   ▲ Use the jog controls to the right of the duration.

   ▲ Click the duration to make it editable and directly enter the desired setting.

3. Use the transport controls in the middle of the window to preview the transition.

4. Close the Video toolbox by clicking the X in the upper-right corner or by reclicking the Video Toolbox icon you used to open the window (Figure 8.24).

✔ Tip

- The Video toolbox is great when you want precise transition times, but the Timeline is more helpful when you're making artistic decisions, because it gives you a much better visual representation.

To reverse a transition effect:

- ◆ In the Transitions Clip Properties tool, click the Reverse checkbox (**Figure 8.26**). Studio reverses the transition effect.

✔ Tips

- A good example of a transition that's significantly affected by reversal is the "Open curtain" transition, located at the top and on the left of page 2 of the Alpha Magic Transitions album. I often open a movie with that transition in the normal direction (opening the curtain), and at the end of the movie I reverse it to close the curtains.

- If you encounter a Reverse checkbox that's dimmed for a particular transition, look for a transition in the library that performs the reverse of the selected transition.

CUSTOMIZING TRANSITIONS

Working with Background Rendering

Most Standard and Alpha Magic transitions are fairly simple. That's why you can get real-time previews on fairly old computers.

However, Hollywood FX transitions, even some of the free ones, are much more complex, making real-time preview challenging.

To accelerate preview, Studio will automatically use the 3D graphics capabilities now embedded in most graphics cards. In Studio 9, you had the option to enable or disable this capability; with Studio 10 it's always on.

Like Studio 9, version 10 also enables background rendering, where Studio renders the actual frames that make up the transition and stores them in a separate file. Although the process takes a few moments, while Studio is rendering I can still be editing elsewhere in the production, and when it's done I can view my transition in real time.

The sidebar "About Background Rendering" discusses other benefits of this feature, and how to select the optimum rendering alternative.

About Background Rendering

Studio is a nondestructive editor, which means that it leaves all captured or imported files untouched and implements your edits by producing a completely new file. This process is called *rendering*, and depending on project duration, complexity, and the speed of your computer, rendering can take quite a long time.

When you render at the end of a project, it's a *foreground* task, which means that the program is totally dedicated to rendering, and you can no longer edit. Virtually all editing and graphics programs work this way. However, Studio also provides an option to render transitions and other effects in the *background*, which means that you can continue to edit while Studio is rendering. When you're ready to output your final video files, the process will be quicker since much of the rendering will already be completed.

As shown in **Figure 8.27**, Studio 10 offers two format choices for background rendering, DV, which is ideal if you're sending your project back to tape, and MPEG-2, which is great for DVD projects that must be rendered into MPEG-2 before recording to disc. Neither alternative speeds your rendering if you're outputting into Windows Media, Real, or another format. However, you still may want to render in the background, using the DV option, because this provides the most accurate preview of your effects.

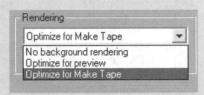

Figure 8.27 Here's where you select your background rendering options.

Note, however, that background rendering may make your system feel sluggish during editing. For example, you may notice that you have to select a video file two or three times before the system responds, that dragging files on the Timeline takes longer than usual, or that scenes in the Album take longer to appear when you select a new video file.

This is because rendering is very computationally intensive, which means that it consumes lots of your computer's processing power. On my 2.4 GHz Pentium 4 HP workstation, I notice very little difference when background rendering is turned on. On my Dell laptop with a 1.6 GHz Mobile Pentium chip, background rendering creates some sluggishness, but it's still worthwhile, because I get to view effects I couldn't preview otherwise and because of the rendering time it saves me on the back end of the project.

So what's the net/net? If your goal is to output to DV tape or DVD, give background rendering a try, using the appropriate format choice. If your goal is to output in some other format, try rendering in the background to DV format. In both instances, be aware that background rendering may slow performance, and if this becomes unacceptable, disable background rendering.

In addition, recognize that rendering in the background stresses the system, which may lead to instability and system crashes. If this occurs, turn off background rendering and see if the situation improves.

WORKING WITH BACKGROUND RENDERING

To render as a background task:

1. From the Studio menu, choose Setup > Project Preferences.

   The Studio Setup Options screen appears, open to the Project Preferences tab.

2. In the Rendering list box at the right (Figure 8.27), select one *of the following options:*

   ▲ No Background Rendering, to disable background rendering

   ▲ Optimize for DVD, to render into MPEG-2 format

   ▲ Optimize for Make Tape, to create a file in DV format

   See the sidebar "About Background Rendering," earlier in this chapter, for assistance with this decision.

3. Click OK to close the Studio Setup Options dialog box.

   Studio will now render all transitions and effects as background tasks.

   After applying background rendering, you'll see a small green bar above all areas on the timeline that require rendering (**Figure 8.28**). When this disappears, Studio has finished rendering the effect or clip.

✔ Tip

■ When rendering in the background, click Shift+Ctrl+Home and you'll see the rendering progress screen shown in **Figure 8.29,** which is useful to chart your rendering progress.

Rendering needed

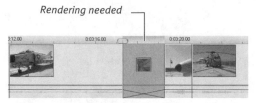

Figure 8.28 Background rendering at work. This bar indicates that video needs to be rendered and disappears once the job is finished. The bar is very faint in the grayscale figure but it's bright green and impossible to miss in the real application.

Figure 8.29 Click Shift+Ctrl+Home to see this rendering progress screen.

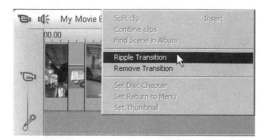

Figure 8.30 Start the ripple transition by dragging the desired transition between the first and second images. Let's use this Page Turn from the Pro collection, which makes my slide show look like a Jane's Fighting Ship manual.

Ripple Transitions for Slide Shows

As discussed in "To create a slide show" in Chapter 7, you can create a slide show from still images by dragging multiple images to the Timeline. As a lovely touch for slide shows, you can add transitions between images, a process that Studio simplifies with a feature called ripple transitions.

Here's how it works.

To insert a ripple transition between slide show images:

1. With your slide show on the Timeline, drag the desired transition between the first and second images (**Figure 8.30**). Studio inserts the transition.

continues on next page

2. Select all slides in the slide show by doing *one of the following*:

   ▲ If your entire presentation is a slide show, choose Edit > Select All from the Studio menu (or press Ctrl+A).

   ▲ If the Timelines contains other assets that you don't want included in the ripple transition, hold down the Shift key and select the first image and then the last image in the slide show.

   Studio highlights all the images in the slide show.

3. Right-click the selected images to reveal the menu and then select Ripple Transition (**Figure 8.31**).

   Studio inserts the transition between all still images (**Figure 8.32**).

✔ **Tips**

■ For most video clips, 2-second transitions (the default setting for video) are fine. But for still images, a 2-second transition can be a bit long, especially at the default 4-second duration for stills. You may want to change the default transition time when you are applying transitions to slide shows; then change it back to the usual 2 seconds for your video work.

■ After you apply a ripple transition, you can customize the duration for any transition as described in "Customizing Transitions," earlier in this chapter.

Figure 8.31 Then highlight all images in the slide show, right-click, and select Ripple Transition.

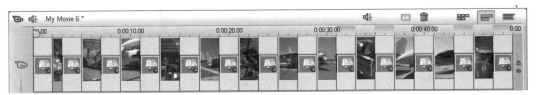

Figure 8.32 Voilà! Multiple transitions, neatly inserted.

APPLYING
SPECIAL EFFECTS

9

Special effects are filters that change the appearance of video either to fix problems (curative special effects) or enhance the video artistically (artistic special effects). Studio has seven classes of special effects: one curative and six artistic classes. Pinnacle calls all effects RTFX (for real-time effects), since you can preview them in real time. You will, however, have to render most effects for high-quality preview and final output.

Studio has standard effects that ship with the program as well as Plus and Pro effects packs that you can buy to add more capabilities. Pinnacle also has opened up Studio's architecture so that third parties can build filters for it.

Pinnacle added a boatload of new effects between Studio 9 and Studio 10, some incorporated in the midterm Studio 9 Plus version, and some with version 10. We're talking Chroma key, picture-in-picture, and the ability to control effects with keyframes, a huge creativity boost.

Another very useful tool is Studio's automatic music video–creation routine, SmartMovie, also covered in this chapter. All this on top of Studio's top-notch color correction and image stabilization.

So let's quick talking about it, and jump right in.

Types of Effects

Studio is a fluid program with multiple versions marketed to different target groups and features that appear in one version and not in another (but check back tomorrow, and that may change). I've learned that the quickest way to render a book obsolete is to try to provide a definitive breakdown of what's in one version and not the other, so I won't do that here.

In general, if I demonstrate a feature that you don't have, you should assume that you have a feature-limited version that can be upgraded to a version with the demonstrated feature. In particular, Pinnacle has reserved the overlay effects and keyframe capabilities for advanced Studio versions.

After an overview of the special effects interface, which applies to all special effects, I'll describe how to use the following types of effects.

- **Cleaning Effects:** These are curative filters that fix problems with the underlying video. Auto Color Correct fixes white balance and other color- and brightness-related issues, while Noise Reduction removes noise, usually caused by shooting with poor lighting or capturing from analog sources (more on this in "Video Rescue 101," later in this chapter). Stabilize minimizes unwanted motion in a video, usually produced by shooting with a handheld camera.

- **Time Effects:** These artistic effects change the speed of the video, either slowing it down or making it faster; these tools are demonstrated in "Varying Playback Speed," later in this chapter.

Figure 9.1 Studio used to present special effects by function.

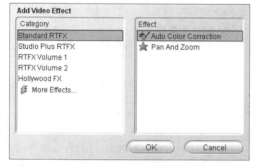

Figure 9.2 In Studio 10, Pinnacle switched to a product view with some special functional categories. Here's what you'd get with the base-level product.

◆ **Still Image Effects:** These tools allow you to rotate your digital pictures and remove red-eye, and then add pan and zoom effects; these tools are demonstrated in "Quick Image Fixes in Studio" and "Inserting Pan and Zoom Effects," in Chapter 5.

◆ **Overlay Effects:** These tools allow you to create picture-in-picture and chroma key effects; these tools are demonstrated in multiple sections starting with "About the Overlay Track," later in this chapter.

◆ **Auto-Movie Effects:** Though not a true effect like others covered in this chapter, this feature automatically converts your footage into a music video-like production, and is explained in "Creating Music Videos Automatically," later in this chapter.

Studio offers additional effects not addressed in this book in the following classes:

◆ **Color Effects:** These artistic effects adjust the color of the video, for example, to black and white or sepia.

◆ **Fun Effects:** These artistic effects change the video in some fundamental way; for instance, the Water Drop effect makes your video look like a pond with water dropping into it.

◆ **Style Effects:** These artistic effects change the style of the video; for instance, Old Film makes your video look like it was shot in the 1940s.

Note that in Studio 9, Pinnacle sorted the special effects by category, as shown in **Figure 9.1**. In Studio 10, Pinnacle presents most effects by Studio version and some by category, while preserving the categorization icons so you can more quickly identify the function of each effect (**Figure 9.2**).

TYPES OF EFFECTS

Before Getting Started

Let's discuss a few points before jumping in. We'll start with setup options, specifically as they relate to background rendering as discussed in "Working with Background Rendering," in Chapter 8.

With background rendering enabled, Studio renders transitions and effects in the background, which speeds final rendering at project completion and provides a more accurate preview of the transitions and effects you've added to your project. If you don't enable background rendering, Studio will preview the effect, but what you will see is only an estimate, not the real effect applied to your actual source footage. For this reason, I generally recommend working with background rendering enabled.

In addition, note that video displayed on a computer monitor usually looks different from the same video displayed on a TV screen. If you're producing video for TV viewing on DVD, and don't preview on a TV or NTSC monitor during development, your results may not be optimal. For this reason, DVD producers should implement some sort of analog preview, either through a DV camcorder or the TV output of a graphics card like the ATI All-in-Wonder. See "Setting Up a Dual-Monitor Display" in Chapter 2 for more details.

Also, be aware that while effects have some similarities in interface and operation (as discussed in the next section "Learning the Special Effects Interface"), each effect, by necessity, looks and works differently. This is especially true of third-party effects created by companies other than Pinnacle.

Space doesn't allow a comprehensive review of all special effects, so this chapter demonstrates only the most widely used. Once you understand the basics, you'll find most other Pinnacle-created effects self-explanatory, though some third-party effects use different interfaces. If you're not comfortable teaching yourself how to use these effects, before buying a third-party effect, you may want to check whether the vendor provides user documentation.

Figure 9.3 Click here to get to the special effects.

Figure 9.4 Here are the Studio Plus RTFX effects.

Figure 9.5 Pinnacle lets you view the effect with a watermark to see if you like it; if so, you can purchase effects from Pinnacle's Web site.

Learning the Special Effects Interface

This section covers the basics of accessing, applying, and configuring special effects, while the next section will describe what keyframes are and how and when to use them. Then we'll move on and explore some of the most commonly applied special effects.

To access special effects:

1. Place the target clip on the Timeline and select the clip with your pointer.

2. At the upper left of the Movie window, click the Open/Close Video Toolbox icon (**Figure 9.3**).

   The Video toolbox opens (**Figure 9.4**).

3. On the left side of the toolbox, click the Add an Effect to a Video Clip icon.

   Studio lists all effects installed and operational on your computer in the Category and Effect tabs. If you elected to Show Premium Content in the Edit Preferences tab (see, "Hiding Premium Content and Features," in Chapter 2), Studio will also show premium content that you can try out, but will contain a watermark to prevent use in a real project (**Figure 9.5**).

To add and configure a special effect:

1. Click the target effect category (**Figure 9.6**).

2. Click the target effect.

3. Click OK.

   Studio applies the special effect. If it's a Studio effect, Studio then opens the Special Effects window (**Figure 9.7**).

   If it's a third-party effect, the Special Effects window either contains the configurable settings or an Edit button that opens the third-party configuration screen.

Figure 9.6 Let's start with a simple Water Drop effect.

Turn effect on/off   Move effect up   Close Special Effects window

Video Effects list   Presets

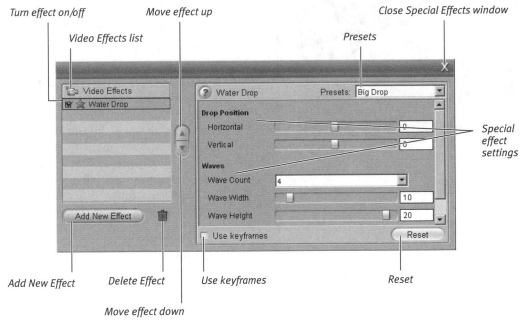

Special effect settings

Add New Effect   Delete Effect   Use keyframes   Reset

Move effect down

Figure 9.7 Once you select an effect, Studio presents its configuration options.

LEARNING THE SPECIAL EFFECTS INTERFACE

Fun effect icon

Figure 9.8 An icon on the clip in the Timeline lets you know what type of effect you've applied.

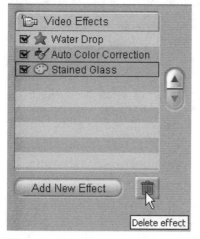

Figure 9.9 Click here to delete effects.

4. To choose special effect settings, while previewing in the Player, do *one of the following:*

   ▲ Choose a value from the Presets list (Figure 9.7).

   ▲ Manually adjust the effect settings.

   Note that you can preview the effect in the Player by clicking Play or by dragging the Player slider around the video.

5. When you are finished configuring the special effect, do *one of the following:*

   ▲ Click the X in the upper-right corner to close the Special Effects window.

   ▲ Click the Add New Effect button to select and configure another special effect.

   Studio saves the first effect and returns you to either the Movie window for additional editing or the Special Effects window so you can choose and configure another special effect.

   Studio adds an icon to the video clip in the Timeline showing the class of special effect applied to the clip (**Figure 9.8**).

✔ Tips

- Note the Reset button in Figure 9.7, which resets all controls and values to their original state.

- To add another effect, click the Add New Effect button beneath the Video Effects list.

To delete a special effect:

1. Select the target effect in the Video Effects list.

2. Click the Delete Effect button (**Figure 9.9**). Studio deletes the effect.

To turn effects on or off:

◆ Click the checkbox to the left of the effect (**Figure 9.10**) to turn the effect on or off for preview and rendering.

✔ Tips

■ It's often useful to turn an effect on or off when attempting to configure another special effect. For example, in Figure 9.10, I'm trying to configure the Color Correction effect, but the waves from the Water Drop effect make this hard to do. By turning the Water Drop effect off (**Figure 9.11**), I get a clear view of the video and can effectively set my configuration options. You won't remove the effect from the clip by turning it off; you'll simply keep it out of the preview.

■ You can adjust the order of special effects by selecting an effect and then clicking the arrows to move the effect up or down (Figure 9.6). You'll see how and why you might want to do this in "Video Rescue 101," later in this chapter.

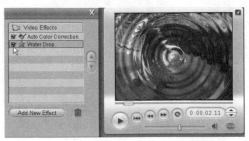

Figure 9.10 Here's how you turn off an effect so you can preview other effects applied to that clip.

Figure 9.11 Now you have a clear view of the video so you can configure another effect.

Figure 9.12 Let's work with the Soften effect.

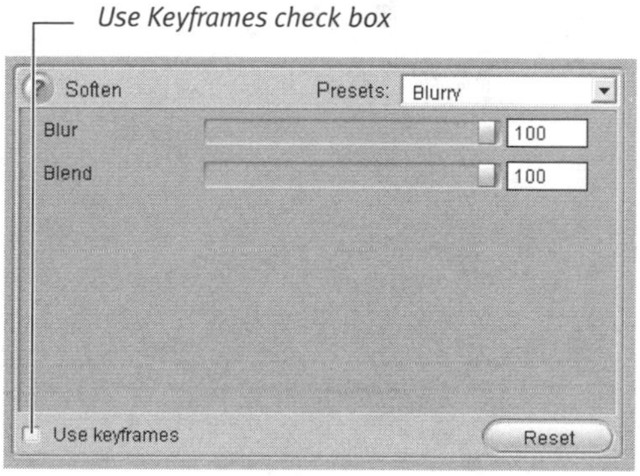

Use Keyframes check box

Figure 9.13 Here are my configuration options, and the Use keyframes checkbox.

Working with Keyframes

Keyframes allow you to vary effect settings over time, essentially animating the effect. The result is a true quantum leap in creative potential.

When I was first learning about keyframes, it took a while for the concept to sink in, so I'll start with a simple application where I'll use keyframes to transition in the application of an effect. Specifically, I'll apply a soften filter to the beginning of a clip and then gradually remove the filter so the video comes into focus. This example will involve three keyframes, one at the start of the video, one at the point where the video becomes clear, and one at the very end.

Then we'll go full bore with a "keep the spotlight on the dancing ballerina" example, which will involve setting about a dozen keyframes. Though it's pretty cheesy, after both examples, you should be in great shape to keyframe your effects with aplomb.

Note that not all effects can be keyframed; in particular, you can't apply keyframes to Studio's Speed effect.

To transition in a fade effect with keyframes:

1. Place the target clip on the Timeline and select the clip with your pointer.

2. At the upper left of the Movie window, click the Open/Close Video Toolbox icon (Figure 9.3).

3. On the left side of the toolbox, click the Add an Effect to a Video Clip icon.

4. Click the target effect category (**Figure 9.12**).

5. Click OK.

   Studio applies the special effect and opens the Special Effects window (**Figure 9.13**).

continues on next page

WORKING WITH KEYFRAMES

6. Adjust the settings to the desired starting value.

When you insert keyframes, Studio inserts the current settings as values for the first and last keyframes. Though you can change the values later, it's easier if you simply adjust them before you insert the keyframes.

I'm happy with the 100/100 values in the Blur and Blend controls in the Soften effect, so I'll start with those.

See the sidebar "Studio's Static and Keyframed Presets," later in this chapter, for a discussion of Studio's effect presets.

7. On the bottom of the Special Effects window, click the Use Keyframes checkbox.

Studio opens the keyframes interface and adds two keyframes, one at the start of the clip and the other at the end (**Figure 9.14**).

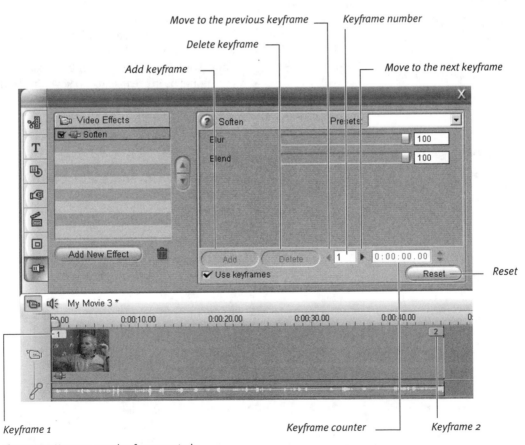

Figure 9.14 Here are your keyframe controls.

Figure 9.15 Now drag the Timeline scrubber to where you want the Soften effect to disappear.

Figure 9.16 Click Add to add a keyframe.

Figure 9.17 There's new keyframe number 2, right under the Timeline scrubber.

8. Grab the Timeline scrubber and move it to the desired end point for the effect (**Figure 9.15**).

   Here I'm moving about 2 seconds in, where I want the video to return to 100 percent clarity. Said another way, I want the Soften effect to stop as of this position.

9. In the Effect Control window, click Add to add a keyframe (**Figure 9.16**).

   Studio adds a keyframe at that position (**Figure 9.17**). This becomes keyframe 2, while the keyframe at the end of the clip becomes keyframe 3.

   Note that when Studio adds a keyframe, it inserts the values from the immediately preceding keyframe.

   continues on next page

WORKING WITH KEYFRAMES

10. In the Effect Control window, drag the Blur and Blend sliders all the way to the left (**Figure 9.18**).

This brings the strength of the effect to zero, ending the transition from soft at the start of the video to completely clear. That's half the job; now, because Studio inserts *both* original keyframes (1 and 2) with the then current values, I have to zero out the values of keyframe 3 to eliminate the Soften effect throughout the clip.

11. In the bottom of the Special Effects window, click the Move to Next Keyframe button (**Figure 9.19**).

Studio moves to the third keyframe.

12. In the Effect Control window, drag the Blur and Blend sliders all the way to the left (**Figure 9.20**).

✔ Tip

■ With shorter clips, you may find it easier simply to move the second keyframe to the desired end point of the effect, rather than inserting a new keyframe and zeroing out the values of keyframes 2 and 3. See the task "To Move Keyframes," later in this chapter.

WORKING WITH KEYFRAMES

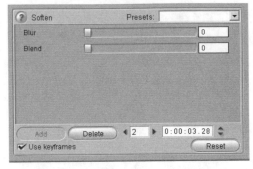

Figure 9.18 Now zero out the effect controls to eliminate the effect. Note the number 2 in the keyframe number box. That tells us which keyframe we're working on.

Figure 9.19 Move to the next keyframe by clicking this button.

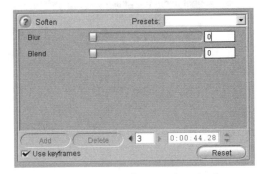

Figure 9.20 Now zero out the controls on keyframe 3.

To apply multiple keyframes to customize an effect:

1. Place the target clip on the Timeline and select the clip with your pointer.

2. At the upper left of the Movie window, click the Open/Close Video Toolbox icon (Figure 9.3).

3. On the left side of the toolbox, click the Add an Effect to a Video Clip icon.

4. Click the target effect category (**Figure 9.21**).

5. Click OK.

   Studio applies the special effect and opens the Special Effects window (Figure 9.21).

6. Adjust the settings to the desired starting value (**Figure 9.22**).

   continues on next page

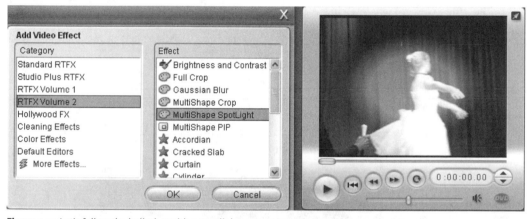

Figure 9.21 Let's follow the ballerina with a spotlight, a more complex exercise.

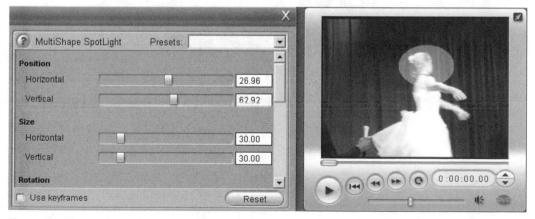

Figure 9.22 First I configure the effect to the desired settings.

WORKING WITH KEYFRAMES

7. On the bottom of the Special Effects window, click the Use Keyframes checkbox.

Studio opens the keyframes interface and adds two keyframes, one at the start of the clip and the other at the end.

8. Grab the Timeline scrubber and move it to the next desired keyframe point.

Here I'm chasing my ballerina wife around the stage with a spotlight, so I'll keep sliding the scrubber over until she moves out of the light (**Figure 9.23**).

9. In the Effect Control window, click Add to add a keyframe (Figure 9.16).

Studio adds a keyframe at that position (**Figure 9.24**). This becomes keyframe 2, while the keyframe at the end of the clip becomes keyframe 3.

Figure 9.23 Oops, she's getting away. Time for a new keyframe.

Figure 9.24 Here's the new keyframe; now I have to adjust the controls.

10. In the Effect Control window, adjust the controls to the new position (**Figure 9.25**).

11. Repeat as necessary throughout the clip, adding keyframes and adjusting the settings of the final keyframe to the desired setting (**Figure 9.26**).

✔ Tip

- When applying multiple keyframes, you'll get the best result if you trim your clip to the desired start and end points before you start keyframing. If you trim after, Studio may adjust keyframe positioning to new frames, which is seldom the desired result.

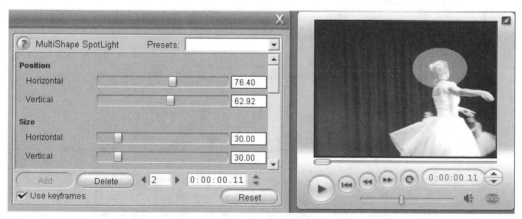

Figure 9.25 Back on track. Now on to the next keyframe.

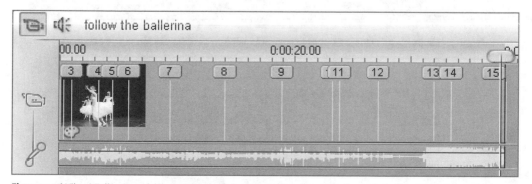

Figure 9.26 Yikes! Following a ballerina around takes a lot of hard work (but you probably already knew that).

To move keyframes:

1. Click the Move to Previous Keyframe or Move to Next Keyframe button to arrive at the target keyframe.

   Here I'm on keyframe 11, which as we can see in the keyframe counter is at precisely 30 seconds (**Figure 9.27**).

2. Do *one of the following:*

   ▲ Adjust position by clicking the Increase by One Frame and Decrease by One Frame icons to the right of the keyframe counter (**Figure 9.28**).

   ▲ Click the time in the keyframe counter and manually type the desired position.

   Studio adjusts the keyframe to the new position in the Timeline.

✔ Tip

■ Clicking Reset (Figure 9.27) while keyframes are enabled either creates a new keyframe with the default values or changes the then selected keyframe to the default values. This seems a bit counterintuitive; since Reset usually means push all parameters back to zero and let's start over. The operation of this button may change as Studio's keyframe feature evolves, but if it doesn't, the quickest way to delete all keyframes and start over is by deleting the special effect (see the task "To Delete a Special Effect," earlier in this chapter) and starting over.

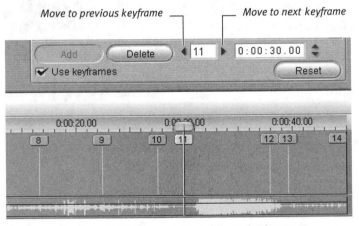

Figure 9.27 Use these buttons to navigate to different keyframes.

Figure 9.28 Change keyframe location by clicking these controls or by simply clicking in the keyframe counter and typing a new time. Note the Delete button, which you can use to delete a keyframe.

To delete keyframes:

1. Click the Move to Previous Keyframe or Move to Next Keyframe button to arrive at the target keyframe.

2. Click the Delete button (Figure 9.28). Studio deletes the keyframe.

Studio's Static and Keyframed Presets

Studio has always provided effect presets that let you quickly select a certain look. As you can see in **Figure 9.29**, Studio now has both Static and Keyframed presets. Static presets are like the presets of old, applying one set of parameters to the entire clip.

Keyframed presets contain keyframes with start and end values to produce a dynamic effect. As you would expect, when you apply a keyframed preset, Studio creates the keyframes and inserts the preset values for you. You can use these as a starting point and modify as desired, or accept them as is and move on to your next edit.

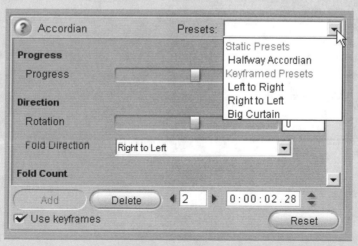

Figure 9.29 Studio now offers both Static and Keyframed presets, the latter a one-click solution for animating effects in your videos.

Studio's Cleaning Effects

One of the benefits of having older siblings is that you get lots of their cool stuff, albeit often after they tire of it and it's a bit worn. Similarly, Studio, with a more full-featured sibling like Pinnacle Liquid Edition, gets lots of cool stuff passed down to it—but without the negatives of hand-me-down clothes.

One of these hand-me-downs is Studio's Auto Color Correct effect, which corrects for improper white balancing and other color deficiencies. Simply stated, this tool is extraordinary, and can help improve the appearance of your videos immensely.

The most frustrating thing about this, of course, is that since the book is in black and white with grayscale images, you have to take my word for most of these kudos. Don't worry, if you try it for yourself you'll quickly see what I'm talking about. Also in the cleaning category are image stabilization and noise reduction effects, both covered in this section.

Note that in Studio 9, Pinnacle grouped all cleaning effects into a single Cleaning category. In Studio 10, the three main cleaning effects are contained in the Standard RTFX category with others contained in a separate Cleaning category.

To apply automatic color correction:

1. Place the target clip on the Timeline and select the clip.

2. At the upper left of the Movie window, click the Open/Close Video Toolbox icon (Figure 9.3).

3. On the left side of the Video toolbox, click the Add an Effect to a Video Clip icon (Figure 9.4).

4. Select the Standard RTFX category (**Figure 9.30**).

5. Select Auto Color Correct.

6. Click OK.

   Studio opens the Auto Color Correct effect (**Figure 9.31**) with its one configurable setting.

7. Adjust the settings as desired; then do *one of the following:*

   ▲ Click the X in the upper-right corner to close the Special Effects window.

   ▲ Click the Add New Effect button to select and configure another special effect.

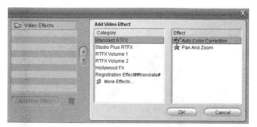

Figure 9.30 Let's start cleaning our video with Auto Color Correct.

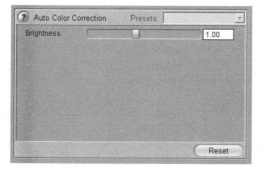

Figure 9.31 Here are the standard controls included with all versions of Studio.

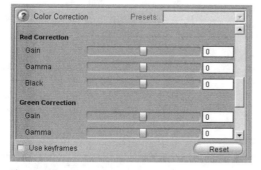

Figure 9.32 If Automatic Color Correction doesn't work, try manual color correction.

Figure 9.33 Or the new White Balance option.

✔ Tips

- Usually, when videos need color correction, they often need to be brightened as well, which is why Pinnacle includes the Brightness setting in Studio. I almost always bump up the brightness a bit once I apply color correction.

- Studio offers (at least) three ways to tackle color correction issues. I always try the Auto Color Correction tool first, which works about 75% of the time. If this doesn't work, I apply the manual color correction tools now found in the Studio Plus version only. Here, I can manually adjust the red, green, and blue values of the clip to correct any color issues (**Figure 9.32**). New in Studio 10 is a White Balance effect (**Figure 9.33**) that works with an eye-dropper control that you use to click on a color in the image that's supposed to be white. With these three tools, you should be able to resolve even the toughest color correction issues in your videos.

- Color correction requires precise adjustments, so I always wait for background rendering to complete before finalizing my decision. If you're applying color correction to a large clip, split out a small segment and apply Auto Color Correct to the segment to identify the proper values. Then apply the effect to the larger clip using the same values. See "Common Tasks" in Chapter 7 for information on splitting clips.

- Pinnacle advises that the Auto Color Correct filter "may introduce video noise into the clip as a side-effect of processing" and recommends that you apply the Noise Reduction effect shown in Figure 9.30, to counteract this problem.

- If you split a clip with special effects, Studio applies all effects to both clips. Studio prevents you from combining two clips if one of them has special effects.

STUDIO'S CLEANING EFFECTS

To apply the Stabilize effect:

1. Place the target clip on the Timeline and select the clip.

2. At the upper left of the Movie window, click the Open/Close Video Toolbox icon (Figure 9.3).

3. On the left side of the Video toolbox, click the Add an Effect to a Video Clip icon (Figure 9.4).

4. Select the Standard RTFX category (Figure 9.30).

5. Select the Stabilize effect (Figure 9.30).

6. Click OK.

   Studio adds Stabilize to the Video Effects list, but presents no user-configurable settings (**Figure 9.34**). To understand how Studio stabilizes the image, see the sidebar, "About Stabilization."

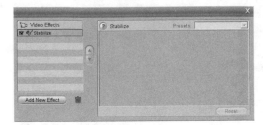

Figure 9.34 Some filters, like Stabilize, have no options.

About Stabilization

Whereas Auto Color Correct addresses poor white balancing, Stabilize bails you out for not using a tripod or for failing to hold the camera steady.

Interestingly, Stabilize works exactly like electric image stabilization (EIS) in a DV camera. That is, most EIS systems capture a larger frame than is necessary for the ultimate video frame. For example, in a DV camera, the CCD may capture an 800 x 600 frame that will ultimately be reduced to 720 x 480 resolution.

Then, when the motion sensor chips in the camera sense motion, the camera compensates by shifting the image within that larger frame. For example, if the camera detects an inadvertent five-pixel jerk to the right, it compensates by shifting the image five pixels to the left.

Similarly, if the algorithms used by Studio detect a five-pixel jerk to the right, Studio moves the image five pixels to the left. However, since Studio doesn't start with a larger-than-necessary frame, it must zoom into the image to free up pixels on the borders to enable the necessary shifting.

This is evident in **Figure 9.35**. On the left is the original frame, and on the right is the frame after stabilization. As you can see, my daughter, the cute blonde in the middle, is noticeably larger in the frame on the right, and the little girl on the left in the original frame has been cut out of the picture. You might also notice that my daughter's face is slightly less sharp on the right.

The key benefit is that the video is vastly easier to watch because Studio eliminated most of the motion injected by my walking alongside my daughter. Though the visible area in the frame and the detail are both slightly reduced, overall the video is much more watchable.

Once you know the trade-offs to look for, you can easily try stabilizing footage with noticeable jerkiness, making sure that the cure isn't worse than the disease. Most of the time, your video will end up looking much, much better.

Original   Post-stabilization

Figure 9.35 Stabilize works by zooming into the image to create space on the top, bottom, and sides to remove minor camera motion. That's why the original clip shows more area than the stabilized version of the same clip.

STUDIO'S CLEANING EFFECTS

To apply the Noise Reduction effect:

1. Place the target clip on the Timeline and select the clip.

2. At the upper left of the Movie window, click the Open/Close Video Toolbox icon (Figure 9.3).

3. On the left side of the Video toolbox, click the Add an Effect to a Video Clip icon (Figure 9.4).

4. Select the Standard RTFX category (Figure 9.12).

5. Select the Noise Reduction effect (Figure 9.12).

6. Click OK.

   Studio opens the Noise Reduction settings window (**Figure 9.36**).

7. Adjust the setting as desired.

   See the sidebar "About Noise Reduction Filters," later in this chapter, for assistance.

8. When you're finished, do *one of the following:*

   ▲ Click the X in the upper-right corner to close the Special Effects window.

   ▲ Click the Add New Effect button to select and configure another special effect.

Figure 9.36 Setting the Noise Threshold for the Noise Reduction filter.

Video Rescue 101

There's no one-size-fits-all cure for poorly shot video, but here's one procedure I used to help correct some footage shot with a single-chip, consumer-quality DV camcorder in a dark restaurant without a light. Hey, it was reunion weekend, and I was definitely not breaking out the good equipment.

Figure 9.37 shows the four stages of the video, with the overly dark original video at the upper left. I first applied Auto Color Correct, with brightness boosted to the max, shown at the upper right. This brightened the image considerably, but it wasn't enough, so I applied manual Color Correction as well.

This brightened the video even more, but also produced significant noise that resembled an indoor snowstorm, which I mostly removed with the Noise Reduction effect. This isn't easy to see in the figure, but it's readily apparent when playing the clip in real time.

continues on next page

Original · *Auto Color Correction*

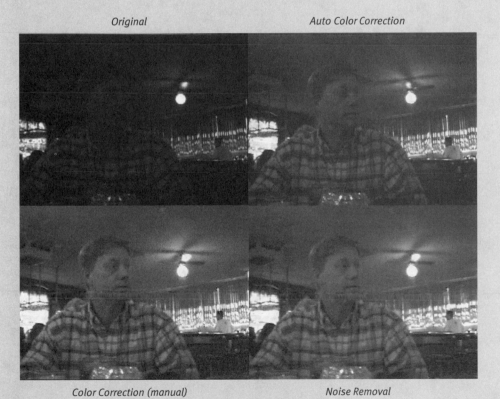

Color Correction (manual) · *Noise Removal*

Figure 9.37 Video Rescue 101, from unusable to reasonably good quality.

STUDIO'S CLEANING EFFECTS

Video Rescue 101 *(continued)*

One interesting part of the exercise was a realization that the order of special effects affects the way in which Studio applies them and the visual result. For example, **Figure 9.38** shows the three filters applied with Noise Reduction applied last; now the video is very dark. **Figure 9.39** shows the same three filters applied to the same source video in a different sequence, with a completely different result. I rendered both files to make sure the previews were accurate, and the rendered files looked just like previews. When applying special effects, order definitely matters.

Move effect up

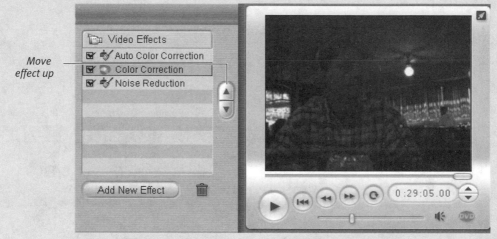

Figure 9.38 Shifting the effect order. Here you can barely see the video.

Figure 9.39 Same effects, different order, completely different result.

About Noise Reduction Filters

Noise reduction filters work by attempting to distinguish between real motion that occurs from frame to frame, like a hand waving or lips speaking, and noise, which is random graininess and other artifacts (video defects) caused by a number of factors, including shooting under poor lighting conditions or using poor equipment.

The slider bar shown in Figure 9.36 sets the threshold between noise and real motion. The farther you move the slider to the right (higher value) the more motion Studio assumes is noise. This increases the filtering, enhancing noise removal, but also potentially producing artifacts caused by the elimination of real motion. Move the slider to the left (lower value), and Studio uses a lower threshold, assumes that more motion is real motion, and removes less noise, reducing the cleansing effect.

Noise reduction can work wonders when you're working with very poor quality video (see the sidebar "Video Rescue 101"), but it must be used judiciously because higher thresholds can and do produce artifacts. This means that you should render in the background to get the best possible preview before selecting your final settings.

Varying Playback Speed

Changing the playback speed of your clips is useful in a variety of circumstances, whether it's to showcase a child's look of delight or slow your golf swing to better reveal its flaws. It's also great for a fun, Chaplin-esque sped-up effect, which I use quite often in my home videos.

If you're an experienced Studio user, you'll like how Pinnacle upgraded this feature for Studio 10. First, there are more options for achieving the optimal appearance of the adjusted video, discussed in the sidebar "Speed with style." Second, you can now make your video play in reverse.

Finally, Studio no longer mutes the audio with all speed adjustments; it slows or speeds the audio with the video. If you like how it sounds, keep it; otherwise you can mute or delete the audio manually (see Chapter 11, "Working with Audio," for details).

To change playback speed:

1. Place the target clip on the Timeline and select the clip.

2. At the upper left of the Movie window, click the Open/Close Video Toolbox icon (Figure 9.3).

3. On the left side of the Video toolbox, click the Add an Effect to a Video Clip icon (Figure 9.4).

4. Select the Studio Plus RTFX category (**Figure 9.40**).

5. Select the Speed effect.

6. Click OK.

   Studio opens the Speed settings window (**Figure 9.41**).

7. To adjust video speed, drag the Speed (%) slider to the desired speed.

   Dragging the speed to the left (below 100%), slows the video and increases its length on the timeline.

   Dragging the video to the right (above 100%) speeds the video and decreases its length on the timeline.

8. If desired, click the Reverse checkbox to make your video play in reverse.

9. Choose the desired blend type (**Figure 9.42**). See the sidebar "Speed With Style" for details.

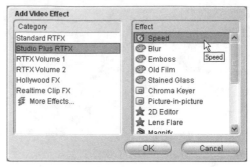

Figure 9.40 Using the Speed controls to slow down my chip shot so that I can visualize my errors.

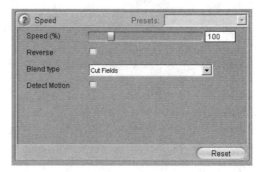

Figure 9.41 The Speed settings window.

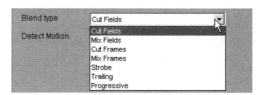

Figure 9.42 Here are your interpolation options when you slow video down.

10. When slowing down the video, click Detect Motion.

This will force Studio to create "tweener" frames to smooth the appearance of the video. This option has no effect when increasing video playback speed, so there is no harm in leaving it checked at all times.

11. When you're finished, do *one of the following:*

▲ Click the X in the upper-right corner to close the Special Effects window.

▲ Click the Add New Effect button to select and configure another special effect.

Speed with Style

Studio now offers multiple blending options to produce the highest-quality image, primarily when slowing video playback down. That's because when you slow video down, Studio has to "make up" frames to create the motion. For example, when slowing speed down to 25%, Studio has to create three new frames between each original frame. Studio makes multiple interpolative techniques available to ensure the highest-quality result.

Here are the definitions from the Pinnacle Edition help files (the Studio help files weren't quite finished when I wrote this book):

◆ **Mix Fields (for video):** Motion is played back more smoothly but is not as sharply focused. In most cases, this is the best choice.

◆ **Cut Fields (for video):** Provides a sharper focus but motion can be slightly jerky.

◆ **Mix Frames (for film):** Provides smooth motion but is less focused.

◆ **Cut Frames (film):** Provides sharp focus but motion is often jerky.

◆ **Strobe Effect:** The Strobe effect is best used for motifs with a great deal of motion. Strobe plays a configurable number of identical frames in succession before repeating the same number of the next frame (omitting those in between). For example: Instead of the standard frame sequence 1-2-3-4-5-6-7 etc., 2-frame-Strobe plays back the sequence: 1-1-3-3-5-5-7-7 etc.

◆ **Trailing:** The Trailing effect makes movements and changes of motif visible by means of "trails" in the frame.

◆ **Progressive:** The Progressive option serves to convert interlaced material to noninterlaced material.

continues on next page

VARYING PLAYBACK SPEED

Speed with Style *(continued)*

The net/net from the help file is that if you're working on video as opposed to film (and I assume that you are), try Mix Fields first, then Cut Fields. Mix and Cut Frames are effects primarily designed for use with film, so stay away from these. Moving down the list, Strobe Effect and Trailing are both "artistic" effects you should use when trying to achieve a certain look. The interlaced to noninterlaced conversion produced by the Progressive option is beyond the scope of this book.

My experience aligns with the direction of the help files. I find that Mix Fields produces the smoothest result, so I always try that first, and then look for two types of artifacts. The first is shown in **Figure 9.43**, where you can see multiple faint shafts of my 60-degree wedge. This isn't the staggering speed of my swing (hey, it's only a wedge); rather, the artifacts are produced by the interpolative technique used to create the frames, and typically appear when the moving figures have sharp detail like a golf club. The other video detritus sometimes produced by Mix Fields is a shimmering artifact that typically occurs in a highly detailed background like the brick wall over my right shoulder.

If I see either artifact, I'll use Cut Fields, which as you can see in **Figure 9.44**, shows only one shaft. However, this alternative produces a slightly choppier look, so I always try Mix Fields first.

Figure 9.43 Note the multiple shafts of my wedge shown in this slo-mo video produced with the Mix Fields selection.

Figure 9.44 Much better—only one shaft (still shanked the shot, though).

About the Overlay Track

Let's discuss the Overlay track, shown in **Figure 9.45**. As you can see, the Overlay track includes both a video and an audio track and sits directly below the original Video and Audio tracks. By default, the Overlay track doesn't appear until you drop a video file into it, though there is a right-click option to keep it open at all time.

In Figure 9.45, the Video track contains a video of my mother, pregnant with my older brother sometime last century. The Overlay track contains a much more contemporary video of my father. However, only the video of my father shows in the Player.

This reflects how Overlay tracks function in video editing programs. Specifically, though an Overlay track may sit *below* the Video track on the timeline, video from that track always sits *above* the video in the main Video track when the video is produced.

Unless you use a technique like Picture-in-Picture or Chroma key to merge the two streams, only the video in the Overlay track will show in the final production. Accordingly, when discussing the two tracks, I'll refer to the video in the Video track as the *Background video*, and the video in the Overlay track as the *Overlay video*.

Note that once you import an Overlay video, you'll probably have to adjust the volume of one or both Audio tracks to produce the desired effect. See "Using the Volume Tool" in Chapter 11, to learn about Studio's options for adjusting volume.

Video track
Audio track
Overlay track
Audio track
Title track
Sound Effect track
Music track

Figure 9.45 Let's have another look at Studio's multiple tracks.

ABOUT THE OVERLAY TRACK

To open the Overlay track:

1. On the Video Scenes tab, hold down the mouse button and select one or more contiguous or noncontiguous scenes (**Figure 9.46**).

   The borders turn from white to blue, and a small hand appears over the scenes.

2. Drag the scenes to the target position on the Overlay track.

   A small plus sign appears below the pointer and a green vertical line marks the position of the video on the Overlay track.

3. Release the mouse button.

   Studio Plus inserts the scenes into the Overlay track and creates a new Title track (**Figure 9.47**).

✔ Tips

- You can edit videos in the Overlay track exactly like those in the Video track, including trimming and applying special effects.

- Unlike videos on the Video track, which always snap to the left to close any gaps in the Timeline, a video clip can be placed on the Overlay track at any location.

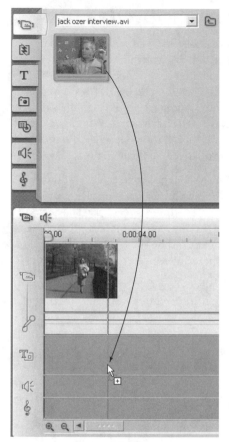

Figure 9.46 To open the Overlay track for the new video file, drag a video file onto the Overlay track.

Figure 9.47 Here are both files in the Timeline.

Applying Picture-in-Picture Effects

Picture-in-picture (P-I-P) effects add a great visual element to your projects. Here, I'm producing a video of my father's life, primarily using videos from an interview I recently shot. While editing the video, I'm weaving in older videos converted from 8 mm film shot back in the day. In this example, he talks about the gestation and birth of my older brother, and I'm using the P-I-P effect so viewers can see my father today and the older, background video simultaneously.

You need to make four basic decisions about inserting a P-I-P:

1. The size and position of the P-I-P window.

2. The size and appearance of the border around the P-I-P, which helps visually distinguish the P-I-P from the Background video.

3. The size and appearance of the P-I-P shadow—another alternative for setting the P-I-P off from the Background video.

4. Whether to customize the transparency of the P-I-P video.

To apply a P-I-P effect:

1. Select the Overlay video.

2. At the upper left of the Movie window, click the Open/Close Video Toolbox icon (**Figure 9.48**).

   The Video toolbox opens.

3. On the left side of the toolbox, click the Edit the Video Overlay Using Picture-in-Picture or Chroma Keying icon (**Figure 9.49**).

   Studio Plus opens the Video Toolbox with the Picture-in-Picture controls tab showing. At this point, as long as the Enable Picture-in-Picture checkbox is selected (the default option), Studio Plus applies the P-I-P effect.

✔ Tips

■ Note the P-I-P effect in the Player on the right in Figure 9.49. This is where you'll preview all of your edits to the P-I-P window as well as the border and shadow attributes.

■ To apply the selected P-I-P values to all clips subsequently placed on the Overlay track, click the Apply to New Clips checkbox in Figure 9.49.

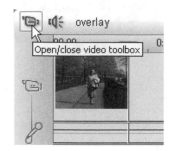

Figure 9.48 Click here to open the Video toolbox.

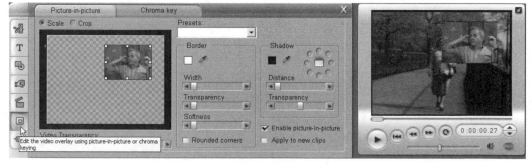

Figure 9.49 Click this tab to open the P-I-P and Chroma key controls.

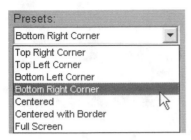

Figure 9.50 You can choose a preset, go completely custom using the individual P-I-P adjustment controls, or customize a preset.

Figure 9.51 Move the image around with this four-headed pointer.

Figure 9.52 Grab any point to make the image larger or smaller.

To customize P-I-P size and location:

◆ To customize the size and the location of the P-I-P, do *one or more of the following*:

   ▲ In the Presets drop-down list, select a preset (**Figure 9.50**).

   ▲ Position the cursor above the P-I-P and drag it to the target location (**Figure 9.51**).

   ▲ Position the cursor over any control point in the bounding box and drag the P-I-P to the target size (**Figure 9.52**).

✔ Tips

■ When selecting the size and position of your P-I-P, use the Timeline scrubber to move through the Background video to ensure that you don't obscure any critical regions in the video. I typically use the same exact positioning (and other parameters) throughout my productions.

■ When positioning your P-I-P, remember that the extreme edges of the video don't show when displayed on a television set. If you're writing your project back to DV tape, or producing a DVD, you should beware of the Title-safe zones discussed in Chapter 10.

To customize the P-I-P border:

1. To choose border color, click the solid-colored box beneath the Color text label (**Figure 9.53**).

   Studio Plus's Color selection dialog box opens (**Figure 9.54**).

2. Choose the desired color by selecting it from the Basic colors or Custom colors palette or by clicking a color on the spectrum.

3. If you want, save your custom color by clicking the Add to Custom Colors button (Ctrl+A). Saving your custom color helps you maintain uniformity as you work.

4. Click OK to close the dialog box.

5. Use the control sliders in the Border box to adjust border width, transparency, and softness.

6. Click the Rounded Corners checkbox to round the corners of the border.

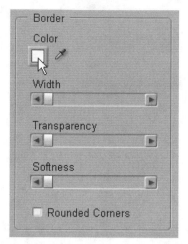

Figure 9.53 Click here to choose a border color.

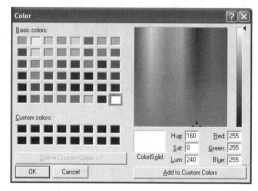

Figure 9.54 Select an existing basic color or choose your own custom color.

✔ Tips

- In addition to choosing the border color via the Color dialog, you can also click the eyedropper beneath the Color text label and then click the desired color in the video showing in the Player (**Figure 9.55**).

- While there are no hard-and-fast rules regarding P-I-P border width, I typically keep them very slender, just enough to set the P-I-P video off from the Background video.

- When selecting P-I-P color, I try to match the occasion and mood of the video. For a child's birthday video, orange or yellow is fine; here, for a more serious video, I'll select a very dark blue.

- I almost always soften the edges of my P-I-Ps with both softness and transparency controls. Otherwise, the edges of the P-I-P just look too harsh. **Figure 9.56** shows the P-I-P positioning and configuration options that I ultimately selected for this project.

- When applying a P-I-P effect, I usually transition into and out of the effect using a dissolve transition. To learn how to apply transitions to the Overlay track, see the section "Using Transitions" in Chapter 8.

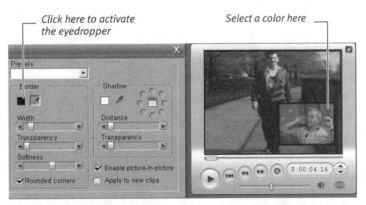

Click here to activate the eyedropper

Select a color here

Figure 9.55 You can also choose your border color by clicking the eyedropper and choosing a color in the Player.

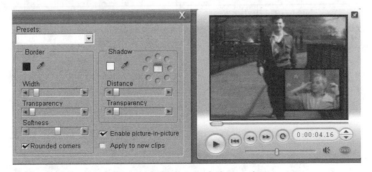

Figure 9.56 Here's my final P-I-P, Dad on Dad, then and now.

To customize the P-I-P Shadow:

1. To choose shadow color, click the solid-colored box beneath the Color text label (**Figure 9.57**).

   Studio Plus's Color selection dialog box opens (Figure 9.54).

2. Choose the desired color by selecting it from the Basic colors or Custom colors palette or by clicking a color on the spectrum.

3. If you want, save your custom color by clicking the Add to Custom Colors button (Ctrl+A). Saving your custom color helps you maintain uniformity as you work.

4. Click OK to close the dialog box.

5. Use the control sliders in the Shadow box to adjust the shadow's distance from the P-I-P video and its transparency.

6. On the upper right of the Shadow box, click a radio button to move the shadow to a different location around the P-I-P video.

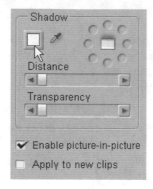

Figure 9.57 Click this icon to choose a color for your shadow.

✔ Tips

- In addition to choosing the shadow color via the Color dialog box, you can also click the eyedropper beneath the Color text label and then select the desired color in the video showing in the Player.

- Shadows, like borders, are generally used to distinguish the P-I-P from the Background video. For this reason, I recommend using either borders or shadows, but not both, since the double dose can make the P-I-P look a bit garish.

To customize P-I-P transparency:

◆ The P-I-P slider starts out on the extreme left, which is zero transparency. To customize the transparency of the P-I-P, adjust the Transparency slider to the right. This makes the P-I-P less visible against the Background video (**Figure 9.58**).

To delete the P-I-P effect:

◆ To delete the P-I-P effect, do *one or more of the following*:

   ▲ Uncheck the Enable Picture-in-Picture checkbox (Figure 9.49).

   Studio Plus deletes the effect and only the Overlay video shows in the Player window.

   ▲ Delete the Overlay video.

   Studio Plus deletes the Overlay video and the Background video shows in the Player window.

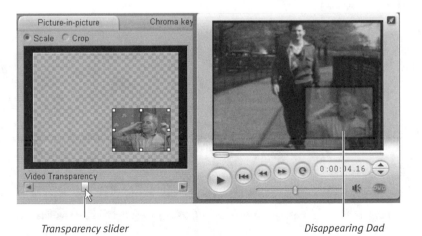

Transparency slider

Disappearing Dad

Figure 9.58 Drag this slider to the right to make the P-I-P more transparent. Now Dad looks like Patrick Swayze in *Ghost*!

Accessing Advanced P-I-P Controls

To a degree, Studio Plus's new P-I-P and Chroma key controls are simply accessible front ends to more advanced controls available via the normal special effects interface (see "Learning the Special Effects Interface," earlier in this chapter). In the case of P-I-P controls, the advanced interface offers controls that extend your creative opportunities beyond simple P-I-P.

For example, in a recent *PC Magazine* article, I tested different methods for digitizing 8 mm film. As with many technology comparisons, seeing the footage side by side often makes it easy to identify the pros and cons of each product offering.

As shown in **Figure 9.59**, using the advanced Picture-in-Picture controls, which you can apply to both the Video and Overlay tracks, you can crop, resize, and position both tracks in a highly customizable, side-by-side display. This is just one example of the effects enabled with the advanced P-I-P controls.

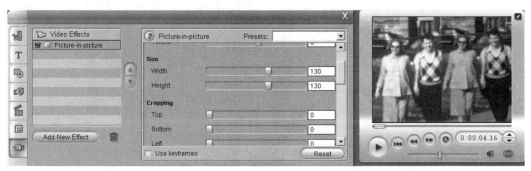

Figure 9.59 The advanced P-I-P controls enable advanced effects like placing videos side by side. That's some snazzy sweater, eh?

Figure 9.60 Click here to access the advanced P-I-P controls.

To access the advanced P-I-P controls:

◆ With Studio Plus open to the Picture-in-Picture controls, click the Add an Effect to a Video Clip icon (**Figure 9.60**).

Studio Plus opens the controls shown in Figure 9.59.

About Chroma Key

The most common application of Chroma keying is on the evening news, when you see the weatherperson standing in front of a weather map. Actually, he or she is video-taped standing in front of a green wall while the weather map is contained in a separate video feed. To combine the two, the video editing program at the TV station eliminates the green background and superimposes the weatherperson over the video containing the weather.

Studio 10 works the same way. After getting the two videos properly placed in the Time-line, you tell Studio Plus which color to eliminate from the Overlay video, usually either green or blue. Then Studio Plus super-imposes the video that wasn't eliminated into the Background video.

Software aside, to produce a high-quality Chroma key, you need to shoot your video correctly.

About Chroma Key Controls

Figure 9.61 contains Studio's Chroma key controls. Since they're unique to the Chroma key operation, I'll define them before getting started.

◆ **Key Color.** The key color is the color you're eliminating from the Overlay video before superimposing the remaining segments into the Background video (e.g., the green wall against which the weatherperson is videotaped). As you'll see, you'll choose the key color by clicking the eyedropper beneath the Key Color text label, and then clicking the background in the Overlay video.

◆ **Color Tolerance.** When shooting video for Chroma key, you shoot against a solid background, usually either cloth or a painted wall. Though you do your best to minimize them, there are always slight variations in the background color due to shadows or minor irregularities, like small wrinkles or folds in background cloth or dirt or paint strokes on painted walls. Increasing the color tolerance tells Studio to eliminate a broader range of colors, which helps eliminate these irregularities.

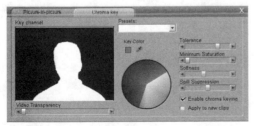

Figure 9.61 Here are Studio Plus's new Chroma key controls.

◆ **Saturation Minimum.** This control increases and decreases the saturation value eliminated by the Chroma key. During my tests, I consistently produced the best result with this slider set all the way to the left.

◆ **Softness.** According to the Studio help file, this slider controls "the density of the underlying video." During my tests, I consistently produced the best result with this slider set all the way to the left.

◆ **Spill Suppression.** In most Chroma key projects, some of the background color from the Overlay video "spills" onto the Background video, almost always at the edges between the two videos (e.g., some fringes of the green wall behind the weatherperson spill onto the weather map in the background). Spill Suppression turns this spillover to gray, making it much less noticeable. During my tests, I consistently produced the best result with this slider set all the way to the right.

◆ **Transparency.** This control affects the transparency of the image in the Overlay track. Drag it to the right to make the image more transparent, à la Patrick Swayze in *Ghost*.

◆ **Enable Chroma Keying.** This checkbox enables and disables Chroma keying.

◆ **Apply to New Clips.** Checking this checkbox applies the same Chroma key values to all subsequent clips dragged into the Overlay track.

◆ **Key Channel.** This provides another view of the effectiveness of the Chroma key controls. When the background is completely black and the edges clean, and the foreground clear of black specs, the controls are set to their optimum positions.

To apply a Chroma key effect:

1. Drag the background video clip to the Video track.

2. Drag the clip shot against the Chroma key background to the Overlay track.

3. At the upper left of the Movie window, click the Open/Close Video Toolbox icon (Figure 9.48).

   The Video toolbox opens.

4. On the left side of the toolbox, click the Edit the Video Overlay Using Picture-in-Picture or Chroma Keying icon (Figure 9.49).

5. Click the Chroma Key tab above the Key Channel window.

   Studio opens the Chroma Key control window (**Figure 9.62**).

Click the eyedropper.   Select a color.

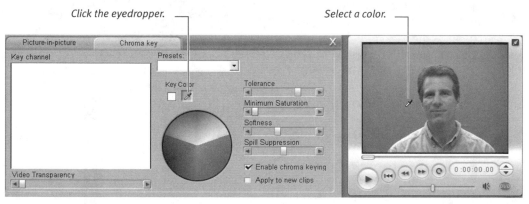

Figure 9.62 Now you're ready to Chroma key out the background.

Figure 9.63 That got most of it; now let's work on the fringe around the edges.

6. If the Enable Chroma Keying checkbox isn't enabled, click the checkbox.

7. Click the eyedropper beneath the Key Color text label and click the background color in the Overlay video in the Player.

Studio should immediately eliminate most of the background (**Figure 9.63**).

8. Adjust the Color Tolerance slider to the right to eliminate the remaining background color from the combined videos. To find the optimum value, do *one or more of the following*:

▲ Use the slider bar beneath the Player window to scan through the entire Chroma key.

▲ Watch for black spots in the white portion of the Key channel as shown on the left in **Figure 9.64**. This indicates that the Color Tolerance value is too high. Adjust the value to the left until the black spots are gone.

continues on next page

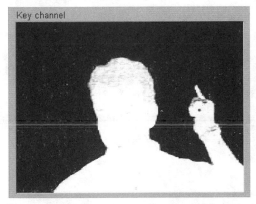 

Figure 9.64 Note the black spots in the image on the left. This means that the Color Tolerance value is too high and is eating into the subject. Better back off by dragging the slider back to the left, producing the result shown on the right.

ABOUT CHROMA KEY CONTROLS

9. Adjust the Saturation Minimum and Softness values all the way to the left.

10. Adjust Spill Suppression all the way to the right.

11. If desired, adjust the Transparency value to the desired levels.

12. If desired, click the Apply to New Clips checkbox to apply the selected values to other clips dragged to the Overlay track.

✔ Tips

■ Most Chroma key sets are slightly lighter at the top because this region of the frame is closer to the lights. You can see this in Figure 9.62, where the background is lighter at the top than on the bottom. For this reason, I choose a color in the middle of the screen, which provides an average value between the brightest and darkest regions. This improves my chances for a high-quality Chroma key.

■ Though Studio has two Chroma key presets—one for a blue screen, one for a green screen—I recommend ignoring the presets and starting from scratch, since even small differences in color values between the presets and your actual footage can produce dramatically different results.

■ You can apply the P-I-P and Chroma key effects to the same video simultaneously.

■ You can access Studio's advanced Chroma key controls by clicking the Add an Effect to a Video Clip icon (**Figure 9.65**). This gives you the ability to add keyframes and an Invert Key checkbox, which reverses the effect, keying out the subject and superimposing the rest of the frame over the background video.

Figure 9.65 The advanced Chroma Keyer controls add the artsy invert key shown in the Player and the ability to apply key frames.

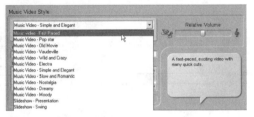

Figure 9.66
Let's create a
SmartMovie.
Click here to start.

Figure 9.67 Pick your music video style here.

Creating Music Videos Automatically

One of the more exciting features of Studio 10 is the ability to create a music video automatically. This capability, called SmartMovie, is ideal for footage like the 30 minutes I shot during our visit to the Charleston Aquarium: footage with no plot, no highs, no lows, nothing to turn into an interesting story. Even condensed, it would be painful for the grandparents to watch.

However, cut it up into short, tasty segments, add a zesty background music clip, and you've got a four-minute music video that will have viewers tapping their toes and clapping their hands. While this could take hours to accomplish manually, Studio does it all automatically.

To automatically create a music video:

1. Drag the target video footage to the Video track.

    Note that the video footage should be at least twice as long as the background music you'll be using. You can (and should) edit out scenes as desired before producing the music video.

2. At the upper left of the Movie window, click the Open/Close Video Toolbox icon (Figure 9.48).

3. On the left side of the Video toolbox, click the Create a Music Video Automatically icon (**Figure 9.66**).

4. From the Music Video Style list, choose the target style (**Figure 9.67**).

    Note the description of the style in the callout box to the right of the drop-down box.

continues on next page

CREATING MUSIC VIDEOS AUTOMATICALLY

5. Do *one of the following:*

▲ Select the Use Clips in Random Order checkbox (Figure 9.66).

Studio will use the clips in random order, promoting smoothness but losing continuity.

▲ Don't select the Use Clips in Random Order checkbox.

Studio will maintain narrative continuity, but this option will limit Studio's choice of clips, which could degrade the smoothness of the music video.

6. Click the add music to your project link to add music to the music track (**Figure 9.68**).

Studio opens the Add Music to Smart Movie window (**Figure 9.69**).

7. Choose one of the three options in Figure 9.69 and follow the prompts to select a music file.

Note that you can choose multiple songs, which Studio inserts into the Music track. The cumulative length of the music you select—whether one song or several—determines the length of the SmartMovie.

8. Enter the opening title and closing credits (**Figure 9.70**).

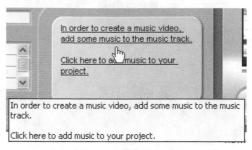

Figure 9.68 Click here to add audio.

Figure 9.69 Choose your option and follow the prompts.

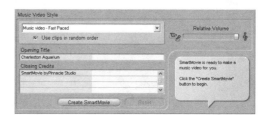

Figure 9.70 Add opening title and credits and click Create SmartMovie.

Figure 9.71 Working! Working!

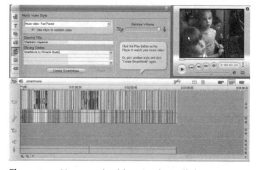

Figure 9.72 Your music video. Look at all those cuts. This would have taken hours by hand.

9. Set the Relative Volume slider completely to the right to prioritize background music over the original audio from the video.

   There may be situations where you want to maintain the original audio, but I can't think of any, since it will be completely chopped up and placed in random order by Studio while creating the music video.

10. Click Create SmartMovie.

   Studio loads the background audio file and then starts creating the SmartMovie (**Figure 9.71**). The techniques used are proprietary, but Pinnacle seems to be gravitating toward all the facial close-ups, using these as the primary video content and then matching the beat of the song to transition and effect timing.

   Studio produces the SmartMovie (**Figure 9.72**).

✔ Tips

- If you don't like the resulting video, you can select another music video style, click Create SmartMovie, and try again. Or, you can click Reset and restore the Timeline and all assets to their pre-SmartMovie condition.

- You can edit any component of the completed SmartMovie as desired, though significant edits, like shifting clips on the Timeline, could result in a loss of synchronization.

DESIGNING TITLES AND MENUS

Studio's Title editor is one of its most important tools, performing double duty to create both titles and DVD menus. Fortunately, the Title editor, formerly known as Title Deko, has always been both elegant and easy to learn.

To start, here's a quick function flyover. First, for all video productions, DVD or otherwise, the Title editor creates full-screen titles, positioned on the Video track, that introduce the movie or new sections, or show final credits.

Second, again for all video productions, the Title editor produces *overlay* titles, positioned on the Title track, which are displayed over your videos. These are useful for adding logos or text descriptions that enhance the video. For example, you could have the title "Billy's First Birthday" running along the bottom of a clip showing the happy child with chocolate cake all over his face.

Finally, the Title editor also produces the menus needed to navigate through and around your DVD titles.

Note that the Title editor works identically for both 4:3 and 16:9 projects. Just be sure to be in the proper mode before starting your title or menu because the dimensions are completely different. See "Working with the Album's Views and Tools" in Chapter 6 for details on switching between the two aspect ratios.

Opening the Title Editor

At last count, there were approximately 6,583 ways to open the Title editor, but I'm sure I missed a few. Just joking, of course, but here are the easy ways to get the job done.

To open the Title editor:

1. Position the Timeline scrubber at the desired title insertion point (**Figure 10.1**).

2. From the Studio menu, choose Toolbox > Create Title (**Figure 10.2**).

   The title creation screen opens (**Figure 10.3**).

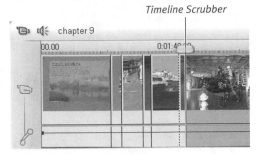

Timeline Scrubber

Figure 10.1 You can open the Title editor from either the Video track or the Title track. First position the Timeline scrubber where you want the title inserted.

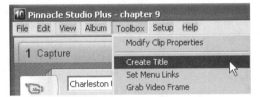

Figure 10.2 One of the many ways to open the Title editor.

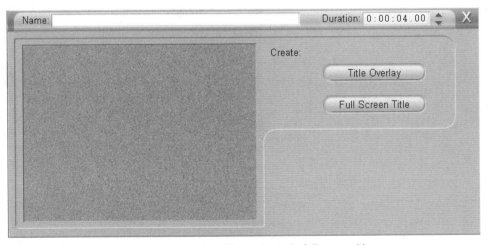

Figure 10.3 Here's where you choose between a title overlay and a full-screen title.

3. Do *one of the following:*

▲ Click the Title Overlay button to create a title that appears over your video on the Title track.

The Title editor opens, displaying the video that will appear behind the title to help you design and place your title (**Figure 10.4**).

▲ Click the Full Screen Title button to create a title that appears instead of video.

The Title editor opens, with no video displayed since the full-screen title displaces the video on the Video track.

Figure 10.4 The Title editor for a title overlay, with the underlying video displayed. Get comfortable; you're going to be here for a while.

To open the Title editor (easier):

Do *one of the following:*

1. From the Edit screen, click the Show Titles icon at the left of the Album (**Figure 10.5**).
   The Titles tab opens (**Figure 10.6**).

2. Select the desired title and do *one of the following:*

   ▲ Drag the title to the Video track to create a full-screen title (**Figure 10.7**).

   ▲ Drag the title to the Title track to create an overlay title (**Figure 10.8**).

3. Once the selected title is on the track, double-click the title (**Figure 10.9**).
   The Title editor opens with the selected title (**Figure 10.10**).

Or

◆ Double-click the Title track at the desired location for the title overlay. The Title editor opens, displaying the underlying video (Figure 10.4).
   Note that this way (the easiest method) works only for overlay titles.

✔ Tips

- The Title track is beneath the Video track. To make Studio display a title over the video, you actually place it under the Video track.

- If you work with titles a lot (and who doesn't?), the F11 (don't save) and F12 (save title) keys become pretty handy. Often it's easier to deep-six a title by pressing F11 and starting over than it is to attempt the multiple undos necessary to get back to square one.

Figure 10.5 Studio includes an album of very useful titles. Here's where you find them.

Figure 10.6 Three pages of time-savers and idea generators.

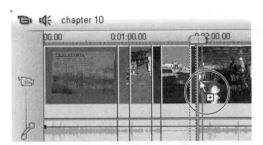

Figure 10.7 Placing the title on the Video track.

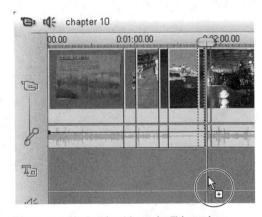

Figure 10.8 Placing the title on the Title track.

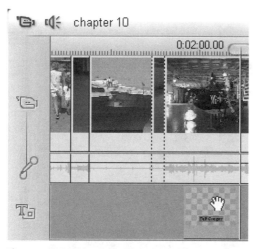

Figure 10.9 Double-click an existing title to open the Title editor.

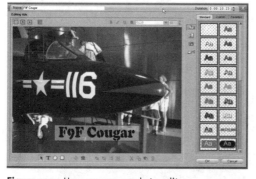

Figure 10.10 Here you go, ready to edit.

Full screen title   Title overlay

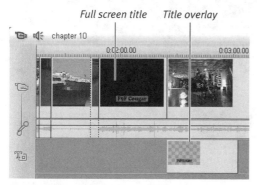

Figure 10.11 Where full-screen titles and title overlays end up on the Timeline.

■ **Figure 10.11** illustrates the positioning of full-screen and overlay titles. As mentioned earlier, Studio places full-screen titles on the Video track, where they displace the video for their duration. In contrast, Studio places overlay titles on the Title track, where they appear over other videos. If you change your mind about whether you want your title to appear in overlay or full-screen mode, but don't want to redo your design, simply drag the title into the other track at the same position in the Timeline.

■ You can only place full-screen titles between scenes, before the first scene, or following the last scene. Drag a title to a position on the Video track and Studio will place it at the nearest scene change. In contrast, you can place overlay titles at any point in the Title track.

To close the Title editor and save your work:

◆ Do *one of the following*:

▲ Click OK in the bottom right corner.

▲ Choose File > Close Title Tool (or press F12).

▲ Click the X at the upper right of the Title editor.

To close the Title editor without saving:

◆ Do *one of the following*:

▲ Click the Cancel button at the bottom right.

▲ Choose File > Cancel Title Tool (or press F11).

Looking at the Title Editor

Once you've opened the Title editor, take a look at its interface and tool sets (**Figure 10.12**). You can access many of these functions by using the Studio menu as well as by clicking the onscreen icons.

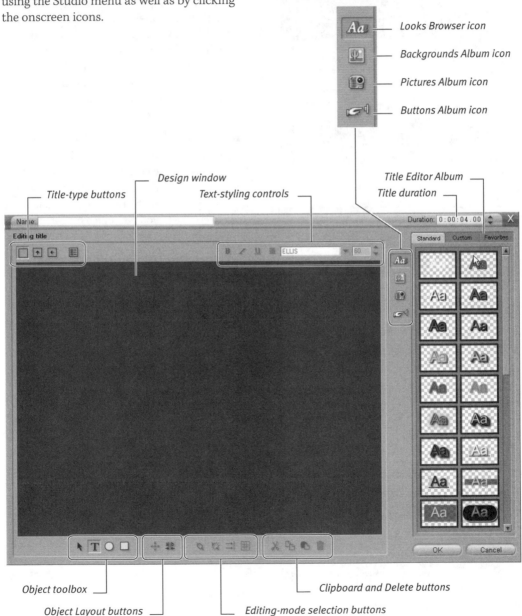

Looks Browser icon

Backgrounds Album icon

Pictures Album icon

Buttons Album icon

Title-type buttons

Design window

Text-styling controls

Title Editor Album

Title duration

Object toolbox

Object Layout buttons

Editing-mode selection buttons

Clipboard and Delete buttons

Figure 10.12 The Title editor for a full-screen title, which takes over the entire screen.

Design window: Studio's Design window is a WYSIWYG (what you see is what you get) design area. When you're designing title overlays, you'll see the underlying video in the Design window (Figure 10.4). But when you're working with full-screen titles, the Design window starts out empty.

Title-safe zones: When creating titles for DVD and other productions viewed primarily on a TV, keep all title elements inside these zones. Otherwise, they may be truncated.

Title-type buttons: These buttons control the type of title: static, rolling up and down, crawling sideways, or DVD menu.

Text-styling controls: These controls are similar to those in most word-processing programs, with the addition of some excellent alignment and word-wrapping tools.

Object toolbox: These controls allow you to create and position text-, circle-, and square-based objects that serve as either design elements or menu buttons.

Editing-mode selection buttons: Use these buttons to switch into and out of advanced editing modes for kerning text and deforming objects.

Object layout buttons: My favorite. Nothing is more irritating than menu components that are out of alignment or not quite the right size. These tools let you group, align, and resize objects for a more uniform appearance.

Clipboard and Delete buttons: When you're designing titles and menus, often the simplest approach is to copy and paste text attributes and other labels. These tools simplify these common tasks.

Title Editor Album: Studio includes libraries of looks, backgrounds, pictures, and menu elements to use in your productions. Generally, you can customize these, add your own, and save them in a Favorites Album.

Title duration: Here's where you can customize the duration of your title (as with still images, you can also accomplish the same goal by dragging the title to the desired length on the Timeline).

Adding and Editing Text

Studio's titles can be composed of text and imported images, as well as circles, squares, and derivatives thereof drawn with the Title editor's own drawing tools.

We'll start with text and then examine other components and how they all work together.

To add menu text:

1. Open the Title editor using any of the techniques described earlier in this chapter.

   You should see an I adjacent to the pointer, indicating that the Text tool is active. If you don't see the I, click the T in the Object toolbox at the bottom of the screen (**Figure 10.13**).

2. In the Design window, click where you want the text to appear.

   Studio displays a bounding box for your text (**Figure 10.14**).

3. Type the desired text.

4. Click anywhere outside the box to set the text (**Figure 10.15**).

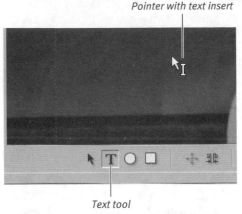

Pointer with text insert

Text tool

Figure 10.13 Click the Text tool to insert text. Studio rewards you with a special text-insert pointer.

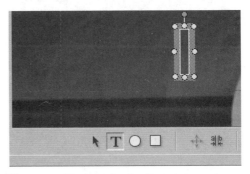

Figure 10.14 The bounding box is ready to receive your text.

Figure 10.15 Pretty bland, eh? We'll spice it up in a minute.

Figure 10.16 Select the box to edit the text. See the thin text-insert pointer after the word *Point*?

Figure 10.17 Studio highlights the text you're about to replace.

Figure 10.18 The new text.

To add menu text:

1. Select the menu text.
   A bounding box appears around the text.

2. Click inside the text at the desired insertion point (**Figure 10.16**).
   You should see a text-entry pointer where you clicked, which you can move using the left and right arrow keys on your keyboard.

3. Type the desired text.
   Studio adds the text.

4. To set your changes, click anywhere outside the box.

To replace menu text:

1. Select the menu text.

2. Drag over the text that you want to replace or hold down the Shift key and use the arrow keys to select the text you want to replace.
   Studio highlights the selected text (**Figure 10.17**).

3. Type the desired text.
   Studio replaces the text (**Figure 10.18**).

4. To set your changes, click anywhere outside the box.

ADDING AND EDITING TEXT

To move text:

1. Select the text.

   A gray bounding box appears around the text object (Figure 10.18).

2. Click the bounding box.

   Yellow control points appear around the box, a green dot appears above the box, and the pointer turns into the move-object pointer (**Figure 10.19**).

   The move-object pointer will disappear if it's moved outside the bounding box.

3. Drag the text to the desired location.

✔ Tip

■ You can use the arrow keys to move text (and all objects) one pixel in any direction— a great way to fine-tune your positioning.

Figure 10.19 Select the text twice to move or resize it. First you get the gray bounding box and then these control points (little dots) on the box outside the title.

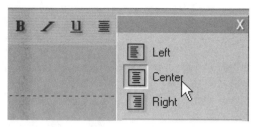

Figure 10.20 Studio's alignment controls work like those in most programs.

Figure 10.21 To change text attributes, simply highlight the text and change the attributes.

Figure 10.22 The Ellis font supplies that painted-on military look.

To change font, text attributes, and alignment:

1. Select the text.

A gray bounding box appears around the text object (Figure 10.18).

2. Click the bounding box.

Yellow control points appear around the box, a green dot appears above the box, and the pointer turns into the move-object pointer.

All text-styling controls are now active. You know the drill for bold, italics, underlining, font, and font size.

3. To change the alignment, do *one of the following*:

▲ Click the Text Justification icon at the top and select Left, Center, or Right alignment (**Figure 10.20**).

▲ From the Studio menu, choose Title > Justify Text. Then choose the desired alignment.

4. To change font or text attributes such as size, boldfacing, italics, and underlining, drag over the text that you want to modify and then choose the desired attributes (**Figure 10.21**).

Studio changes the attributes (**Figure 10.22**).

✔ Tip

■ The Title editor's shrinking, scaling, and word-wrap options are discussed later in this chapter, since most users pick their styles before fine-tuning their text.

ADDING AND EDITING TEXT

Using Studio's Styles

There are more extensive text-editing capabilities to explore, but if you're like me, you'll produce the most professional-looking titles by using styles contained in Studio's Looks browser.

When you create your first text title, Studio applies the default style at the top left of the Looks browser (**Figure 10.23**), which is open by default when you open the Title editor. Otherwise, to open the Looks browser, click the Looks icon at the left of the browser window or go to the Studio menu and choose Title > Album > Looks.

As you scroll down the Looks browser, you'll see increasingly creative title presets. The upcoming tasks show you how to apply and customize Studio's Looks. Note that changing styles doesn't affect font, font size, alignment, or any other text attribute.

To apply a new look to text:

1. Select the text to adjust and click the gray bounding box to display the control points (Figure 10.19)

2. Using the scroll bar on the right of the Looks browser, scroll down to the desired style (**Figure 10.24**).

3. Select the style with the pointer.

   As soon as you select the style, Studio applies it to the selected text.

✔ Tip

■ If you hover your pointer over any style, Studio displays a submenu containing eight styles with different combinations of color, edge, and shadow (**Figure 10.25**). Move your mouse, and the submenu disappears, or you can click the X in the upper-right corner.

Figure 10.23 Studio's styles are a real blessing for creatively challenged individuals (like me); you can apply them to text and other objects.

Scroll bar

Figure 10.24 Select the text to change; then select a new style, and you're done. Use the scroll bar on the right to scroll down the browser.

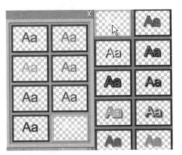

Figure 10.25 Hover your mouse over a style to see a submenu containing eight similar styles.

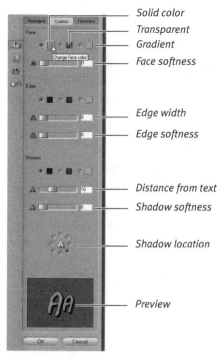

Solid color
Transparent
Gradient
Face softness

Edge width

Edge softness

Distance from text

Shadow softness

Shadow location

Preview

Figure 10.26 Wait, there's more! You can even customize the styles. Note the Solid color, Gradient, and Transparent color swatches for the text face, edge, and shadow.

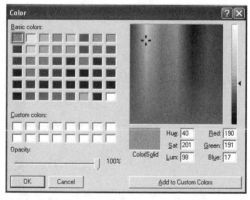

Figure 10.27 Studio's Color selection dialog box. You can store your custom colors, a useful feature when you need to repeat them.

Figure 10.28 Here's where you edit the gradients. Each color box opens the Color Selection screen.

To customize a solid text color:

1. Select the style to customize (Figure 10.24).

2. In the Looks browser, select the Custom tab (**Figure 10.26**).

3. In the Face section, select the radio button next to the solid-colored box with the Tool Tip Change Face Color.

4. Click the solid-colored box.

   Studio's Color selection dialog box opens (**Figure 10.27**).

5. Choose the desired color by selecting it from the Basic Colors or Custom Colors palette or by clicking a color on the spectrum.

6. If you want, save your custom color by clicking the Add to Custom Colors button (Ctrl+A).

   Saving your custom color helps you maintain uniformity as you work.

7. Click OK to close the dialog box.

To customize a gradient text color:

1. Select the style that you want to customize.

2. In the Looks browser, select the Custom tab.

3. In the Face section, select the radio button next to the gradient-colored box.

4. Click the Gradient box.

   Studio's Gradient Selection dialog box opens (**Figure 10.28**). The boxes at each corner of the Gradient preview box control the gradient blend.

5. Click any box to open its Color Selection dialog box. You can configure each of the four colors independently.

6. Click the X in the upper-right corner to close the Gradient Selection dialog box.

USING STUDIO'S STYLES

299

To adjust text softness:

1. Select the style that you want to customize.

2. In the Looks browser, select the Custom tab.

3. In the Face section, select the solid or gradient radio button and adjust the face softness with the Face slider, viewing the results in the Preview window (**Figure 10.29**).

   Softness controls the definition of the text face. At 0 the face is completely sharp, while at 30 it's very indistinct, causing the text to blend into the background.

   If you have text selected in the Title editor, Studio applies these modifications to the title in near-real time.

To adjust text edges:

1. In the Edge section, select the solid or gradient radio button and then change the text color as described in "To customize a solid text color" or "To customize a gradient text color" earlier in this section.

2. Use the Edge sliders to modify the edge width and softness.

   Width refers to the width of the edge, while edge softness, like face softness, relates to how sharply Studio defines the edge. The easiest way to get a feel for this is through experimentation.

Face softness

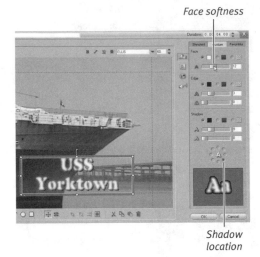

Shadow location

Figure 10.29 Use the softness sliders to control text strength; click the desired radio button to set shadow location.

Figure 10.30 The Favorites Album can come in very handy, especially when you decide to change a style.

Figure 10.31 Click the Suitcase icon to save your current style.

Add the current look to Favorites

Delete the selected look

Figure 10.32 See the new style added to your Favorites.

To adjust text shadows:

1. In the Shadow section, select the solid or gradient radio button and then change the text color as described in "To customize a solid text color" or "To customize a gradient text color" earlier in this chapter.

2. To modify the distances of the shadow from the original text and shadow softness, use the Shadow sliders.

3. To change the position of the shadow, click the button for the desired Shadow location.

✔ Tip

■ There are no customization options for the transparent text style.

To add a style to the Favorites Album:

1. Select the Favorites tab to open the Favorites Album (**Figure 10.30**).

2. Click the Suitcase icon to add the currently selected style (**Figure 10.31**).
   Studio adds the style to the Favorites Album (**Figure 10.32**).

To delete a style from the Favorites Album:

1. From within the Favorites Album, select the offending style.

2. Click the Trash Can icon to delete the style.

✔ Tips

■ Saving styles in your Favorites Album is very convenient when you're changing the styles of multiple objects. Otherwise, you have to hunt through the Looks browser each time you apply the style.

■ You can save any style in the Favorites Album; it doesn't have to be one that you've edited.

■ Think twice before deleting a style, because you cannot bring the style back with Undo.

About Text Scaling and Word Wrapping

Studio's text-resizing and word-wrapping controls (**Figure 10.33**) can be confusing at first, so I'll explain a couple of concepts that made them easier for me to understand.

First, the top two controls, Shrink to Fit and Scale to Fit, are alternatives for managing text appearance, typically used when a text string doesn't fit into the desired space. This is shown in the top of **Figure 10.34**, where the text "Aiken-Rhett House" has too many characters to fit in the same space as "Beach and Pool" beneath it. Since they're both text menu buttons on the same page, I want their appearance to match as closely as possible.

One way to solve the problem is to remove characters from the title (like the word "House," for example) and fit it that way, and I may ultimately choose that approach. However, the Shrink to Fit and Scale to Fit functions provide two alternatives.

Figure 10.33 Your shrinking, scaling, and word-wrap controls.

As shown in the middle of Figure 10.34, Shrink to Fit shrinks the text to fit it into the horizontal space without distorting the font. Obviously, the text size is slightly smaller, but the overall size and appearance is very similar to the Beach and Pool text string we're trying to match.

In contrast, with Scale to Fit, Studio scales the text to fit the available horizontal and vertical space, producing the larger, slightly distorted look on the bottom of Figure 10.34. This looks nothing like the "Beach and Pool," so it's not a good alternative in this application.

The word-wrapping controls operate like this. When you select Word Wrap On and then resize the text box, Studio resizes the box and

Starting point

Shrink to fit

Scale to fit

Figure 10.34 Shrink to Fit doesn't distort the letters in any way, while Scale to Fit does.

About Text Scaling and Word Wrapping *(continued)*

rewraps the words to make them fit, but does not change the size. **Figure 10.35** illustrates this point, working from the same starting point as Figure 10.34. Here, I selected Word Wrap On and made the box smaller. As you can see at the top of the figure, the text size is the same, but Studio adjusted the word wrap to make the text fit.

Then I selected Word Wrap Off, and Studio disabled Word Wrap and converted a two-line title to a one-line title.

Between you, me, and the fencepost, I find Studio's word-wrapping controls unintuitive and not particularly useful, and I rarely use them. Instead, I insert carriage returns in my titles to control word-wrapping directly.

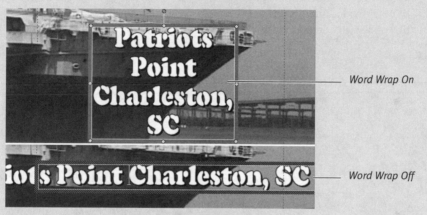

Figure 10.35 Select Word Wrap On, and Studio wraps your text for you, but doesn't change font size. Word Wrap Off returns you to the status quo.

Resizing and Justifying Text

Even after applying Pinnacle's wonderful styles, you still may have to resize and/or justify your text. When resizing, note that Studio will adjust your text differently depending on which scaling, shrinking, or word-wrapping option you've selected. See the preceding sidebar, "About Text Scaling and Word Wrapping," for details.

To justify text, you use a control to place the text in one of nine divided areas, a simple way to ensure consistency among menus.

To resize text:

1. Select the text that you want to adjust and click the gray bounding box to display the control points.

2. If the Move, Scale, and Rotate tool isn't selected at the bottom of the Title Editor window, click the icon to enable the tool (**Figure 10.36**).

3. To shrink or expand the text, do *any of the following:*

   ▲ Hold the pointer over a corner control point of the bounding box to convert it into a two-sided arrow (**Figure 10.37**). Press the mouse button and drag the control point in or out to shrink or expand the text as desired. If you've selected Shrink to Fit or Word Wrap On, you can freely resize the height and width of the text, but if you've selected Scale to Fit, Studio restricts your scaling so that the aspect ratio of the text doesn't change.

Figure 10.36 Click the Move, Scale, and Rotate tool to resize your title text.

Figure 10.37 With this double arrow, you can adjust both the text height and width.

Figure 10.38 Note the small double-arrow pointer on the right control point. Drag this to adjust width but not height.

Figure 10.39 You knew this was coming. The small double-arrow pointer on the bottom is used to adjust height but not width.

Figure 10.40 Use the Justify tool to place your text in one of nine positions.

Figure 10.41 Note that Studio respects the title-safe zone when it justifies the text.

▲ Hold the pointer over the left- or right-side control point to convert it into a two-sided arrow (**Figure 10.38**). Press the left mouse button and drag the control point in or out to shrink or expand the text.

▲ Hold the pointer over either the top or bottom control point to convert it into a two-sided arrow (**Figure 10.39**). Press the left mouse button and drag the control point in or out to shrink or expand the text.

To justify text:

1. Select the text that you want to adjust and click the gray bounding box to display the control points.

2. Do *one of the following:*

▲ On the Title Editor toolbar at the bottom of the screen, click the Justify tool, which looks like a tic-tac-toe board (**Figure 10.40**).

▲ From the Studio menu, choose Title > Justify.

3. Select the desired area in the Justify tool. Studio aligns the text accordingly (**Figure 10.41**).

After positioning your text, the Justify tool displays a black dot in the selected spot, reflecting the current positioning.

✔ Tip

■ The Justify tool is easily confused with the Text Justify (text alignment) tool discussed in "To change font, text attributes, and alignment" earlier in this chapter. The Text Justify tool justifies or aligns the text within the text object itself, like the alignment tools in a word processor. In contrast, the Justify tool aligns the text object to a location in the menu or title.

RESIZING AND JUSTIFYING TEXT

Kerning and Leading Text

Occasionally you may want to adjust the space between letters or characters, a process called *kerning*, or change the vertical space between lines of text, called *leading*. Here's how.

To kern text:

1. Select the text that you want to adjust and click the gray bounding box to display the control points.

2. On the Title Editor toolbar at the bottom, click the Set Kerning. Leading, and Skew tool (**Figure 10.42**).

3. Position the pointer over one of the side control points.

   The pointer changes to the kern pointer (**Figure 10.43**).

4. Drag the pointer in or out to achieve the desired spacing.

   Studio changes the distance between the letters (**Figure 10.44**).

To change the leading between text lines:

1. Select the text that you want to adjust and click the gray bounding box to display the control points.

2. On the Title Editor toolbar at the bottom, click the Set Kerning, Leading, and Skew tool (Figure 10.42).

3. Position the pointer over either the top or bottom control point (not the corner).

   The pointer changes to the kern pointer.

4. Drag the pointer up or down to achieve the desired spacing.

   Studio changes the distance between the words (**Figure 10.45**).

Figure 10.42 This font is too compressed for my taste. I'll fix it by clicking the Set Kerning, Leading, and Skew tool.

Figure 10.43 Place the kern pointer over a control point on the right or left and stretch out the text.

Figure 10.44 Note how much more space there is between the letters.

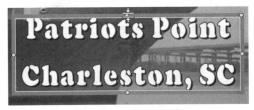

Figure 10.45 Place the kern pointer over the top or bottom control point to change the leading.

Figure 10.46 Use the top control point to rotate the text.

Figure 10.47 Rotate your text to the desired position.

Figure 10.48 You can also skew your text. Just grab and stretch.

Figure 10.49 Here's what happens.

Rotating and Skewing Text

Here are two additional design options: rotate and skew.

To rotate text:

1. Select the text that you want to adjust and click the gray bounding box to display the control points.

2. If the Move, Scale, and Rotate tool isn't selected, click the icon to enable the tool (Figure 10.36).

3. Move the pointer over the green control point atop the text object.

   The pointer changes to the rotate pointer (**Figure 10.46**).

4. Drag the pointer to rotate the text to the desired position.

   A dotted-line bounding box follows your progress.

5. Release the pointer when your text is in the desired position (**Figure 10.47**).

To skew text:

1. Select the text that you want to adjust and click the gray bounding box to display the control points.

2. On the Title Editor toolbar at the bottom, click the Set Kerning, Leading, and Skew tool (Figure 10.42).

3. Position the pointer over one of the control point corners.

   The pointer changes to the skew pointer (**Figure 10.48**).

4. Drag the text to the desired location.

   A dotted-line bounding box follows your progress.

5. Release the pointer when your text is in the desired position (**Figure 10.49**).

Using Full-Screen Titles

As you may recall, a full-screen title is any title that lives on the Video track, since it replaces the video completely, taking up the full screen. All full-screen titles initially have black backgrounds (**Figure 10.50**). You can go with that minimalist approach, or you can add a background, which can be a solid color, gradient, or full-screen image.

You can choose from Studio's range of useful background images or use your own. Just remember: all images used as a background run full screen and can't be resized and used as foreground design elements such as logos. For information on using images as logos, see "Adding Logos to Video" later in this chapter.

To create a single-color background:

1. In the Title editor, do *one of the following:*

    ▲ Click the Backgrounds icon at the left of the Title Editor Album (**Figure 10.51**).

    ▲ From the Studio menu, choose Title > Album > Backgrounds.

    The Backgrounds Album opens (**Figure 10.52**).

Figure 10.50 Here's what a full-screen title looks like when you first create it. It has no background—but we'll fix that in a hurry.

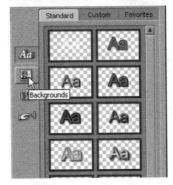

Figure 10.51 Getting to the Backgrounds Album.

Single-color background

Gradient background

Transparent background

Click to browse for
background images

Image background

Backgrounds library

Figure 10.52 Your four choices for menu backgrounds: solid, gradient, transparent, and image.

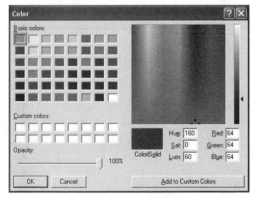

Figure 10.53 The familiar Color Selection dialog box.

2. Select the single-color background radio button (Figure 10.52).

3. To change colors, click the colored box next to the radio button.

Studio's Color Selection dialog box opens (**Figure 10.53**).

4. Choose the desired color by selecting it from the Basic Colors or Custom Colors palette or by clicking a color on the spectrum.

5. If you want, save your custom color by clicking the Add to Custom Colors button (Ctrl+A).

Saving the custom color helps you maintain uniformity as you work.

6. Click OK to close the dialog box.

Studio replaces the background with the selected color.

To create a gradient background:

1. In the Title editor, click the Backgrounds icon at the left of the Title Editor Album (Figure 10.51).

   The Backgrounds Album opens (Figure 10.52).

2. Select the gradient background radio button.

3. To change colors, click the colored box next to the gradient radio button.

   Studio's Gradient Selection dialog box opens (**Figure 10.54**). The boxes at each corner of the Gradient preview box control the gradient blend.

4. Click any box to open its Color Selection dialog box (Figure 10.53). You can configure each of the four colors independently.

5. Click the X in the upper-right corner to close the Gradient Selection dialog box.

   Studio replaces the background with the selected gradient.

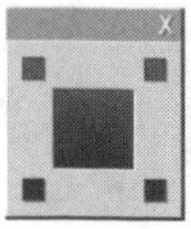

To create a transparent background:

1. In the Title editor, click the Backgrounds icon at the left of the Title Editor Album (Figure 10.51).

   The Backgrounds Album opens (Figure 10.52).

2. Select the transparent background radio button.

   This is the default setting for the background, for which there are no options. The background simply appears as black behind the menu or title components.

Figure 10.54 This is where you choose your gradient colors.

Figure 10.55 To change the background, just select the image you want.

Figure 10.56 You can use the images supplied by Pinnacle, or insert your own.

To select an image background:

1. In the Title editor, click the Backgrounds icon at the left of the Title Editor Album (Figure 10.51).

   The Backgrounds Album opens (Figure 10.52).

2. Select the image background radio button.

3. Do *one of the following:*

   ▲ To use an image from the Album, select the desired image.

   Studio replaces the background with the selected image (**Figure 10.55**).

   ▲ To use an image from another location, click the Folder icon to browse for images elsewhere (Figure 10.52). In the standard Open dialog box that appears, navigate to and select the desired image file.

   Studio replaces the background with the selected image and populates the Image browser on the right with the new files (**Figure 10.56**).

✔ Tips

■ The original location of Studio's excellent background images is Program Files > Pinnacle > Studio 10 > Backgrounds, should you need to find these images again.

■ If a selected image doesn't fill the screen in either height or width, Studio stretches the image proportionally (without distorting it) to fill either height or width, whichever is closer. For the most predictable results, prepare your background image files at your target output resolution, using 640 x 480 pixels for DVD, the resolution used for Pinnacle's background files.

■ For a complete discussion of image preparation, see "Editing Still Images" in Chapter 5.

USING FULL-SCREEN TITLES

Adding Logos to Video

Placing logos over videos is a nice professional touch, though in this situation Studio
presents a minor catch-22. Simply stated,
from the Title editor, you can place, move,
and resize a logo over your video, but you
can't make it transparent.

Alternatively, you can drag an image to the
Title track from the Still Images tab in the
Album and make it transparent (assuming
that you follow the rules discussed here), but
you can't move or resize the image or it
becomes a full-screen logo.

These are the general rules; this section
describes how to work within them. An
exception to the rules is discussed in the
sidebar "The Art of Being Transparent," later
in this chapter.

To overlay a logo on video:

1. Double-click the Title track at the desired
   location for the logo overlay.
   The Title editor opens.

2. In the Title editor, do *one of the following:*

   ▲ Click the Pictures icon at the left of
   the Title Editor Album (**Figure 10.57**).

   ▲ From the Studio menu, choose Title >
   Album > Pictures.

   The Pictures Album opens (**Figure 10.58**).

Figure 10.57 Click
the Pictures icon
to open the
Pictures Album.

Click to browse for pictures

Figure 10.58 The
Pictures Album.

Figure 10.59 Drag the image into the Design window. Unlike a background image, an image dragged from the Pictures Album can be scaled or moved.

3. If necessary, click the Folder icon to navigate to the directory containing your logos.

4. Drag the image into the Design window (**Figure 10.59**).

5. Move and resize the image as described in "To resize text" earlier in this chapter. Note that you can't skew or rotate the image, only resize and move it.

✔ Tips

■ Although you can't argue with the sheer elegance of the logo shown in Figure 10.59 (pretty cheesy, eh?), you probably wish the black background would go away. The sidebar "The Art of Being Transparent," later in this chapter, describes how to accomplish this.

■ The program of choice for creating titles and logos is Ulead Systems' Cool 3D Production Studio, available at www.ulead.com. Using one of Cool 3D's supplied templates, I created the logo shown in Figure 10.59 in about two minutes.

To make a logo transparent:

1. From the Still Images tab, drag the logo to the Title track (**Figure 10.60**).

   In the Player, Studio zooms the image to full screen and makes it transparent, so you can see segments of the video behind it.

2. Double-click the logo to open the Title editor (**Figure 10.61**).

   The logo is full screen and shows no transparency in the Title editor. In addition, selecting the logo raises no control points. The image looks fuzzy (though perhaps not in your small version of it) because the 160 x 120–resolution image was zoomed to full screen.

Figure 10.60 To make an image transparent, you must load it from the Album. See how this logo is transparent now?

Figure 10.61 Notice how the same logo shows no transparency in the Title editor.

Figure 10.62 Since you can't resize images placed on the Title track from the Album, you have to pre-make your logo files like this.

Figure 10.63 Here's how the logo looks in use.

✔ Tips

■ Studio assumes that the top-left pixel is the transparent color and eliminates this color when displaying the logo. In the Ozer Productions logo, the top-left pixel is black, the same color as the background to be eliminated. When you want to make an image transparent, computer-generated images work best, or real-world images carefully edited to produce a single, consistent background image.

■ Since you can't resize the logo when pulling it down from the Album, the best solution is to create a full-screen (640 x 480) image with the logo as a small component in the desired location (**Figure 10.62**). Remember to observe the title-safe zones when creating images in this fashion. **Figure 10.63** shows the image overlaying the video.

ADDING LOGOS TO VIDEO

The Art of Being Transparent

This section's introduction describes Studio's catch-22 when it comes to transparent logo overlay: if you drag in an image from the Title editor, you can move and resize it, but you cannot make it transparent; if you drag in an image from the Still Images tab of the Album, you can make it transparent, but you cannot move or resize it.

Not to worry; there is one undocumented exception to this catch. If you create a 32-bit image with an alpha channel for the desired transparency region, Studio recognizes and eliminates this region from the Title editor, allowing full moving and resizing control.

For example, of the three logos in **Figure 10.64**, two are transparent—including the Ozer Productions spinning globe, which has active edit points, proving that the logo is both resizable and movable. These were produced as 32-bit video overlays in Targa (TGA) format in Ulead's Cool 3D Studio. The third logo was output as a simple 24-bit bitmap file, and as you can see, it's not transparent. Note that Studio displays the two images as transparent in the Looks browser (it also displays another transparent logo not used in this example), showing a checkered gray pattern behind them instead of the pure black backgrounds of the other images.

In retrospect, it's not surprising that Studio recognizes a transparent alpha channel in images, since the program uses this technique to recognize transparent areas in DVD buttons (see "Working with Buttons" later in this chapter).

The bottom line is that if you understand how to produce 32-bit images with an alpha channel in programs like Cool 3D Studio and Adobe Photoshop, you can make your images transparent in Studio so that you can move and resize them at will in the Title editor. Check www.doceo.com/Studio9 for details on creating a transparent logo in Cool 3D Studio and Photoshop.

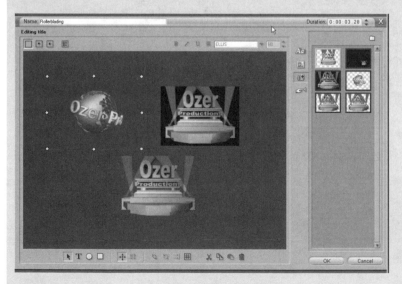

Figure 10.64 The Title editor can recognize transparency masks on 32-bit images with an alpha channel, providing the best of both worlds.

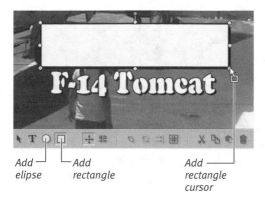

Add —┐   ┌—Add   Add —┐
elipse   └ rectangle   rectangle
                                     cursor

Figure 10.65 Studio lets you draw ellipses and rectangles in your titles. Click the desire shape and drag the desired area.

Creating and Editing Title Objects

Now that you're comfortable with text, it's time to describe how to add and edit title objects: ellipses and rectangles that you can use in your titles. Title objects serve quite nicely as text backgrounds or as stand-alone design components. You can assign Looks to Studio's title objects, and customize, skew, resize and reposition them at will, using the same techniques that you learned for text objects.

Let's study objects by creating a background for a text title. If you like consistent fonts and placement in your titles, and I definitely do, you're almost always going to need a solid background. Otherwise, at some point in the project, the background video will conflict with the title text, making it hard to read.

I'll show you how I like to create my backgrounds; you're obviously free to create your own look. In most instances, however, you will want to use a transparent box, since it's less obtrusive than a solid color.

To create a rectangle:

1. From the Title editor, click the Rectangle icon in the Object toolbox (**Figure 10.65**).

2. In the Design window, drag the pointer to draw the object (Figure 10.65).

   If you're creating a background for text, draw the object about the same height and width as the text.

✔ Tip

■ Studio applies whatever style you have selected when you draw the object. That's why the image in Figure 10.65 has both a shadow and black edge, neither of which I want in my text background.

To create a title background:

1. In the Custom panel, drag both Edge sliders all the way to the left (**Figure 10.66**). Studio removes the edge around the box.

2. Drag both Shadow sliders to the left. Studio removes the shadow from the box.

3. Click the Change Face icon. Studio opens the Color window.

4. Drag the Opacity control to approximately 50%.

5. Click OK to close the Color window.

6. Drag the box behind the title text (**Figure 10.67**).

7. Resize and reposition the text box to achieve the desired look and fit around the text.

✔ Tip

■ If the new object appears over the text title (instead of behind), you can adjust this with the layer controls discussed in "To Change Object Layers," later in this chapter.

Figure 10.67 This title will be legible irrespective of the content in the background video.

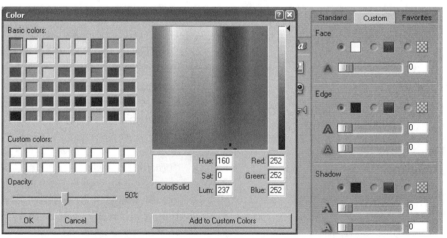

Figure 10.66 To create the ideal text background, lose the edges and shadows and make the rectangle about 50% transparent with the opacity slider.

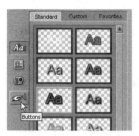

Figure 10.68 Time to start authoring! Step 1: open the Buttons Album.

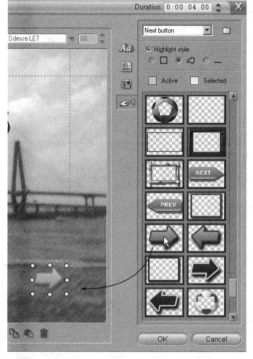

Figure 10.69 Drag the button from the Buttons Album to the Design window.

Working with Buttons

Buttons are interactive links on a menu that let viewers play content like video or a slide show, or jump to other menus. Studio supplies an album of buttons, and you can convert any ungrouped object to a button. Once you add a button to a title, it magically becomes a menu. Like titles, menus can be either full screen or overlays displayed over an underlying video track.

Studio's Title editor is a great place to produce attractive, custom menus, but you can also choose from an extensive range of customizable menus on the Disc Menus tab of the Album, accessible from the Edit menu. The easiest way to get started is to use the supplied templates, described in "Using Menu Templates" in Chapter 12, which also describes how to link content to buttons. The current chapter focuses exclusively on the mechanics of menu creation.

To add a button to a title:

1. In the Title editor, do *one of the following*:

   ▲ Click the Buttons icon at the left of the Title Editor Album (**Figure 10.68**).

   ▲ From the Studio menu, choose Title > Album > Buttons.

   Studio opens the Buttons Album.

2. Drag the desired button into the Design window (**Figure 10.69**).

   Studio inserts the button into the title.

✔ Tip

■ If you've created your own album of buttons, use the folder to the right of the drop-down menu at the top of the Buttons Album (Figure 10.71) to navigate to the appropriate folder.

To convert an object to a button:

1. Select the object that you want to convert and click the gray bounding box to display the control points (**Figure 10.70**).

2. At the top of the Buttons Album, open the drop-down menu (**Figure 10.71**).

3. Choose Normal Button.

   Studio converts the text to a button and highlights it with the default-selected color (**Figure 10.72**). When you return to the Menu view, you'll see that the Menu track is now active, and that the label M1, for Menu 1, appears at the top of the menu (**Figure 10.73**). Congratulations; you're now authoring a DVD!

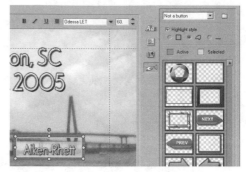

Figure 10.70 Or convert any menu object—text, rectangle, image—to a button. Start by clicking the object. Note that it's "Not a button" in the button selection tool.

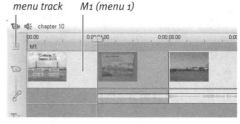

Figure 10.71 The four button types: Normal, Thumbnail, Previous, and Next.

menu track   M1 (menu 1)

Figure 10.73 Adding a button converts a title to a menu. Now the Menu track is activated, and Menu 1 (M1) is in place.

Figure 10.72 After converting text to a button, Studio highlights it with the default-selected color. This is the faint shadow you see beneath the highlighted text.

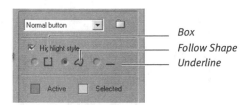

Figure 10.74 Buttons can have three highlight styles, shown here.

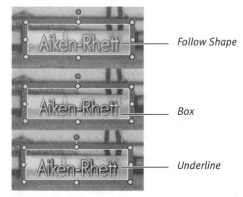

Figure 10.75 Here's what the three highlight styles look like when applied to a title. It's tough to see in this grayscale image, but the differences will be clear once you start to experiment.

To set a highlight style for a button:

1. Select the button that you want to modify and click the gray bounding box to display the control points (Figure 10.72).

2. At the top of the Buttons Album, choose *one of the following highlight styles* (**Figure 10.74**):

   ▲ **Follow Shape:** Makes the highlighting follow the object's shape.

   ▲ **Box:** Displays a box around the button.

   ▲ **Underline:** Underlines the button. **Figure 10.75** shows the styles.

✔ Tip

■ Studio provides no feedback in the Title editor after you select the button style, so you have to preview the buttons in the Clip Properties tool.

A Taxonomy of Buttons

As you can see in the drop-down menu in Figure 10.71, Studio has the following four button types:

Normal Button: Links to a video, slide show, or another menu.

Thumbnail Button: Links to a video or slide show and displays a thumbnail inside the button (usually shaped like a frame).

Next Button: Links to the next menu page. Appears on all but the final page of multi-menu productions automatically created by Studio from menu templates.

Previous Button: Links to the previous page. Appears on the second and subsequent pages of multi-menu productions automatically created by Studio from menu templates.

If you're building your own menus one by one, always select either the Normal or Thumbnail Button option, even when creating links to previous or next pages.

Use the Previous and Next Button options *only* when you're creating menu templates for auto-completion by Studio (see "Creating DVD Menu Templates" later in this chapter). Studio uses these buttons to enable navigation between menus that it automatically creates from these templates.

WORKING WITH BUTTONS

To set active and selected colors:

1. Select the button that you want to modify and click the gray bounding box to display the control points (Figure 10.72).

2. At the top of the Buttons Album, choose the color box next to the state (Active or Selected) that you want to change (**Figure 10.76**).

   Studio's Color Selection dialog box opens (**Figure 10.77**).

3. Choose the desired color by selecting it from the Basic Colors or Custom Colors palette or by clicking a different color on the spectrum.

4. If you want, save your custom color by clicking the Add to Custom Colors button (Ctrl+A).

   Saving your custom color helps you maintain uniformity as you work.

5. Click OK to close the dialog box.

Figure 10.76 You can customize the highlight color for the active or selected state.

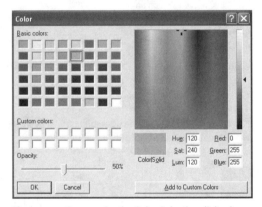

Figure 10.77 Once again, the Color Selection dialog box.

Working with Multiple Objects

Studio includes a wealth of grouping, alignment, sizing, and sequencing tools that can be used with all text, graphic, and other objects. You will find them especially helpful for DVD menu design, where they can shave countless minutes off work time you would otherwise spend ensuring that objects are properly sized, spaced, and aligned.

This section explores these features while creating a DVD menu that you will save as a Studio template.

To make objects the same size:

1. Select the objects that you want to resize by doing *one of the following:*

   ▲ Hold down the Ctrl key and click each object; the last object you select should be the one whose size you want the others to replicate.

   ▲ Drag an area that includes only the objects to be resized; the last object you select should be the one whose size you want the others to replicate.

   Studio places white highlights around each object except the last one selected; it places yellow highlights around the final object (**Figure 10.78**).

continues on next page

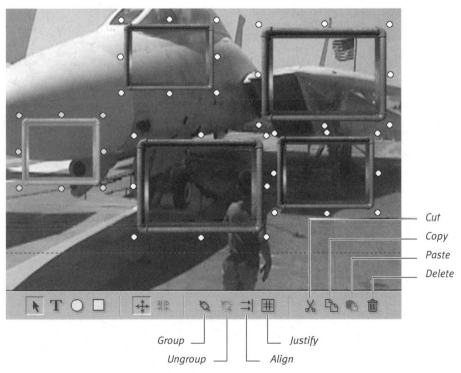

Cut
Copy
Paste
Delete

Group
Ungroup
Justify
Align

Figure 10.78 To make all objects the same size, select them, choosing last the one you want all the others to conform to (it should have a yellow bounding box around it).

WORKING WITH MULTIPLE OBJECTS

2. Click the Align icon at the bottom of the Design window.

Studio displays the Align menu (**Figure 10.79**).

3. Select Make Same Size at the bottom of the Align menu.

Studio resizes all objects to the size of the last object selected (**Figure 10.80**).

✔ Tips

■ This method works best if you've already made your objects and need to resize them en masse. But often it's easier to copy and paste buttons and other objects to ensure that they're identical (see "To copy and paste objects" later in this chapter).

■ The Align menu also includes options for making objects the same height and width. Use the same procedures described in the preceding task to operate these functions.

■ You can also access sizing functions from the Studio menu by choosing Title > Align.

■ In truth, these controls have worked sporadically for me in the past. If you find that they're not working for you, use the copy and paste method discussed in the first tip if you can; otherwise, mutter (quietly) under your breath and resize your objects manually.

Align icon

Figure 10.79 Click the Align icon; then select Make Same Size at the bottom of the menu.

Figure 10.80 All of the objects are the same size now!

Figure 10.81 Now to get the objects evenly spaced, first move the two outside boxes to the desired locations. Studio spaces the images inside these extremes.

Figure 10.82 Now that the objects are spaced evenly, time to get them aligned. When selecting the images, choose the one in the desired position last (it should have a yellow bounding box).

To evenly space objects vertically or horizontally:

1. Move the two outside objects to the external boundaries for all the objects that will be spaced.

2. Select the objects that you want to space by doing *one of the following:*

   ▲ Hold down the Ctrl key and click each object.

   ▲ Drag an area that includes only the objects to be spaced (**Figure 10.81**).

3. At the bottom of the Design window, click the Align icon.

   Studio displays the Align menu (Figure 10.79).

4. Select Space Even Across.

   Studio spaces all objects evenly between the two objects at either extreme (**Figure 10.82**).

✔ Tips

■ Studio does not space the objects evenly on the page, only between the objects at either extreme. To obtain the desired spacing, place the two outside objects at the desired location, and Studio spaces all other selected objects evenly between these two.

■ The operation is identical when spacing objects vertically.

■ You can also access spacing functions from the Studio menu by choosing Title > Align.

WORKING WITH MULTIPLE OBJECTS

To align objects vertically or horizontally:

1. Select the objects that you want to align by doing *one of the following*:

   ▲ Hold down the Ctrl key and click each object; the last object you select should be the object with which you want the other objects aligned (Figure 10.82).

   ▲ Drag an area that includes only the objects to be aligned; the last object you select should be the object with which you want the other objects aligned.

   The object with the yellow control points will be the reference object. All other objects will shift to align with this object.

2. Click the Align icon at the bottom of the Design window.

   Studio displays the Align menu (Figure 10.79).

3. Click the desired alignment—in this case, Align Bottom.

   Studio aligns all objects on the bottom of the reference object (**Figure 10.83**).

✔ Tips

- The operation is identical when using the other alignment functions.

- You can also access the alignment functions from the Studio menu by choosing Title > Align.

Figure 10.83 Alignment achieved.

WORKING WITH MULTIPLE OBJECTS

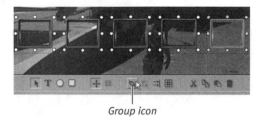

Group icon

Figure 10.84 Group the objects so you can position them en masse. Use the Group icon.

To group and ungroup objects:

1. Select the objects that you want to group by doing *one of the following:*

   ▲ Hold down the Ctrl key and click each object.

   ▲ Drag an area that includes only the objects that you want to group.

2. Click the Group icon at the bottom of the Design window (**Figure 10.84**).

   Studio groups the objects together. To ungroup the objects, click the Ungroup icon next to the Group icon.

✔ Tip

■ Once you've grouped the objects, you can perform extensive edits that affect all the objects. For example, with the thumbnail buttons shown in Figure 10.84, you can modify the size, active color, and highlight style for all grouped objects at once—a very efficient editing procedure.

WORKING WITH MULTIPLE OBJECTS

To copy and paste objects:

1. Select the objects that you want to copy by doing *one of the following:*

   ▲ Hold down the Ctrl key and click each object.

   ▲ Drag an area that includes only the objects to be copied (**Figure 10.85**).

2. Click the Copy icon at the bottom of the Design window.

3. Click the Paste icon to paste the objects. Studio pastes the objects directly on top of the original objects.

4. Drag the pasted objects to the desired location (**Figure 10.86**).

In the next task, a frame (a rectangle object) was created after the thumbnail button was created and thus obscures the thumbnail when dragged to the same location. Here's how to place the frame behind the thumbnail.

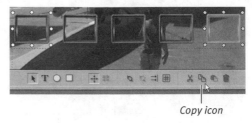
Copy icon

Figure 10.85 To copy two of the objects to move them above the others, select them and click the Copy icon.

Paste icon

Figure 10.86 Next, paste them atop the originals using the Paste icon. Then drag them to the desired location.

Figure 10.87 Suppose you want to use a rectangle as a frame for this thumbnail button. The problem is that when you create the rectangle, Studio places it over the thumbnail.

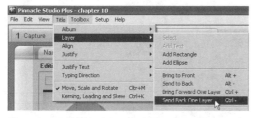

Figure 10.88 Use these controls to move objects to different layers.

Figure 10.89 Now the frame is behind the button, where you can move it to serve as a frame for the thumbnail button.

To change object layers:

1. Select the object or objects that you want to move forward or backward (**Figure 10.87**).

2. From the Studio menu, choose Title > Layer; then choose the desired action—in this case, Send Back One Layer (**Figure 10.88**).

   Studio moves the object back one layer, displaying the thumbnail button over the frame (**Figure 10.89**).

WORKING WITH MULTIPLE OBJECTS

Creating DVD Menu Templates

One of Studio's coolest features is its menu template function. You can create menu templates that Studio automatically populates when you add videos to the Timeline. Through your work in the previous section, "Working with Multiple Objects," the template is almost complete.

A complete template has three components: buttons for linking content, Next buttons, and Previous buttons. These allow Studio to automatically create menus and controls for navigating. Text and cute backgrounds are nice but not required. Our template-in-progress already contains the buttons for linking content; you will now see how to add the Next and Previous buttons.

See Chapter 12 for more on DVD menus.

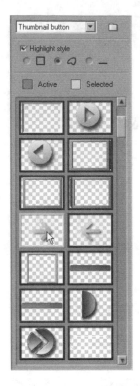

Figure 10.90 To complete the template menu, you need Next and Previous buttons.

To use existing Next and Previous buttons in your template:

1. Browse the Buttons Album until you find suitable buttons with the words *next* or *previous* in the name (**Figure 10.90**).

2. Drag the buttons to the desired locations (**Figure 10.91**).

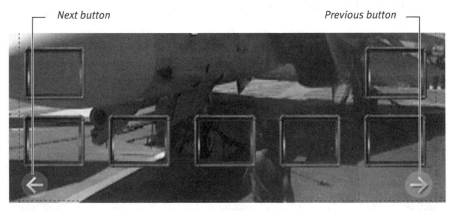

Next button   Previous button

Figure 10.91 Drag the Next and Previous buttons to the desired locations.

CREATING DVD MENU TEMPLATES

Figure 10.92 You also could use any object as a Next or Previous button and simply assign it the appropriate value.

Figure 10.93 Save the template.

To create your own Next and Previous buttons:

1. Create the desired text or object.

2. Open the drop-down menu at the top of the Buttons Album and choose Next Button (**Figure 10.92**).

3. Repeat Steps 1 and 2 to create the Previous button.

To save a menu as a template:

1. From the File menu, choose File > Save Menu As.

   Studio opens the Save Menu As dialog box.

2. Name the file and save it in the Program Files > Pinnacle > Studio 10 > Menus > My Menus folder (**Figure 10.93**).

   Studio should default to this menu location; you should need to hunt for it only if you've saved menus before in another location.

Creating Rolls and Crawls

After all this work, there's only one way to close this chapter: with "The End" rolling onto the screen, or crawling across the screen—you pick. The grandparents are screaming for this DVD.

With rolls, you place the title object where you want it to end up, and Studio moves it from off-screen at the bottom of the window to the specified location.

With crawls, Studio moves the title object from off-screen on the right to off-screen on the left. You set the object at the desired height, and Studio does the rest.

To create a rolling title:

1. In the Title editor, position the title object at the desired stopping point (**Figure 10.94**).

2. Among the title-type buttons at the upper left, click the Roll icon.

   Studio produces the effect, which you can preview only in the Movie window.

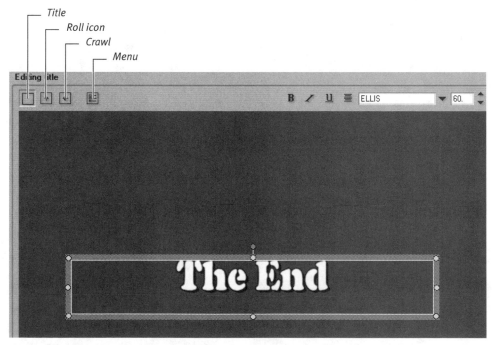

Figure 10.94 The perfect way to end this chapter: a rolling "The End" title.

To create a crawling title:

1. In the Title editor, position the title object at the desired height.

2. Among the title-type buttons at the upper left, click the Crawl icon (Figure 10.94).

   Studio produces the effect, which you can preview only in the Movie window.

✔ Tips

- To make the title roll or crawl more slowly, simply make the title longer by dragging it on the Timeline or entering a longer duration in the Title editor as shown in Figure 10.12.

- You can easily mix effects—for instance, a scrolling title that fades to black—by placing two titles sequentially on the timeline. Be sure that the text in the second title aligns precisely with the stopping point of the text in the first title. Make this happen by copying the first title, pasting it into the Timeline next to the first title, and then reversing the motion on the second clip as described in the following tip.

- To reverse a crawl or a roll and convert back to a static menu, click the Title icon among the title-type buttons (Figure 10.94).

- Menus (that is, titles with buttons) can't roll or crawl.

- Studio includes a "The End" title in the Titles Album, which provides the easiest way to create this effect.

Working With Audio

The last ten chapters have focused largely on video, perhaps leading the casual observer to believe that audio is less important. However, as serious producers will tell you, this just isn't so. The Internet experience is probably the best barometer: Many viewers will tolerate grainy, postage stamp-sized video, but let the audio drop out once or twice, and satisfaction quickly wanes.

Studio offers up to four audio tracks, the audio associated with the original and overlay videos, and two others for your choice of narration, sound effects, or background music. It also provides tools for taking music from CD tracks and converting them to sound files (a process known as ripping), and recording narration.

But what sets Studio's audio capabilities apart are three features. First is SmartSound, which produces thematic background music of any customizable length. Also exceptional is Studio's Volume tool, a real-time mixer that lets you customize audio volume on all tracks simultaneously. Finally, Studio now offers audio effects for critical functions like noise removal and equalization, allowing producers to improve sound quality dramatically. Together, these tools let you easily create and integrate professional-quality audio into your productions.

About Audio Tracks and Workflow

Studio's timeline can handle up to four audio tracks (**Figure 11.1**), which operate as follows:

◆ **Original Audio track.** This track always starts with audio from the video file above it. If you lock the Video track, you can delete the original audio file and insert an audio file from the Album or drag one from any other track.

◆ **Overlay Audio track.** This track always starts with audio from the video in the Overlay track. If you lock the Video track, you can delete the original audio file and insert an audio file from the Album or drag one from any other track.

◆ **Sound Effect track.** Studio places narrations created with the Voice-Over tool in this track. By designation, Pinnacle also suggests that sound effects should be placed in this track, but you can place the sound effects in any open track. The Sound Effect track is referred to as the Sound Effect and Voice-Over track in some Studio Help files.

◆ **Music track.** Studio places files from both the CD Audio tool and SmartSound tool in this track, which can otherwise contain any audio file. It's referred to as the Background Music track in some Studio Help files.

You can place any audio file from the Album in any track, but you should reserve the designated tracks for their namesake items if you plan to create narration or background audio files. Once Studio creates these files, it lets you move them to any track, thus providing additional design flexibility.

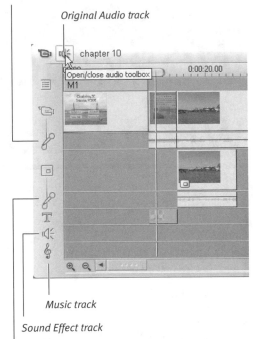

Audio Toolbox button

Original Audio track

Music track

Sound Effect track

Overlay Audio track

Figure 11.1 Studio has up to four audio tracks: one for the audio included in the captured file, one for the Overlay track audio, one for sound effects and voice-overs, and one for music. At the top is the Audio Toolbox button.

ABOUT AUDIO TRACKS AND WORKFLOW

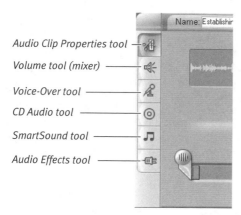

Audio Clip Properties tool

Volume tool (mixer)

Voice-Over tool

CD Audio tool

SmartSound tool

Audio Effects tool

Figure 11.2 The Audio toolbox contains six tools.

Getting audio to the Timeline

As we've seen, Studio populates the Audio track with audio associated with the video file.

You can add only the audio from any video file by dragging the file from the Album to either the Sound Effect track or the Music track. (For details, see "Working with Audio Files" in Chapter 7.)

Studio can also import WAV and MP3 files for dragging to the audio tracks. (For details, see the section "Working with the Sound Effects Tab" in Chapter 6.)

The Audio toolbox

Studio's Audio toolbox, accessed by clicking its namesake button at the top of the Movie window (Figure 11.1), contains the various tools used to create, edit, and mix audio on the respective tracks (**Figure 11.2**). Here are those tools (top to bottom):

◆ **Audio Clip Properties tool:** For trimming audio files.

◆ **Volume tool (mixer):** For adjusting the volume of the various audio tracks.

◆ **Voice-Over tool:** For recording narration segments placed on the Sound Effect track.

◆ **CD Audio tool:** For ripping CD audio tracks that are placed on the Music track.

◆ **SmartSound tool:** For creating background music placed on the Music track.

◆ **Audio Effects tool:** For adding audio effects to any audio track.

✔ Tip

■ Create your audio tracks last, after all your video edits are finalized. That way, adjustments to the video tracks won't throw off the synchronization of the Music and Sound Effect tracks with the video.

ABOUT AUDIO TRACKS AND WORKFLOW

Setting Recording Options

In addition to simply importing audio files into Studio, you can also import tracks from a CD-Audio disc and record a voice-over narration. This section describes the setup options for both of those activities.

To choose a drive for CD-ripping:

1. From the Studio menu, choose Setup > Video and Audio Preferences.

   The Pinnacle Studio Setup Options screen opens to the Video and Audio Preferences tab (**Figure 11.3**).

2. In the lower-right corner of the screen, select the drive containing the CD-Audio disc.

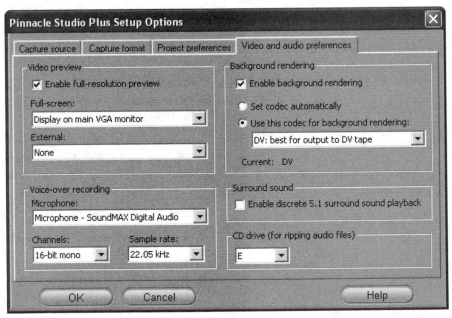

Figure 11.3 Here's where you select the drive for ripping CD tracks and set other recording options.

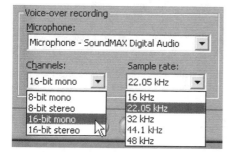

Figure 11.4 Setting Voice-over recording options. Start by selecting your microphone input.

Figure 11.5 Set capture parameters next.

To set voice-over recording options:

1. Follow Step 1 of the previous task.

2. In the Voice-Over Recording section on the right, make sure the Microphone drop-down menu is set to the correct microphone input source (**Figure 11.4**).

3. Click the Channels drop-down menu and choose 16-bit mono (**Figure 11.5**).

4. Click the Sample Rate drop-down menu and choose 22.05 kHz.

5. Click OK to close the dialog box.

✔ Tips

■ Pinnacle recommends using 16-bit mono at 22.05 kHz for narration because speech is less complex than music, and this format saves space without any perceptible change in quality. If the quality isn't good enough for your ear, or if you record your audio with music in the background, bump it up to the 16-bit stereo, 44.1 kHz, used for ripping CD tracks. It'll cost you an extra 128 KB per second, or about 3.5 percent of what DV video costs you.

■ When you rip a CD or create narration, you're creating auxiliary audio files, and it helps to know where the system is storing them so that you can reuse or delete them. See "Working with Auxiliary Files" in Chapter 2 for details.

Ripping CD Audio

If you're used to fully functional jukebox products like those from MusicMatch, Microsoft, and RealNetworks, Studio's CD Audio tool will seem mundane. But while it doesn't compare to these products in flash and features, at least you'll know the files you create using the CD Audio tool will be compatible with Studio.

To rip a CD audio track:

1. In the Movie window, place the Timeline scrubber where the audio should be inserted (**Figure 11.6**).

2. To open the CD Audio tool, do *one of the following*:

   ▲ Click the Audio Toolbox icon (Figure 11.1), then click the CD to switch to the CD Audio tool.

   ▲ In the Studio menu, choose Toolbox > Add CD Music.

   The Audio toolbox opens to the CD Audio tool (**Figure 11.7**).

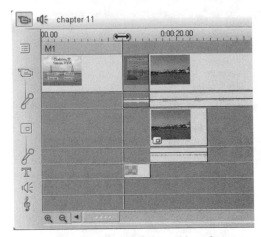

Figure 11.6 Position the Timeline scrubber where you want Studio to place the ripped CD audio.

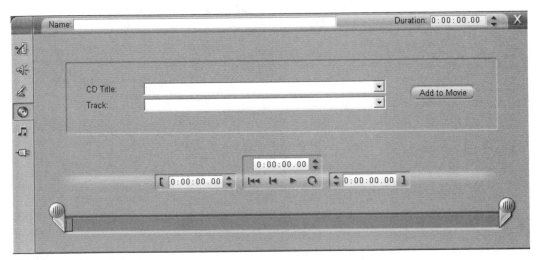

Figure 11.7 The CD Audio tool.

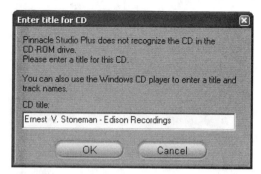

Figure 11.8 Studio tracks your CDs by the title you enter here.

3. Place a CD in the CD drive.

Studio performs one of the following actions:

▲ If the CD is new, Studio prompts you to enter the name of the CD (**Figure 11.8**). Enter the appropriate name.

▲ If you've ripped tracks from this CD previously, Studio automatically recognizes the CD and inserts the name (**Figure 11.9**).

4. Select the desired track.

5. If desired, select the Start and End locations by doing *one of the following*:

▲ Slide the Trim calipers to the desired location.

▲ Type the desired setting in the transport controls or use the Trim scrubber to move to the desired location, and then click the controls that set your Start and End locations.

▲ Use the Jog buttons next to the Start and End Location counters.

continues on next page

Trim scrubber   Name field   Transport controls   Duration field

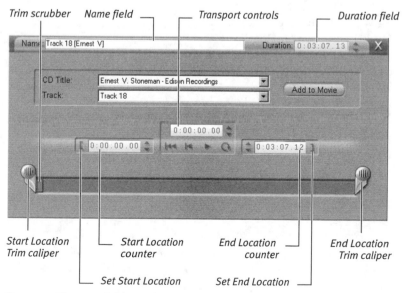

Start Location Trim caliper   Start Location counter   End Location counter   End Location Trim caliper

Set Start Location   Set End Location

Figure 11.9 The second time you load the CD, Studio remembers it.

6. Click the Add to Movie button.

Studio rips the CD-Audio track (**Figure 11.10**) and adds the track to the selected location (**Figure 11.11**).

✔ Tips

■ There's usually some silence at both the start and end of a CD audio clip. It's a good idea to eliminate this before you rip a track; otherwise it's another step with the Audio toolbox (Figure 11.9).

■ If you're a digital audio aficionado, you'll probably be much happier using any of the players from the companies I mentioned in the introduction to this section (MusicMatch's Jukebox, Microsoft's Media Player, or RealNetworks' RealPlayer) to rip tracks from your audio CD. All these programs can search the Internet and name your CDs and tracks, and rip the files for instant use and later reuse. But many people will probably find that the CD Audio tool works just fine.

■ If you use a third-party player, note that Studio can be finicky during import, and might fail to load MP3 files that are not 128 Kbps, or WAV files that are not 16-bit stereo at 44.1 kHz (the standard for CD-Audio). If you use another tool, rip a track or two and see if Studio can load it before ripping your entire soundtrack. And remember, Studio can't load RealMedia files or QuickTime, so don't even think about it.

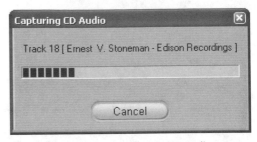

Figure 11.10 Studio is capturing the CD-Audio to your hard disk.

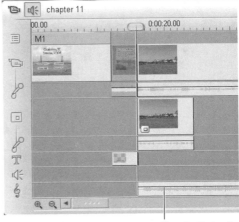

New Audio track

Figure 11.11 Studio adds the captured audio to the music track.

RIPPING CD AUDIO

Creating Background Tracks Using SmartSound

With the buildup I gave it in the intro, SmartSound can't possibly live up to its billing. So, I'll try the low-key approach, walk you through the tool quickly, and let you decide for yourself.

I used country legend Pop Stoneman to set the mood for some of the older ships at Patriots Point. Now I need background music for our visit to the Charleston Aquarium.

Let's see what SmartSound has to offer.

To add SmartSound background music:

1. To select the scenes to which SmartSound can synchronize the audio, do *one of the following*:

   ▲ Holding down the Shift key, select contiguous scenes with the pointer (**Figure 11.12**).

   ▲ Starting with any unpopulated area on the Timeline, drag a box around the scenes.

   ▲ From the Studio menu, choose Edit > Select All (Ctrl+A) to select the entire Timeline.

   Studio turns the selected tracks blue.

continues on next page

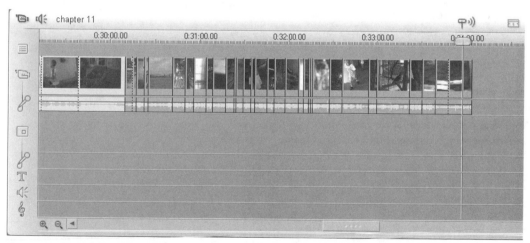

Figure 11.12 Studio's SmartSound creates background music for all selected tracks, so start by selecting the tracks. Here I've selected all the dark gray clips.

CREATING BACKGROUND TRACKS

2. To open the SmartSound tool, do *one of the following*:

   ▲ Click the Audio Toolbox icon (Figure 11.1), and then click the SmartSound Tool icon, which is the second from the bottom on the left of the Audio Toolbox panel (Figure 11.2).

   ▲ From the Studio menu, choose Toolbox > Generate Background Music.

   The SmartSound tool opens (**Figure 11.13**).

   If you didn't install SmartSound during installation, Studio prompts you to insert the setup disc.

3. Choose a style from the Style list.

4. Choose a song from the Song list.

5. Choose a version from the Version list.

6. Click the Preview button anytime to listen to your selection.

   You can change your selection and preview again anytime.

7. When complete, click the Add to Movie button.

   Studio adds the background audio track to the selected clips (**Figure 11.14**).

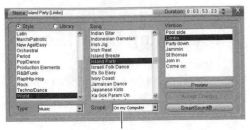

Scope drop-down list

Figure 11.13 The SmartSound tool. Studio ships with a lot of choices, and you can buy additional tracks at www.smartsound.com.

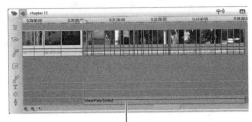

New SmartSound track

Figure 11.14 Studio adds the track to the selected videos.

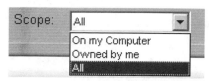

Figure 11.15 Here's how you set the search parameters for SmartSound tracks.

✔ Tips

- Each time you change the duration of the videos on the Timeline, Studio adjusts the duration of the SmartSound track, creating noticeable delays on longer projects as Studio creates the new audio track. This is another reason to add audio as the last editing step.

- Note the Scope drop-down list in the bottom center of the SmartSound window, which controls the location of music that populates the window (**Figure 11.15**). If you choose All, Studio will populate the window with every available track, though you may need to download the preview, and will probably have to pay to use the tracks. If you choose On My Computer, Studio will display all clips on your computer, whether download demos or clips you can actually use in a production. The most restrictive option is "Owned By Me," which displays only those clips on your computer that you own and can actually use in a production.

Recording Narrations

Narrating your videos and slide shows is a great way to add context to the visual presentation, and Studio makes narrations simple to create and use. Even with an inexpensive microphone, you can create high-quality audio, but with the wrong gear or wrong setup, you'll be disappointed with the quality. For more details, see the sidebar "Getting the Most from Your Narrations."

To connect for narration:

1. Connect your microphone to the microphone port on your sound card or computer.

   Note that the internal settings for line-in are different from those for the microphone jack, so you're not likely to get good results using this connector.

2. Connect your headphones (if available) to the speaker port on your sound card or computer.

✔ Tip

- Many computers (like my Sony VAIO) designate the microphone connector with a red plug, which sometimes matches the plug on the microphone itself.

Getting the Most from Your Narrations

There are two aspects to a good-quality narration: technical and artistic.

From a technical perspective, you can achieve great results with an inexpensive microphone, but I recommend that you use a microphone that's part of a headset. Microphones and headsets are often sold together for use in Internet video-conferencing.

If you're using a stand-alone microphone, ditch your external speakers and use a set of headphones during recording. Otherwise, you'll produce feedback—an annoying screeching sound caused by the microphone picking up output from the speakers.

From an artistic standpoint, you'll get the best results by scripting your narration and trying multiple takes until you get it right. Keep your comments short and to the point, or you'll complicate both the scripting and the performance.

If you're going to wing it without a script, adjust your expectations downward. While you may strive to emulate the baritone splendor of James Earl Jones, the fluidity of Bryant Gumble, or the mellifluous tones of yoga maven Tracey Rich, you'll never get finished if you insist on that level of perfection.

Finally, there are tools out there that can stretch or compress your narration to the duration of the corresponding video with minimal pitch change or distortion. They'll save you oodles of time compared to re-recording a four-minute track to shave 15 seconds either way. Sony Media Software's CD Architect is a good place to start (www.sonymediasoftware. com).

RECORDING NARRATIONS

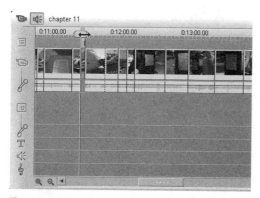

Figure 11.16 Start your narration by positioning the Timeline scrubber where you want the narration to begin.

To record your narration:

1. In the Movie window, position the Timeline scrubber to the desired insert point (**Figure 11.16**).

   There must be at least one video or still image on the Timeline to record a narration, and there can't be audio in the Sound Effect track at the desired insert point.

2. To open the Voice-Over Narration tool, do *one of the following*:

   ▲ Click the Audio Toolbox icon (Figure 11.1), and then in the Audio toolbox, click the icon for recording a voice-over narration—the third icon from the top.

   ▲ From the Studio menu, choose Toolbox > Record Voice-over.

   The Voice-Over Narration tool opens (**Figure 11.17**).

   The volume meter on the right is completely unlit, meaning the microphone is hearing no audio—a good thing. When you have a noisy room or a poor microphone, the meter jumps, signifying noisy audio.

continues on next page

RECORDING NARRATIONS

Volume adjustment

Too high (red)
Target range (yellow)

Too low (blue)

Figure 11.17 The Voice-Over Narration tool. Use the Volume Adjustment tool to customize recording volume.

3. Speak into the microphone, and use the Volume Adjustment tool on the right to position the audio level so that it is at the top of the blue level or into the yellow level, but never touches the red.

   Touching the red may clause clipping, which often sounds like a mechanical click on the audio, or it can distort your voice.

4. After setting the appropriate level, click the Record button to start the recording.

   Studio first lights a "Standby" sign in the Recording box, then numbers count down from three, to two, to one. Then the Recording light turns on, and blinks slowly during the recording (**Figure 11.18**).

   While recording, watch the audio levels to maintain the appropriate volume.

   If the Recording button doesn't light up, it's most likely because the Timeline scrubber is positioned above a point in the Sound Effect track that already contains audio. So move, edit, or delete the old audio, or change locations to a blank place in the track.

5. Press Stop to stop recording (Figure 11.18).

   When Studio stops recording, it creates and stores the audio file (you'll see the word Standby light for a moment), then posts the file in the Sound Effect track (**Figure 11.19**).

6. In the Player, press Play to hear your recorded audio.

   Since the proper levels haven't yet been set for the narration and other tracks, it may be difficult to hear the narration over the other tracks. To learn how to set the respective volumes, see "Using the Volume Tool" later in this chapter.

   After you've finished recording, the narration track is just like any file that you can trim, split, move, or delete. For example, if you don't like the recorded track, simply select it, press Delete, and it's gone.

Figure 11.18 Once you're recording, try to keep the level predominantly in the upper green and lower yellow, avoiding the red at all costs.

New Narration track

Figure 11.19 The completed narration track.

RECORDING NARRATIONS

File open

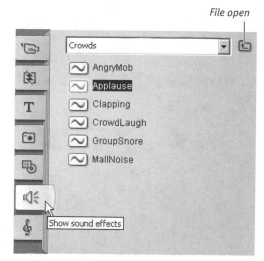

Figure 11.20 Studio's sound effects.

Using Studio's Sound Effects

Pinnacle includes a range of sound effects with Studio, which you access by clicking the Audio Files tab on the left of the Edit Album. I'm not a big sound effects guy, but every once in a while they come in handy, like the chewing effect I used to spice up a slide show on sharks, or adding applause to my daughter's gymnastics exercises.

The first time you run Studio, the list of sound effects is displayed when you open the Sound Effects Album (**Figure 11.20**). However, if you change folders to import other files, Studio doesn't automatically return to this default view. Assuming you installed Studio using all default file locations, you should be able to reload the sound effects into the Album by clicking the yellow Folder icon (Figure 11.20), which produces the Open dialog box, and then navigating to C:\Program Files\Pinnacle\Studio 10\ SoundEffects.

Editing Audio Clips

Chapter 7 described how to edit audio files on the Timeline. All of those principles apply equally to audio files created by the three tools discussed earlier.

In addition, you can edit audio files with Studio's Clip Properties tool, also discussed in Chapter 7. Since the Audio Clip Properties tool presents a slightly different face when editing a CD-Audio clip and a SmartSound clip, I'll address each separately below.

To edit Audio from a CD:

1. Double-click the Audio track in the Movie window to edit (**Figure 11.21**).

   Studio opens the CD Audio Clip Properties tool (**Figure 11.22**).

2. Make the desired edits.

3. To save edits, click the X in the upper right to close the Clip Properties tool or touch another tool.

To edit a SmartSound clip:

1. Double-click the track to edit it.

   Studio opens the SmartSound tool (**Figure 11.23**).

2. Make the desired changes and click the Accept Changes button.

   Studio makes the changes.

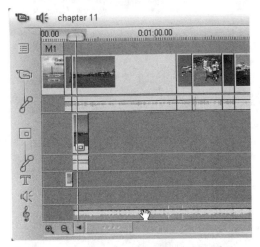

Figure 11.21 To edit the track, double-click it. What opens?

Figure 11.22 The Clip Properties tool.

Figure 11.23 Change your style, then click Accept Changes.

EDITING AUDIO CLIPS

Using the Volume Tool

Now that you've created these multiple audio tracks, it's time to blend them into a synergistic audio experience by adjusting their relative volume.

Studio offers two tools, the Volume tool discussed here, and the adjustment handles on the Timeline discussed in the next section. Both tools are designed to complement each other, so you can use the adjustment handles on the Timeline to modify any adjustments you made using the Volume tool, and vice versa.

There are up to four sets of volume controls, one each for the Original and Overlay Audio tracks, the Sound Effect track, and the Music track. Here's how they operate:

◆ **Mute:** Mutes the entire track.

◆ **Global Volume:** Adjusts the volume of the entire track.

◆ **Volume Adjust:** Adjusts the volume at the current edit location. This tool is best used in real time with the audio playing, so you can listen to the volume and adjust as necessary.

◆ **Volume Meter:** Reflects track volume at that location.

◆ **Fade-in and Fade-out:** Perform their namesake tasks at the current edit location.

◆ **Balance:** Adjusts the audio balance between the left and right speakers, and the position of each track front to back as perceived by the listener (this is also called a fade).

To open the Volume tool:

◆ Do *one of the following*:

▲ Click the Audio Toolbox icon in the Movie window (Figure 11.1), and then click the Speaker icon on the left of the Audio Toolbox panel.

▲ In the Studio menu, choose Toolbox > Change Volume.

The Volume tool opens above the Movie window (**Figure 11.24**).

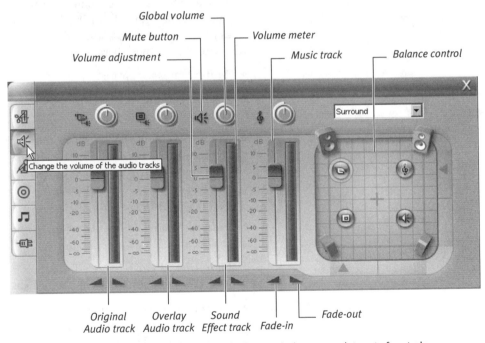

Figure 11.24 Studio's cool Volume mixer. Each of the four tracks has a complete set of controls.

USING THE VOLUME TOOL

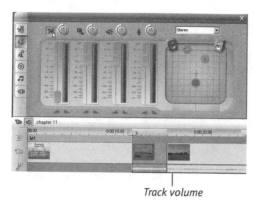

Track volume

Figure 11.25 A muted track. Note the line at the bottom of the Audio track—it will be more easily visible when you try this on your projects.

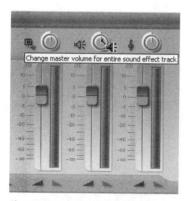

Figure 11.26 This control adjusts volume for the entire audio clip.

To mute a track:

1. Follow Step 1 of the previous task.

2. Click the Mute button for the respective track.

   Studio places a red line over the Mute button and adjusts track volume to zero, placing a red line at the bottom of the track (**Figure 11.25**).

To adjust track global volume:

1. Follow Step 1 in "To open the Volume tool."

2. Adjust the Global Volume tool to the desired level by turning it clockwise (to increase volume) or counterclockwise (to decrease volume) (**Figure 11.26**).

   Studio adjusts the volume of the entire track and places a blue line at the adjusted level (**Figure 11.27**).

Original
Post volume decrease

Volume line

Volume line

Figure 11.27 The adjusted audio track. Note the uniform level of the volume line, especially compared with Figure 11.29, where I create adjustment handles to edit track regions, rather than the entire track.

To adjust track volume:

1. Follow Step 1 in "To open the Volume tool."

2. Position the Timeline scrubber at the target location.

3. Move the volume adjustment downward or upward (**Figure 11.28**).

   Studio creates an adjustment handle and adjusts the clip volume on the track at the target location (**Figure 11.29**).

   Once Studio creates the adjustment handle, you can move it around manually. As you'll see in the next section, you can also create adjustment handles directly on the Timeline.

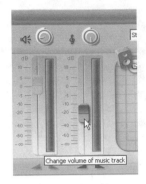

Figure 11.28 This control adjusts volume *at that location,* as opposed to uniformly over the entire clip.

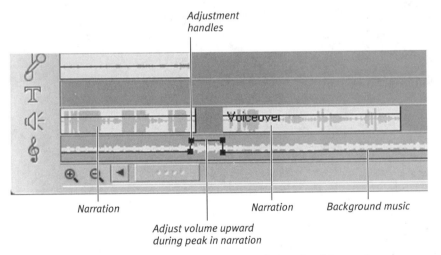

Adjustment handles

Narration

Adjust volume upward during peak in narration

Narration

Background music

Figure 11.29 Here I'm adjusting the Music track upwards during a break in narration.

USING THE VOLUME TOOL

To fade in audio:

1. Follow Step 1 in "To open the Volume tool."

2. Position the Timeline scrubber where the fade-in should start—that is, the point where volume should be zero before it starts to increase (**Figure 11.30**). Normally, this is the absolute start of a scene or audio clip.

continues on next page

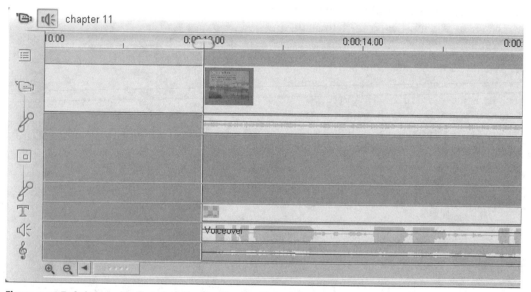

Figure 11.30 To fade in audio, first place the Timeline scrubber where you want the fade-in to start—that is, where audio volume is set to zero. Normally, this is the start of the audio file.

3. Click the Fade-in icon for the target audio track (**Figure 11.31**).

Studio fades in the audio using the default fade-in/fade-out duration (**Figure 11.32**). To adjust this default setting, see "Setting Default Durations" in Chapter 2.

✔ Tips

■ If your track has multiple files and you want each to fade in, you have to apply the effect separately to each audio file. For example, if you have multiple CD-Audio or narration tracks and want each to fade in, you must apply the fade-in to each file manually.

■ When you apply transitions between clips, Studio automatically creates a cross-fade between the two original audio tracks, unless you apply the fade transition (in which case Studio fades the first track out and fades the second one in). Note that you can customize this cross-fade manually—see "Adjusting Volume, Balance, and Fade on the Timeline," later in this chapter.

■ If the track's Fade-in control is not active, click the target track with your pointer to make it the active track. Studio will turn the Fade-in and Fade-out controls black and make them active.

Figure 11.31
Click this button to produce the fade-in.

Adjustment handle

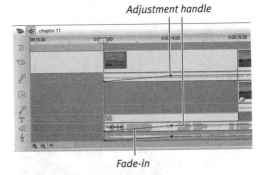

Fade-in

Figure 11.32 Fade-in accomplished. Again, note the small blue dot, which is the adjustment handle you can manually move.

USING THE VOLUME TOOL

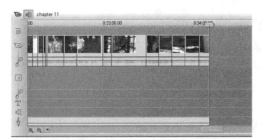

Figure 11.33 To fade out, place the Timeline scrubber at the point you want volume to be set to zero— normally, the end of the clip.

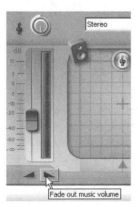

Figure 11.34 Click this button to fade out.

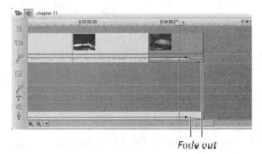

Fade out

Figure 11.35 Fade-out accomplished.

To fade out audio:

1. Follow Step 1 in "To open the Volume tool."

2. Position the Timeline scrubber where the fade-out should end—that is, the point where volume should be set to zero (**Figure 11.33**).

   Normally, this is the absolute end of a scene or audio clip.

3. Click the Fade-out icon for the target audio track (**Figure 11.34**).

   Studio fades out the audio (**Figure 11.35**) using the default fade-in/fade-out duration. To adjust this default setting, see "Setting Default Durations," in Chapter 2.

✔ Tip

■ If your track has multiple files and you want each to fade out, you have to apply the effect separately to each audio file. For example, if you have multiple CD-Audio or narration tracks and want each to fade out, you must apply the fade-out to each file manually.

USING THE VOLUME TOOL

About the Balance Control

The Balance control adjusts two characteristics of an audio clip: the clip's position with reference to the left and right speakers (called the balance, or pan) and its position front to back (or the fade) as perceived by the listener.

These controls are useful under several circumstances, including the following:

◆ If you recorded the left and right audio tracks of an event separately (balance).

◆ To change the perceived location of a sound, such as a train or car, from one direction to another to create the impression that the train or car was moving from left to right (balance).

◆ To make a clip sound more faint toward the end (fade).

◆ To place background music clearly behind the Audio or Sound Effect track (fade).

◆ To place a voice narration track more clearly in front of the audio from the video clip.

It's important to note, however, that Studio doesn't provide track-wide balance or fade control in the same way it does with the other volume adjustments.

For example, if you're not at the first frame of an audio file when you adjust the balance or fade using the Balance control, Studio creates an adjustment handle and adjusts the balance or fade value from that position forward, which is often not the desired effect. But if you position the Timeline scrubber at the absolute start of an audio clip and then adjust the Balance control, Studio adjusts the balance or fade values for the entire clip.

So if you use balance and fade controls extensively, you may find it easier to make these adjustments on the Timeline rather than using the Balance control (see "Adjusting Volume, Balance, and Fade on the Timeline" later in this chapter for more information). The easiest way to set the Timeline scrubber to the absolute start of an audio clip is to position it a few frames before the start of an audio clip, and then press the right arrow key, which is the shortcut that directs Studio to select the next clip.

Note that all three tracks start at the same exact position in the Balance control, front and center. Each track is represented by the same icon that represents the track in the Timeline (**Figure 11.36**). To select the track to adjust, either click the desired icon in the Balance control or click the target track in the Timeline.

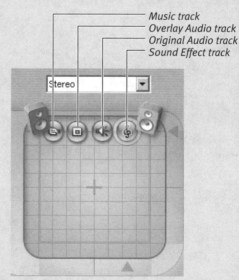

Figure 11.36 A close up of the Balance control. Note the icons for the four tracks.

About the Balance Control *(continued)*

Note also that the balance control has three modes, Stereo, Surround, and Dialog. Here's how each operates.

Stereo is shown in **Figure 11.37**, and is the simplest. This assumes that you have only two speakers, left and right, and are limited to pan adjustments between the left and right speakers.

Dialog mode (**Figure 11.38**) is optimized for dialogue. In this mode the center channel takes priority over the front left and right channels, ensuring that dialogue is clearly audible in the center at all times.

When a stereo clip is panned to dead center, the left and right channels are combined and sent to the center speaker. The right channel is also sent to the right rear speaker at half the level as is sent to the center speaker and the left channel is sent to the left rear speaker at half the level as is sent to the center channel. As the clip is panned to the front, the audio level sent to the rear speakers is decreased. As it is panned to the rear, the audio level sent to the center speaker is decreased.

As the clip is panned to the left or right of center, audio is sent to the front right and front left speakers as appropriate. A mono clip is panned in the same manner: with a mono clip panned dead center sent to the center, right rear, and left rear speakers

Surround mode (**Figure 11.39**) is optimized for sound effects. This mode does not use the center channel, and allows panning anywhere between the left front, right front, left rear, and right rear channels. In this mode, when a clip is panned to dead center, the audio will be heard equally from each of the four speakers. As it is panned to one speaker, the volume for that speaker will increase while the volume of the other speakers decreases.

Figure 11.37 Balance control in Stereo mode, with only two speakers.

Figure 11.38 Balance control in Dialog mode, which uses five speakers, including one directly in front of the listener, to focus the audio.

Figure 11.39 Balance control in Surround mode, which uses four speakers.

To adjust balance using the Balance control:

1. Follow Step 1 in "To open the Volume tool."

2. Position the Timeline scrubber where the balance adjustment should begin: at the start of the audio clip for clip-wide adjustments, or at any other position to adjust the value from that position forward (**Figure 11.40**). (See the sidebar "About the Balance Control" for more information.)

3. Do *one of the following* to select the track to adjust:

   ▲ Click the target track on the Timeline.

   ▲ Click the Target icon in the Balance control (Figure 11.36).

   To access the icon in the Balance control directly, you may have to move one of the other icons out of the way, which obviously changes its balance value. So, remember to move it back to the desired value after you've adjusted your target track (just another reason why it's easier to adjust these values on the Timeline).

4. Do *one of the following* to adjust track balance:

   ▲ Click the icon and move it to the left or right (**Figure 11.41**).

   ▲ Click the green triangle beneath the Balance control and move it to the left or right.

   Studio adjusts the track's balance.

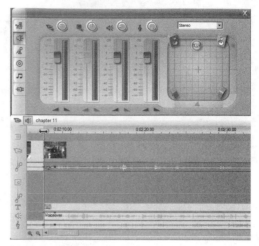

Figure 11.40 To adjust balance, place the Timeline scrubber at the point to adjust.

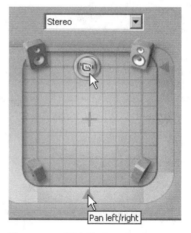

Figure 11.41 Click the icon for the target track and move it to the left or right, or use the green triangle beneath.

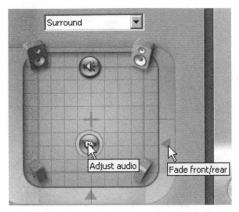

Figure 11.42 To fade a track, either grab it directly or use the brown triangle.

To adjust fade using the Balance control:

1. Follow Step 1 in "To open the Volume tool."

2. Position the Timeline scrubber where the fade adjustment should begin: at the start of the audio clip for clip-wide adjustments or at any other position to adjust the value from that position forward (Figure 11.40). (See the sidebar "About the Balance Control" for more information.)

3. Click the drop-down box at the top of the Balance control and choose Dialog (Figure 11.38) or Surround (Figure 11.39).

4. Do *one of the following* to select the track to adjust:

   ▲ Click the target track on the Timeline.

   ▲ Click the Target icon in the Balance control (Figure 11.40).

   Note that to access the icon in the Balance control directly, you may have to move one of the other icons out of the way, which obviously changes its balance value. So, remember to move it back to the desired value after you've adjusted your target track (just another reason why it's easier to adjust these values on the Timeline).

5. Do *one of the following* to adjust track fade position:

   ▲ Click the icon and move it in front of the other icons or behind them (**Figure 11.42**).

   ▲ Click the brown triangle to the right of the Balance control and move it to the front or back.

   Studio adjusts the track's fade position.

To perform real-time, multitrack audio mixing and balance adjustments:

One of Studio's best features is the ability to adjust volume, balance, and fade for all three tracks in real time, which is the fastest and easiest way to produce the desired values.

1. Follow Step 1 in "To open the Volume tool."

2. Position the Timeline scrubber where you'd like to start adjusting the volume, fade, and balance (**Figure 11.43**).

3. In the Preview window, press Play.

4. As you listen to the audio, adjust the volume, balance, and fade position for each track using the appropriate controls in the Volume tool.

   Studio creates adjustment handles and adjusts the three parameters in real time (**Figure 11.44**). Don't feel like you need to make this perfect; you'll learn how to fine-tune these settings manually in the next section.

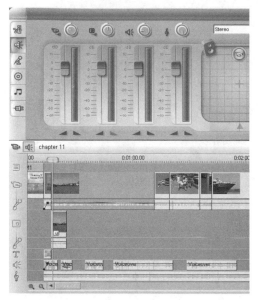

Figure 11.43 Now for some fun: real-time, multitrack mixing. Position the Timeline scrubber at the starting point.

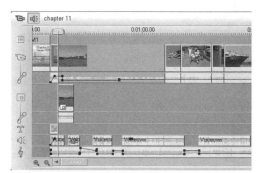

Figure 11.44 The adjusted volumes.

Figure 11.45 When the pointer looks like this hand, you can move the file to a different location on the track or a different track.

Figure 11.46 When the pointer looks like a speaker, you can create and move the adjustment handles.

Adjustment handle

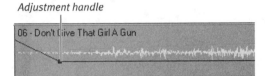

Figure 11.47 You can create an adjustment handle by touching the volume line, and dragging the volume down.

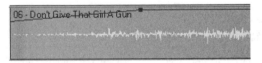

Figure 11.48 Here I've increased the volume.

Adjusting Volume, Balance, and Fade on the Timeline

You can use the Timeline to modify the adjustments you made using the Volume or Balance controls or create your own adjustment handles and edit them manually. This section shows you how to do both (and how to delete unwanted adjustment handles).

To adjust audio volume:

1. Touch the target track.

   Studio turns the track blue. Note that the cursor has two states for audio editing. The cursor resembles a hand when hovering over any part of the audio track except the blue audio level line (**Figure 11.45**). In this state it's called the Location Adjustment cursor, and it lets you move the track to a different location on the same track or to a different track.

   When you hover the pointer over the blue audio level line, it converts to a speaker and becomes the Volume Adjustment cursor, which you can use to create or adjust the levels of adjustment handles (**Figure 11.46**).

2. With the Volume Adjustment cursor, do *one of the following*:

   ▲ To create an adjustment handle and adjust the volume, touch the audio line and move it to the desired volume level.

   Studio creates an adjustment handle and adjusts the level (**Figure 11.47**).

   ▲ To adjust a previously created adjustment handle, touch and drag it to the new volume level (**Figure 11.48**).

   You can drag the adjustment handle in all four directions: up, down, left, and right.

To delete an adjustment handle:

◆ With the cursor in Volume Adjustment mode, touch an adjustment handle, drag it straight down quickly, and release (**Figure 11.49**).

Studio removes the adjustment handle.

Figure 11.49 To delete an adjustment handle, just grab it and pull it down quickly.

To remove all volume changes:

1. Select the track or multiple tracks on the same Timeline (**Figure 11.50**).

2. Right-click and choose Remove Volume Changes (**Figure 11.51**).

Studio removes all volume changes on the selected track (**Figure 11.52**).

✔ Tip

■ Removing volume changes only works on a single track. Studio lets you select clips on different tracks and activate the tool via the right-click menu, but only removes volume changes from the top track.

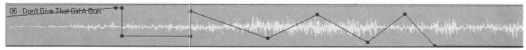

Figure 11.50 Say you don't like these adjustments and simply want to start over. First select all the affected clips.

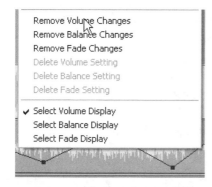

Figure 11.51 Then choose Remove Volume Changes from the right-click menu.

Figure 11.52 You're back at square one with a pristine volume line.

ADJUSTING VOLUME, BALANCE, AND FADE

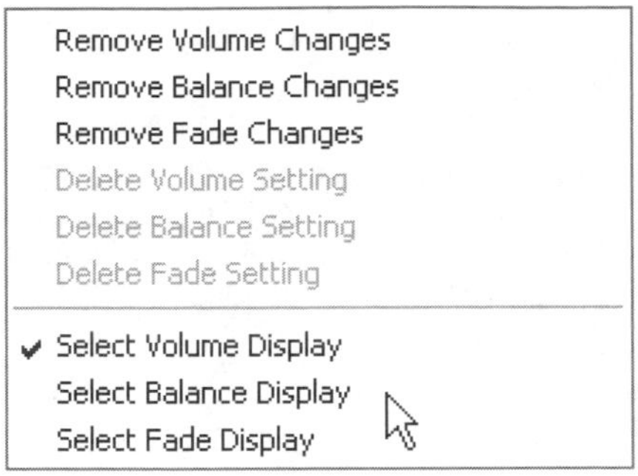

Remove Volume Changes
Remove Balance Changes
Remove Fade Changes
Delete Volume Setting
Delete Balance Setting
Delete Fade Setting

✔ Select Volume Display
Select Balance Display
Select Fade Display

Figure 11.53 Here's how you switch between the different Track displays.

To switch track displays:

1. Select the target track.

2. Right-click and choose the target display (**Figure 11.53**).
   Studio switches to the selected display.

✔ Tips

■ Studio color-codes the displays: The Volume display is blue, the Balance display green, and the Fade display a ghastly orange (where's the *Queer Eye for the Straight Guy* crew when you need them?).

■ As you would expect, moving the volume line up increases volume while moving it down decreases volume. Similarly, moving the fade line down pushes the audio toward the back, while moving it upward brings the audio closer to the front. Moving the balance line toward to the top moves the audio to the left, while moving it downward shifts the audio to the right.

■ You can delete all balance and fade changes to a track by right-clicking on the track and choosing Remove Balance Changes or Remove Fade Changes. The technique is identical to the steps outlined in the previous task, "To remove all volume changes."

ADJUSTING VOLUME, BALANCE, AND FADE

Using Adjustment Handles: A Primer

Let's make it sound like a train is moving from left to right as an exercise on how to use adjustment handles. If you're interested in following along, you'll find the train sound in the Vehicles folder of Studio's sound effects, though you can practice these techniques on any Audio track. Once the target Audio track is on the Timeline, switch to Balance display as described in "To switch track displays." Your track should look like **Figure 11.54**.

Figure 11.54 Starting point for panning a train.

Let's start by moving the Audio track all the way to the left. Click the balance line near the start on the left to create an adjustment handle (**Figure 11.55**). Then drag the adjustment handle as far as possible to the left and to the top of the track (**Figure 11.56**). While you're not at the precise start of the track, you're close enough that your viewers won't hear the difference.

Figure 11.55 Click the balance line to create an adjustment handle.

Figure 11.56 Then drag it to the upper left, which represents the right speaker.

Go to the end of the audio clip, create an adjustment handle (**Figure 11.57**), and drag it to the bottom-right corner (**Figure 11.58**). Play the clip by pressing Play in the Preview window, and if you have stereo speakers set up, you should hear the train moving from your left speaker to the right. You can use the same procedure (in Fade display) to move a sound from front to back.

Figure 11.57 Create your adjustment handle on the right.

I use the Volume and Balance controls primarily for real-time mixing, but find working on the Timeline more effective for track-wide effects.

Figure 11.58 And drag it down to the bottom, representing the left speaker.

Using Studio's Audio Effects

In addition to the video effects discussed in Chapter 9, Studio includes several audio effects that perform both curative and artistic functions. It also supports third-party audio effects that conform to the VST plug-in specification, so you can supplement the audio effects that ship with the program using additional effects from Pinnacle and third-party vendors.

This last section of the chapter begins with an overview of the audio effects included with Studio, and then provides a general description of how you select, configure, and operate them. As you would expect, these effects operate very much like Studio's video effects, so if you're familiar with those, you'll have no problem working with these. The section concludes by showing you how to use Studio's new Noise Reduction filter.

What's in the box?

Once again, what Studio offers here depends upon your product version. If you don't see effects described here in your program, you may want to upgrade to the Plus version or consider buying the additional effects. Notable effects that should be included with the Plus version include these three types of cleaning effects:

◆ **Noise Reduction:** Removes unwanted background noise from your audio.

◆ **Equalizer:** Allows you to fine-tune your audio across ten supported bands, similar to controls on receivers and amplifiers (**Figure 11.59**).

◆ **Leveler:** For standardizing the volume of all audio clips included in a production.

Studio's artistic effects are more varied; here are some highlights.

◆ **Grungelizer:** Adds noises like the crackle from a record player, electric static, or the hum of AC current to your audio to provide a dated feel.

◆ **Reverb:** Simulates the audio from a range of environments, such as a concert hall, car, church, corridor, or cavern.

◆ **Karaoke:** Removes the vocals from a song so that you can sing along with the background music.

You can apply and test any audio effect in real time, which makes them very simple to sample and configure.

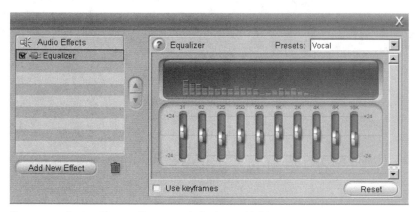

Figure 11.59 Pretty nifty equalizer control, don't you think?

USING STUDIO'S AUDIO EFFECTS

Figure 11.60
You know the
drill—click
here to open the
Audio toolbox.

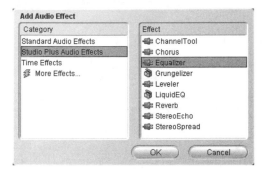

Figure 11.61 Click the desired effect, and then OK.

The audio effects interface

Let's take a look at how to access, apply, and configure audio effects. As you'll see, operation is very similar to Studio's video effects (see Chapter 9), so if you're familiar with their operation, you can skip this part.

To access audio effects:

1. Place the target audio clip on the Timeline and select the audio clip with your pointer.

2. In the upper-left corner of the Movie window, click the Open/Close Audio Toolbox icon.

3. On the left side of the Audio toolbox that appears, click the Add an Effect to an Audio Clip icon (**Figure 11.60**).

   In the Add Audio Effect section on the right side of the screen (**Figure 11.61**), note the two types of effects, indicated by the little icons to the left of each category name in the Category window: The Broom and Dustpan icon represents cleaning effects, while the Electric Plug icon with the VST label represents plug-in effects.

To add and configure an audio effect:

1. Follow Steps 1 through 3 of the preceding task.

2. In the Category window, click the target category of the type of effect you want to use (Figure 11.61).

3. In the Effects list on the right, click the target effect (Figure 11.61).

4. Click OK.

   Studio applies the special effect and, depending on the effect you chose, will either open a Settings window with configuration options (**Figure 11.62**), or a screen with a button for opening a different configuration screen (**Figure 11.63**).

   You can see the option to use keyframes to customize your audio effects. See "Working with Keyframes" in Chapter 9 for details.

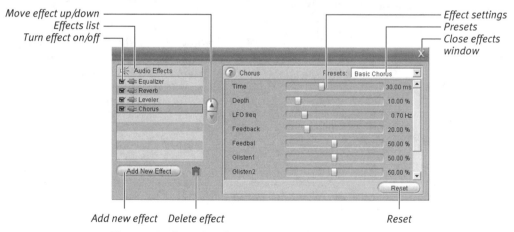

Figure 11.62 The Audio Effects Settings window.

USING STUDIO'S AUDIO EFFECTS

Figure 11.63 If the adjustments aren't in the Settings window, you'll typically see an Edit button like you do here.

5. To adjust the audio effect settings, do *one of the following*:

   ▲ Choose a value from the Presets list box (Figure 11.63).

   ▲ Manually adjust the effect settings.

   Note that you can preview at any time by pressing Play in the Player window.

6. When you're finished configuring the audio effect, do *one of the following*:

   ▲ Click the X in the upper-right corner to close the Special Effects window (Figure 11.62).

   ▲ Click the Add New Effect button to select and configure another special effect.

   Studio saves the first effect and either returns to the Movie window for additional editing or to the Audio Effects window to choose and configure another special effect.

✔ Tip

■ The Reset button (Figure 11.63) resets all controls to their initial values.

USING STUDIO'S AUDIO EFFECTS

To delete an audio effect:

1. Follow Steps 1 and 2 of "To access audio effects."

2. Select the target effect in the Audio Effects list with your pointer (Figure 11.62).

3. Click the Trash Can icon (Figure 11.62). Studio deletes the effect.

To turn an effect on or off:

◆ Deselect the Effect On/Off checkbox to turn the effect off for preview and rendering, or select the checkbox to turn it on (**Figure 11.64**).

✔ Tips

■ It's often useful to turn an effect on or off when attempting to configure another audio effect.

■ You can also adjust the order of special effects by selecting them and then clicking the Move Effect Up or Move Effect Down arrows (Figure 11.62). The order does impact how the resultant audio sounds, so you should experiment with the order to achieve the desired effect.

Figure 11.64 This control turns the effect on and off so that you can fine-tune other controls.

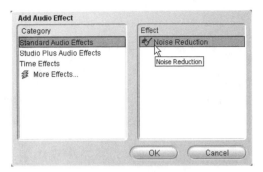

Figure 11.65 Getting to Studio's Noise Reduction effect.

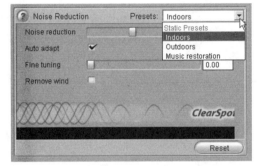

Figure 11.66 The controls for Studio's Noise Reduction effect.

Cleaning Your Audio

Studio's Noise Reduction audio effect attempts to remove unwanted background noise from your audio files. The key word here is attempts. It generally works best on consistent noises like the hum of air conditioning or the recording noise from your camcorder, and works poorly, if at all, with random noises like a dog barking or a car horn.

You should never count on any Noise Reduction effect—Studio's or any other—as a curative that can fix any problem. The best course is to eliminate the background noise before shooting, because Noise Reduction is never a sure thing.

To apply the Noise Reduction effect:

1. Place the target audio clip on the Timeline and select the audio clip with your pointer.

2. In the upper-left corner of the Movie window, click the Open/Close Audio Toolbox icon (Figure 11.1).

3. On the left side of the Audio toolbox, click the Add an Effect to an Audio Clip icon (Figure 11.60).

4. Click the Studio Plus Audio Effects category (Figure 11.61).

5. Click the Noise Reduction effect (**Figure 11.65**).

6. Click OK.

   Studio opens the Noise Reduction settings window (**Figure 11.66**).

7. Do *one of the following*:

   ▲ Choose one of the three presets (Indoors, Outdoors, or Music Restoration) and proceed to Step 9.

   ▲ Manually adjust the controls as described in the next step.

continues on next page

CLEANING YOUR AUDIO

8. If you're manually adjusting the controls:

▲ Adjust the Noise Reduction setting to match the noise in the video, setting it higher for loud background noises and lower for slight hums.

▲ Select the Auto Adapt option to have the effect automatically modify itself for changing conditions.

▲ Adjust the Fine-tuning control to specify the level of cleaning.

▲ Select the Remove Wind option when background wind is the problem.

Preview the effect frequently while modifying these settings. The most commonly experienced problem is distortion, which can make the audio sound heavily metallic or hollow. Also preview at different points in the audio clip to test for distortion, especially if conditions change.

9. Do *one of the following*:

▲ Click the X in the upper-right corner to close the Special Effects window.

▲ Click the Add New Effect button to select and configure another special effect.

Studio saves the first effect and returns to either the Movie window for additional editing or to the Audio Effects window to choose and configure another special effect.

✔ Tip

■ If Noise Reduction produces unacceptable distortion, try using the Equalizer control and reducing levels in one or more bands (Figure 11.62). If the offending background noise is mostly contained in one or two bands, often you can remove the background noise without distorting the original audio.

12

DVD Authoring

The problem with linear video is that it's so, well, linear. While it can seemingly take forever to create a 30-minute video from your four hours of vacation tapes, you still might have trouble quickly locating that cute spot where little Sally and cousin Johnny were holding hands, watching the 4th of July parade.

That's the beauty of DVD. It's pretty much infinitely linkable, allowing you to find the most important scenes quickly. And, though you can dress up your videos as much as you like, you can also choose to break them into scenes (or let scene detection do the work for you) and create menus with links to the good parts.

It's a parent's dream: simple, fast, and better-than-VHS quality, with tape-like playback simplicity. Just open the player and pop in the disc. With recordable drive and media prices dropping every time you turn around, it's also alluringly inexpensive.

Whereas Springsteen was "born to run," Studio was born to author DVDs, the first program ever to offer an integrated editing and authoring environment. It's enough to get my creative juices flowing—how 'bout yours?

About DVD Authoring

With a buildup like that, it's a letdown to start in tutorial mode, but you gotta walk before you can run. So spend some time learning about DVD authoring before diving in.

When planning your DVD, you have two basic issues to consider: video flow and menu structure.

Video flow

Video flow relates to the way the video plays over the course of the DVD. There are two extremes, with many points in between.

◆ **Linear production:** At one extreme is a linear movie that simply happens to be on DVD. You've designed it to flow from beginning to end, like a Hollywood movie, and you're using DVD simply as a convenient distribution medium, perhaps in addition to dubbing to VHS tape. Maybe you want viewers to be able to jump in at certain points, but once the video starts, it will play from start to finish unless interrupted by the viewer.

When planning a linear production, you have to build the entire movie on the Timeline first and then start adding the interactivity. The key link between DVD menus and the video content on the Timeline are chapter points that connect menu buttons with the video scenes you select during authoring. Studio makes these chapter points easy to spot by creating flags on the menu track, which are labeled sequentially, starting with C1 (**Figure 12.1**). At the end of each chapter, you can also choose whether viewers automatically continue on to the next video scene or return to the menu so that they can choose another option. If you choose the latter approach, Studio places Return to Menu flags on the Menu track.

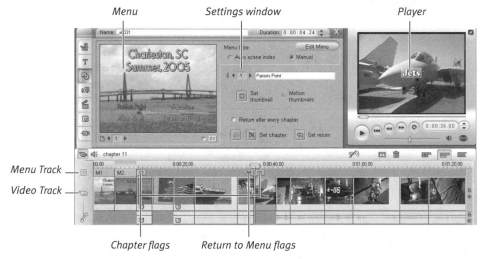

Menu   Settings window   Player

Menu Track

Video Track

Chapter flags   Return to Menu flags

Figure 12.1 Studio's DVD authoring interface. Note the Menu Track icon above the Video Track icon, and the Menu Clip Properties tool, where you'll do most of your linking and customization.

ABOUT DVD AUTHORING

♦ **Disparate videos or slide shows:** The opposite of linear productions are collections of related but essentially disparate videos or slide shows that don't flow from start to finish. Perhaps you're converting your three-month tape from last summer, which covered Johnny's trip to the Little League World Series, Sally's diving championship, and that ridiculously expensive trip to Disney World. In addition to the videotapes, you also shot pictures with a digital still-image camera, and you'd like to build them into a slide show viewable from the DVD.

You'll spend some time consolidating scenes from each event into a discrete movie, but you don't expect viewers to watch the video from start to finish. After each movie or slide show, you want viewers to return to the original menu so that they can choose another sequence.

When planning this second type of production, you start by building all individual movies and slide shows on the Timeline. You again use chapter flags to link to the various movies and scenes within the movies. Then, using techniques discussed in this chapter, you insert Return to Menu flags (Figure 12.1), which return viewers to a menu after the video or slide show finishes.

The net-net is that two tools control video flow. Chapter flags allow viewers to jump to any spot in the video, and Return to Menu flags let you direct where viewers go after watching any particular video.

Irrespective of the production type you choose, it's best to get the video and slide show production done first and then start your DVD authoring.

Some Words of Advice

The best advice I can give to those new to DVD authoring is to be unambitious. In general, most DVD authoring tools, like Studio, offer a cornucopia of development options. Once you start to experiment, development time can go through the roof, and advanced options like video thumbnails and menus lengthen rendering time drastically. With your first DVD projects, it's better to be unambitious and finished than frustrated with no end result.

And while Studio is a mature, tenth-generation video editor, it's only a third-generation DVD authoring program. If you scan the Pinnacle message boards, you'll notice a disproportionate share of messages that relate to exotic DVD authoring attempts. In my experience, with all authoring programs, not just Studio, the more you push the design envelope, the more likely you are to find yourself immersed in untested waters. So get a few simple and successful projects under your belt before going crazy on the authoring front.

Menu structure

Menu structure determines the way menus link to each other. Studio uses three basic types:

- **Linear menus:** Linear menus flow sequentially backward and forward, as shown in **Figure 12.2**. You create these by using any Studio template or by building your own template, as described in Chapter 10.

  When you use a linear menu, Studio automatically builds enough menus so that each chapter in your video has a

link. Viewers move through the menus sequentially, using links between the menus that Studio automatically inserts. Because Studio does all the work for you, using linear menus is fast and easy.

However, though linear menus are acceptable for linear movies, they're poor choices for collections of loosely connected, nonsequential content. For example, if the trip to Disney World was the last event of the summer, you may have to toggle through 10 menus to see that killer sunset from the hotel room balcony—definitely not optimal.

Figure 12.2 Linear menus flow sequentially. Studio builds them automatically, making them easy to create, but viewers have to navigate through them sequentially, which can get old.

The Two Faces of DVD

Recordable DVDs have two basic roles in life. The first is to serve as a place to store data, similar to a CD-recordable disc but with a 4.7 GB or 8.5 GB capacity rather than 650 MB or 700 MB.

More to our interests, however, is the recordable DVD's second role, as a medium for playing back interactive productions on DVD players connected to TV sets and computers with DVD drives and the necessary player software.

Whereas any program capable of writing data to a disc can use DVD-R and DVD+R discs in their first capacity, only an authoring program like Studio can produce titles that play on DVD players.

◆ **Custom menus:** When working with disparate collections, you may want to consider building your own custom menus, which have direct links from one to many menus, as shown in **Figure 12.3**. In my production, I created separate pages for different sites in Charleston, including Patriots Point, the Aquarium, the (supposedly haunted) Aiken-Rhett House, and a page for beach and pool shots. If viewers want to jump to the haunted house videos, they need click only twice rather than multiple times.

Studio provides tremendous flexibility in this regard, allowing you to customize menus and link menu to menu at will. Though you'll get vastly improved navigation, the obvious downside is you have to build multiple menus and perform most of your linking manually. You'll also have to build links from these pages back to the home page and insert Return to Menu flags at the end of each main sequence.

continues on next page

Figure 12.3 You build 'em, you link 'em—custom menus are more work, but are customized for your content, enhancing the playback experience.

ABOUT DVD AUTHORING

◆ **Hybrid menus:** The third menu structure, shown in **Figure 12.4**, is a hybrid structure that includes both linear and custom menus. This is the structure used in my Charleston vacation project, because several of the menus had more sequences than I could fit on one page.

For example, the Patriots Point section contained eight videos, requiring two menu pages. Since I used a linear rather than a custom menu, Studio built the second menu for me, along with links back and forth between the first and second locations menus.

If you study the custom menus in Figure 12.4, you'll notice they all look somewhat similar. That's because to speed production, I created the first menu by hand, saved it, and then swapped the background image and title by section, saving each menu as I went along. (Total production time for the five custom menus was about 10 minutes.)

Figure 12.4 Hybrid menus offers the best of both worlds: they provide great navigation, and Studio handles some of the linking for you.

About DVD Authoring

For a $100 program, Studio is surprisingly adept at authoring, with elegant touches such as displaying only linked buttons on a menu and hiding those that are inactive, as shown in the Player window on the right in **Figure 12.5**.

In the figure, the Menu Clip Properties window on the left shows the linear menu template, and the Preview window on the right shows how the menu will look during playback. The single unpopulated video icon (with *??* at the upper right) is not displayed during playback, and neither are the Previous (left arrow) and Next (right arrow) buttons, which are unnecessary because this section has only one menu.

On the other hand, Studio also lacks link-checking capabilities and didn't notice the *??* in the bottom left of the page, which is supposed to be a link back to the home page. Had I produced this disc without the link, the viewer wouldn't have been able to navigate back to the main menu using menu links, though the Menu button on their remote would certainly get the job done. To avoid producing a disc with incomplete links, you need to preview and check links thoroughly before burning the disc. You'll learn how later in this chapter.

Linear menu template   Menu Clip Properties window   Player window

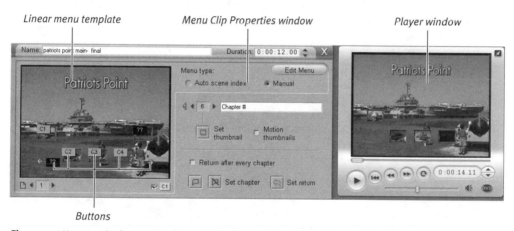

Buttons

Figure 12.5 Here are the linear menu template (left) and the Preview window (right). Note that unpopulated buttons (those with ?? instead of letter/number markers) don't show up in the Preview window.

Using Menu Templates

If you're a new Studio user, I recommend that you produce your first few DVD projects using templates. Keep in mind that the key to success with template-based DVD authoring isn't what you'll learn on these pages, as production is largely automated, but how you've prepared your videos beforehand.

Specifically, Studio automatically inserts chapter flags at the start of each scene. If you have too many scenes, you'll have multiple menu pages, which are cumbersome to navigate. To avoid this problem, combine scenes in the Album (see Chapter 6) or the Movie window (see Chapter 7) before starting your DVD. Also see "Creating DVD Menu Templates" in Chapter 10 for more on menus.

The one downside of this approach is that you can't trim or place transitions between scenes and then combine them. If this limitation prevents you from combining your scenes into usable chunks, you should tell Studio not to create chapter links automatically when you drag in your first menu, and simply create the links manually (see "To create a chapter link" later in this chapter).

As it turns out, the template approach worked well for a concert DVD I produced while writing this book, Galax's own No Speed Limit rocking the Fabulous Rex Theater (pronounced thee-a-tor around these parts). I'll use this project to demonstrate the use of templates and then get back to Charleston for the rest of the chapter.

Figure 12.6 All concert videos are on the Timeline.

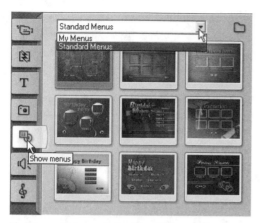

Figure 12.7 Welcome to the Menu Album. Note that the menus you create are stored in a separate folder.

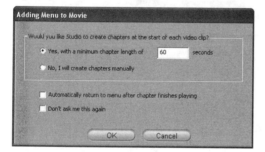

Figure 12.8 Select Yes, and Studio practically builds the DVD for you.

To use a menu template:

1. In Edit mode, place all project assets on the Timeline (**Figure 12.6**).

2. Click the Show Menus icon to open the Disc Menus tab of the Album (**Figure 12.7**).

   If you've created your own menus, you access them by choosing My Menus from the list of menus.

3. Drag the desired menu to the front of the project, placing it on the Video track.

   Studio opens the Adding Menu to Movie dialog box (**Figure 12.8**).

4. Click Yes to create links automatically to each scene after the menu.

   Note the option to insert a minimum chapter length in seconds. This can be really helpful if automatic scene detection produced lots of small scenes that really don't need separate chapter points. My take is to combine the scenes beforehand into the desired chapters, which makes this control superfluous.

   Studio automatically creates as many menus as necessary for all video scenes, inserts the Next and Previous buttons where necessary, and populates the thumbnail buttons with videos from the Timeline.

5. If desired, Click Automatically Return to Menu After Chapter Finishes Playing.

   In a concert video like this one, I want the viewer to move from song to song, so I won't select this option. If you think your viewers will want to consume your video in short chunks, rather than from start to finish, select this option.

   continues on next page

✔ Tips

■ Studio automatically uses the first video frame as the menu thumbnail, not the thumbnail you've selected for either the Album or the Timeline (see Chapter 10).

■ When you use a menu template, Studio shows only one copy of the menu on the Timeline, even though the program may ultimately produce multiple menus. See "To select the next menu page" later in this chapter for information on navigating through these pages in the Menu Clip Properties window.

■ Studio enables four options when you select a menu, as shown in **Figure 12.9**. I stick with the default option, Ask If Chapters Should be Created, so that I can easily opt out of Studio's automatic menu creation, which I usually do. To access this dialog box, choose Setup > Video and Audio Preferences from Studio's main menu.

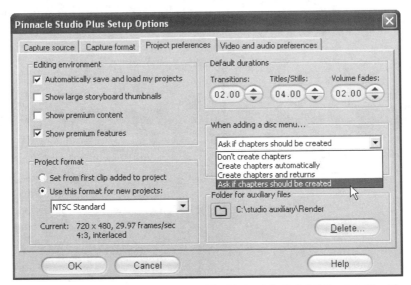

Figure 12.9 Chapter and return options. I stick with the default, Ask If Chapters Should Be Created.

To edit the menu:

1. Double-click the menu.

   Studio opens the Menu Clip Properties tool (**Figure 12.10**).

2. At the upper right, click Edit Menu.

   The Title editor opens (**Figure 12.11**). See Chapter 10 for editing details.

3. Make your edits; then do *one of the following:*

   ▲ At the lower right, click OK (or press F12) to save the menu and return to the Edit window.

   Studio overwrites the original menu on the Timeline, but doesn't change the menu in the Menu Album.

   ▲ Choose File > Save Menu As to save the file using a unique name, preserving the original Studio menu for reuse. Then click OK to return to the Edit window.

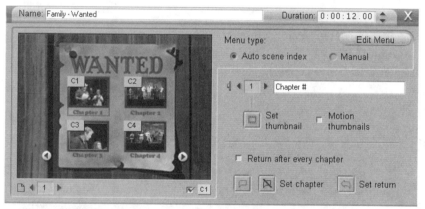

Figure 12.10 The initial menu showing the first four chapter links.

Figure 12.11 The Title editor, where you can customize this template.

USING MENU TEMPLATES

To create a chapter link:

1. Using the Timeline scrubber or the Player controls, navigate to the target starting point of the new chapter (**Figure 12.12**).

2. Do *one of the following:*

   ▲ Right-click the Menu track and choose Set Disc Chapter (**Figure 12.13**).

   ▲ Right-click the Video track and choose Set Disc Chapter.

   Studio inserts chapter link 3 (C3) at the insertion point, and creates a new link (C4) where C3 was previously located (**Figure 12.14**).

✔ Tip

■ You can move a chapter flag by dragging it to any location on the Menu track. See "Previewing Your DVD" later in this chapter for details.

Figure 12.12 To create a chapter flag, drag the Timeline scrubber to the desired frame.

Figure 12.13 Right-click the Menu track and click Set Disc Chapter.

Figure 12.14 The new chapter link is created.

USING MENU TEMPLATES

Maintaining Order—Or Not

If you elect to have Studio automatically create chapter points at all scenes (Figure 12.8) and then later add chapter points at other locations on the Timeline, Studio automatically places each new scene in its chronological sequence. For example, in Figures 12.12 through 12.14, I added a chapter point between C2 and C3, which Studio automatically named C3; Studio then renumbered all subsequent chapter points on the Timeline, increasing each one by one number. In Studio parlance, this means that the menu type is Auto Scene Index, which you can see at the upper right of Figure 12.10.

In contrast, if you elect to assign chapter points manually and then insert a chapter point between two current chapter points, Studio inserts the next available chapter point at the selected location and doesn't automatically reorder the chapters. This is shown in **Figure 12.15**, where I added all chapter points manually. Here, the inserted chapter point is C13, rather than C5. This means that this chapter point will be out of sequence when played from the menu. This menu type is Manual, shown at the upper right of Figure 12.10.

Note that you can convert from Manual to Auto Scene Index at any time by clicking the Auto Scene Index checkbox in the Menu Clip Properties window, and Studio will reorder the chapter points into sequential order. This process is described in "To change menu type" later in this chapter.

Here's the lesson: So long as your videos are laid out sequentially on the Timeline in the order you want your viewers to access them, and you have a reasonable number of scenes, you can have Studio automatically assign chapter points. This approach is also easier if you delete chapter points, since Studio will automatically reorder all subsequent videos and close any gaps in the menu.

On the other hand, if you want to customize the menu order of the chapter points, you have to use the second approach and manually assign all chapter points. Note that if you delete any chapter points under this approach, Studio doesn't automatically fill the gaps, and you'll have unassigned buttons in your menus. You can easily address this issue by switching to Auto Scene Index mode, but then all chapter points will be assigned sequentially, and you'll lose the custom order you've already created.

Figure 12.15 Here's how the link would look if I selected Manual rather than Auto Scene Index.

To assign chapter points manually:

1. In Edit mode, place all project assets on the Timeline (Figure 12.6).

2. Click the Show Menus icon to open the Disc Menus tab of the Album (Figure 12.7).

   If you've created your own menus, you can access them by choosing My Menus from the list box shown at the top of Figure 12.7.

3. Drag the desired menu to the front of the project, placing it on the Video track.

   Studio opens the Adding Menu to Movie dialog box (Figure 12.8).

4. Click No to create links manually to each scene after the menu.

5. At the bottom of the Menu Clip Properties tool, click the Show chapter numbers checkbox (**Figure 12.16**).

Show chapter numbers check box

Figure 12.16 Click here to see the chapter links (or the absence of links).

USING MENU TEMPLATES

Figure 12.17 Drag the scene into the target frame to create the link.

6. Link scenes to the menu buttons by doing *one of the following:*

   ▲ In the Timeline, drag the target scene into the target button frame (**Figure 12.17**).

   ▲ Click the target button frame in the Menu Clip Properties tool (Studio highlights the frame). Click the target scene on the Timeline (Studio highlights the scene). Then click the Create Chapter Link button in the Menu Clip Properties tool (**Figure 12.18**).

   Studio lists C1 in the button frame and C1 on the Timeline and places the first frame of the video as a thumbnail (**Figure 12.19**).

7. Repeat Step 6 until you populate all button frames on the first menu.

continues on next page

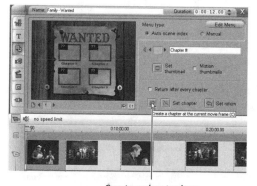

Create a chapter icon

Figure 12.18 Or click the frame and then the scene and then click here.

Figure 12.19 The C1 on the button identifies the chapter point the button is linked to on the Timeline.

USING MENU TEMPLATES

8. At the bottom of the Menu Clip Properties tool, click the Show Next Page icon (**Figure 12.20**). Studio advances to the next menu page, identified as Menu Page 2 in the page selector (**Figure 12.21**).

9. If Studio doesn't automatically advance to the next page, use the page selector icons to advance to the next menu.

You have to create the new chapter link before attempting to advance to the next menu page because Studio won't create the page until necessary to host all chapter points.

10. Repeat Steps 6 through 9 until all desired scenes are added to the menu.

Figure 12.20 Once you create all links on a menu, click here to see the next menu page.

Figure 12.21 Here we are at Page 2. Now you can start inserting links here as well.

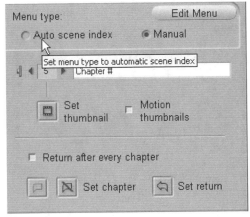

Figure 12.22 To place chapter flags in numerical sequence, click Autoscene index.

Figure 12.23 Order restored. Compare this figure to Figure 12.15.

Figure 12.24 To clear chapter links (and delete chapters), select the chapter and then click the Delete the Current Chapter icon.

To change menu type:

◆ In the Menu Clip Properties tool, select Auto Scene Index (**Figure 12.22**).

Studio sorts the chapter flags sequentially and updates all affected menus (**Figure 12.23**).

To delete chapter links:

◆ To delete chapter links, do *one of the following*:

▲ In the Menu Clip Properties tool, select the button linked to the target chapter link. Click the Delete the Current Chapter icon or press V (**Figure 12.24**).

▲ On the Menu track, select the chapter flag, right-click, and choose Delete.

▲ On the Menu track, select the chapter flag and press the Delete key.

Studio deletes the chapter flag and clears the menu link (**Figure 12.25**).

Figure 12.25 The chapter flag and link created in Figure 12.14 are both gone.

To change a button caption:

1. Select the button in the Menu Clip Properties tool; then select the button caption description to make the field active.

2. Insert the new text.

3. Press Enter to save the text (**Figure 12.26**). Studio saves the new description and changes the menu.

✔ Tip

■ If you don't press Enter, and simply click outside the box or move to the next chapter, Studio won't save the new text description. You must press Enter.

To change a button thumbnail:

1. Select the button in the Menu Clip Properties tool; then use the Timeline scrubber or Player controls to navigate to a new thumbnail frame.

2. Do *one of the following:*

▲ Right-click the Video track and choose Set Thumbnail.

▲ In the Menu Clip Properties tool, click the Set Thumbnail icon (**Figure 12.27**).

Studio replaces the default image with the new thumbnail.

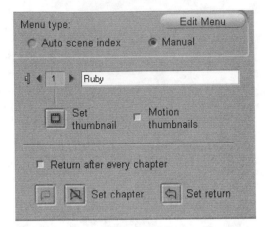

Figure 12.26 Enter the button title here.

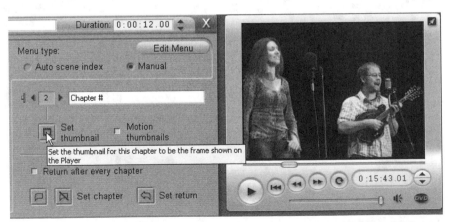

Figure 12.27 To change the thumbnail, navigate to the target frame and click Set Thumbnail.

USING MENU TEMPLATES

Button selection control

Create Motion
Thumbnails check box

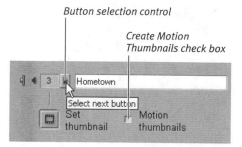

Figure 12.28 Use the button selection control to move from button to button.

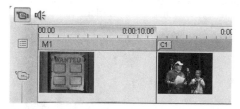

Figure 12.29 Expect some rendering time when you select Motion Thumbnails, especially with multi-menu productions.

To select another button to edit:

◆ In the Menu Clip Properties tool, do *one of the following*:

▲ Click the button to edit.

▲ Use the button selection control to move to the button you want to edit (**Figure 12.28**).

To create video buttons:

◆ In the Menu Clip Properties tool, select Motion Thumbnails (Figure 12.28).

Studio replaces the still-image thumbnail with a tiny version of the video, creating a video button.

✔ Tips

■ The video button will play for the duration of the menu and then restart. Video buttons are most aesthetically pleasing when menus have a duration of at least one minute. See "To change menu duration" later in this chapter.

■ Because video buttons must be separately rendered before they appear, these won't immediately show up when you preview your video. If you selected background rendering (see Chapter 8), you'll see the green bar above the menu that indicates that it's rendering (**Figure 12.29**).

■ Maybe it's just me, but I find video buttons irritating. They take a long time to render, and slow the computer when rendering in the background. These head my list of "don't try this at home" features.

To select the next menu page:

◆ In the Menu Clip Properties tool, click the Show Next Page icon (**Figure 12.30**).

✔ Tips

■ Use this procedure to move through the sequential menus automatically created by Studio, to access all linked chapters.

■ To select a completely different menu, double-click that menu on the Timeline.

To set Return to Menu links:

1. On the Menu track, double-click the target menu.

   Studio displays the menu in the Menu Clip Properties tool.

2. Click the video that, after playback, should return the viewer to the target menu (rather than automatically moving to the next scene on the Timeline).

3. Do *one of the following:*

   ▲ In the Menu Clip Properties tool, click the Return to This Menu icon (**Figure 12.31**).

   ▲ Right-click the Menu track and choose Set Return to Menu.

   ▲ Right-click the Video track and choose Set Return to Menu.

   ▲ Click the Return After Every Chapter checkbox to return to the menu after each chapter finishes playing.

   Studio sets the Return to Menu flag (**Figure 12.32**).

✔ Tip

■ Studio always sets the Return to Menu flag at the end of the video, figuring you'd probably never want to interrupt playback of a clip in the middle. If your intent is to interrupt the clip in the middle, simply drag the flag to the desired location.

Figure 12.30 Click here to display the next menu page.

Figure 12.31 To set Return to Menu links, double-click the menu to open it in the Menu Clip Properties tool and then click this icon or press M.

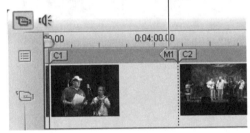

Figure 12.32 Whatever method you use, look for the flag. It should be the same number as the menu you want to return to (in this case, M1 = Menu 1) and blue.

USING MENU TEMPLATES

Figure 12.33 You can set the menu duration here, or simply drag the menu to the desired length, just like a still image.

To change menu duration:

◆ To change the menu duration, do *one of the following*:

▲ Select the menu and drag it to the desired length (see Chapter 7 for details).

▲ At the upper right of the Menu Clip Properties tool, change the Duration field by typing the desired duration or using the controls to the right of the field (**Figure 12.33**).

Using Custom Menus

Before starting work here, you should have at least two menus: a main menu (**Figure 12.34**) with buttons to link to your section menus, and the section menus themselves (**Figure 12.35**).

The section menus should have three navigational button links: Previous and Next buttons that link to the namesake pages, and a Home button to link to the main menu.

I'll start by getting your menu and section menus on the Timeline. Then I'll cover how to link the menus to scenes on the Timeline and then to each other.

Figure 12.34 Here's the main menu for my DVD.

Previous button —
Home button —
(link to main menu)

Next button
Links to scenes

Figure 12.35 Here's one of five section menus. Note the Next and Previous buttons, which handle navigation if Studio creates multiple menus, and the link to the main menu.

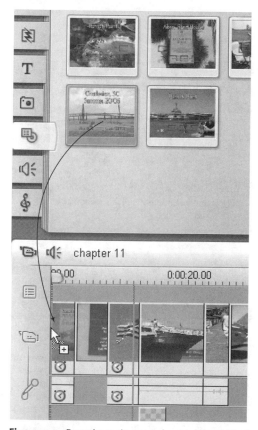

Figure 12.36 Clicking the Show Menus icon opens the Disc Menus tab.

Figure 12.37 Drag the main menu down to the front of the Timeline.

To insert the main menu:

1. In Edit mode, place all project assets on the Timeline (Figure 12.6).

2. Click the Show Menus icon to open the Disc Menus tab in the Album (**Figure 12.36**).

3. At the upper left of the Menus Album, choose My Menus from the list box (**Figure 12.37**).

   Studio opens the Album that contains your custom menus.

4. Drag the main menu to the front of the project, placing it on the Video track (Figure 12.37).

   Studio opens the Adding Menu to Movie dialog box (Figure 12.8).

5. Click No to manually create all links.

   Studio inserts the menu and opens the Menu Clip Properties tool to the Set Menu Links window (**Figure 12.38**).

Figure 12.38 Oops—look at all those question marks, representing open links. You'll fill them in a moment.

To insert and link a section menu:

1. From the Disc Menus tab, drag the section menu to the Timeline in front of the first video clip you will link to this menu (**Figure 12.39**).

2. Click No to create all links manually. Studio inserts the menu (**Figure 12.40**).

3. If Studio doesn't automatically open the Menu Clip Properties tool, double-click the menu to open it.

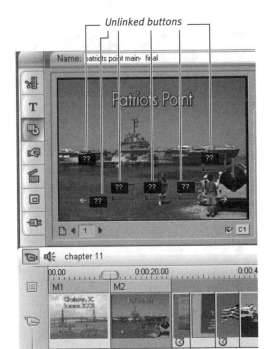

Unlinked buttons

Figure 12.40 Here's the section menu, begging to be linked. Note that the next and previous buttons don't have question marks, because Studio links these automatically. However, the "home" button, alongside the previous button, shows question marks, which we'll eliminate by linking this button to the main menu.

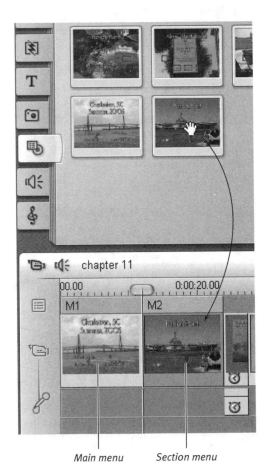

Main menu   Section menu

Figure 12.39 Drag the section menu to the Timeline.

Figure 12.41 Drag the main menu to the Home link, just to the right of the previous icon.

Figure 12.42 The M1 tells you that the link is created.

4. Drag the main menu to the Home button in the section menu (**Figure 12.41**).

   Studio links the main menu to the section menu, allowing the viewer to navigate back to the main menu from the section menu (**Figure 12.42**), and places an M1 on top of the link because the Show Link checkbox, at the bottom right in the figure, is checked.

   I find that links can get disorganized if I don't complete the menu links first, which is why I do this first.

continues on next page

5. To link project assets on the Timeline to the menu buttons, do *one of the following:*

- ▲ Drag a video to a button in the Menu Clip Properties tool (**Figure 12.43**).

- ▲ Select a button in the Menu Clip Properties tool; then right-click the Menu track at the desired location and choose Set Disc Chapter.

- ▲ Select a button in the Menu Clip Properties tool; then right-click the Video track at the desired location and choose Set Disc Chapter.

- ▲ Select a button in the Menu Clip Properties tool; then select the target video and click the Create a Chapter Link for the Selected Button icon (**Figure 12.44**).

Studio creates the new chapter flag, in this case C1 (**Figure 12.45**), and links the chapter flag to the selected button.

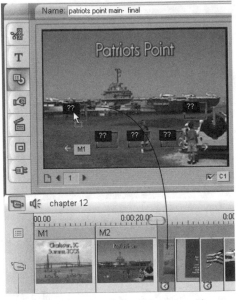

Figure 12.43 Start dragging and dropping videos on the buttons.

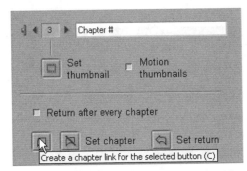

Figure 12.44 Or select a menu button, select a video, and click this button. This is the best method when Studio gets a bit balky and refuses to set the link.

Figure 12.45 Link accomplished. While you can't see it in this black-and-white image, the C1 link in the Menu Clip Properties tool is coded the same color as the menu.

Figure 12.46 All buttons on the first section menu are now linked. Time to move on to the next menu.

6. Populate the rest of the buttons on the section menu using these same procedures (**Figure 12.46**). If you need more than one menu, click the Show Next Page icon, shown in Figure 12.46, or the Select Next Button icon, shown in Figure 12.28.

7. Add and populate any other section menus.

✔ Tips

- At times, Studio gets a bit finicky about accepting a link via drag and drop. When this happens, select the target button and then the target scene and click the Create a Chapter Link for the Selected Button icon.

- If Studio won't let you turn the menu page, it's because you haven't linked all buttons on that menu yet. When this happens, it's usually the Return to Home button that's still unlinked.

- Studio resets the chapter flag number for each menu and color-codes menus, chapter links, and Return to Menu links.

USING CUSTOM MENUS

To link section menus to the main menu:

1. Double-click the main menu.

   Studio opens the main menu in the Menu Clip Properties tool (**Figure 12.47**).

2. Drag the section menu to the appropriate link on the main menu (**Figure 12.48**). Studio creates the link.

3. Repeat Step 2 for all section menus or videos linked directly to the main menu (**Figure 12.49**). Menus are shown as M2, M3, M4, and M5.

Figure 12.47 Time to link the section menu to the main menu. Double-click the main menu to open it in the Menu Clip Properties tool.

Figure 12.49 Menus linked and ready for duty.

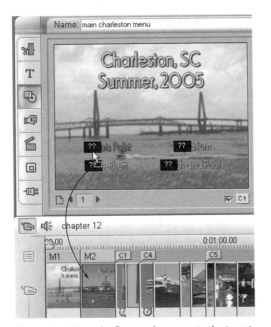

Figure 12.48 Drag the first section menu to the target button.

USING CUSTOM MENUS

Link to the main menu

Figure 12.50 If you're using a hybrid menu structure, you have to link *each menu* to the Home page. Here we turn to page 2 of this menu, and the link to Home is empty.

✔ Tips

■ If you're using a hybrid menu structure and your section menu has multiple pages, you'll have to link the first and all subsequent menus to the main menu to enable viewers to return to the main menu from each menu. For example, Figure 12.46 shows the menu link to the main menu as complete (as indicated by the M1 designation), but once you turn to the next menu page, the link (like all the others) is empty (**Figure 12.50**).

■ Again, sometimes Studio gets a bit finicky about accepting a link via drag and drop. In these instances, make sure the target link is selected in the Menu Clip Properties tool, select the target asset, and then click the Create a Chapter Link for the Selected Button icon (Figure 12.44).

USING CUSTOM MENUS

To set Return to Menu flags:

1. Double-click the target menu.

   Studio displays the menu in the Clip Properties tool.

2. On the Timeline, select the final video linked to that menu (**Figure 12.51**).

3. Set the Return to Menu link using one of the techniques described earlier in "Using Menu Templates."

   Studio sets the Return to Menu link for that menu (**Figure 12.52**).

4. Set Return to Menu links for all section menus.

✔ Tip

■ If the Return to Menu flag has a number that's different from the menu number, you may be returning to the wrong menu—obviously okay if you wanted to return to a different menu than where you started from, but also a fairly common mistake.

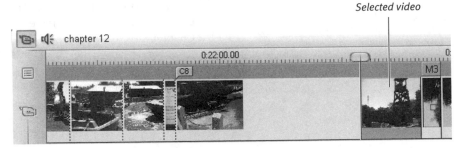

Selected video

Figure 12.51 To set a Return to Menu flag, choose the last video in the section.

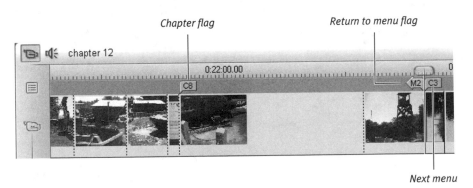

Chapter flag *Return to menu flag*

Next menu

Figure 12.52 Return to Menu link set.

USING CUSTOM MENUS

Figure 12.53 Click here to start the DVD preview.

Figure 12.54 Look at that DVD control—makes me want to grab a beer and put my feet up!

Previewing Your DVD

Given Studio's DVD design flexibility, it's difficult to set rules for previewing your titles. Generally, I like to check the major inter-menu links first, because if these are wrong, viewers won't be able to access certain menu pages. Then I check the Return to Menu links and finally the video links themselves.

Note that even if you let Studio build the production for you from a template, you should check the inter-menu links, especially if you created your own template. That way, if you made a mistake creating the menu, you'll catch it before you burn your DVD.

Basically, the best practice is to go through each link on each menu. It's not so much the media cost that will kill you if you have to re-burn your DVD; it's the rendering and production time, which can easily take hours, even for short productions.

To preview your DVD:

1. In the Player window, click the Start DVD Preview icon (**Figure 12.53**).

   The Player switches to DVD Preview mode with DVD-specific playback controls (**Figure 12.54**).

continues on next page

PREVIEWING YOUR DVD

2. Check all links from the main menu to the section menus (**Figure 12.55**).

3. Check all links back to the main menu from the section menus (**Figure 12.56**).

4. From each section menu with multiple pages, check the links between each menu (Figure 12.56 and **Figure 12.57**).

5. If you inserted Return to Menu flags, play the last video in each section to test whether you return to the proper menu.

You can use the Timeline scrubber to move to near the Return to Menu flag and then click Play, which may be faster than waiting for the video to play (**Figure 12.58**).

6. Check each movie link in each menu.

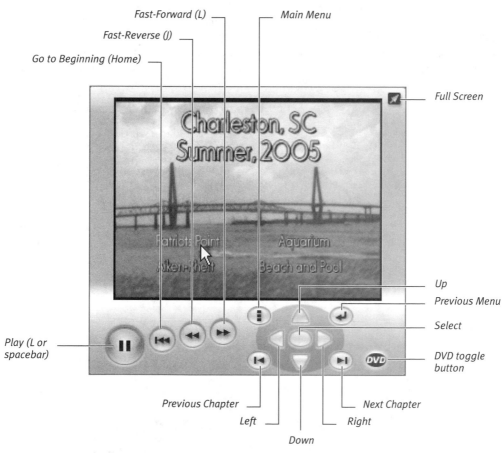

Figure 12.55 Start by checking all links to section menus.

Return to
Main Menu   Next Menu

Figure 12.56 And then back to the main menu.

Return to Previous menu

Figure 12.57 After clicking to the next menu, click here
to return to the previous menu.

✔ Tips

■ If your chapter flags aren't in the desired
locations, you can drag them to any
frame desired (**Figure 12.59**).

■ If you toggle to full-screen mode during
preview, you no longer have access to any
of the preview controls. Press Esc on
your keyboard to return to the main
Studio menu.

■ Studio may stall and simply stop playing
during preview at times. If this occurs,
toggle out of Preview mode by clicking
the Start DVD Preview icon (Figure 12.53)
and then toggle back in and try again. If
that doesn't work, try rebooting (saving
your work first, of course).

PREVIEWING YOUR DVD

Timeline scrubber

Figure 12.58 Drag the Timeline scrubber to the end
of the video to speed things up.

New chapter
flag location

Figure 12.59 You can drag chapter flags to new locations,
watching the video in the Player as a guide.

Creating Audio Menus

Many Hollywood DVDs play audio while displaying the menu, an effect that Studio can duplicate with ease. You can use any audio track you create or import into Studio (see Chapter 11) as background for your menu tracks.

For simplicity, the tasks here will use a WAV file already in my Music album, but you can rip tracks at will or use SmartSound to create audio for your menus.

Few things are as irritating as music repeated over and over every 12 seconds. So if you're going to use audio menus, remember to extend the duration of your menus to at least one minute, preferably longer.

To create an audio menu:

1. Double-click the target menu.

   Studio opens the menu in the Menu Clip Properties tool (**Figure 12.60**).

2. Extend the duration of the menu to at least one minute (**Figure 12.61**).

   (See "To change menu duration" earlier in this chapter for instructions.) The one-minute rule is for aesthetics, not any limitation in the Studio program. You can run a menu for the entire length of your chosen audio track, if you desire.

3. At the upper left of the Movie window, click the Camcorder icon to close the Video toolbox (**Figure 12.62**), or click the X in the upper-right corner of the Menu Clip Properties tool.

Figure 12.60 To add audio to your menu, start by double-clicking the menu to load it in the Menu Clip Properties tool.

Figure 12.61 Extend the duration to at least one minute (for aesthetics, not due to a Studio limitation).

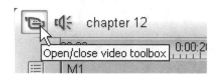

Figure 12.62 Close the Video toolbox.

Figure 12.63 I'm using a killer song from No Speed Limit called "Wayfaring Stranger" as background for my menu.

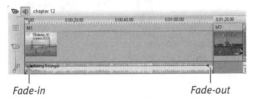

Fade-in   *Fade-out*

Figure 12.64 Fade the audio in and out for a bit of extra polish.

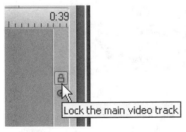

Figure 12.65 To drag an audio file to the Original Audio track, you first have to lock the Video track.

4. Do *one of the following:*

   ▲ To find an audio file to use as background music, click the Show Music icon to open the Music tab in the Album (**Figure 12.63**).

   ▲ To use the audio from a video file as background music for the menu, click the Show Videos icon.

5. Drag the desired audio track to either the Sound Effect track or Music track and trim to the same duration as the DVD menu using techniques discussed in "To change the duration of an audio file on the Timeline" in Chapter 7.

6. If you like, fade the background audio in and out. See "Using the Volume Tool" in Chapter 11 for details (**Figure 12.64**). Note that to drag the audio track to the Original Audio track (where it is shown in Figure 12.64), you first have to lock the Video track (**Figure 12.65**).

✔ Tips

■ Audio backgrounds work automatically with templates; Studio inserts the audio into all sequential menus. However, the track starts over each time you move between menus, which may prove irritating. (This is a limitation of the DVD format, not Studio.)

Creating Video Menus

Motion menus have video playing underneath the buttons to amuse viewers while they're making their menu selection. Video menus come with the same caveat as audio menus: when they're short and repetitive, they get irritating. Plan on using video clips of at least one minute for your video menus, or generic videos like clouds blowing or flags waving where it isn't obvious that they're restarting.

Essentially, a video menu is just like a regular menu, but instead of inserting a still image as background, you insert a video. For a complete recap, review "Using Full-Screen Titles" in Chapter 10, particularly the section "To select an image background." Here, I'll just cover the highlights.

Note that you must insert a video file from your hard disk, rather than a video scene in the Album or video clips on the Timeline. This means you have to select, edit, and output the video background into the final form, most preferable a DV AVI file, before using it in a menu. See Chapter 14 for details on producing AVI files.

You can either create a new video menu, or convert a menu with an image in the background to video. For simplicity, I'll perform the latter.

To create a video menu:

1. Drag the menu to the Video Track (**Figure 12.66**).

2. Right-click the menu, and choose Go To Title/Menu Editor (**Figure 12.67**).
   Studio opens the Menu Editor.

3. In the upper-right corner of the Menu Editor, click the Backgrounds icon (**Figure 12.68**).
   Studio opens the Backgrounds library.

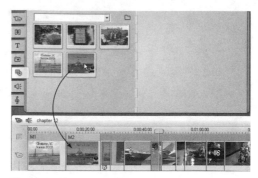

Figure 12.66 Insert the menu video onto the Video track.

Figure 12.67 Right-click and choose Go to Title/Menu Editor to swap out the backgrounds.

Backgrounds   Browse icon

Figure 12.68 In the Title Editor, click the Backgrounds icon, and then the Browse icon.

Figure 12.69 Now we tell the Menu Editor we want to load a video background by choosing AVI files as the file type.

Figure 12.70 Here's the flag video I'll use in the background.

4. Click the Browse icon in the Backgrounds library (Figure 12.68).

Studio opens the Open dialog box (**Figure 12.69**).

5. On the bottom of the Open dialog box, click the Files of Type drop-down list and select the format of your saved video file. You can use either AVI or MPEG video files; I prefer the former since they are generally less compressed than MPEG.

Studio populates the Backgrounds library with files of the selected type (**Figure 12.70**). In the example, I have only one such file.

continues on next page

6. Click the desired background video. Studio inserts the video as background for the menu (**Figure 12.71**).

7. In the upper-right corner of the Title Menu, enter the title duration (**Figure 12.72**).

8. Choose File > Save Menu As and name your new menu.

9. In the bottom-right corner of the Menu Editor, click OK to close the window and return to the Timeline.

Studio adds the new menu to the menu library (**Figure 12.73**). The logo on the bottom right of the new menu (compare to Figure 12.66) indicates that it's a video menu.

10. If Studio didn't replace the original menu on the Timeline with the new menu, drag the new menu to the Timeline and delete the original menu.

11. Create the links to the content and other menus as normal.

✔ Tip

■ Video backgrounds work automatically with templates; Studio inserts the video behind all sequential menus.

Figure 12.71 This looks beautiful as background for the Patriots Point menu.

Figure 12.72 I like a duration of a minute or longer for audio and video menus.

Figure 12.73 The logo on the bottom right of the menu icon indicates that this is a video menu.

Choosing Your DVD Recorder

In the beginning, there was DVD, and it was good. Then DVD-R and DVD-RAM. Then DVD+RW. Then (in nonsequential order) DVD-RW, and DVD+R. Then DVD+R/RW/-R and DVD-R/RW +R/RW and DVD-RAM/-R, and DVD+R DL and DVD−R DL. It's enough to make your head swim.

This is not a misprint—in fact, I'm sure I've forgotten a few formats. Overall, if the DVD industry set out to confuse potential buyers of DVD recorders, it couldn't have done a better job.

But here are the details you need to know—appropriately enough—in random order.

◆ Recorders that burn in −R/+R, or +RW/-RW or +R DL or −R DL can all produce discs that play on your living room player. Recorders that burn solely in -RAM format (if you can find one) can't.

◆ The technologies used in −R and +R discs are different, but not meaningfully so to you as end user, or to your audience, for that matter. Neither is better than the other; different patent holders get paid when you buy different disc formats, but the practical differences end there.

◆ Recorders that support only −R/-RW can burn only −R/-RW discs, while recorders that support only +R/+RW can burn only +R/+RW discs. Be careful when shopping that you buy the right format for your burner. Fortunately, most recorders burn all four formats.

◆ All recordable discs have some risk of incompatibility with desktop players. More on that in the sidebar "The Dark Side of Recordable DVD" at the end of this chapter.

◆ If you're buying a new drive, opt for one that supports both +R/RW and −R/RW. That will increase the odds that you can burn a disc that grandma can play.

◆ Many new drives support DVD+R DL, and a few support DVD-R DL. Both of these formats store data on two layers on a single side of a disc, which increases capacity from 4.7 GB to 8.5 GB. This is not a new concept; the DVD movies you rent at Blockbuster have been using dual-layer media to include more content for years. But mass-produced, store-bought DVDs are a different animal from recordable media, and the recordable guys only got into the dual-layer (DL) game last year. The DL discs are more expensive, but if you can't possibly think of a way to cut your project down below two hours, DL media will allow you to do so without having to degrade video quality to fit more video on the disc. There are some playback compatibility issues with these discs (no surprise since they're still relatively new); more on that in "The Dark Side of Recordable DVD".

Burning a DVD Title

The big moment has arrived; you've created, previewed, tinkered, and then tinkered some more. The babies are crying, the spouse is complaining, and the grandparents are doubting they'll ever see this DVD. It's time to shoot the videographer and ship the movie.

Let's burn, baby, burn.

To burn a DVD title:

1. Put blank media in your DVD burner.

2. Do *one of the following:*

    ▲ At the upper left of the program window, click Make Movie (**Figure 12.74**), then click Disc (**Figure 12.75**), and then click Settings.

    ▲ From the Studio menu, choose Setup > Make Disc (**Figure 12.76**).

    Studio enters Make Movie mode, and the Pinnacle Studio Setup Options dialog box opens to the Make Disc tab (**Figure 12.77**).

Figure 12.74 Click Make Movie to start the DVD production process.

Figure 12.75 Click Disc to display the Diskometer.

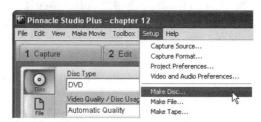

Figure 12.76 Or choose Setup > Make Disc.

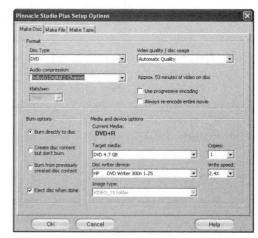

Figure 12.77 Decision central for DVD production.

Figure 12.78 Choosing the type of disc to burn.

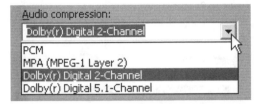

Figure 12.79 Choosing an audio format.

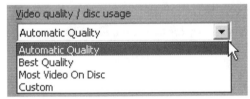

Figure 12.80 Go with Automatic unless you really know what you're doing.

3. In the Output Format section, choose DVD.

4. In the Format section, choose *one or more of the following:*

▲ **Disc Type:** Set to DVD (**Figure 12.78**).

▲ **Audio Compression:** Set to Dolby Digital 2-Channel for stereo recording and Dolby Digital 5.1-Channel if you've used the Surround Panner to customize the pan and fade location of multiple tracks (**Figure 12.79**).

▲ **Video Quality/Disc Usage:** Set to Automatic (**Figure 12.80**).

This tells Studio to automatically determine the optimal data rate for the amount of content on your disc, which is the simplest of the four options. If you select Best Quality, Studio encodes at 8 Mbps but limits your disc to about 59 minutes of video. If you select Most Video on Disc, Studio encodes at 3 Mbps, which allows up to approximately 124 minutes of video, but will encode at 3 Mbps even if you have less video, which is suboptimal. Or you can choose Custom and set your own target data rate.

For progressive encoding, do *one of the following:*

▲ If producing a DVD for playback on a progressive scan DVD player and high-definition (HD) TV, click the Use Progressive Encoding checkbox.

▲ Otherwise, don't enable progressive encoding.

▲ Don't enable Always Re-encode Entire Movie.

continues on next page

BURNING A DVD TITLE

5. In the Burn Options section, choose *one of the following:*

▲ **Burn Directly to Disc:** Choose this to render and burn the current project directly to DVD.

▲ **Create Disc Content but Don't Burn:** Choose this to render the current project and save it to your hard disk.

▲ **Burn from Previously Created Disc Content:** Choose this to burn from previously created content. Studio burns the content from the currently open project; this option is available only if the project was already burned to disc or saved as a disc image.

6. Check Eject disc When Done unless you have a good reason not to.

7. In the Media and Device Options section, do *one of the following:*

▲ Select your target media from the drop-down list (**Figure 12.81**).

▲ From the Disc Writer Device list, choose the target DVD-Recordable drive (**Figure 12.82**).

▲ From the Copies list, choose the number of copies you want to produce (Figure 12.77).

Studio will create the set number of copies sequentially, prompting you for additional discs when required.

▲ From the Write Speed list, choose the maximum speed supported by the recordable drive.

See the sidebar "The Dark Side of Recordable DVD" later in this chapter for details.

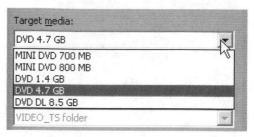

Figure 12.81 Studio can burn to a number of formats; choose the type of disc you've inserted.

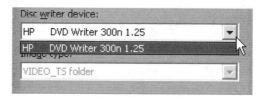

Figure 12.82 If you have more than one recorder on your system (you lucky dog), locate it in the drop-down and choose the one you want to use here.

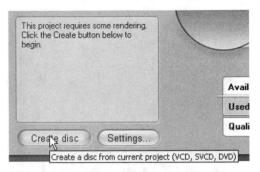

Figure 12.83 Click here to start the process.

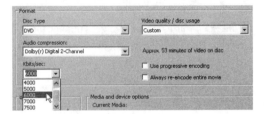

Figure 12.84 Here's where you select a custom data rate for your projects.

8. Click OK to close the Pinnacle Studio Setup Options dialog box.

Studio returns to the Make Movie window, and a Status box appears. You'll see an error message if the project is too large to fit on the recordable disc or if the hard disk doesn't have sufficient space to stage the disc image. Studio will also alert you if additional rendering or encoding must be performed to produce the disc (**Figure 12.83**).

9. Click Create Disc to start encoding.

✔ Tips

■ Though technically Studio can burn projects of any length, once you go over 80 minutes or so, Studio must increase compression to fit the video on the disc, degrading quality. All DVD authoring programs have this issue, not just Studio.

■ If you're having problems playing your DVDs, particularly if they stutter and stop during playback, you may want to encode at a lower rate (see the sidebar "The Dark Side of DVD" later in this chapter). Try encoding between 6000 and 7000 Kbits/second, selecting Custom for Video quality/disc usage and manually choosing the data rate in the Kbits/sec drop-down box (**Figure 12.84**).

BURNING A DVD TITLE

What's happening?

After you start the DVD burn process, Studio has three tasks to perform:

- ◆ **Encoding:** Studio has to convert the video and other assets to the proper formats. Depending upon the length of content and speed of your computer, this can take anywhere from several minutes to several days. While encoding, Studio moves the Timeline scrubber through the Timeline and updates the Player to show the video being encoded (**Figure 12.85**).

- ◆ **Exporting:** Studio converts the encoded files to DVD-formatted files and stores the files to disk. This is called the Exporting frame stage, as shown in **Figure 12.86**.

- ◆ **Burning the DVD:** Studio updates the Status screen and reports "Writing disc content" (**Figure 12.87**).

When the process is completed, Studio ejects your freshly minted DVD. Time to address the envelope, lick the stamps, and get this disc off to the grandparents. If you elected to create more than one DVD, Studio will ask you to insert another blank disc.

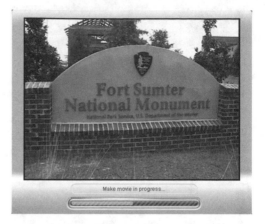

Figure 12.85 This bar shows progress through the encoding, compilation, and disc burning processes.

Figure 12.86 The next step is rendering, or encoding the content to be burned to DVD.

Figure 12.87 Then writing disc content (burning). Getting close now.

✔ Tip

■ Occasionally, especially with more complex projects, Studio may crash while encoding and writing to disc. When this occurs, I typically reboot and give Studio another try. If it crashes again, I remove the menus from the project and render the entire video as an AVI file using the DV format for video and 48 KHz for audio (see "To encode a project in DV format" in Chapter 14 for details). Then I insert the completed AVI file into the project, split the video where I need to insert menus, and insert and re-link all menus. Then I try to burn the project again; invariably, the problem is resolved, and Studio produces the DVD.

High-Def DVD? Not Quite Yet

So you've been shooting high definition (HD) video with your new HDV camcorder and you're wondering when you'll be able to produce high-definition DVDs? Well, unfortunately, not quite yet, primarily because there is no standard for producing or playing back high-definition video on DVD players. While there has been lots of talk about the two competing high-definition DVD formats, HD DVD and Blu-ray, even the companies who hold the patents on the formats like Toshiba and Sony don't expect the technology to reach the mainstream until 2008 or beyond.

For this reason, when you produce a DVD with HDV source material, Studio automatically scales the video down to standard definition (SD) resolution before encoding and burning the DVD. That way, you can play it on your current DVD player.

So how can you actually play the HD video your HDV camcorder creates? Well, your first option is to connect your HDV camcorder to your high-definition television set (HDTV) using the component cables, which send the HD signal across. Check the manuals that came with your HDV camcorder and HDTV set for details.

Alternatively, you can produce Windows Media Video files in high definition and view the files on your computer. See "What About HD?" in Chapter 14 for details.

About VideoCD and Super VideoCD (S-VCD)

In theory, VideoCD and Super VideoCD (S-VCD) are CD-R-based formats that play on computers and DVD players. Sounds great, and sounded even better back in the day when DVD recorders cost $5,000 or more.

In practice, however, using a variety of programs, I've had poor luck creating VideoCDs or S-VCDs that play reliably on either computers or DVD players. And since DVD recorders now cost under $200, I have pretty much given up on both formats.

If you're going to burn these types of discs, stick strictly to the default settings that Studio selects for you, to optimize your chances for compatibility.

The Dark Side of Recordable DVD

Okay—so you work for 10 hours getting your masterpiece on disc and then ship it off to the grandparents. What are the odds that it will play?

Well, it varies substantially according to format and player, but here are some general truths:

◆ No single recordable format or disc brand will play on all DVD players. Period.

◆ In general, -R/+R is most compatible, followed closely by –RW/+RW with Dual Layer (DL) technologies trailing significantly. You have to be very, very brave to send a DL disc out for the first time to friends and family.

What's a budding videographer to do? Here are the steps that I follow:

◆ Use name-brand media. I exclusively use Verbatim and Ridata.

◆ If you have problems playing back on some players, override Studio's Automatic encoding controls and produce at a combined data rate of no more than 7.5 Mbps.

◆ Send all discs out with a caveat, something like "These recordable DVDs don't work on 100 percent of the drives out there; let me know if you have a problem, and I'll come up with a plan B." That way, if the disc doesn't play, the recipient knows it's a fact of life, not my foul-up.

◆ Plan B is pretty simple: try another brand or format. Blank DVDs are cheap these days, and spending a few extra dollars to match player and brand is a lot better than giving up on your DVD masterpiece and sending it out as VHS. If Verbatim DVD+R didn't work, try Verbatim DVD-R, or Ridata DVD-R, etc. The bad news is that there's no rhyme or reason to what will or won't play on a given player; the good news is that name-brand DVD-R and DVD+R media enjoy about 90 percent compatibility on consumer DVD players these days, and I'm really just preparing you for the worst.

◆ DVD+R DL and DVD-R DL are a different story. The most recent testing at EMedialive.com showed DVD+R DL playback compatibility at around 60 percent for Verbatim and just under 40 percent for Ridata. DVD-R DL was just introduced this spring, and there's not much data on it yet, but you can expect it to have the same uphill climb. Proceed with caution in either case.

Finally, once you find a burner/media combination that works on most of your target players, don't change just to save a penny or two.

Part IV:
Other Output

13

WRITING TO TAPE

Most video producers render to tape to distribute or archive their productions.

When you work in DV and write to DV tape, typically you will then dub to VHS or some other widely supported analog format for distribution to the grandparents.

When you work in analog video, you'll want to write each distribution tape directly from Studio, rather than dubbing one tape to VHS and then dubbing additional tapes from there. This approach avoids the quality loss associated with analog-to-analog copies, which is like photocopying a photocopy.

Writing to tape is a three-step process. First you set up your hardware, which is nearly identical to connecting for capture. Then Studio renders the project, essentially implementing all of your editing work, inserting transitions, mixing audio, and overlaying titles. Sounds like hard work, doesn't it? But it's all transparent; no user intervention required. When rendering is complete, you begin the final stage: actually writing the video to tape.

Setting Up Your Hardware

Hardware setup involves three discrete actions: getting connected to your camera or deck, getting the camera or deck ready, and getting your computer ready.

To set up your hardware:

1. Connect your camera or deck to the computer.

   For more information on DV capture, see Chapter 3; for more information on analog capture, see Chapter 4.

2. Make sure the camera or deck is in VTR, VCR, or Play mode.

3. If the camcorder has an LCD display, open the LCD and use the camcorder controls to display all tape location and recording/playback information (if available).

   Sony camcorders usually have a Display button that reveals this information.

4. If the camera or deck has an Input/ Output selector, select Input.

   I haven't seen this in a while, but my venerable Sony Hi-8 CCD-TR81 had an Input/Output switch that needed to be set before writing to tape.

5. If there is no LCD, or you're writing to a stand-alone deck, connect a television or other analog monitor to the camera or deck.

The only way to be sure you're actually writing to tape is to see the video in the camera or deck. If you don't have an LCD or TV you can connect, you should be able to track progress in the viewfinder.

6. Check the time codes of the tape in the deck to make sure you have sufficient space for your production.

7. Check that any copy-protection features on the tape are disabled.

   Most DV tapes have a copy-protection tab on the back panel, a great way to make sure you don't overwrite your valuable video.

   In my tests, Studio didn't detect that copy protection was enabled and played the video out to the DV camera anyway. No harm was done, as the camera didn't overwrite the video, but nothing got recorded either.

8. Close all extraneous programs on your computer and don't perform any other tasks on the computer while writing to tape.

✔ Tip

- Like capture, writing to tape is an extremely demanding process, and one slip can ruin the tape. Try not to touch the computer or camera over the course of this procedure.

Figure 13.1 Click the Make Movie tab to get started.

Writing to Tape

You may want to consider some minor adjustments when converting a DVD production to tape-based output (see the sidebar "Outputting DVD Projects to Tape" later in this chapter), but otherwise your project should be on the Timeline, complete and itchin' to be written.

To write your project to tape:

1. Do *one of the following:*

   ▲ At the top of the Studio interface, click Make Movie (**Figure 13.1**). Then, at the upper left of the Make Movie panel, click Tape (**Figure 13.2**).

   ▲ From the Studio menu, choose Setup > Make Tape (**Figure 13.3**).

   Studio displays the Make Tape controls in the Make Movie window.

   Note that Studio will immediately compute the project's disk requirements and warn you in the Status box if you don't have the necessary disk space.

continues on next page

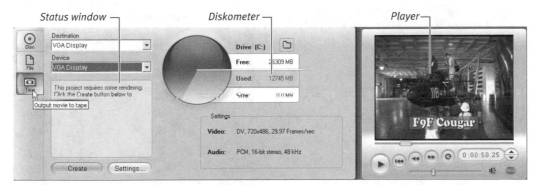

Figure 13.2 The Make Tape controls. Note the Status window, which delivers instructions and warnings; the Diskometer, which details disk requirements and capacity; and the Player, which controls writing to tape.

WRITING TO TAPE

2. Below the Diskometer in the middle of the Make Movie window, click Settings.

The Pinnacle Studio Setup Options dialog box opens to the Make Tape tab (**Figure 13.4**).

3. Choose the appropriate audio and video output devices:

▲ If outputting DV, as in Figure 13.4, choose DV Camcorder.

▲ If outputting analog video, choose both the device and the audio output (**Figure 13.5**). I'm sending my video out through the ATI All-in-Wonder, which Pinnacle sees as a second VGA display, which is why only that option is enabled.

4. For a DV camcorder, select the Automatically Start and Stop Recording checkbox to allow Studio to control the DV camera, and adjust the Record Delay Time value, if necessary.

All DV camcorders have a short delay between the time they receive the Record command and the time they start recording. Stick with the default (1 second, 27 frames), unless you notice that your camcorder is not capturing the first few moments of the video; then you should extend the duration.

For an analog camcorder or deck, the automatic recording option won't be available (Figure 13.5); you'll manually start the recording.

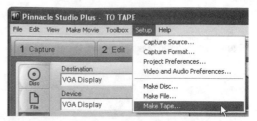

Figure 13.3 Another route to the Make Tape controls is the Setup pull-down.

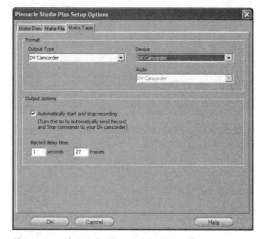

Figure 13.4 The Make Tape tab in DV mode.

Figure 13.5 The Make Tape tab in analog mode.

WRITING TO TAPE

Figure 13.6 Studio tells you when it's rendering.

Figure 13.7 You can track your progress by watching the Timeline scrubber, or the progress bar under the Player.

Figure 13.8 Itchin' to be written!

5. At the bottom of the Status box in the Make Movie window, click Create (Figure 13.2).

Studio starts to render the project. The Status box presents the message "RenderProgress" (**Figure 13.6**), the Timeline scrubber moves through the production as it's rendered, and the status bar under the Player reflects progress through the project (**Figure 13.7**).

When rendering is complete, Studio displays the message shown in **Figure 13.8**.

continues on next page

6. If you have an analog camcorder or deck
(or are manually cueing your DV deck),
start your device recording now.

If you selected Automatically Start and
Stop Recording, Studio will start and stop
the DV tape automatically.

7. Click Play in the Player to start playback
(**Figure 13.9**).

Studio starts playing the video out the
device selected in Step 3.

You should see video in the camcorder
LCD panel and/or on the television or
other monitor attached to your analog
device. You should generally also see a
red light or other indicator on your camcorder to show that the video is being
recorded.

If you don't see video, it's likely because
you're not sending the video out to the
device, so you should recheck your setup.

Figure 13.9 Click Play to start writing back to tape.

WRITING TO TAPE

✔ Tips

- To stop Studio during rendering, click Cancel in the status window (Figure 13.6). To stop Studio while rendering to tape, click the Pause button in the Player or press the spacebar.

- Studio saves all temporary files created during rendering, so if you want to write another tape, simply load the project, enter Make Movie mode, and everything should be rendered and ready to go.

- Some older DV cameras use nonstandard commands to start and stop recording and may not recognize Studio's commands. If Studio doesn't automatically start your DV recorder, uncheck the Automatically Start and Stop Recording checkbox and manually set the record function.

- Before recording a long segment to tape, try a one- or two-minute sequence, just to make sure everything is working. Writing back to tape is one of those "tough to get it right the first time" activities, at least for me, so test your setup with a shorter project to catch any errors.

- Previous versions of Studio could write disk-based files to disk, but Studio 10 can't. No worries; simply create a new project, import the file into Studio, drag it into the Timeline, and then write to tape.

Outputting DVD Projects to Tape

So, you've created this awesome DVD and then realized Aunt Janie hasn't made the leap to DVD. VHS will just have to do.

What's the absolute bare minimum you have to do to convert your DVD project to tape output? Well, actually, nothing. You're in great shape. Studio simply treats the menus as still images and compiles them into the video normally.

Of course, the menus may look a bit bizarre, with all those windows and links and such. So you may want to delete the menus before writing to tape. Probably best to save the project to another name first because otherwise you may forget to undo your deletions and return later to your DVD project to find your menus gone.

CREATING
DIGITAL OUTPUT

Chapter 12 addressed DVD creation, and Chapter 13 covered writing back to tape. This chapter covers producing digital files for playback on your hard disk, copying to a CD or DVD, or posting to a Web site.

A key component of digital video output is compression, so I'll start by defining some compression-related terms to make sure we're on the same page. Then we'll look at Studio's format options, which have increased in Studio 10, and I'll give you my thoughts on their relative strengths and weaknesses. Next we'll take a task-oriented view of encoding, where I'll identify the format and preset I would use for a variety of compression tasks.

With this as background, we'll learn how to produce files with all available formats, from AVI to 3GGP and three flavors of MPEG in between.

Note that this chapter discusses CD and DVD as data-storage devices, not specialized formats that play in a player attached to your television. That is, if you want to produce a Windows Media file to copy to a CD or DVD to send to a friend to play on a computer, you're in the right place. If you want to author a production that can be viewed on a DVD player and TV set, go to Chapter 12.

Decoding Your Compression Parameters

Before you start encoding, take a quick look at the parameters you'll be selecting, using the main encoding screen, **Figure 14.1**, as a guide.

File Type: Starting at the top, your first choice, in the Format box, will be File Type. As we'll discuss in the next section, "Studio's Format Options," Studio offers a range of file types including AVI, MPEG, Real Video, Windows Media, and others. Each file type typically has its own extension, or the letters after the dot in the file name, like AVI, MPG, RM, and WMV. This identifies the file for Windows, Macintosh, or Unix computers so the operating system knows which program to use to play the video.

Note that each file type comes with presets that I'll encourage you to use, located to the right of the File Type drop-down list. The last preset is always "custom," which lets you free-lance a bit with other parameters.

Also note that sometimes your file type decision will dictate compression technology as well. For example, choose MPEG-2 as a file type, and your only option in the Compression box is MPEG-2. Ditto for all other compression technologies except for AVI, where you have your choice of two compression technologies.

Compression: Compression technologies **CO**mpress and **DEC**ompress video, and are often called codecs. As mentioned earlier, usually when you choose the file type, the compression choice is made for you. You'll see that there are drop-down lists for both Video and Audio compression, both usually dictated by your File Type selection.

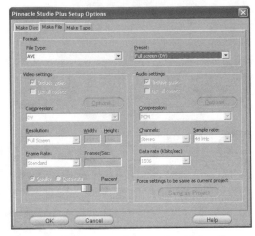

Figure 14.1 This setup option screen contains all relevant encoding options. Don't worry, though, we'll be using presets for most encoding runs, which won't involve this many choices.

Resolution: Resolution refers to the number of horizontal and vertical pixels in a video file. By way of reference, DV video starts life at 720 pixels wide and 480 pixels high, or 720 x 480. You capture and edit in this format to maintain the best possible quality, and then you generally *scale* to a lower resolution to distribute your videos.

Why scale the other formats to lower resolutions? Generally, when video is compressed to lower data rates, the individual frames look better when you start with lower-resolution frames. That's why most Web-based videos have a resolution of 320 x 240 or less, especially those distributed at modem speeds.

Frame rate: The frame rate is the number of frames per second (fps) included in an encoded file. Video starts life at 29.97 fps, and most higher-end codecs like MPEG-2 and DV output at that same rate. When producing for Web distribution, most codecs drop the frame rate to produce fewer frames at a higher quality.

Data rate: Data rate is the amount of data associated with a specified duration of video, usually one second. For example, MPEG-2 usually has a data rate of between 4000 and 8000 kilobits per second (Kbps), while streaming formats like RealVideo and Windows Media can be as low as 22 Kbps.

The most important factor in determining data rate is the capacity of the medium over which the video is played. If you exceed this capacity, the data can't keep up, and playback is interrupted, something we've all experienced with Internet-based video.

DVDs are capable of retrieving more than 10 megabits per second (Mbps) leaving a comfortable margin over the 4 to 8 Mbps used for most DVDs. On the other hand, if a computer is connected to a Web site via a 28.8 Kbps modem, retrieval capacity is down to around 22 Kbps, requiring the much lower rate.

Now that we understand the lingo, let's look at Studio's encoding options.

Studio's Format Options

With Studio 10, Pinnacle expanded output support to include eight different formats as shown in **Figure 14.2**. The flexibility this offers is great, but you as producer need to know when to use each codec.

I take a fairly conservative view of new codecs and don't use them just because they're cool or *au courant*. I use three or four for various applications, and that's it. But I recognize that others feel differently, and applaud Pinnacle for extending support so broadly.

Still, for those readers seeking direction, here's my take.

◆ **AVI files:** AVI was the first Windows compression format, but its day as a distribution format has come and gone. The only reason to produce AVI files is to export a file you can import into another editing or authoring program, or back into Studio to act as a video background. In these roles, you'll want to produce the file using the DV preset.

◆ **DivX:** This format was the flavor of the month a couple years back, and it's still popular among online movie file-sharers, but I've never liked it because quality was always inferior to Windows Media or Real and encoding was always a chore. There, I've said it, now I'll have to cancel my subscription to *Wired* and discard all my black clothes. Part of the problem with DivX is that it's based on an early version of the MPEG-4 codec, and MPEG-4 itself has improved since then while DivX has remained trapped in time. I prefer Windows Media to DivX (and current MPEG-4, for that matter) at all data rates for all uses.

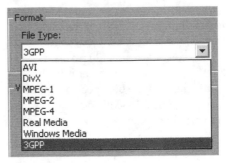

Figure 14.2 Yikes, a compression cornucopia. Which should I use first?

- **MPEG-1:** Another great codec whose day has passed. Produce MPEG-1 files only for VideoCDs; choose Windows Media for all other uses.

- **MPEG-2:** Produce MPEG-2 files for including in DVDs or SuperVideoCDs; use Windows Media for desktop playback and other uses.

- **MPEG-4:** See DivX above, and my column "The Moving Picture: MPEG-4 is Dead," at:

  http://www.emedialive.com/Articles/PrintArticle.aspx?ArticleID=8425.

  That's all I have to say about that!

- **Real Media:** Though Real Networks' codecs are slightly better than Windows Media at most data rates, the advantage has narrowed. In addition, while Real Player is very popular, Windows Media Player is practically ubiquitous, especially on the Windows platform. I would consider Real only if producing for folks on Unix or very old Macintosh computers (like OS 7).

- **Windows Media:** This has become my general go-to codec for desktop playback and streaming. If you're curious as to why, check out my article and codec comparison in "Framing B2B Video," here:

  http://www.eventdv.net/Articles/PrintArticle.aspx?ArticleID=8422

- **3GPP:** This stands for the 3rd Generation Partnership Project (3GPP), which is dedicated to producing standards for mobile devices. If you're producing video to display on a cell phone, this is your choice (and let the force be with you).

STUDIO'S FORMAT OPTIONS

A Task-Oriented View

That's my take on formats. Now, I'll present this information in a task-oriented way. You pick your goal, I'll supply the codec and preset.

◆ I want a file to watch from my computer. I don't really care about file size; I just want the best possible video.

Go with Windows Media, High Quality NTSC preset shown in **Figure 14.3**.

◆ I want a file to load back into Studio as background for a DVD menu or to load into another program.

I recommend an AVI file in Full Screen DV format as shown in **Figure 14.4**.

◆ I want a file to post to a Web site.

If you're uploading to a video server (like in a business), check with your webmaster. If uploading for casual use on your own Web page, go with Windows Media, but your specific selection depends upon the connection speed of your target viewer.

If your audience is likely to view the file at modem rates, choose the Custom preset (more on this in "Creating Windows Media Files," later in this chapter) to access the profiles for Video for Web servers at 28.8 Kbps or 56 Kbps. If they connect via broadband, go with Video for Broadband NTSC 256 Kbps (my favorite) (**Figure 14.5**).

Understand that if you encode at 256 Kbps, and a viewer with a modem connection tries to play the file, it may take a long time to download, but they *will* be able to view and play the file.

Files encoded at 28.8 or 56 Kbps will generally look pretty awful, but viewers will eventually see video worth waiting for. Encode at modem speeds, and they'll see ugly video no matter what.

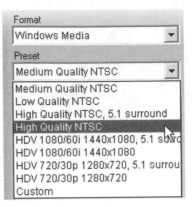

Figure 14.3 This is my choice for hard disk–based playback.

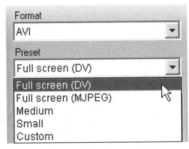

Figure 14.4 Use this when producing files to re-input back into Studio or into another authoring or editing program.

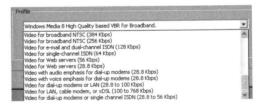

Figure 14.5 We'll have to dig into the Windows Media Profiles to find a good format for Web video delivery.

With streaming servers, which deliver video live in real time, it's a different story. 256 Kbps video streamed to a dialup modem will choke and sputter. If you know your site is streaming-based, encode at multiple bitrates (see "Creating RealVideo Files" and "Creating Windows Media Files," later in this chapter) or confine your encoding rates to your target audience's download speed.

◆ I want to compress a DVD's worth of video onto a single CD.

This is the supposed sweet spot for DivX, but I would still choose Windows Media, using the Video for Broadband NTSC (768 Kbps) setting, which should deliver about 120 minutes of video on your CD.

◆ I want to produce a file to send to a buddy on CD. Size is an issue.

I would select Windows Media, varying the data rate by the length of the content. You can get about an hour of video on CD at 1500 Kbps, and about 45 minutes at 2000 Kbps.

◆ I want to produce a file to input into a DVD, VideoCD, or SuperVideoCD project.

I recommend that you output an AVI file in DV format and let your authoring program encode to your project's final format. This virtually guarantees compatibility with that program (sometimes authoring programs don't accept MPEG files produced in other programs). It also lets the authoring program manage the critical data rate issue to fit all the video on the disk at optimum quality.

For example, if you encode into MPEG format in Studio, and encode at too high a data rate, your authoring program might have to re-encode the MPEG file to fit all the video on the disc, decreasing quality. Encode at too low a rate, and quality isn't as good as it could be.

These concerns notwithstanding, if you decide to go the MPEG encoding route, here are my recommendations. For DVD or SuperVideoCD (SVCD), encode into MPEG-2 format, using the appropriate preset (**Figure 14.6**). If encoding to input into a VideoCD, use the MPEG-1 format and the Video CD Compatible preset (**Figure 14.7**).

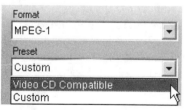

Figure 14.7 Same here; if encoding for VideoCD, use the preset.

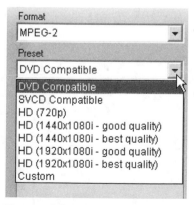

Figure 14.6 If you must encode to MPEG-2 format, stick to the presets.

General Encoding Parameters

Now that we know which codecs and presets to use and when, let's look at the general encoding parameters, which work with all format options except RealVideo and Windows Media. I'll cover only how to apply a preset because that's what I recommend for most users, and because the custom options vary significantly between the technologies.

To encode into any format other than Real or Windows Media using a preset:

1. After completing your project, do *one of the following:*

   ▲ At the top of the Studio interface, click Make Movie (**Figure 14.8**). Then, at the left of the Make Movie panel, click File (Figure 14.8).

2. Click the Format drop-down list and choose the target format (**Figure 14.9**).

3. Click the Preset drop-down list and choose the target preset (**Figure 14.10**).

   Studio computes the project's disk requirements and warns you in the Status box if you don't have the necessary disk space (**Figure 14.11**). Studio also displays the currently selected encoding parameters for both audio and video.

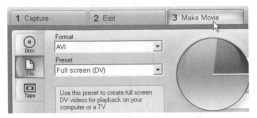

Figure 14.8 OK, let's get started. Click Make Movie, then File.

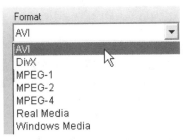

Figure 14.9 Choose your format first.

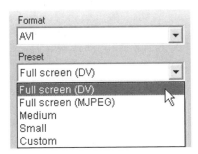

Figure 14.10 Then pick a preset.

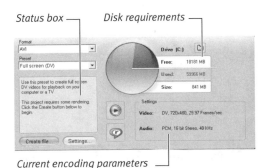

Figure 14.11 Studio identifies the encoding parameters, checks disk space, and advises you of any issues.

GENERAL ENCODING PARAMETERS

Figure 14.12 Name the file and choose the location.

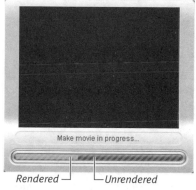

Rendered ──┘ └──Unrendered

Figure 14.13 Then sit and wait while the file renders.

Windows Media Player

RealPlayer

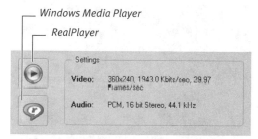

Figure 14.14 Studio will play your file after encoding. Use the RealPlayer for RealVideo, the Windows Media Player for every other format.

4. Beneath the Status box, click Create File (Figure 14.11).

   Studio opens the Save File As dialog box (**Figure 14.12**).

5. Type the file name and change the location if desired.

6. Click OK to close the dialog box.

   Studio starts encoding. You should see the Timeline scrubber moving through the video, the video updating in the Player, and progress in the bars beneath the Player window (**Figure 14.13**).

   Depending upon the codec and the rendering stage, the Player may be black, as shown, or may show the frames being encoded.

7. To play the video after encoding, click the Windows Media Open File button in the Make Movie window (**Figure 14.14**).

Creating RealVideo Files

The RealVideo format was created by Real-Networks. To view files encoded in this format, viewers need the RealPlayer, which is available for free download at www.realnetworks.com.

Though functional, Studio's tools for RealVideo encoding lack filtering, variable-bitrate encoding, and other advanced options available in Real's free encoding tools. Studio is great for encoding videos for email and for other casual projects, but for high-volume production and real-time encoding (which Studio doesn't perform), you're better off using other tools.

To create RealVideo files:

1. After completing your project, click Make Movie at the top of the Studio interface. Then, at the left side of the Make Movie panel, click File (Figure 14.8).

2. Click the Format drop-down list, and choose Real Media (**Figure 14.15**).

3. Below the Status box, click the Settings button.

   The Pinnacle Studio Setup Options dialog box opens with Real Media as the File Type and Custom as the preset, since all Real Media encodings are custom (**Figure 14.16**).

4. Type title, author, and copyright information.

   This information will appear when the file is played (**Figure 14.17**).

5. Type the desired keywords in the Keywords box.

   If the video is posted to a Web site, this information will be used to categorize the video by Internet search engines.

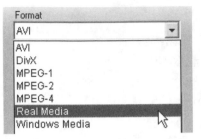

Figure 14.15 Now let's encode a RealVideo file.

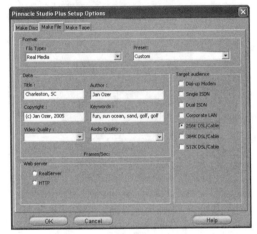

Figure 14.16 Every encoding choice is a custom job with RealVideo.

└─ *Title and author information*

Figure 14.17 Here's the title and author information in the RealPlayer.

Figure 14.18 Choose how you want your video to look.

Figure 14.19 Also choose how Studio should encode your audio.

6. In the Video Quality list (**Figure 14.18**), do *one of the following:*

   ▲ To produce a clip with no video, choose No Video.

   ▲ For clips with normal motion (no extremely high motion or low motion), choose Normal Motion Video. During encoding, RealVideo will balance frame rate and image clarity.

   ▲ For talking-head and similar clips with very limited motion, choose Smoothest Motion Video. During encoding, RealVideo will produce a higher frame rate and smoother motion.

   ▲ For high-action clips, choose Sharpest Image Video. During encoding, RealVideo will reduce the frame rate and produce fewer frames of higher quality.

   ▲ For slide shows, choose Slide Show. During encoding, RealVideo will reduce the video to a series of high-quality still photos.

7. In the Audio Quality list (**Figure 14.19**), select the description that best matches your audio content.

   During encoding, Studio will use the appropriate audio codec and data rate for your audio content.

continues on next page

8. In the Web Server section (Figure 14.16), do *one of the following:*

   ▲ If the ISP hosting the video has a RealServer installed, choose RealServer. Streaming files with RealServer is the preferred method, since it provides several valuable options, including the ability to create files that serve multiple target audiences and the ability to adjust playback performance to changing line conditions. If you don't know whether RealServer is installed, ask your ISP.

   ▲ To stream videos from an HTTP server without RealServer installed, choose HTTP; however, this produces a file that serves only one connection speed. This is the most general-purpose option; unless you absolutely know that your ISP has a RealServer and you'll be streaming from the server, choose this option. Also use this option for files created to play from disk or to distribute via email.

9. In the Target Audience section (Figure 14.16), choose the connections that your viewers will use to view the video.

   If you selected RealServer in Step 8, you can choose multiple options and produce a file that can serve a diverse range of connection speeds.

   If you selected the HTTP option in Step 8, you can select only one profile.

10. Click OK to return to the Make Movie window.

11. Beneath the Status box, click Create File (Figure 14.11).

    Studio opens the Save File As dialog box (Figure 14.12).

12. Type the file name and change the location if desired.

13. Click OK to close the dialog box.

    Studio starts encoding. You should see the Timeline scrubber moving through the video, the video updating in the Player, and progress in the bars beneath the Player window (Figure 14.13).

    Depending upon the codec and the rendering stage, the Player may be black, as shown, or may show the frames being encoded.

14. To play the video after encoding, click the RealPlayer Open File button in the Make Movie window (Figure 14.14).

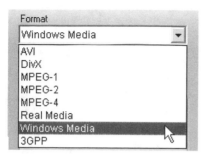

Figure 14.20 Getting started with Windows Media.

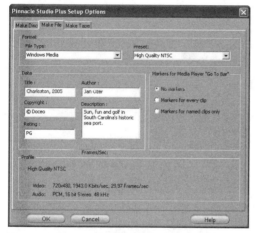

Figure 14.21 Here's the main Windows Media encoding screen.

Creating Windows Media Files

As the name suggests, Windows Media Video is Microsoft's video compression technology. To play files encoded in this format, viewers need Microsoft's Windows Media Player, which ships with all Windows computers and is freely downloadable at www.microsoft. com/windowsmedia. Microsoft offers players for all relevant Windows flavors and Macintosh (8.01 to OS X), but no Linux or Unix version (*quel surprise!*).

Like the RealNetworks technology, the Microsoft technology can produce files that support multiple-bitrate connections, but only when streaming from a Windows Media server (which is available only for Windows XP) or from a RealNetworks Helix server. Microsoft's most recent release of Windows Media 9 supports multiple-resolution files within the multiple bitrates, but if you're working at this level, you should use Windows Media Encoder, not Studio. Studio is a great tool for casual Windows Media encoding, but doesn't expose all relevant encoding controls and doesn't support real-time encoding.

To create Windows Media files:

1. After completing your project, click Make Movie at the top of the Studio interface. Then, at the left side of the Make Movie panel, click File (Figure 14.8).

2. Click the Format drop-down list, and choose Windows Media (**Figure 14.20**).

3. Below the Status box, click the Settings button.

   The Pinnacle Studio Setup Options dialog box opens with Windows Media as the File Type (**Figure 14.21**).

continues on next page

CREATING WINDOWS MEDIA FILES

4. Type information in the Title, Author, Copyright, Rating, and Description boxes. This information will appear when the file is played (**Figure 14.22**). If the video is posted to a Web site, the description will be used to categorize the video by Internet search engines.

5. In the Preset drop-down list, select *one of the following*:

   ▲ Any preset other than Custom, and proceed to Step 6 (**Figure 14.23**).

   ▲ Select Custom, and proceed to Step 5. Studio opens the Profile drop-down list (**Figure 14.24**).

6. In the Profile drop-down list, select the target profile.

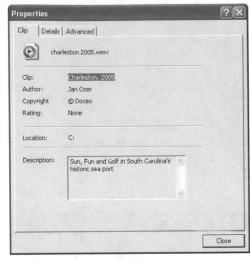

Figure 14.22 Windows Media Player displays author and content information in the Properties screen.

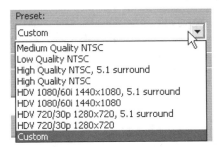

Figure 14.23 Either choose a Preset here, or go Custom.

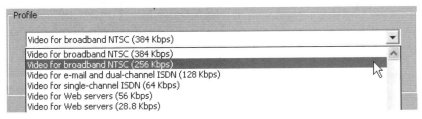

Figure 14.24 If you choose the Custom route, select your Profile here.

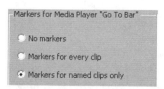

Figure 14.25 File markers are definitely cool for longer videos.

Figure 14.26 Markers let your viewers jump to the scenes they really want to see in your video.

Figure 14.27 Windows Media markers are the only reason I know for naming your clips in the Clip Properties tool. Enter the name in the Name box on top of the Clip Properties tool.

7. In the Markers for Media Player "Go To Bar" section, select the desired option (**Figure 14.25**).

   If you insert markers in the clip, viewers can jump to these markers using a menu in Microsoft's Windows Media Player (**Figure 14.26**).

   If you enable markers and don't name your clips, Studio will enter a default name based on the project name and clip start point.

   To name your clip, open it in the Clip Properties tool and enter the desired name in the Name field (**Figure 14.27**). See "Trimming with the Clip Properties Tool" in Chapter 7 for more information on the Clip Properties tool.

8. Click OK to return to the Make Movie window (Figure 14.11).

9. At the bottom of the Status box, click Create File.

   Studio opens the Save File As dialog box (Figure 14.12).

10. Type the file name and change the location if desired.

11. Click OK to close the dialog box.

    Studio starts encoding. You should see the Timeline scrubber moving through the video, the video updating in the Player, and progress in the bars beneath the Player window (Figure 14.13).

12. To play the video after encoding, click the Windows Media Open File button in the Make Movie window (Figure 14.14).

CREATING WINDOWS MEDIA FILES

What About HD?

Okay, so you bought the Sony HDR-HC1 or maybe even the HDR-FX1 (you lucky dog), and you're happily shooting in HD. You know you can only produce standard-definition DVDs in the short term, but you want to view high-resolution files on your computer. What output format should you choose? Well, by now you must be thinking that I wake up every morning reciting "Use Windows Media," but to paraphrase Ronald Reagan, "Here I go again."

Though you can produce HD files in MPEG-2, Windows Media produces better video at a lower data rate. As shown in **Figure 14.28**, there are even presets to simplify the process. Both of the Sony camcorders mentioned above record 1080/60i video (1080 lines of horizontal resolution, 60 interlaced fields of video per second), so use that preset to output your files. My tests confirmed that Studio delivered the promised 5 Mbps data rate with very good quality. Other HDV camcorders record at 720/30p (720 lines, 30 noninterlaced frames per second); use this Windows Media preset to reduce the data rate to a cozy 4 Mbps.

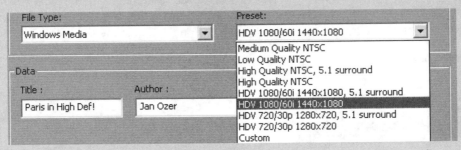

Figure 14.28 Your best bet for exporting HDV at either of its native resolutions is Windows Media. Definitely use the presets.

In my tests with a Beta version of Studio, it did not successfully downsample a 1080i file to 720p, though it produced several other non-HD files (like Windows Media, High Quality NTSC) without a problem. If you can't successfully play 1080i files on your computer, you might try downsampling to 720p and see if it's working. If not, use the High Quality NTSC preset.

CONVERTING TAPES TO DVD

Video editing is great, but sometimes what you really want to do is drop a tape in, click some buttons, leave your PC to work its magic, and return to find a finished DVD.

If one-click conversion is your goal, Pinnacle Instant DVD Recorder is your tool. Note that the program offers two modes of operation, Advanced and Wizard-based. To break this explanation into the most logical chunks, I'll describe the steps needed to work in Advanced mode, in the order presented in the Wizard. That way, no matter which approach you choose, you should be able to follow along in the chapter.

A couple of caveats. First, the DVDs you can create with the Instant DVD Recorder are primitive in several respects. For example, all menus are sequential, and you have limited ability to customize their appearance. In addition, you can only add chapter points at regular time intervals like every five minutes, so you lack the precision offered when producing DVDs in Studio. Still, Instant DVD Recorder is much more efficient for quick-and-dirty conversions to DVD than going through the traditional capture, editing, and authoring process.

This chapter assumes that you have your camera connected to your computer already and are prepared to capture video. If not, Chapter 3 and Chapter 4 can get you hooked up.

Working in Advanced Mode

Advanced mode sounds, well, advanced, but it's really just a one-window presentation of the four major tasks you work through in the Wizard. Same stuff, different presentation.

In this fly-through, I'll assume that you will select either no menu or a standard menu. Then, in the next section, "Customizing Your DVD Menus," I'll work through Instant DVD Recorder's customization options.

To run Pinnacle Instant DVD Recorder:

Do *one of the following*:

▲ Choose Start > Run > Programs > Studio 10 > Pinnacle Instant DVD Recorder > Instant DVD Recorder.

▲ If the Studio Launcher is running, click Instant DVD Recorder (**Figure 15.1**).

The Launcher runs Pinnacle Instant DVD Recorder (**Figure 15.2**).

If you don't see the Instant DVD Recorder option in your Studio Launcher, it means that the program is not installed on your computer. There are three possible explanations: the program didn't come with the version of Studio that you acquired, you didn't install the program during setup, or you have since removed (uninstalled) the program from Windows.

Figure 15.1 Click Instant DVD Recorder in the Studio Launcher to start converting tape to DVD.

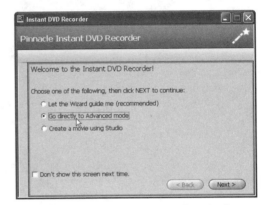

Figure 15.2 Once you master Advanced mode, the Wizard is a breeze.

WORKING IN ADVANCED MODE

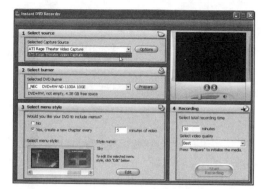

Figure 15.3 Choose your video source here.

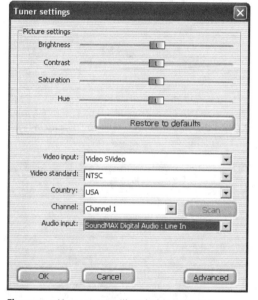

Figure 15.4 Your screen will probably look a bit different, but should present most of the same options

Figure 15.5 Choose your video input, favoring S-Video when available.

To select and configure your source video:

1. Click the Go Directly to Advanced Mode radio button (Figure 15.2).

2. Click Next.

   The Instant DVD Recorder program opens (**Figure 15.3**).

3. In the Select Capture Source list box, choose your video source.

4. Click the Options button (Figure 15.3).

   Instant DVD Recorder opens the Tuner Settings screen for your capture device (**Figure 15.4**). Note that this will be different for all analog capture devices; here I'm showing the options for the ATI All-in-Wonder, which uses ATI's Rage Theater Video Capture driver.

5. In the Video Input drop-down list, choose the appropriate input (**Figure 15.5**).

   When capturing analog video, as opposed to via DV, always use S-Video (designated "Video SVideo" here) when available, since that delivers the cleanest video signal.

   continues on next page

6. In the Video Standard drop-down list, choose the appropriate standard (**Figure 15.6**).

7. In the Country drop-down list, choose your country (**Figure 15.7**).

8. In the Channel drop-down list, do *one of the following*:

▲ If capturing television input from a TV station, choose the channel.

▲ If capturing from a camcorder, choose Channel 1 (**Figure 15.8**). If you don't see video in the display window in Step 9, try another channel (this control should have no effect since you're not capturing from TV input; I tested several channels with the ATI card and they all worked).

9. Click Play on your camcorder to send video to the capture card.

You should see video playing in the preview window (**Figure 15.9**). If not, check your configuration options and try again.

Figure 15.6 Then choose your video standard (NTSC here in the U.S.).

Figure 15.7 You probably won't see this one unless you're capturing with a TV tuner.

Figure 15.8 Choose your channel when capturing from live TV. Otherwise, this selection should be irrelevant.

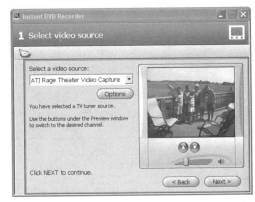

Figure 15.9 Houston, we have video! You're now ready to check audio.

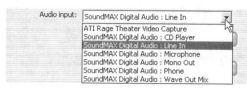

Figure 15.10 Choose your audio source here.

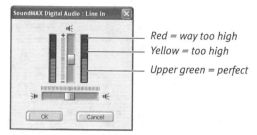

Figure 15.11 You know the drill; keep the audio volume in the upper green, touch the yellow, stay out of the red.

10. In the Audio Input drop-down list, choose the appropriate input (**Figure 15.10**).

11. In the Tuner Settings screen, just below the Audio Input drop-down list, click Audio Input (Figure 15.4).

    Instant DVD Recorder opens the volume control (**Figure 15.11**).

12. Click Play on your camcorder to send audio to the capture card.

    You should see the volume meters reacting to changes in the audio volume. If not, check your configuration options and try again.

13. Adjust the volume control so that the lights occasionally reach into the yellow bar, but never into the red bar.

14. Click OK to return to the Tuner Settings window.

15. With your camcorder playing, adjust the Picture Settings (Brightness, Contrast, Saturation, and Hue) as necessary.

16. In the Tuner Settings screen, just below the Audio input drop-down list, click Audio Input (Figure 15.4).

17. Click OK to close the Tuner Settings window and return to the Instant DVD Recorder application.

WORKING IN ADVANCED MODE

To select and prepare your burner for recording to disc:

1. In the Selected DVD Burner drop-down list, choose the target DVD recorder (**Figure 15.12**).

2. Click Prepare.

   If there is no disc in the drive, the program will open the window shown in **Figure 15.13**. Insert a disc and click OK to clear the window.

   If there is a DVD-Rewritable disc that is not blank in the drive, the program will display the window shown in **Figure 15.14**. Click Yes to erase the disc, or No and then replace the disc with either a new recordable or rewritable disc.

   Before preparing a recordable (write-once) disc for burning, Instant DVD Recorder displays the warning shown in **Figure 15.15**. If this is your first time recording a DVD, you might consider recording to your hard drive first (Figure 15.12) just to test the waters, or using a rewritable disc.

3. Click OK.

   Instant DVD Recorder prepares the disc for burning.

Figure 15.12 Choose your burner here. When first starting out, you may want to record the movie to your hard drive first, just to get some experience without creating any coasters.

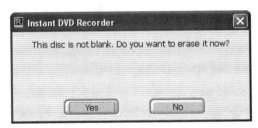

Figure 15.13 Looks like you forgot to put in a disc! Do so and click OK.

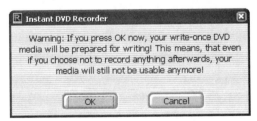

Figure 15.14 Recording on rewritable discs isn't a bad idea, either. Instant DVD Recorder handles them well, and can erase them to burn anew.

![Instant DVD Recorder warning dialog: "Warning: If you press OK now, your write-once DVD media will be prepared for writing! This means, that even if you choose not to record anything afterwards, your media will still not be usable anymore!" with OK and Cancel buttons]

Figure 15.15 Once you "prepare" a recordable (write-once) disc, you can't use it for other purposes.

WORKING IN ADVANCED MODE

Figure 15.16 Click No if you don't want a menu.

Slider bar

Figure 15.17 If you opt for a menu, this is where you choose chapter interval and menu style.

Figure 15.18 We'll customize in a bit; here I just want to insert the right title in the menu.

To select and configure a menu style for the disc:

1. In the Select Menu Style window, do *one of the following:*

   ▲ If you don't want a menu on your DVD, click the No radio button, and move to the next task, "To Record Your DVD" (**Figure 15.16**).

   ▲ If you choose this option, when you insert the DVD into a player, no menu will appear and the video will immediately start to play.

   ▲ If you want a menu on your DVD, click the Yes radio button (**Figure 15.17**) and move to Step 2.

2. Type the desired duration in the minutes of video text box.

3. Click to choose the desired menu style.

   You can browse through the styles using the slider bar on the bottom of the Select Menu Style window.

4. Click the Edit button.

   Instant DVD Recorder opens the Create Custom Menu screen (**Figure 15.18**). I'll detail all options in the next section, "Customizing Your DVD Menus"; for now, I just want to name my DVD something other than My Home Video.

   continues on next page

WORKING IN ADVANCED MODE

5. In the DVD Menu, click the title to make it active (**Figure 5.19**).

6. Type the desired text title.

7. In the Style Name text box, type the desired style name (**Figure 5.20**).

8. Click OK to return to the main Instant DVD Recorder application.

✔ Tip

■ When I tried to save a new menu title, Instant DVD Recorder kept redisplaying My Home Video as the title when I closed the active text box, which was obviously disconcerting. However, when I burned the DVD, Instant DVD Recorder had inserted the correct title (**Figure 5.21**).

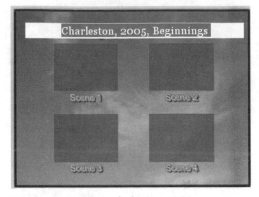

Figure 15.19 Typing the desired menu title.

Figure 15.20 Then the style name.

Figure 15.21 It looks like the title doesn't take, but clearly it did, as seen in the screen shot of the completed DVD.

WORKING IN ADVANCED MODE

Figure 15.22 Choose your recording options here.

To record your DVD:

1. In the Recording window, type the target recording time in the designated text box (**Figure 15.22**).

   Instant DVD Recorder will stop the recording after the designated time.

2. In the Select Video Quality drop-down list, select the desired video quality.

   Quality options control the duration of video you can store on the disc. With Best quality selected, you can store up to 93 minutes; with Better selected, you can store up to 109 minutes; and with Good selected, you can store up to 133 minutes.

   Choose the top quality setting that can store the duration entered in Step 1.

continues on next page

WORKING IN ADVANCED MODE

3. Cue your camcorder to a few seconds before the desired starting point and press Play to start playback.

4. Click Start Recording.

   Instant DVD Recorder starts recording and burning up to the selected duration. You can stop the process at any time by clicking Stop Recording (**Figure 15.23**). The process is not real time, and continues after the video capture stops, with total processing time dependent upon processor speed.

   When complete, you'll see the window shown in **Figure 15.24** and Instant DVD Recorder will eject the disc. Click Start Over to start another project, or Exit to leave the program.

✔ Tip

- This process is extremely processor-intensive, and susceptible to failed discs if interrupted. For this reason, you shouldn't use the computer for other tasks while converting tapes to DVD.

Figure 15.23 DVD burning is under way. You can stop at any time by clicking Stop Recording, but if you do, your recordable disc is a goner.

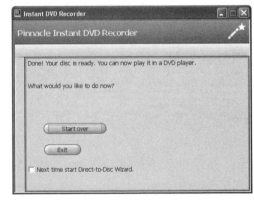

Figure 15.24 Task completed. What do you want to do now?

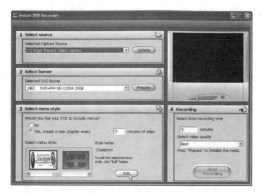

Figure 15.25 Let's customize our menu. Click here to edit menu styles from the main Instant DVD Recorder application.

Figure 15.26 Click here to use the Wizard.

Figure 15.27 Here's the Background tab. Note how the frames are obscuring the background image, making it tough to find the ideal background image.

Customizing Your DVD Menus

While not as flexible as the main Studio application, Instant DVD Recorder offers some useful configuration options you can incorporate into a "style" that you can save and reuse. I'll detail these options here.

I'll start with choosing the background image, as should you, since this sets up all other choices. Then I'll describe all other menu-creation options.

To open the Create Custom Menu window:

Do *one of the following*:

▲ If you're working in Advanced mode, click the Edit button on the bottom right of the Select Menu Style panel (**Figure 15.25**).

▲ If you're working in Wizard mode, click Edit in the Select Menu Style window (**Figure 15.26**).

Instant DVD Recorder opens the Create Custom Menu window (**Figure 15.27**).

To create a custom menu:

1. In the Create Custom Menu window, click the Background tab.

2. Click the desired background image.

   The program automatically inserts it into the preview window.

   In the upper-right corner of the Create Custom Menu screen, click Import to import other background images. Use the slider bar beneath the backgrounds library to browse through all images. Consider your layout options before spending hours finding the ideal image, since many layouts tend to obscure major portions of the image.

3. Click the Frame tab (**Figure 15.28**).

4. Click the desired frame.

   The program automatically inserts it into the preview window.

   Use the slider bar beneath the frame library to browse through all frames.

5. Click the Layout tab (**Figure 15.29**).

6. Click the desired layout.

   The program automatically inserts it into the preview window.

   Use the slider bar beneath the layout library to browse through all layout options. When choosing a layout, consider both the placement of the frames on screen, and the number of frames in the layout. For example, if you plan to insert frequent chapter points, use a layout with six or more frames; otherwise, the number of menus in the project will be very large, which makes navigation clunky.

Figure 15.28 Choose the frame you want included in the menu.

Figure 15.29 Here are your frame layout options.

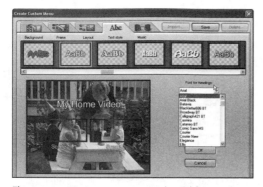

Figure 15.30 Here are your text style and font options.

Figure 15.31 You can insert background music for your menu here. Have a listen to the "Lithium" file; it really lives up to its name.

7. Click the Text Style tab (**Figure 15.30**).

8. Click the desired text style.

   The program automatically applies it to the preview window.

   Use the slider bar beneath the Text Style library to browse through all styles. When choosing a style, keep readability in mind. For example, styles with black edges, like that shown in the figure, help distinguish the letters from the background, enhancing readability.

9. If desired, click the Font drop-down menu, and choose a different font for your title.

   Once again, readability is key here. Choose a simple font that will display well on relatively low-resolution TVs and won't make grandma squint when trying to read the text.

10. Click the Music tab (**Figure 15.31**).

11. Click the desired background music for the menu.

    When you click the song, the program will preview it for you.

    Use the slider bar beneath the music library to browse through all audio files.

    In the upper-right corner of the Create Custom Menu window, click Import to import other songs or background audio files (note that the program only accepts WAV files).

continues on next page

Customizing Your DVD Menus

12. In the DVD Menu, click the title to make it active (Figure 5.19).

13. Type the desired text title.

14. In the Style Name text box, type the desired style name (Figure 5.20).

15. Click OK to return to either the Instant DVD Recorder application or the Wizard.

Instant DVD Recorder saves the style, and inserts it into the menu style library for selection and reuse (**Figure 5.32**).

✔ Tip

■ To delete a style, select it in the Instant DVD Recorder (or Wizard), and click Edit and then Delete in the upper-right hand corner of the Create Custom Menu window (**Figure 5.33**).

New style

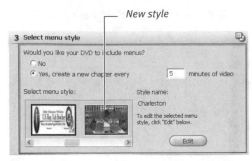

Figure 15.32 Instant DVD Recorder saves all styles in a library for later reuse.

Figure 15.33 To delete a style, select it in the Instant DVD Recorder or Wizard, click Edit to get to this screen, and choose Delete.

CUSTOMIZING YOUR DVD MENUS

INDEX

INDEX

INDEX

INDEX